Date Due

THAT DAY ALONE

Also by Pierre van Paassen:

DAYS OF OUR YEARS
THE TIME IS NOW!

THAT DAY ALONE

BY PIERRE VAN PAASSEN

When Justice seals the gates of heaven and hell
The rest—that day, that day alone, will tell.
—JAMES MONTGOMERY

THE DIAL PRESS

NEW YORK · 1941

D
443
.V35

59535

CONTENTS

v

THAT DAY ALONE

I

Farewell to France

WHENEVER I dropped in at the Lion d'Or, those last few weeks in France, I found the bar lined with strangers. Most of them, to judge by their accent and their clothes, were peasants, small shopkeepers, and *petits fonctionnaires* from neighboring villages and hamlets, who had come to Bourg-en-Forêt to catch a train for the mobilization centers. There seemed to be a good deal of uncertainty and confusion among them as to whether the next passenger train would halt long enough to pick them up. For the expresses that roared through our station night and day since the first day of mobilization were all packed with men and boys from points farther up the line. All the way to Paris, more-over, the tracks and sidings were cluttered up with long strings of flatcars carrying English war-material: tarpaulin-covered artillery, crated airplanes, field kitchens, search-lights, ambulances, and things of that sort. There were reservists in the barroom who said they had been wander-ing around Bourg for days.

I was stopped on my way to the back room, where I knew my old friend, M. Tisserand, the librarian, to be in virtual permanent session with the elders and notables of our community, by a sign from the host, who stood behind the bar wiping some wineglasses. With a nod of his head he drew my attention to a railroad worker who was telling all and sundry that the government had been storing vast quantities of pressed-paper coffins in the cellars of the rail-way stations and in other public buildings of the capital.

In the crypt of Notre-Dame, he was saying, and in the catacombs of the Denfert-Rochereau district, he had seen fifty thousand of those coffins stacked up that very day— seen them with his own eyes.

"What are they for?" asked one of the peasants naïvely.

"Not for you and your kind," shot back the *cheminot,* who probably thought that with his question the peasant had meant to cast doubt on that fantastic story. "They are for the air-raid victims."

"Parbleu," said the peasant, "who in hell wants to be buried in a paper coffin? And then," he added suddenly, in a comical burst of anger that flushed his face a deep red, "I consider it unfair, quite unfair what you say, why should a distinction be made between civilians and us soldiers?"

The crowd was silent for a moment. Some men took sips from their glasses and replaced them with almost furtive gestures on the counter. Others exchanged significant glances with their neighbors. The question of equality had been raised, albeit in a somewhat macabre way. But that meant that the conversation was about to take a political turn.

"You don't understand, I can see that," resumed the *cheminot,* now mollified. "Do you want me to tell you," he said in a slightly bragging tone, "why they bury civilians in paper coffins? That's for the morale, my friend. They can't be seen carrying the fragments of civilians around in tin pails or bed sheets, can they, now? A sight like that would demoralize the average city dweller in a minute."

"I don't like it," insisted the peasant with a kind of drunken man's stubbornness. "I don't like it and I will have nothing to do with it, *figurez-vous,* paper coffins for those ladies and gents. Is that what we're paying our good taxes for?"

Everybody laughed at this, but the *cheminot* bent his head towards the bar and, looking sideways at the red-faced peasant five or six places away from him, called out: *"Ne t'en fais pas, mon vieux,* don't worry, old boy, you're in the infantry, no? Well, they will have a nice and shiny new Boche tank plow you under. . . ." The peasants seemed to be struck speechless by this cynical remark, but one of them said: "It's evident, smart boy, that you were not at the Chemin des Dames in the last war! . . ."

I found M. Tisserand sitting on one of the small marble-topped tables in the rear of the billiard room. He was talking to Élie, the bald-headed old waiter, who stood in front of him, arms crossed, shifting his weight from one painful foot to the other. M. Tisserand seemed very excited. In spite of that, I noticed that the other men in the room, all of them prominent in our community—*monsieur le notaire,* the pharmacist, the architect, and a couple of big landowners—strangely enough paid but slight attention to M. Tisserand's words.

"Do you know, Élie, old friend," he was saying, "what my nephew just tells me? *Eh bien,* he was in Maisons-Laffitte yesterday—you know the little town where there is a race track? He was there on business, my nephew, and what does he see there? A scandal, I tell you, a scandal as has never yet happened in this France of ours. He was walking up the Avenue Longueil, and what does he see there?" M. Tisserand was now speaking very slowly and not looking at Élie at all but at his friends, who were obviously pretending not to be interested and busily playing cards. "He sees there a long file of civilians—men, women, and children—loaded down with baggage—suitcases, sacks, boxes, I don't know what else—and those civilians escorted by Senegalese soldiers, bayonets fixed. . . ."

"Des espions, sans doute," shot out Élie indignantly, and I noticed that the notary vigorously nodded his head at the waiter's remark.

"Spies, nothing!" shouted M. Tisserand, who now jumped down from his table and began to pace the floor in long strides. "Spies, nothing! Those men were political refugees, men who had sought asylum here in France from Hitler and Mussolini. And those men were being marched to a concentration camp!"

"A concentration camp here in France, *maître?* That does not seem possible!" said Élie, aghast.

"I thought that would astonish you," said M. Tisserand calmly. "Your astonishment honors you, Élie, *mon ami!"*

But now the notary spoke up. "Monsieur," he said to the librarian, "your language is irresponsible. These prisoners are aliens, aliens of the German enemy. The government does well to intern them. We must watch our internal security as well as our borders. Who knows the private records of these men, or what they are up to? *D'ailleurs,"* he went on, "they will be well treated, better, you may rest assured, than those of our soldiers who will have the misfortune of falling into the hands of the Boche. . . ."

"But, monsieur," interrupted Tisserand, "my nephew is like myself a librarian. He knew some of those prisoners by sight. *Il y avait là Monsieur Werfel et Monsieur Leonard Frank et Monsieur Feuchtwanger. . . ."*

"What barbaric names!" sneered the notary.

"What do names matter? Besides, those names are no more barbaric than that of Paul Karageorgevich, who, as you know, as Regent of Serbia, is the honored ally of the French Republic, we hope. . . . But these of whom I am speaking are distinguished men, eminent writers, citizens of Europe. . . ."

"Citizens of Europe, *mon Dieu,* I thought so, I thought you would call them that," came back the notary. "That appellation covers a lot. I suppose you would call those half-million Spanish rascals we entertain in our southern camps also citizens of Europe?"

Tisserand almost burst with indignation at this contemptuous reference to the Loyalist refugees, while Élie, who was an old Front Populaire adherent, started slapping with his napkin at a fly that was buzzing on the window-pane.

"Yes, citizens of Europe," flung back M. Tisserand. "They, the Spanish democrats as well as the prisoners of Maisons-Laffitte. They fought the powers France faces to-day, long before we rallied to the struggle. When they were overwhelmed at home, they came to us to warn us. They are our friends. . . . They should have the rank of honor among our allies. They should certainly not be sent to concentration camps. . . ."

"We do not need allies of that kind," returned the notary coolly.

"No," flared back Tisserand, now thoroughly aroused, "your allies are the Francos, the De la Rocques, the Weygands, the utility trusts, the *grande presse,* and the Jesuits, all those true and tried champions of freedom, equality, and brotherhood. . . ."

"Why don't you include M. Hitler?" the notary snarled back sarcastically.

"I do include M. Hitler!" said Tisserand with emphasis. "Hitler is your best friend. He is your Fuehrer as much as he is the Fuehrer of the German *bourgeoisie.* For years you and your friends have maintained that Hitler is the bulwark against disorder in Europe. You fawned on him and you applauded when his brigands smashed the labor organizations in Germany. You smiled when he burned the German Reichstag, which you called the equivalent of 'our hot-air factory' at the Palais Bourbon. When the Front Populaire came to power, your papers screamed: 'Rather Hitler than Blum.' Your leaders sent felicitations to Berlin on the occasion of the Munich surrender. Now you say you're going to fight Hitler," continued Tisserand, thoroughly excited. "I don't believe it. I don't believe it. I believe you and your class are merely going through the semblance of war in order to deprive the French people of its civil liberties and then throw them as a sop to your god in Berlin. This war is a pretense, a gruesome pretense; the French people are being led into a trap. . . ."

That was the last of the debates at the Lion d'Or. Never again, I knew, would the old men sit down pleasantly for a game of dominoes or whist. The abyss had suddenly yawned between them. M. Tisserand died a few months later . . . in jail, where he had been sent for the duration of the war on the charge of "using language calculated to obstruct the national effort."

Since the departure of most of the men for the armies, our vast parish church of Saint Louis of the French, where in normal times you could distinguish but a few bowed heads in the afternoon's half-darkness, was now filled each day to its uttermost nooks and corners. All day long an endless procession of sabots click-clacked back and forth over the hollowed-out granite steps that led up to the weather-beaten but still massive iron doors. It seemed as if all that remained of the population of Bourg was seeking refuge in that crumbling old edifice. People sat or stood in the side chapels, in the baptistery, even in the worm-eaten wooden galleries that had been condemned as unsafe many years before. When the Benediction of the

Blessed Sacrament was to be given, many peasant women, too, from neighboring hamlets and estates would come shuffling in, after covering their heads with handkerchiefs or shawls, and kneel down on the flagstones and on the slabs of yellowed marble in the aisles that covered the graves. The blue-colored windows above the high altar threw a wan and gloomy light on the assembly, giving the faces of the worshipers a pale, almost ghostlike appearance.

Only one corner of the church, a small area on the right of the intersection of transept and nave, opposite the pulpit, stood out in brilliant illumination. There rose the statue of Joan of Arc, patron saint of France, warlike and victorious, in one hand a silken fleur-de-lysed banner and in the other an unsheathed sword. The figure of the Maid was almost hidden from view by superimposed tiers of blazing candles. From a distance it looked as if she was hemmed in by protective rings of fire.

As the Abbé de la Roudaire, in his pleated alb, mounted the pulpit amid great stillness, to recite the rosary, I recognized many of the women whose sons and husbands were away in those regions on the borders of France which might at any moment be turned into a screaming inferno. The response to the Abbé's invocations rose and fell with the sound of breakers on the shore, fervently, and in rhythmic cadence. Some girls near me were fingering their beads nervously, many women wept; others, quite oblivious to their environment, kept their eyes closed and prayed with an intensity that brought to their features an expression of deepest suffering. "Pray for us! . . . *Ayez pitié de nous!* . . . Have mercy on us! . . . Hear us! Lord, hear us!" At times the sea of voices turned into a collective lament; poignant, sobbing, making the heart shrink with the anguish of its insistent, repetitious appeal.

Would God hear? Would the cup of sorrow pass by this time, or would it have to be drained once more to the last bitter dregs by those tired and weary souls as it had been only a short twenty years before? *"Coeur de Jésus,"* I heard the Abbé say in his deep plaintive voice, "Heart of Jesus, have mercy upon us!"

But what of the hearts of men? What of the value of human life and the value of our humanity? "What think ye of man?" Pontius Pilate had once asked the Jews in another decisive moment of history. I was innerly so perturbed by what was going on around me that I felt like hurling that same old question at the Almighty. Is our human destiny nothing more than forever to be mere flotsam and jetsam on an ageless tide?

Their disquietude and misery weighed on those people around me like a great, incomprehensible necessity. They were beyond hope and consolation. But was not the essence of man's sorrow that, in spite of all his progress, technique, science, and all the things created by his hard will and his fearless intellect, in spite of all his wealth and riches, he had turned up the wrong road, a road morally wrong, wrong in principle?

That question was pressed back after the last war, after the tension of the fighting years relaxed and exploded in a wave of idealism. Then the League of Nations had looked like a first step towards the realization of an international order based on justice. Antiwar sentiments and pacifism were growing in every land. Women's societies and workers' clubs and international congresses were passing unanimous resolutions against war. The vision of a new culture had become discernible on the horizon. Did we not sing and believe in our churches that the gentle way, the way of love and reason, would triumph in the end? But thereafter the old question whether or not our society and our Western culture, which had placed the modern, self-sufficient man in the center of things, were not on the wrong track, returned with renewed insistence when the fog cleared and we realized that even after the signing of peace we were still in a state of war.

There were times, in the feudal era, when man was closely associated with nature, when the rhythm of nature determined his life, when he accepted the changes of birth and death as self-evident and as things not to be questioned. Why should he fear death and life, when these were part and parcel of a divinely instituted order? Moreover, the ancient church, which had absorbed the rhythm of nature in its organization, promised him and actually gave him a measure of security and certainty in both life and death.

Modern man, who has lost all contact with nature, the modern city dweller especially, who only contemplates nature but no longer lives in and with its rhythm, who has lost belief in the spiritual basis of his own and the world's existence, and who thinks belief in God an antiquated myth, this man becomes obsessed with a fear that in times of social crisis grows to an unreasoning, blind anguish. And when this anguish takes on mass characteristics (which occur when the mass is cut loose from its economic, social, and spiritual moorings), confusion and chaos appear. Fear leads to bestiality. Fear, too, is more easily mastered by brutality than by the spirit. Hence, the leader who ruthlessly seizes power and holds power without qualms of conscience is glorified and almost deified because of his brutality.

Max Scheler said after the First World War that for the first time in a human history of ten thousand years man has become a problem to himself. Man no longer knows who he is and what he is; worst of all, he knows that he does not know. Indeed, we can no longer distinguish between what is human and what is bestial. We no longer know what is inner freedom and the supremacy of conscience. For is not conscience being enslaved and the inner freedom being sacrificed in the name of freedom?

Never in the course of history has man appeared so hopelessly pathetic a playball of blind forces as he does at present. Does anyone, anywhere, know what to do? Are we not all being swept along by a nameless, impersonal, inescapable current? There is a paralysis of the will, an abdication of reason, an abandonment of common sense, that makes one land after another a ready-made victim for conquest by the forces of evil. In France they did not know whether or not to fight back when Hitler appeared on the borders. For eight months, after Poland had been swept away and the German armies were poised to strike westerly, everybody sat still. The whole nation seemed struck with moral and physical impotence. Men, seemingly mesmerized, watched while Hitler calmly straddled the wave of the future and came bearing down on them riding its crest. In the confusion, Hitler and his philosophy were themselves taken to be the wave of the future, whereas he was merely its conductor and had perforce to be its conductor because no one disputed him that place and his self-assumed rank.

Where were those who knew the difference between light and darkness, between the truth and the lie, when the totalitarians started on their rampage, first gingerly, as if on tiptoe, cautiously feeling their way? Did we protest or make our voices heard when democracy and democratic ideals were assailed as the worthless inventions and trash of the Jews? What aid did we give to the fighters for freedom and decency in human relations when they were at grips with the monstrous emanations from the nether depths? We abandoned them to their fate. We covered their assailants—the assailants of our own most holy possessions—with our silence. We threw back those who were tired of the battle and who had escaped its ferocity as if they were tainted with some horribly contagious disease. We closed our doors to them and we did not know that in doing so we opened our hearts to the spirit of oppression and locked out mercy and compassion.

When I left the church I ran into Camille Villetorte, the gravedigger. I asked him to drink a glass at the *bistro* on the corner of the Rue de la Paroisse.

"Who's dead?" I asked, for I noticed that he wore his best suit, something he did only when he came to town to obtain burial instructions from the undertaker.

"Who's dead? Well, *pardi,* Monsieur Fayolle is dead. Didn't you know?"

"I know nothing!"

"You don't know? *Pourtant,* it happened yesterday," said Camille, sucking the red *pinard* from his moustaches. "It happened in a flash, too."

"What happened in a flash? Was he killed?"

"Killed? Yes and no. That is to say, he killed himself. . . ."

"Monsieur Fayolle committed suicide?"

"Yes, a rich man, too, at least so they say. He did it because of his horse."

"Why do you speak in riddles?" I said. "I don't understand."

"Nobody else does," came back Camille. "But it is the

truth I am telling you. Last week they took his horse away, for the mobilization, of course. He was so attached to the old beast that he went around moping and worrying about it. He asked the military to let him accompany the horse to the *dépôt* at Bougival. But they refused. They told him they'd take good care of his horse. Fayolle pleaded, it seems, that the horse was too old and quite useless for work. He told them he'd gladly pay them the price of a young strong horse. But they told him to be off. . . ."

"And so?"

"And so, when the news came yesterday morning that his horse had died—the animal had refused to eat or drink after being separated from its master—Fayolle went to Bougival, found the dead horse, kissed it on the snout, pulled out his revolver, and shot himself. . . . It's Pierre Péguy who told me. He saw the whole thing."

"It's very sad," I said.

"Sure, *c'est triste*," assented Camille, shrugging his shoulders, "but what's sadder still is that I, old and crippled with rheumatism, as you know me, must leave for the mobilization *dépôt* myself on the eleventh day. . . ."

"I thought you were *réformé*, no longer fit for the service?" I said.

"Fit I am not, except to dig a few more graves here in our *commune*, certainly not to dig trenches under fire. I had half my left haunch shot away in the last war—here, feel this," he said, grabbing my hand and putting it on the seat of his trousers. "What can a man with half a backside do in a war, I ask you now?"

"They will probably put you in some warehouse in the commissariat department. What I wonder at though," I said, "is who is going to slaughter the pig for us this fall." For Camille earned a little money on the side, and some tripes and livers, by doing a little butcher's work privately.

"Don't worry about that," he said reassuringly. "Nobody will eat any pork next winter in Bourg-en-Forêt. Only the army will eat pork, or anything else, for that matter—that is, if the army is victorious. Else the Boche will eat everything, and especially pork . . . they are fond of that, *messieurs les Allemands,* fond of pork, that is. I remember in the last war. . . ."

I have since those days often wondered why I did not simply stay home in Bourg-en-Forêt hidden behind the high walls of our garden, gathering the plums, which were extraordinarily plentiful that summer, or making myself useful in another way—for instance, by constructing a communal bombproof shelter of the kind we soldiers, under the watchful eye of Captain David Windsor, dug in the chalk back in '17 for the Canadian nurses at the base camp of Etaples. In doing so I might at least have set a good example to my neighbors who bungled that job completely, going about it, as they did, in so haphazard and inefficient a manner—one shovelful today and another to-morrow—that one might well have thought that the Germans were massing in the Gobi Desert instead of actually standing next door, trampling with impatience and thirsting for the spoil.

The truth is that nobody did a stroke of work for months. We stood about gossiping, speculating, and rumor-mongering all day and far into the night—and this for weeks on end. And that is the way it was in every community in France. Instead of passing the time of day in idle chatter and futile debate that way, a million of us, native sons and foreigners alike, should have been sent north to build an extension of the Maginot Line along the Belgian frontier to the North Sea as a second line of defense behind the Albert Canal. This would have stopped the gap through which the armored divisions were to come pouring into the plains of Champagne and through the valleys of Artois a few months later.

Now we know that its deliberate laxity in taking essential precautions for defense and plain treason on the French side enabled the Germans to break through with comparative ease in July, 1940. In December, 1939, however, and again in the following June, when the news came of two massive German concentrations in the same regions—one on the Netherlands border and one around Aix-la-Chapelle—we looked at the map with anxiety amounting to panic. One did not have to be a graduate of the War College to know that once the Germans had overcome Holland's fragile defense positions and thereafter, or simultaneously, outflanked the Belgian line by marching through Luxembourg and Flanders, northern France would lie wide open before them.

"Ah, that is when we go back into the trenches and stop them," said the old men around the coffeehouse tables.

"If only we have time to dig trenches," I replied, for I was well aware, because of my frequent automobile trips to and from Holland, that not a trench had been started anywhere in Belgium or France.

In August I ventured to speak to M. Daladier about my worries of the open road in the north. It happened this way: the bureau of the Grand Orient sent me regularly its bulletin about activities in the various Masonic lodges in France—notices of lectures, speeches, and visits by prominent scientists, philosophers, politicians, and the like. Back in 1925 I had been elected a member of the Saint-

Germain-en-Laye lodge and although I had seldom attended the sessions, my interest was now aroused anew by
an announcement in the bulletin of a forthcoming convention of the lodges of the *Département* of Seine et Oise
in which Saint-Germain is located. The convention was to
be held in Versailles, the capital of the *département,* and
the chief speaker was to be Édouard Daladier.

I telephoned the old doctor in Saint-Germain who had
been one of the sponsors at my initiation and arranged
with him to drive out together on the appointed day. We
had not much hope of Daladier's showing up, overloaded
with War Office work as he must have been in a time of
general mobilization; but halfway through the session he
nevertheless dropped in. He was given the floor at once
and pronounced the usual set speech of politicians the
world over: about democracy, humanity, freedom, the
splendid morale of the French people, and the loyalty of
France's allies, the British and the Poles.

After the formal session, when there was an opportunity
to speak to him semiprivately, I remarked to the Prime
Minister that I wished he had said something about our
Belgian friends and the situation up north. I made it clear
that I was not speaking as a foreign newspaperman but as
a friend of France and as *"une frère."* "It is clear," I said,
"that with the Maginot Line protecting the eastern frontier, the Germans will be forced to make their attempt at
invasion at another spot, through Belgium again, for instance."

"The Belgian defenses are quite formidable," returned
Daladier. "Their line of the Albert Canal is really quite
strong. Their fortifications in Liége province right up to
the Dutch border are most impressive. . . . There is the

system of Eben-Emael, right at the southern tip of the Dutch province of Limburg, which is considered as strong as our Maginot Line. . . ."

"But that is where the line of defenses ends, does it not?" I asked.

"True," came back Daladier. "If the Germans attack, they will most likely strike north of that point."

"Against Holland?"

"Yes, against Holland," he agreed.

"In other words, the way that line of defense has been built, along France's eastern border and continuing into Belgium, it really constitutes an invitation to the Germans to make Holland the gateway of their invasion?"

"Quite, but they won't get far!" he replied laughingly.

"Do you expect the Dutch army to stop them?" I laughed in turn.

No, the Dutch, he intimated, would merely fight a delaying action until reinforcements could be sent, and then the Germans would be up against the Albert Canal and the Franco-Belgians, and then there was the Little Maginot Line. . . .

"Holland is then to serve as a sacrifice battalion, so to speak?"

Daladier pursed his lips and cocked his head a little at this question. "Suppose," I went on somewhat impertinently perhaps, "suppose the Dutch do not like the idea and, seeing the futility of a struggle against the Reich, they surrender or give Hitler passage, as Luxembourg did in the last war. . . ." I could not finish the sentence.

"You do not know the Dutch," Daladier interrupted, lighting a cigarette.

"Yes, I think I do know the Dutch," I said. "I believe they will fight, but will the French fight?"

"Why do you say that?" he asked suddenly, staring at me.

"*Monsieur le ministre,*" I said, "you must forgive me for speaking frankly, but I would not be a true friend of France if I did not say to you that I and many others have grave misgivings about the sentiment in the country. It is not like 1914. The people are apathetic, strangely so. Perhaps they do not understand the issue at stake. . . ."

"The issue is plain enough, *d'ailleurs,*" he interrupted again, pulling at his cigarette with a wry face. "Hitler menaces Poland and threatens to throw Europe upside down. If they break loose again, the Germans, they must be made to fight on their own territory. That is the task of the Franco-British allies. The war will be fought in Germany. That's it. *Voilà!* They will not be permitted to set foot in France again. It's across the Rhine that the contest will be waged. . . ."

"I am glad to hear you say that, *monsieur le ministre,*" I said. "It gives me new hope."

Some of the other lodge members had gathered about to listen to the Prime Minister's words. Several of them gravely nodded their heads when they heard him say that if war broke out it would be fought on German territory. Since Daladier did not seem to be in a hurry, I chanced another question.

"If the war is to be fought in the enemy's country, we may perhaps attack any day now?"

"*Comment?* What do you mean?"

"France will strike at the Germans," I said, "before they are ready to deliver their first blow!"

"Where could we strike?" Daladier asked with a shrug of the shoulders.

"*Eh bien,* along the Mediterranean shores," I said.

"Against Italy?"

"Of course. That's the most vulnerable spot in the Axis lines. The French Army of the South could smash the Italians in a month, occupy the Po Valley and the industries of northern Italy, and drive the Italian forces back on Naples, capturing the naval base of Spoleto on the way. Such a move would greatly upset the calculations of the German general staff. It might save Poland, to begin with. . . ."

Daladier laughed. "You are quite a strategist," he said. "But you forget that we are not at war yet and that Italy is not likely to join Germany. Italy is not menacing us."

"Mussolini is having his boys parade the streets shouting for Savoy, Nice, Corsica, Djibouti. . . . Italy is mobilized and a member of the Axis. France may not consider herself at war with Italy, but Italy is at war with France just as much as Germany is at war with France, although not a shot has been fired yet. I think it would electrify Europe if France struck at Italy right now instead of waiting for the first blow to fall on Poland."

"France desires peace," said Daladier. "We will not fight till all ways of reaching a peaceful solution have been exhausted. . . . War is no frivolity, no little game, you know. The French people are peace-loving."

"I know that, *monsieur le ministre,*" I said, "but while you and the French diplomats look for means to avoid war, Germany is concentrating her armies on the borders of Poland, Holland, Belgium, and France. It is true you do not need to fight. The Germans will be glad not to have you fight. But the only case in which they won't fight is if France surrenders."

"You seem to be quite sure it is going to be war," he said a little sarcastically.

"Positively, *monsieur le ministre,*" I said, "that's why

I would like to see France take the initiative by striking across Italy to effect a juncture with the Yugoslavs: I would like to see France strike the first blow and make it so terrific that the Axis snaps in two. . . ."

It became more and more difficult to go to Paris. In the first place, you never knew when there would be a train, while most of the buses on the cross-country runs had been commandeered "provisionally" by the military. In addition, the government placed every day more restrictions on the movements of foreigners, so that before long a person was virtually confined to his own place of residence. Still and all, circumstances called for my presence in the capital nearly every day, for I was broadcasting at the time from a government-owned station for NBC in America.

It was in vain that I pleaded with officials of the Quai d'Orsay for some kind of *laissez-passer* from the military authorities, so that I might avoid the daily delays and annoyances on my way to work. For each municipality between Bourg and Paris had its full complement of bayoneted guards stationed at the town limits, and every time I passed their way each set of guards seemed to consider it a patriotic duty to conduct me to a *mairie* or a military post for thoroughgoing questioning.

Fortunately at the time I still had a Canadian passport. This circumstance, coupled with the fact that my hair, both on the passport photo and in reality, was parted on the left side, seemed to have a soothing effect on inquisitorial spirits. Only, all this harassing red tape made the short trip to Paris a long and arduous journey, for there were no less than thirteen towns, villages, and hamlets to traverse, to say nothing of crossing innumerable heavily guarded bridges and passing through neighborhoods where more than the usual precautions had been taken, with tanks and assault cars stretched across the roads and entire battalions of homeguards disposed in defense position, evidently to guard some important (though to me invisible) military objective.

In short, the walk to Paris became, more or less, an obstacle race. But it had an inspiring effect. More than once I thought, as I saw the military precautions taken in such towns as Saint-Dénis, with its working-class population, that if France was half as well prepared on the borders as it was against possible revolutionary outbreaks in the interior, the situation was far from hopeless.

One reached Paris in an exhausted condition, only to discover that the troubles on the road had been merely a prelude to dodging members of the corps of black-coated and black-helmeted Mobile Guards, which Édouard Daladier, onetime leader of the Popular Front, had organized to keep the adherents of that same Popular Front in check. I could not sit in any restaurant, café, or hotel, for every public establishment of that sort was invaded from time to time by squads of these troopers, who came to verify the identity of guests. Some of the guests I saw being led away, often amidst the wails and sobs of wives and children, seemed to have been roused from their beds or from some peaceful occupation. Where were they taken? God only knows! And who were they? Reservists from the provinces caught lingering around Paris for a day or so before reporting at *dépôts*, spies detected in the act of rigging up a signaling station on the roof, just ordinary *types louches*, or—who could tell?—newspapermen on their way to a broadcasting station? I could not be sure, nor did I inquire. I had no business being around at all, for my identity card stated specifically that my presence outside Bourg-en-Forêt exposed me "irrevocably to immediate arrest" by any policeman, civil or military—that is to say, without further ado or explanation.

It was a miserable job wandering about the half-deserted city, blacked-out after nightfall. All the great squares were empty and soundless. The palaces and monuments stood gaunt and ghostly in their loneliness. You felt as if you were left alone with tombstones in a moonlit cemetery. The rare Parisians venturing abroad walked with hesitant, muffled step, on tiptoe almost, as if they were fearful to disturb the unnatural, unholy silence. There was something so oppressive, so portentously disturbing in that vast stillness, that it stabbed your mind like a dagger. And none of the official reassurances which came with every *communiqué* was able to banish that strange, unreasoning apprehension from your mind. It clutched at your throat with spectral fingers. You knew as well as Daladier and Gamelin, whose voices could be heard through the radios behind the shuttered windows, that the Maginot Line stood there far to the west, a formidable bastion of unimaginable power, bristling with steel and ready to spew death at the invader at an instant's notice. But of what avail, one wondered, would be the most impregnable fortifications, if the spirit of resistance should be found lacking?

I crossed the Seine bridge and watched the river by the pale glow of a covered lantern coiling its way between the quays like a gigantic bottle-green snake. But the face of Saint Geneviève's statue, turned in the direction of the barbarian invasions, was shrouded in a black mist that did not arise from the stream. It was as if the patron saint of Paris had lost her head and had no way of seeing the approaching danger.

Whence came the fear, the all-pervading undertone of indifference, the *je-m'en-foutisme* of the masses? And was it really fear? Could one be sure of that? When, ere this, had Frenchmen been afraid to face fierce, even overwhelming odds, or had they hesitated to die for freedom? In the semiobscurity of the great North and East railway stations, I watched the departure of the levies for the advance posts. Soldiers and officers—Bretons, Flemings, Basques, Alsatians—were pouring through in never-ending streams. Whether you came at noon or in the dead of night, it was always the same scene, men, men, and still more men, marching by, trotting, stamping, tramping. Packed troop trains were leaving every minute for the front. But not once did I hear a cry, not once a shout of patriotism, not once did I see a show of ardor or feel a ripple of enthusiasm. In a crowd of thousands of spectators and relatives of the departing soldiers, not ten individuals, I noted, saluted the battle flags and the regimental emblems as they went by.

Were these the sons of the Revolution, of the Year II of Liberty? Were these boys in horizon-blue the children of the barefooted sans-culottes who had thrown back the coalitions of Europe's reaction, without thought of danger or of hunger? Were these the descendants of the heroes who had marched off like lions sniffing the tempest, to efface the frontiers of Europe and to perform prodigies of heroism under Marceau and Joubert? "Volunteers!" the ancestors of these men cried out, "let us go and die to liberate the peoples of Europe!" To that cry a million men had responded. Now their sons marched by sullenly, automatically, listlessly, scarcely glancing to left or right, obviously contemptuous of the double hedge of Mobile Guards through which they had to pass. Not a smile, not one shout of encouragement, not once a cheer. Why weren't the huge glass domes overhead reverberating with the thunder of the *Marseillaise* or the *Jeune Garde*—or *Madelon,* for that matter? Was the danger less than in the days of Veuillot or Verdun?

I had stood near a middle-aged citizen in the crowd of spectators. Almost simultaneously turning to leave, we looked into each other's eyes, quizzical, disturbed, intuitively asking for an expression of opinion.

"*C'est bien morne,*" I blurted out involuntarily. "It's dreary, that spectacle!"

"*Non,* monsieur," he corrected me, "it is sinister!"

Then back into the streets, down the lugubrious Boulevard de Strasbourg, where I myself had marched with the Canadian battalions, twenty-two years before. Our place had been taken by a procession of caterpillar tanks rumbling over the broken pavement. The vehicles stretched as far as the eye could reach and beyond the blue arc light at the intersection of the Grands Boulevards. In the semi-darkness they looked like one of those black serpentine monsters in the Japanese prints: a small head with an endless tail. Some of the soldiers were sound asleep on top of the steel lids. In the trailers, lying in clusters, pell-mell on each other, they made you think of little children being carried home after a day's picnic in the woods.

At the corner of the Rue du Château-d'Eau a group of prostitutes were talking excitedly with two night watchmen of the cycle corps.

"I have my rights," shouted a big blonde girl, whom

one of the policemen held by the arms. "I have my rights, and I intend to have my rights respected."

"T'as pas des droits, ma fille," said the big cop. *"T'es putain, c'est tout!"* (You have no rights, girlie, you are only a whore!)

For answer she struck him across the lips so that the blood trickled into his moustache.

The other cop lifted his bicycle and knocked the girl down. She was on her feet in a flash and screamed like a fury. Her arm had been broken. As she was led away, she yelled: "Bread and peace! *Vive la République!*" The soldiers on the tanks, awakened by the shouting, rubbed their eyes and stared as if they had heard a blasphemy.

I walked down the Boulevard Saint-Michel, where some students were sitting on the terraces of the Café d'Harcourt and the Chope Latine. They were talking in whispers, but squads of gendarmes were watching them from across the street. I bought some English newspapers at the kiosk facing the closed Luxembourg Gardens and learned from a man signing himself "Diplomatic Correspondent" that the morale of the French Army was higher than in the days of Verdun. The headlines announced that Gamelin would break the Siegfried Line the moment the signal was given that the war had started.

A green bus swung suddenly out of the Rue de Médicis. Its destination was marked in front in luminous letters above the driver's seat: *Gare Montparnasse.* That was my direction, and I jumped on board. There were about ten or twelve passengers inside and two men standing on the rear balcony.

A man dressed in a dilapidated overcoat and a derby hat that had seen better days took off his pince-nez with a gesture of evident dismay, folded up the newspaper he had been reading with the aid of a small pocket torch, and exclaimed with so deep a sigh that all the passengers looked at him with surprise: *"Quelle époque!"*

"To what epoch do you refer—to this time in which we are living?" an individual, who was sitting directly in front of the man who had made the doleful exclamation, asked in a shrill piping voice.

"Obviously," came back the first speaker. "What other epoch could I have in mind, *parbleu?* Do you think I'm talking about the Middle Ages?"

"We live in the time we deserve," said the second individual, who wore a painter's blouse and a beret.

"Even so, the cost of living is going up frightfully, *tout qui augmente,* would you say honest folks deserve that?" insisted the doleful one.

"Oh, the cost of living, is that what you mean? But that is not true either. The cost of living is not rising as rapidly as it was under Poincaré, for instance. Not by any means. Besides, the trouble with us is not the high cost of living. That is definitely not a fundamental issue today. What is much graver is our lack of idealism and the materialization of our whole life."

"*Ça, pooh-pooh!* That's a very old story," interjected the conductor, who had overheard the colloquy as he moved through the car punching our tickets. "I heard my grandmother complain of the decline of idealism when I was a child. You both see things from the dark side, that's clear. I don't," the conductor went on. "Privately, I think there is hope . . . privately, you understand. But I don't say so. Why don't I say anything, do you think? Simply because it is dangerous to speak optimistically."

"Why dangerous?" asked the erstwhile newspaper reader, stopping abruptly in the act of running his tongue along the edge of the paper of a cigarette he had just rolled. "What danger, *je vous prie*, is there in an expression of optimism?"

"There is danger," explained the conductor. "Public optimism, you see," he went on, dropping his voice to a mysterious whisper, "public optimism would unquestionably be of advantage to this government of nincompoops, you will readily agree to that. I grumble, not because I want to, but because it's the last right I have. I say: let's all grumble!"

Everybody laughed. But Painter's Blouse pulled the conductor's sleeve and, motioning significantly with his head in the direction of the rear of the bus, said: "Don't let those two on the back platform hear you grumble."

The conductor looked at the rear balcony, threw up his shoulders quickly, and said: "*O, là, là!*"

At the Raspail intersection we came to a halt. Troops were passing. They had the right of way. We waited five minutes, ten minutes, a quarter of an hour, and still the road was not clear.

The passengers grew nervous and fidgety, they began to consult their watches.

"How long will this last?" said one man.

Another said: "I didn't know there were so many horses in France. Poor beasts!" And shrugging his shoulders, he added: "At least we can say that there has been no decline in the birth rate of horses!"

Still another chimed in: "This delay will make me miss my train! It's damned inconvenient, I must say."

"Messieurs, messieurs," came the reassuring voice of another passenger, who had not said a word up till then, *"ne vous en faîtes pas,* don't worry. *Laissez passer la prison ambulante,* let the walking prison go by."

The words were not out of his mouth before the two men from the rear balcony stepped inside the bus.

"Your papers, please!" they demanded icily.

"I have no papers," said the man who had made the remark about the army. "I have no papers. I am the son of the Unknown Soldier!"

They took him off the bus right then and there, and one of them blew a whistle for the police.

The bus was off again. It veered around Kleber's statue and the Clôserie des Lilas, where the clock showed it to be a few minutes before midnight. The conductor called out the stations mechanically, in a droning voice, as if he were reciting a litany: "Saint-Michel, Grande Chaumière, Notre-Dame-des-Champs. . . ." In front of the Montparnasse station the bus slowed down, the wheels grated against the curb, and the old engine, hissing and spluttering like an asthmatic man after a fast run, with a last shuddering spasm stopped dead. "Terminus!" sang out the conductor, and the tone of relief in his voice made it sound like a welcome amen at the close of a long prayer. He jumped to the pavement, pulled up his trousers, and tightened his belt.

I walked across the square, past the Restaurant Lavenue, where I noticed Georg Bernhard, the former editor of Berlin's *Vossische Zeitung,* at table on the terrace with a French officer in the uniform of the intelligence service. The German journalist greeted me with an almost imperceptible move of his hand.

On a wooden street bench, in front of the coffeehouse, sat the old beggar, who had long been a fixture of this neighborhood, where I also had resided for years. If you gave him a couple of francs, he would dance with glee and run off as fast as his feet could carry him—to fill up on Pernod at a taproom.

"*Tenez,*" he said, as he caught sight of me, "why so late in our gay city?" He looked like one of those horrible creatures in the illustrated editions of Victor Hugo's *The Terrible Year,* the gnomes and phantoms who came up out of the sewers and the catacombs to haunt the deserted streets of the famine-stricken metropolis. The beggar, commonly called "Papa Pitrou" by those who knew him, had deteriorated a great deal since I had seen him last. His long hair had fallen down in greasy curls to his shoulders; his white beard was streaked with yellow, while his clothes were a bundle of rags held to his body with a rope. He looked up to me with the reddish, wicked eyes of an albino as he filled his mouth with snails, which he had probably pilfered from one of the stalls across the way. He picked the snails from their shells with a broken fork.

"Do you still live at Number Nine?" I asked him, for I remembered that when I resided in the quarter, the concierge at one of the apartment houses on the Rue Saint-Romain used, of a wintry night, to give him asylum midst the garbage cans in the cellar.

"No," he answered, his mouth full of the succulent delicacy. "No, at Number Nine I dwell no more. I now spend my days in this very square, and my nights, too. One sleeps rather well on these benches. One feeds well, too, as you may observe. Moreover, the view is pleasant. What animation, *n'est ce pas?* It's greatly to my liking. I am absolutely content. I take a supreme delight in watching the panic."

"What panic?" I asked in surprise.

"What panic?" he returned, looking up with a horribly

malignant twinkle in his eyes. "The panic of the *bourgeoi-sie,* of course! Look around you, *mon ami!* Can't you see it and sense it? They're in a mortal funk. They've lost all hope. For years they knew that this would come. They put it off as long as they could. They did not want a renewal *(une renaissance).* They wanted to continue, to hang on to what they had, to their poor little dirty, decrepit possessions and survive, just survive, just sneak through for another generation. After us, the deluge! *Eh bien,* the deluge is not waiting any longer. It's upon them. Ha, ha, ha!" he laughed loudly.

"*L'heure a sonné,*" he resumed in a solemn voice. "The hour has come at last. . . . It's the end of the end that is approaching now. . . . The great whore is about to face judgment!"

"By judgment you mean Hitler?"

"Monsieur Hitler," he railed. "No, not Monsieur Hit-ler! *Je m'en fous de cet homme, et je m'en contrefous!* I don't care a damn for him." He snapped his crooked fingers in contempt. "Monsieur Hitler is just part of the combination. It's the world that is cracking, our world. The supports are rotten. . . . Do you know why?" he added. "It's because the worms, I mean people like me, the lice-covered *malheureux,* the syphilitic, tubercular garbage eaters, the great unwashed, it's we who have gnawed away the substance, the core of the pillars. We have been eating away for ages, for centuries, we have been chewing at the pillars of society since the foundation of the world, you might say. Do you know what you are walking on?" he went on breathlessly. "From Val-de-Grâce to the Santé Prison, from the Réservoir to the Porte de Châtillon and far to the west, you are walking on the void. That's what you are doing. There is nothing beneath your feet, absolutely nothing but a thin crust. Everything is hollow down below here, emptied out, burrowed, mined and countermined, excavated, what am I telling you? . . . It is scooped out, so to speak. The collapse is due any minute now. It's here now. . . . The farce is over. There's going to be a jubilee in hell." He laughed exultingly, with a shrill, frightening sound that was more bark than laugh. Then he fell to coughing.

"Do you ever see Tarzan nowadays?" I asked, so as to change the subject which was becoming risky in a land where the government itself warned you by posters on the billboards that the walls have ears. Tarzan was the concierge at Number Nine, Rue Saint-Romain, a huge, ape-like man, who had been given that nickname by the neighbors because of his gaunt and hairy appearance.

"Tarzan," the beggar shook his head. "No, that fool is mobilized. His wife is for the taking. It was she, in fact, who put me out of the cellar. I asked her the night after her husband left: 'Well, Madame, you and I, we are not going to let the human race become extinct, are we?' "

"*Parbleu,* you offended the lady! No wonder you lost her hospitality," I said.

"Ah, no," he came back quickly, "I knew what I was about. I had my peekholes in that cellar a long time. I knew what was going on."

I gave him his dole—two francs—and started to move away. "Make it five tonight," he called me back. "You'll not see me for a long time."

"I'm staying," I protested. "I'm not leaving France, no matter what happens."

"You had better go, *mon ami,*" he said quietly. "*Ça va barder!* There's going to be hell to pay. Take my word for it. Earthquakes are nothing compared to what old Europe is going to see. This is not a war that's coming—it's the Devil with a big broom. And he's going to sweep clean this time. Not a speck of the old will remain!"

"You forget the Maginot Line," I said, noticing that some people were approaching.

"The Maginot Line, ha, ha, that's a good one!" he called back. "*Merde,* do you hear? *Merde,* that's the Maginot Line!"

The breeze swept a bitter smell of anise and fried potatoes down the Rue de la Gaîté. A raucous loud-speaker brayed a song about a soldier who had left his girl without saying a word of tenderness. At the corner stood some taxicabs. One of the drivers approached me to say that he knew a good show in the Étoile quarter. "A show in the black-out," he whispered. Before I could answer him I saw a patrol of the political police closing the street at both ends and beginning to question passers-by, holding passports and identity papers under the electric lamps that hung from their tunics. I dived into a doorway and found myself in a *café chantant.*

The place was crowded with soldiers and noncommissioned officers. On the stage was a clown playing an accordion. The glare of a fierce yellow light, coming from a square aperture above the entrance door and streaming across the hall like a searchlight beam, beat unmercifully on his painted features. He blinked and smirked alternately under the impact. At the table nearest to the door were three artillerymen and their girls. They clapped their hands in rhythmic accompaniment to the clown's music. At other tables men and women were beating out the measure with tumblers and bottles.

Soon the clown withdrew under a hail of applause, and his place on the stage was taken by a small orchestra— a drummer, a saxophone player, and a pianist. The light changed to red, tables were pushed aside, and everybody got up to dance. A fourth artist climbed on to the stage and began to sing through a microphone. His voice sounded like a tornado. He sang: *Elle-avait-de tout-petits michons.* Bellowing, the crowd took up the refrain in chorus: *Valenteene, Valenteene!* Presently one soldier lifted his dancing partner to his shoulders. She was a swarthy Haitian girl with a red ribbon in her hair. While sitting on the tramping cavalier's neck, she discarded her gown, flung it toward the stage where the saxophone player caught it, and, swinging her arms upward, began to tear down the colored balloons and artificial flowers suspended from the ceiling. One by one, the other girls were swung aloft by their partners. They followed the dark girl's example of undressing and joining in the whirling chase of the balloons and confetti.

The light burned lower and lower until the illumination in the hall was a mere glow of dying embers. In the feeble red twilight the dancers seemed like weird, fantastic shapes executing some primitive saraband in a jungle clearing: centaurs and satyrs and nymphs and double-headed apparitions. The screaming and singing were hushed; the horde now whirled in suggestive silence.

"*C'est la danse de la mort,* the dance of death," said the doorman, who stood by my side looking on. A giant with a grizzly moustache, he wore the threadbare uniform of the Don Cossacks and an Astrakhan hat.

"Is that what it is called," I asked, "the dance of death?"

"No, I call it so," he said. "The nearer they come to death, these young men, the more they feel the need of female companionship. it's a natural urge: nature is trying in advance to make up for the empty places there are going to be in a few weeks, *c'est tout*. That's the psychological significance of a scene like this. . . ."

"You are a philosopher," I said.

"No," he came back, "I am just an old soldier. . . . I fought for the Czar in 1905 in Manchuria, I know what I am talking about. . . . It's always just before the battle that Venus has her busiest hours. . . . There wasn't a soul in this place for months. Now we are crowded from sunset to sunup. It's the smell of battle that drives them here, the smell of blood. . . ."

The light turned to green as we spoke, and a young woman, completely nude, walked on to the stage. She was a brunette of great charm, ardent and lascivious. The saxophone player announced that she was going to present an Oriental number. She danced alone. In the motions of her beautiful arms, her breasts, and her abdomen, in the expression of her eyes and in her smiles, she achieved so complete and marvelous a harmony that she made you think of the serpent of Beaudelaire.

The laughter in the hall died down. It became as still as in a church.

I stopped at Louis Tschann's bookshop, thinking that I could there write out the script for my broadcast, which came at three in the morning. It was shortly after midnight, and I had almost three hours, but I also had to pass the censor before I could speak.

Louis Ferdinand Céline, the author of *Journey to the End of the Night,* was in the bookshop, telling a young regimental doctor that France had been sold out by the Jews and hence was "*fichue, foutue dans la purée, dans la merde du diable.*" Céline, a giant with a black beard, was spouting obscenities and filth, as usual.

"The English," he roared, "the English are Jewish swine. It's Israel that rules the roost on the Thames. We're caught between Abraham and Joseph of Moscow."

"I don't like the English myself," said the young medical man, "and as to the Jews, you know my sentiments, but I would remind you that the Communists have been charged with warmongering ever since the Popular Front came into existence. They urged us to smash at the Boches when it would have been easy to crack them in the Paris-Moscow nutcracker."

"It's the Jews, I tell you, who are responsible for all this," Céline insisted. "They have led us by the nose step by step until today we are standing on the brink of disaster. Tomorrow they will push us into the abyss."

"Why should they?" the young doctor shrugged his shoulders. "If we go into the abyss, the Jews will go with us, willy-nilly. Do you imagine the Jews do not know what to expect from Hitler? They are his chosen people, chosen, that is, for the most atrocious torments. . . ."

"That's why they're pushing us into war. They want us to do the fighting," came back Céline.

"Somebody is pushing us to war," chimed in the shopkeeper. "Of that there is no doubt. There isn't a man in France who wants to fight, and still everybody is grabbing his gun and moving up the line. I myself leave on the ninth day of the mobilization—that is to say, the day after tomorrow. . . . It's the English who are pushing us in, that's my opinion," he added.

"Well, that's the same thing," shot back Céline. "England—that is, the City, the international bankers, the same old crowd. In London it's Israel who commands, everybody knows that. Do not the English claim to be descended from the ten lost tribes of Judah?"

"Pourtant," interjected the doctor, "they do not look like Semites. No two peoples on earth look so much alike as the Germans and the English. Does that make the Nazis Jews, too? No," he continued, "the English are driving us into this war for an entirely different reason. They figure that so long as France fights, their empire is safe. Since Hitler wants nothing from France and has solemnly promised not to attack us, the English were in a quandary until they made Poland the issue. . . . The Poles are our allies, to be sure, but the Poles are an arrogant lot. Their generals talk of seizing East Prussia and of marching on Berlin. England backs them up in that threatening attitude, not to plunge Poland into war, but in order to make us take the plunge. The English care not a rap for Poland. And as long as we fight, England will have her way in Europe."

I took down a book from the shelves. It's title was *Au Seuil de la guerre*—On the Threshold of War—published in 1933. I opened it to a page showing an illustration of the city of Strasbourg, with the cathedral and principal buildings of the Alsatian city allegorically bound in a thick chain of steel. The caption read: "Never will Germany rest so long as these symbols of German-Alsatian grandeur are in the hands of the degenerate French." The illustration was a reproduction from the *Völkischer Beobachter*, Adolf Hitler's own paper.

"In his speeches," I said, "the Fuehrer tells you that he has no claims on France. But this is what his paper says." I showed them the illustration. "Once he is given Alsace, he will be across the border, inside France, and he'll ask for more. He has made that very clear in the case of

Czechoslovakia. When he was given the Sudeten regions, he guaranteed the inviolability of what was left of Czech national territory. He broke that solemn engagement on the pretense that nothing was agreed about it in Munich. At the bottom of all of Herr Hitler's arguments there is one doctrine, this: Germany has rights, and Adolf Hitler has been sent by Providence to claim those rights and fulfill German destiny. Germany, the Fuehrer says, only asks for what belongs to her. But what belongs to her?

"It turns out that Hitler claims everything that belonged to the Holy Roman Empire of the German Nation in the Middle Ages, every bit of land in Europe that Germans occupied in the course of history or merely traversed, in addition to every inch of territory that was ever so slightly influenced by Teutonic civilization. The unhappy Czechs, for instance, have been condemned to absorption because it is officially stated in Berlin that they squatted on land that was long ago abandoned by German barons or because German emperors once lived in Prague and because a great number of cathedrals and castles in their country clearly show the influence of German architectural styles. On that basis, France would have a right to all the imitation palaces of Versailles in the world, and she could claim all the rich country homes in the United States that were modeled on French châteaux.

"Hitler said in his last speech that Germany once dominated the Western world. You will not be able to find one serious historian to tell you when this occurred, nor will you be able to discover historical justification for that other assertion of his that 'even before the formation of the Brandenburg-Prussian state, Germany was a world empire.' These things are simply lies. But what does the

Fuehrer care? With these declarations he seeks to justify in his own mind and in the minds of his followers the Third Reich's claims to the mastery not only of Alsace-Lorraine, but of the world."

"Of the world?" exclaimed Céline sarcastically. "Now you exaggerate. All the Fuehrer wants from France is the right to help us get rid of our Jews."

"He will probably do that," I said, "that is, if you let him in. But he will rid you of much more besides, once you do let him in.

"There was a time," I continued, "when Herr Hitler said he merely wanted to liberate Germany from the *Diktat* of Versailles. One by one, the clauses of that treaty were abolished by the victor nations of the last war. Not because these nations feared Herr Hitler. Some of the clauses had been abolished at a time when Hitler was no more than an unemployed paperhanger. They were abolished because liberals everywhere considered the burdens of Versailles unjust and insupportable for the German people. It was the liberals who brought about a mitigation of the burdens of Versailles.

"Then Herr Hitler raised the racial question and demanded that Germany's frontiers should correspond with the limits of German race, language, and blood. It was an absurd doctrine, confused and, in the light of history, downright ridiculous, but at least it still set a certain limit to German ambitions. The occupation of Czechoslovakia proves that he now goes beyond race limits, for the Czechs and the Slovaks are Slavs. The Lorrainers are French, and they are to be incorporated in the Reich, too. The Dutch and Danes are now called nations speaking a Germanic idiom. This means they have no longer a right to an independent national existence—in other words, sooner or later they must be assimilated into the German Reich and pass under the sway of their big brothers, the warriors of the Third Reich, who draw their revolvers when they hear the phrase 'national culture' and who pride themselves on having shaken off 'the nightmare of intellectualism.'

"Today Herr Hitler rejects all limits and makes his own all the delirious theories of Pan-Germanism: race, language, grammar, verb conjugation, living room, means of communication, military exigencies, density of population, the shape of roofs, artistic influences, the length of skulls, and the prehistoric epochs. Whithersoever a dinosaur in the preglacial period wandered from the area where Herr Hitler reigns at present, whether in the direction of the Ukraine or Norway or to the lost continent of Atlantis, there is Germany, and there the Nazi power intends to install itself. Wherever a German pioneer cut down a forest, built a road, or forded a river, even if that pioneer fled from Germany to escape oppression and misery, wherever he settled, whether in Milwaukee, Brazil, or Pretoria, there is a milepost to direct the Third Reich in its march to world power.... You say in your books, Monsieur Céline, that Hitler is a genius because he rid Germany of the Jews and thus set an example to all Christian states. Have you ever considered that this Fuehrer is the antithesis of the European spirit and that if those theories of race and blood should prevail, there would be an end to the Christian era and all its treasures: justice, truth, morality, art, philosophy and religion? . . ."

But Céline was waving his hand in a deprecating gesture. "All I care about," he said, "is that we get rid of the Jews, yes, and incidentally I was also glad to hear you say that the Fuehrer includes America in his scheme of conquest. That is really good news. . . ." I was going into the back room to write my script for the broadcast. But he called after me: "I am so glad, in fact, that I would willingly open him a road across France to march against the Anglos, for if there ever was a contemptible race, there you have it."

I had scarcely started to write my notes when Tschann came into the back room carrying a copy of the *Journal officiel.* "Here," he said, "is a report of the meeting of the Senate this afternoon. It may be useful to you in your broadcast."

The report said that the President of the Senate, after discussing the international crisis, and on the motion of M. Daladier, the chief of the government, had proposed a resolution declaring the people of France "solidly with our English allies in the position they have taken in the matter of the Reich's claims on Danzig." Jules Jeanneney, the President of the Senate, had just put the motion, the report went on to say, when the Senator for the *département* of Seine-et-Marne, Pierre Laval, rose in his seat and asked for the floor.

"*Mais non,* M. Laval," said the *président,* "really, this is not the time to talk. This is the time to act. In this hour we must show by our unanimity that the country is united, that we no longer quarrel, that we are one in word and deed."

"But I insist on my rights as a Senator," M. Laval had replied, "I must speak. . . ." There were some cries of dissent at this point, the *Journal officiel* reported, but in the end Laval had his way. He said that in this solemn moment he wanted to remind the Senate and the people of France of the "great and eminent service rendered to France by that great statesman, Signor Mussolini, in the month of February, 1934."

"To what 'great and eminent' service did Monsieur Laval refer," Tschann asked me over my shoulder.

"In that month," I replied, "Adolf Hitler flew to meet Mussolini. He wanted to know what the Duce thought of a plan that had been conceived by Goering. Goering had thought that France could be paralyzed and knocked out by one surprise blow. Without a declaration of war, Paris and other great cities, rail centers, and industrial areas were to be laid under a blanket of poison gas, all in a single night."

"*Eh bien?*" questioned Tschann.

"*Eh bien*, Mussolini, who had been sworn to secrecy by his friend from Berlin, immediately telephoned Franklin-Bouillon, the head of the Military Commission in the French Chamber, who was stopping at the Lido-Venice at the time. Franklin-Bouillon telephoned Pierre Laval, and that's all."

It had started to rain when I left the old bookshop. Tschann insisted on my taking his umbrella, for it would be a long walk to the Hotel Continental, where the censors had lately installed themselves. "And besides," he said in parting, "you never know: an umbrella may serve you in lieu of a *permis de circulation*. An umbrella is a badge of respectability these days, therefore a guarantee of security, like the red bonnet in the time of the Revolution.

"But wait," he called, as I started to move off, "what book are you carrying under your arm?"

"This book?" I asked. "Why, it's the one you just sold me. It's *Lucien Jacques' Diary*. . . ."

"You must not take that tonight," he said with a note

of disquiet in his voice, as he tried to take the volume away from me. "I'd rather have you take that some other day. I would not like to see you being questioned by the police with that volume in your possession. . . ."

"But it is nothing more than the diary of a stretcher-bearer in the last war—what harm can there be in that?" I protested.

"Precisely, the diary of a stretcher-bearer: isn't that sufficient to make it a dangerous volume to be seen with, especially for a foreigner? Just take your umbrella—it will be much safer, I assure you."

"No, I take the book, too," I said, breaking away hastily.

And so I was off at last. I walked rapidly down the Rue Notre-Dame-des-Champs, past the house where Saint-Beuve had once lived, and turned into the Boulevard Raspail. I noticed from afar that the lights were burning in the military prison of Cherche-Midi. Covered trucks drove up before its entrance and discharged batches of civilians and soldiers, clearly the Mobile Guard's evening catch of reservists whose papers had not been found in order or soldiers who should have been away at the front. Some aliens, too, no doubt. . . .

I gave a wide berth to that sinister old dungeon with all its disturbing memories. *"La cage aux hommes"*—the cage for men—Francis Carco had called it in one of his books. I had no desire to be seen by one of those troopers who were herding their shuffling prisoners into the gate. It would have been hard enough to explain my presence in Paris, contrary to regulations, particularly at that unearthly hour. But now with that script for the broadcast in my pocket, full of military terms as it was, the situation was apt to be twice as painful if I should be apprehended. Of course, I was not a spy or anything of the kind, and, in the event of arrest, I would immediately have got in touch with the Canadian legation or with acquaintances in the government, such as Anatole de Monzie, Ludovic Frossard, or M. Daladier himself. But I knew from a previous experience, when M. Laval had decreed my expulsion from France, how long it takes to get redress. Moreover, now it was war time and I was definitely not *en règle*. I felt more like breaking into a trot than keeping to my even walking pace.

At that moment four municipal policemen flew by on their bicycles. They were going my way, and I followed them with my eyes, wondering what could be up. I was not long left in doubt. At the next intersection, half a block ahead, I saw them suddenly dismount, throw their machines against the sidewalk, and rush into the side street. When I reached the Rue de Varenne, I saw three of the policemen locking handcuffs on two men, neither of whom resisted or protested with so much as a word. One of the prisoners, a mere boy in a frayed cotton shirt, was calmly lighting a cigarette while he casually watched the fourth nightwatch, who held up an electric torch, trying to scrape a freshly pasted-up poster from the wall. On the sidewalk stood a pail containing paste and a couple of long-handled brushes and, a short distance away, their pedals poised on the curb for an immediate getaway, two more bicycles. The two prisoners had been caught in the act of putting up a poster.

The chief of the night patrol had a hard time tearing the poster off. He seized one of the brushes and used its handle as a scraper, but broad strips of the thick paper clung stubbornly to the wall. The red-colored headline that ran across the top of the now-lacerated proclamation resisted all attempts at erasure. It still clung there as the policemen and their quarry made ready to move off. I could only read the two top lines: "Frenchmen-Brothers! *Contre le Fascisme—Oui! Mais à condition que c'est contre le Fascisme partout!* Against Fascism—Yes! But on condition that it is against Fascism everywhere!" And then these words still remained: "Are you sure that the government of bankers and utility magnates, who betrayed our Czech allies at Munich, is sincere this time?" That was all that remained of the ten-foot poster.

I walked on, greatly upset. What, I asked myself, was happening to France and to the people of France who had so often in the past been humanity's forerunner and Europe's voice and conscience in seasons of most poignant agony? My anxiety over the future had been superseded, in recent days and nights of vigil, by a deepening disquietude over what was taking place right then and there. An awareness was growing on me that the present hour, and not what might or might not occur thereafter, was the blossomtime of fate, the almost palpable turning-point in the evolution of Western civilization.

Suddenly that night, as I glanced up at the somber mass of the War Department on the Rue Saint-Dominique, before which a number of diminutive Tonkinese sentries were pacing to and fro and giggling at each other, I knew that there, behind those blue-papered windows and a few blocks beyond, in the salons of the Quai d'Orsay, the building dimly outlined by the mysterious light of the emergency lanterns, the battle for the future was being waged. Not on impending battlefields, amid the clash of steel or in the inferno of gunfire of some Maginot Line or other, but here in the stillness of the night, in this sinister procession of shadows which was Paris, the decision would fall or had fallen already. Whatever debasement and suffering and darkness mankind was to endure in years to come would be the consequence of words spoken and deeds done in this very hour.

The sentiment of gloom, which gradually overwhelmed me, did not find its nourishment in the minor incidents and the petty annoyances of French life thrown suddenly out of balance, as it was, by the imminence of the enormous menace on the frontiers. France had faced great tempests in the past and faced them with equanimity. Nor was it the possibility of defeat that unnerved me. It is better to be defeated in a great cause than not to have fought at all. For the graveyard alone, as Nietzsche says, is the condition of resurrection. In the past the French people had always, and precisely in moments of high historical tension, regained a consciousness of its ultimate and deepest power and had risen, even from spiritual debasement and poverty, to advance into the future for the conquest of new possibilities. In the tumults of history, France had never before lost its faith. The idealism in the soul of France, which cannot be explained by the Marxist doctrine of economic determinism, had always, no matter how deep the humiliation or how disparate the odds, lifted it to the stars, to storm the heavens, as it were, and to reach out for goals that seemed humanly unattainable. In a terrifying burst of enthusiasm, the French people had once set out to bring the message of freedom, equality, and brotherhood to the enslaved peoples of Europe. They had always been in the vanguard in the struggle for human emancipation. No matter how often hurled back, they were always willing to throw themselves anew into the fray or under the guillotine for the ideal. Had they now succumbed to discouragement, bowed their souls to the merely inevitable?

Had they lost the wonder-working faith that had sustained them in the greatest trials?

As I walked over the Pont de la Concorde, that bridge whose arches and piles are built from the debris of the Bastille, the very stones reminded me of the many times that the People of Paris had stood on the barricades, unflinching in the face of injustice, violence, and terror, shouting in the teeth of tyrants: you have the soldiers and the cannon, you have the big battalions and the power. The whole earth is yours. Even so: war it is! We accept the issue! You fight for oppression, we for freedom!

Whence had come the immense lassitude of the present hour? Did Hitler's legions seem so small an evil that their advance could be ignored? Was Paris so drugged as to be insensible of the mortal danger now looming on the horizon?

The city which had dazzled history with its light, which had abolished the throne and the altar, the city of Voltaire and Jean-Jacques, of Victor Hugo and Zola and Jean Jaurès, lay there as if devoured by a mortal ennui—indifferent, impotent. Was Paris an eagle asleep that could yet be roused to terrible combat or was it an eagle caught and imprisoned in the black net of the fowler's intrigue?

Everything pointed to the imminence of war. Diplomatic relations with Berlin and Rome were rapidly deteriorating. The issue would soon be decided and the suspense of months broken. Guns, tanks, and men were streaming toward the frontiers. Passenger traffic on all the railway lines north, east, and west of Paris had been suspended to give right of way to the allies from Britain, who were pouring across the Channel in their hundreds of thousands. On the roads running in the direction of Belgium, Germany, and Luxembourg moved an uninterrupted chain of trucks and caissons and kitchens and artillery. Blenheims, Spitfires, and Hurricane fighters and bombers had come to join the Farmans and the Renaults in the French sky. Every road crossing, every bridge, every factory in France, was under heavy guard, and every farmhouse in the border regions was wrapped in coils of barbed-wire entanglement. Daladier, to spike the rumors that France lacked mechanized equipment, declared that there was not the least warrant, "not a shred of justification," for anxiety and that the fatherland could be proud and sure of its defenses, which were "more formidable, more efficient, and a hundred times more impressive than in 1918. . . . To the West stands the Maginot Line," he said, "unassailable, impregnable, and unconquerable," and nearer by, around Paris, like a ring of steel-mouthed watchdogs, another row of forts: Nogent, Issy, Valérien. . . .

But the people, playing a *jeu de mots* with those names, whispered: *"Nos gens d'ici ne valent rien*—our fellows here are not worth a hoot." France was ready, France was calm, France was invincible—you heard those affirmations repeated with every turn of the dial, yet never in history had there been so deep and universal an anxiety, such a feeling of gloom and of impending disaster as at that moment.

Once, but that was three years earlier, when the Popular Front came into power, there had been an upsurge of national sentiment and patriotism such as no one had ever seen before. Then the future had looked promising. Then the sun of France had shone brightest, and men had gone about their tasks with joy and hope in their hearts and with a song on their lips. In that hour, with Gallic *bravoure*, they would have flung a challenge to the universe at the least threat. For then France had seemed well worth defending: the promise of democracy seemed about to be fulfilled. The French people had hope and courage—and faith in the future.

But that was three years ago. Now hope had departed, courage had been vitiated, and faith in the future had turned into sullen indifference. The people had been robbed of their ideals. The operation of democratic institutions had been suspended. Spontaneous *élan* had been supplanted by regimentation. The vital current of idealism had been diverted into sterile channels of frustration and disillusionment. Now men went around as if they were crushed by some terrible enormity, as if they had lost interest in life itself. A secret worm was gnawing at their hearts, sapping courage, devouring their energy. Not once, anywhere, did one hear so much as a single word of enthusiasm for the impending struggle, though the government kept insisting that it would be "a struggle for freedom."

The Chamber had been sent on vacation. The Prime Minister, who had conferred on himself the symbolic title of *"Taureau de Vaucluse*—Bull of Vaucluse," in imitation of Clemenceau's "Tiger of France," had moved his bed into the War Department. He had taken things in hand. He was ruling by decree, by threats, and by the nozzles of machine guns. Not a single political party in France had by so much as a word opposed the voting of war credits or had expressed disagreement with the government's decision to go to war if Germany should invade Poland. The Left merely had protested that a stand should have been made long before, when Czechoslovakia's forty-five divisions were still intact and when Spain was being overrun by the Condor Legion and the *terribili* of the Fascio.

Yet, the Left was treated as if it were in league with the enemy, upon whom Daladier himself had fawned at Munich. Reading Leftist newspapers was forbidden to the troops. Editors who expressed a feeble hope that the crisis could perhaps still be solved in a peaceful way were gagged or thrown into jail. The police were padlocking printing houses. Assemblies were prohibited. No *attroupements* were allowed in the streets—that is to say, gatherings of more than three individuals, even of three total strangers reading a news bulletin in front of a newspaper office, were broken up. Martial law went into effect in one province after the other. Schools and theaters were closed. The Bull of Vaucluse was in command, now as feverishly applauded by the bankers and the trust magnates as he had been execrated by the same class when he led the Popular Front to victory. There was to be no more talk of appeasement, no more questioning, no debate, no discussion, no more weakness. France had to look the future in the face fearlessly, sure of itself.

But the people of France could not be stirred. They remained unmoved by the appeals that came more and more insistently from those who now held the state's levers of control in their hands. Nothing seemed capable of rousing the French masses from the mental lethargy in which the country had been stagnating since the dissolution of the Popular Front. It was as if the men of France, who had on dozens of occasions in the course of history built barricades and ventured their all for the defense and extension of democratic rights and for the clarification of human thought, had suddenly lost (or, rather, had been deprived of) the quintessential parts of those almost demoniacal powers of theirs which they had so often deployed in the cause of Europe's regeneration.

It must not be thought that anyone denied or minimized the immense and mortal danger to which the Republic had become exposed by the resurgent militarism of Germany. Nobody doubted that the Reich would some day carry out the threat of its leaders and make a thorough-going attempt to eliminate what they had for years been calling "the putrid source of democratic liberalism on the European continent." France—that is, democratic France, the land and the people that had constituted the revolutionary crater from which all the fiery currents of liberty had splashed over Europe—had long been marked as the major obstacle in the New Order's path. No Frenchman doubted this. No Frenchman, therefore, had refused the government's call to take down his gun and rally around the tricolor.

Still, there was something fundamentally wrong with France. There was an outer conformity to the mobilization decrees, but you felt intuitively that innerly there was a strong current of passive resistance to the trend of affairs. The people were suspicious of the government's intentions. They were wondering whether the government, which was made up of appeasers and admirers of Hitler's antidemocratic convictions, was not taking them into war not so much to crush the Nazi régime as to rob the French people of their last remaining instruments for achieving a genuine democracy and for establishing brotherly relations with a German democracy on the ruins of the Nazis' totalitarian colossus.

The words on the torn poster came back to my mind: "Are you sure that the government . . . who betrayed our Czech allies . . . is sincere this time?" Was it sincere in declaring that France was now determined to oppose Germany's intentions to seize Danzig by force of arms? Was

Poland so precious an ally as to warrant the sacrifice of millions of French lives? Only a few months before, Colonel Beck, the Polish Foreign Minister, had switched back from close collaboration with Germany into the camp of the Anglo-French allies, after helping Hitler in reducing the formidable Czechoslovak military bastion located right on Germany's flank and after refusing passage to the Soviet's armies, which had been offered for the defense of Prague. Who had sabotaged the principle of collective security more than the leaders of France, who had allowed Hitler to annex Austria without even a word of protest, Mussolini to attack Ethiopia and to annex Albania, and Duce and Fuehrer together to crush the democratic republic of Spain, France's best friend?

Would a democratic Spain, with its not inconsiderable reservoir of man power and its great heroism, not have been a positive asset to France at the present moment? Was not its substitute brought into existence also by French collusion—Francisco Franco's "model Christian state" now wallowing in blood and abject poverty—a definite menace to French security? If the French leaders were sincere, why were they not sitting down in sackcloth and ashes and bewailing or freely acknowledging the ghastly errors and crimes of the past? Were men like Daladier, Laval, Bonnet, Reynaud, Flandin, Weygand, Pétain, and the other political and military chiefs now at last determined to oppose the further Fascistization of Europe with all their might? Then, why were the reactionary newspapers conducting a campaign against the public schools in France and the whole liberal educational system, and why did General Weygand say that "it would be a godsend if someone would put an end, once and for all, to the democratic nonsense in Europe"?

Was not that precisely Herr Hitler's declared intention?

The absence of a logical, coherent program of action was visibly throwing the French people into confusion. Mussolini had his *arditi* demonstrate in front of the French consulates and shout for Nice, Savoy, Corsica, and Tunis, but when democratic newspapers in Paris criticized that sawdust Caesar as a mere vassal and cork puller of Adolf Hitler, their plants were closed by the government and their editors prosecuted for endangering the security of the French state by insulting the chief of a friendly government. In answer to the Duce's taunts and threats, Édouard Daladier kept on repeating before the radio that France was calm and self-possessed and ready for all eventualities, but at the same time the French ambassador in Italy, M. François-Poncet, who was fellow director with Franz von Papen of a Franco-German munition trust,* signaled in distress from Rome that Mussolini was animated with the best of sentiments toward France. It was a mere question of offering the Duce something, the Ethiopian railway, for instance, or Djibouti, or representation on the directorate of the Suez Canal.

The French people were being mobilized to fight the menace of totalitarianism (or so they were told), but Pierre Laval was conferring in Rome with the Duce on the possibility of erecting a bloc of Latin states, not to oppose or check Germany's expansionist program, but to collaborate with Hitler in setting up a Fascist order in Europe. Paul Reynaud, Daladier's financial expert, was making similar representations to Dr. Schacht and Joachim von Ribbentrop in Berlin, while Philippe Pétain, Marshal of France, who had been sent as ambassador to the Axis lackey in Madrid, because he alone, Daladier said, understood

---

*The Berghütte.

the noble qualities of the Caudillo (Pétain, indeed, had seen Franco at work in his bloody war in 1925 during the Riff revolt in Spanish Morocco), was sending back the touching news that Franco's daughter recited her evening prayers half in French and half in Spanish. Was that not evidence of Franco's dependability and a guarantee that not only would he not stab France in the back but that he would be her advocate and mediator with his employers in Berlin and Rome?

To back Pétain's mission of peace with the executioner of Spanish democracy, Daladier had sent to Madrid Marcel Béranger, one of the leading figures in the secret terrorist Order of the Cagoulard. Béranger had just completed a sentence in jail for complicity in the Order's Fascist bomb outrage committed in the latter days of the Popular Front administration.

Avowed and unavowed Fascists, men who had been quite frank and outspoken in their approval of Hitler's labor politics and Mussolini's corporate state, were one by one placed in positions of command. The conduct of the affairs of the French state was put into the hands of utility magnates, clericals, and international trust magnates who had never made any bones about their profound antidemocratic sentiments. They made no pretense of being converted to democratic ideas. They hated democracy. They had spewed it out as filth. They execrated its hopes and ideals. They had said so, and they kept on saying so while the German guns pointed menacingly at the national borders. They and their newspapers had gloated over the fact that the Popular Front had been smashed. And yet, those were the men who now were to lead the French people in a war against totalitarianism in the name and under the banners of democracy.

Is it surprising that the French people were bewildered, that the troops departed for the front in sullen silence, that the masses were asking whether they were to fight to maintain France's position in the international field as a first-class power, merely that she could collaborate with Hitler as a sovereign equal in the establishment of the new totalitarian order in Europe?

Every democratic or liberal refugee escaping into France from Germany or Italy was now thrown into jail without further ado. In the days of the Popular Front, these men had been received with brotherly solicitude as fellow warriors against tyranny and oppression. Now, too, the valiant defenders of Spanish democracy, who had sought asylum on French soil in their tens of thousands, but who had been herded in prison kraals where conditions were worse, according to Emmanuel Mounnier, editor of the Catholic periodical *Esprit,* than in Himmler's concentration camps, were given over to the opprobrium and vituperation of the French conservative press as "breechless vermin and bandits" who should be handed over to Franco "for merited punishment"—punishment, that is, for having loyally defended the legally constituted government of their country.

It was in these and suchlike unchivalrous, not to say scurrilous terms that the respectable press, the dignified newspapers, spoke of the fathers and brothers of the hundreds of thousands of Spanish children whom the simple folk of France, the peasants and the workers and the *petits gens* in general, had taken into their homes in a spirit of spontaneous solidarity and fine Christian solicitude.

Charles Maurras, the editor of *l'Action française,* the journal of the monarchist nobility and of the clerical-minded General Staff, had gone straight from jail, where he had served a sentence for incitement to the murder of the trade-union leaders and prominent democrats "beginning with Édouard Herriot," to be Franco's guest in Madrid.

From there the learned academician sent dispatch after dispatch, urging the return of the Spanish prisoners so that the Caudillo might deal with them, as he wrote sarcastically, in that *caballero's* own "generous Christian way" —that is to say, to have them confessed by his priests and then slaughtered wholesale, in the manner of the Inquisition, in autos-da-fé for the good of their souls. Furthermore, he advocated the immediate return of the waifs and orphans so that, as he said, they might be withdrawn soon enough from the nefarious influence of the godless system of French education and be handed back to the priests and monks of Catalonia and Castille, who were in a position to give them the right kind of instruction.

Thus Charles Maurras, incidentally an athiest himself, but also the most vociferous champion of war with Germany in the French Academy and in the *salons* of the Faubourg Saint-Germain. Was it to be wondered at that men were asking whether these fine gentlemen, the molders of public opinion in France (two of the administrators of two of the most influential newspapers had just been convicted of being in the pay of the German and Italian foreign offices), were not urging war so that their political opponents—the democrats and Socialists—might be killed off as speedily as possible? "Let them enlist with the Loyalists," one reactionary member of the Chamber had called out to Daladier during a debate on aid to Spain. "Let them enlist. Whomever Franco kills we won't have to slaughter later on!"

Was that the purpose of the war which loomed on the

horizon—to get rid of or to break, once and for all, the
strength and the idealism of what was potentially the
strongest anti-Fascist force in Europe: the French working
class?

I do not think there is a precedent in history for the actions of the French government in the critical days of 1939.
The government assumed an attitude of menace and suspicion toward the people of France, as if it considered the
masses a greater potential danger than the German enemy
at the gates. More than half of the mechanized military
equipment—the lighter tanks and the *chars d'assaut*—were
kept away from the firing lines patrolling the cities and the
rural regions, as if a civil disturbance was on the verge of
breaking out. Every manifestation of the popular will
was smothered by the restrictive measures of a police force
that equaled the German Gestapo in numbers and ruthlessness. Why? What had the government to fear? The
masses had rallied to the colors as one man, without a murmur. Mussolini had said to Kurt Schuschnigg but a few
months before: "You are mistaken if you think the German army such a wonder. France has the finest and best-
equipped army in Europe."

Could the French government not look events calmly in
the face and await the hour of decision with tranquillity instead of behaving as if it did not know what course to pursue? The confusion of the time is summed up in the following imaginary dialogue, which might easily have taken
place between the people and the government of France:

THE GOVERNMENT: "Get ready to fight! And don't let
there be any skulking or hesitation about it!"

THE PEOPLE: "Why do you say this? Have we ever refused to fight when the Fatherland was in danger?"

THE GOVERNMENT: "Don't talk back. The time for discussion is past. France must show that it is united in the face of the enemy!"

THE PEOPLE: "Which enemy? Hitler? But we have always wanted to fight him, and you have always in the past prevented us. Do you really consider him the enemy now? You didn't last year, you know. You fawned on him and sent him telegrams of congratulation when he crushed our friends in Czechoslovakia. You rejoiced when he bombed our friends in Spain into submission. Your newspapers said that they preferred Hitler to Blum. You called our Popular Front the enemy, and our democracy you fought tooth and nail. What game are you playing?"

THE GOVERNMENT: "France must be unified now and be ready!"

THE PEOPLE: "Ready for what? To fight? Or to collaborate?"

THE GOVERNMENT: "Be silent. You are giving the world the impression France is in turmoil. Carry out instructions, that's all."

THE PEOPLE: "By the way, what is Pierre Laval doing in Rome? It is rumored he is seeking a compromise and that he would like to see France enter the Axis to collaborate in Hitler's new order. Is that true?"

THE GOVERNMENT: "Monsieur Laval is a patriot. He is working for the good of France."

THE PEOPLE: "It makes no sense. Laval and Mussolini are bosom friends. They hate democracy. How can any good then come from seeking friendship with the Axis?"

THE GOVERNMENT: "Hold your tongue! Hold your rifles high so that Hitler can see that France is ready."

THE PEOPLE: "Ready for what? Ready to join him as a partner?"

THE GOVERNMENT: "No more talk now. We have other worries than your senseless prattle!"

Inasmuch as the soldiers posted in front of the Hotel Continental did not by so much as a word challenge anyone wishing to enter, I concluded that they served more of a decorative than a defensive purpose and that the flash of their bayonets was merely intended to heighten the prestige of the censors inside. I therefore marched in bravely enough. Red arrows on the walls in the hallways and on the staircase pointed towards a huge waitingroom on the third floor, where a scene reminiscent of that depicted in Gustave Doré's famous engraving of the confusion of tongues at Babel was being enacted. Here were gathered representatives of the press from all parts of the compass. I recognized newsmen and editorial writers and commentators of all schools of thought and of all shades and colors of political doctrines, tenets, and presumptions, which are, like dyes, injected into that dark and mysterious brew which is designed to create and mold public opinion.

Near the door, as I entered, stood the correspondents of the English metropolitan journals, a few of them still dressed in dinner clothes, although it was morning now. They had probably just dropped in from some social function or other. Keeping very much to themselves, as had always been their wont in international journalistic gatherings, whether in Paris, Geneva, or Moscow, they were viewing the scene around them with that detached and baronial air of superiority the Briton habitually affects when circumstances beyond his control bring him into the presence of creatures of a lesser breed. Near them was a group of loquacious and gesticulating Arabs. The rasping, harshly aspirated consonants in their speech sounded

like the crackle of small arms above the zooming undertone of the general conversation in the room. Then there
were small parties of Scandinavians, of Belgians, and of
Dutchmen, the latter two standing quite apart, of course,
as they always do, but this time eying each other with more
than the usual suspicion, I thought. Next came three
Japanese gentlemen, who were conversing excitedly in
whispers, as if anyone in that room could have understood
their singsong speech, had they spoken out loud. Negroes
from the colonies, dressed in frock coats, were speaking
French with the flawless precision and dignity of the masters of the Sorbonne.

Some animation was provided by a Polish journalist, the
representative of the *Warzawska Kurier,* who was generally reputed to be a poet of distinction, although he looked
more like the caricature of the Prussian *Junker* with which
Erich von Stroheim has made us familiar than anyone I
know. He wore his hair closely cropped—millimetered, as
they call that style in the German army—and stared at all
and sundry through a square monocle that sharply accen-
tuated the steely blueness of his eyes. He was also very
excited and was waving his silver-knobbed cane like a
rapier as he proceeded to translate in a loud voice to some
stolid-faced South Slavs the report of a hell-raising chauvinist declaration by Marshal Smigly-Rydz. The fiery,
challenging, and uncompromising remarks of the Polish
commander in chief, which were addressed to Adolf Hitler and the German High Command, caused everyone to
turn in the speaker's direction and then look away more
concerned than ever.

There were, furthermore, representatives of all the fifty-
odd Parisian dailies, many of them muttering, *rouspétant,*
and snorting their indignation over having to line up with

all those aliens; plenty of Americans, too, anxiously consulting their watches and swearing about deadlines, and finally, most worried of all, the editors of the German and Italian refugee papers, who, it appeared, had been summoned to hear the death sentence pronounced on their periodicals. I moved about the room greeting an acquaintance here and there, until I caught sight of Ilya Ehrenbourg, *Izvestia's* versatile correspondent, the creator of the fascinating Julio Jurenito. I had not seen Ehrenbourg since the siege of the Alcazar in Toledo, whither we had marched together from Madrid with a battalion of Loyalists. The Russian correspondent was occupying the only seat in the room, a comfortable armchair of the type called *fauteuil Voltaire,* and was calmly reading a copy of *The Church Times.*

"What are you doing here?" I asked, shaking his hand. "Surely you do not expect the censor to look with favor on the dispatches of a Communist?"

"I am here just to be sociable," said Ilya with an ironic smile. "I have not much longer in Paris. That is why I am seeing all I can. A spectacle such as we are about to witness occurs only once in a thousand years—I mean the disintegration and collapse of a civilization. No, I have not come to see the censor. He does not want to see me, nor do I have to see him. I have no dispatches to send. I haven't sent anything for a long time. Tass takes care of the spot news. As for me, they do not need my enlightenment in Moscow, for they know perfectly well, and they have known for a long time, how this story is going to unfold."

"How long, would you say, have they known?" I asked.

"Oh, since Moscow's offer of assistance to Czechoslovakia was turned down."

"And how is it going to unfold, this story?"

"War, of course." He shrugged his shoulders.

"It does not take any magic clairvoyance to see that," I objected. "But aren't they a little fearful over in Moscow to be drawn in?"

"Fearful, no! Why should they be?"

"If they are in doubt about Hitler's intentions, they only have to read *Mein Kampf*.

"Ah, *Mein Kampf,* is it? That is what you take as your guide?" he asked mockingly. "Excellent book, incidentally, really first-class Machiavellianism. It fooled all of the bourgeois ink spillers. You took it for gospel truth, and that is precisely what the author or authors wanted you to do. . . ."

"Still, the chart is there," I objected: "Austria, Memel, the Saar, Czechoslovakia. . . ."

"Sure enough, but it is about the Soviet Union we were talking, was it not?"

"Yes?"

"Well, the Soviet Union is not going to be drawn into this war. It isn't in the cards, you see!"

"That depends on Hitler," I said, "not on Stalin."

"Hitler," explained Ilya a little pontifically, "has had everybody believing for years that he rearmed Germany for the sole purpose of destroying the Soviet Union. Because that was his declared intention, the English tories and their friends here in France gave him not only carte blanche, but they assisted him in every way they could. The man could never have obtained the permission of London and Paris to build up a new army, had he not made it abundantly clear that he planned to use that army against us. When he told Sir John Simon that he might not be able to finish the job with an army alone and that he would need a fleet to cover certain landing operations, say in the neighborhood of the Gulf of Finland, Britain at once gave him permission to start building a fleet up to a third of her own strength. They were overjoyed in London to learn that German aspirations to markets and colonies were to be satisfied by an eastward march. That was the famous *Drang nach Osten.* They liked the idea in England, for they were familiar with it. *Die Leute haben auch selbst sehr viel nach Osten gedrängt,"* he added in German. "The English know their way in the East. Moreover, a proposed drive by Hitler in that direction conveniently diverted attention from the German colonies England held in mandate. And then they fondly imagined in London that Hitler would exhaust both himself and Russia in the war that was to follow. Now Hitler has unmasked. Or, rather, he unmasked after they had handed him Czechoslovakia. London and Paris surrendered that country with the intention of clearing Hitler's way to the Soviet Union. When he did not continue his march to the East after Munich, it dawned on them at last that they had been fooled.

"No, we are not going to be drawn in," he wound up. "In the first place, Hitler does not want to fight, and, in the second place, Britain and France have refused to have us help them."

"Have they refused?" I asked.

"Well, they have refused through Beck. Beck of Poland does not want the Red army in Poland to defend the country, and so, also, say the great statesmen of the Baltic republics. Didn't you hear that Polish poet just now?" asked Ilya. "Poland is fully capable of holding her own and doing a little more in the bargain. Didn't you hear him quote

Smigly-Rydz? The Polish marshal has told the Germans that he is going to march into Silesia and East Prussia. England is betting on the Polish horse. We are not wanted."

"After Poland may come Russia," I said.

"After Poland the last obstacle in the East is removed before Hitler can move west," Ilya corrected me.

"Well, Poland will put up a stiff fight!"

"No doubt, no doubt," he assented with a comical nod of the head, and he asked: "By the way, have you ever seen the Polish mechanized forces?"

"No, I haven't!"

"Neither have I," said Ehrenbourg, "for the simple reason that they do not exist. They are going to fight the Panzer divisions with farm carts. . . . Yes, and the dive bombers with popguns. Very brave, no doubt, very Polish, very much in line with what we may expect, but hardly practical."

"But France has been providing billions for Polish rearmament for years. Where did the money go?" I asked.

"That is a question you must ask of the boyars and the *Junker* of Poland," said Ilya, and he added: "Here is *The Church Times* I picked up in this room. There is an article in it worth reading. Here it is," he said pointing out a column. "It deals with the efforts of Lord Halifax's father to bring about a reunion between the Anglican church and Rome."

"Fine," I said, "but why did you come here?"

"To watch the agony of the bourgeois world. Isn't it charming, this helplessness?"

"How does one get to see the censor here?" I asked, breaking off the apologia for the Soviet.

"You will have to force that line over there," replied Ehrenbourg, pointing to a pair of gold-framed suite doors before which a half-dozen sweating dragoons, steel-hatted, booted, spurred, and armed with carbines, stood guard.

As he spoke, one of the doors swung open to let out four or five men from the room beyond. At the same time, everybody in the waiting room pressed forward, but the soldiers allowed only five or six to enter.

One of the men to come out was Marvin Meredith of the London *Chronicle*. He was a blond giant who had lost a foot in the last war. He held up a few sheets of typescript, which were heavily lined with black pencil stripes.

"There isn't much left," I remarked, looking at his mutilated copy.

"No," came back Meredith. "The gentleman cut out all references to diplomatic negotiations still in progress. He also asked me if I was aware that a war was coming on, and I asked him in return whether it was those damned Afghans again. I don't think he quite understood me, but he took revenge by making his little pencil scratch the more."

"Was he somebody from the Foreign Office?" I asked.

"Oh, no, it's all military in there now. Intelligence Service, I presume, for they don't know ten words of English among the lot of them. . . ."

I told him I was in a hurry, for my broadcast was due in less than an hour. How could I get in?

"Look here," he said, "I will get you in. Take this letter. It's from Daladier. It's two years old and merely a note of acknowledgment to the congratulations I sent him when he succeeded Herriot as head of the party. Just show those soldiers the Prime Minister's signature and they will let you by. It worked with me. Send the note back to me in the morning, for I shall need it again tonight, when, I hope, the guard will be changed.

"By the way," he said, "did you hear that they arrested Lucien Jacques?"

"No, why was he arrested?"

"It appears he wrote a book of his reminiscences as a stretcher-bearer in the last war."

"Is this the book?" I asked, pulling it out of my pocket.

"That's it! Where did you get it?"

"I bought it this evening!"

"That's the most dangerous little book in France today. Anyone found with it in his possession goes straight off to jail, and any bookseller peddling it loses his license and his liberty...."

Daladier's crumpled old note worked like magic.

"*Lettre du président du conseil,*" I said to the sergeant of the dragoons, "a letter from the President of the Council...."

"*Passez,*" he said, saluting.

I was inside at last. Another large room, the floor strewn with newspaper proof sheets; one large table in front of the fireplace and three officers sitting behind it.

An orderly approached me. "Letter from Monsieur Daladier," I repeated. The three officers looked up. "Take him in to see *un de ces messieurs,*" one of the officers ordered.

The military guide let me through a maze of hallways, up another flight of stairs, down some other steps, and finally stopped in front of the open door of an ordinary guest room from which the bed and dresser had been removed.

In the room I could see a young major. He had his back

turned to me and was telephoning. He was lying back in a low armchair and had his legs up on the desk, his spurs firmly hooked into the smoothly polished surface of the table. He was saying: *"T' as diné avec lui?* You dined with him?" But catching sight of the soldier and me in the long Venetian mirror, he interrupted his conversation to shout over his shoulder: *"Eloignez-vous,* get out of the way!" We walked back into the hallway, out of earshot.

"C'est à sa poule qu'il parle," volunteered the orderly. "He's talking to his sweetie."

After we heard him hang up, we approached again.

"Gentleman from the American press, *mon commandant,"* announced the orderly.

"Let him come in," said the officer.

"What is it?" he asked me.

Script in hand, I explained my presence.

"Let's see!" he said, picking up a pencil at the same time. He began to scratch immediately.

"Why do you say the sentiment of our soldiers going to the front is grim and determined?" he asked abruptly.

"Because that is the way their sentiments appeared to me," I said.

"Nonsense!" he snorted. "What do you know about soldiers?"

"I know human beings," I said, "and I remember my own feelings in going up the line with the Canadians."

He mellowed a little at that. "You were with the Canadian army, were you?" he muttered without looking up from the paper, where he presently saw something else that caused him to scowl.

"Look here," he said. "All this is nonsense. You say here that all hope is not lost and that the British ambassador is on his way to Berlin with new proposals. . . . This must not be said. We don't want the American people to think we are still dickering with the Germans. We have no proposals to make. Let Hitler make proposals if he wants to. We are ready to fight and the quicker the better. The whole tone of your dispatch has, I don't know what, a defeatist flavor. . . . There is no anxiety. . . . There is no indecision. . . . There is no hesitancy. . . . This is not a critical hour. . . . All that is wrong. I won't let it pass. It's Hitler who is trembling. We are absolutely calm and collected because we are sure of our defense. One move against Poland, and we march to Berlin."

"I hope so," I said.

"Do you doubt it?" he asked.

"Not in the least," I lied.

"Well, why don't you say so then?" he shot back. "I don't see," he went on, "why any foreigners should be given the use of our radio at all at this time. Why can't Frenchmen be utilized? It's France that is going to do the fighting. France should therefore be the only one to speak."

Again he scratched busily. The passages he deleted dealt with a reference to strong British reinforcements being sent to the Near East and a prediction of mine that one of the most crucial battles of the coming war would be fought for possession of the Suez Canal.

"Don't you realize that if ever a battle is fought there, it will be after Hitler is victorious in Europe?" he asked.

"Not necessarily," I said. "If Hitler is not able to break through in the west, he will most probably turn east."

"That would mean defeating Yugoslavia and Rumania and Turkey. . . . We cannot allow any such totally crazy supposition to go out."

"As you like," I said, taking my script, more than half of which had been cut away.

"And don't forget," he called after me, "if you by so much as one word deviate from your corrected script we cut you off just like that," he snapped his fingers.

The Place Vendôme was a gleaming black mirror in the first yellow glow of daylight. The steady drizzle announced one of those days of interminable rain under a low, colorless sky, a day when the pigeons go into hiding in the deep recesses of the sculpture on Notre-Dame's façade. How cold is the dawn after a sleepless night, even in summer! The strange, almost unearthly silence made me think of the boy in the Dutch storybook who, on his way home from the fair, turned around at every step to see the lights in the merry-go-round and in the booths grow smaller and smaller and who, as the distance lengthened, heard the crashing music of the barrel organs sink to a confused, drowsy murmur, full of melancholy and nostalgic regrets.

In that moment I knew that I would not be able to stay in France.

The streets were still full of shadows, but they were of a lighter, more ethereal substance than the black shapes of the midnight hour. In front of the open cellar windows of the bakeries fantastic colors moved over the sidewalk; ruddy tongues of flame that shot out voraciously the one moment and danced harmlessly in measureless rhythm the next. In the small illuminated areas before the ventholes the million sprinkling raindrops looked like a moving curtain of gauzy orange.

Such mornings set one a-dreaming. They bring memories of a vague universe of innocence and security and freshness, of a summer-vacation atmosphere and, further

back, of fairy things in a happy never-never land of somewhere, a realm of perpetual childhood joy—memories we
guard as precious treasures in our hearts and of which we
hesitate to speak to anyone, unconsciously fearful to see
the thread of recollection broken under a profane and
uncomprehending touch. Perhaps it is true, as someone
said, that the malady of our age is an excess of remembrance
and that amnesia and forgetfulness would be better.

But is not memory, too, a preventive to keep the wheel
of life from turning in the void? Without memory there
can be no refreshing of the spirit and no pardon and no
new beginning. Is remembrance not a primary condition
to inner perfection?

I heard the trumpets in the barracks of La Pépinière
blow the reveille: *"Ta femme fait la putain, brigadier; ta
femme fait la putain! . . ."* Where had I first heard that
ribald tune? Was it in Havre, upon landing with the
Canadians in 1916, or the morning after sleeping in the
crypt of Amiens with a French colonial regiment that had
lost sixty per cent of its effectives in a futile attack on the
ruined refinery of Souchez, which we were to try again the
next day with no better results? And what was that lieutenant's name who had sat with me the night before in one
of the town's taverns and had anticipated the black-shirted
transalpine philosopher in the Palazzo di Venezia by declaring that wars are necessary to keep the peoples from
being devoured by boredom and ennui?

It is nothing less than magic the way a man's thoughts fly
hither and yon, over seas and mountains, back into time
and far into the future. Marching through the rain toward
the broadcasting station, I found myself planning to look
up the yellow, brittle pages in front of the old family Bible
wherein my forefathers, one after the other, wrote in

archaic lettering the names of their wives and children and then, toward the end of their existence, penned with faltering hand a brief confession of their faith as the sum total of their achievements on earth. When will the time come for me to add my contribution, I thought, and what shall I write in the last blank space? That I believe in the resurrection? But I do not. That I expect to find eternal refuge under the shadows of God's wing and therefore have no fear of death, as one of my ancestors wrote in 1795? That would be a little too simple, too Mohammedan, too easy-fatalistic. But what then? Or, must I write at all? Why not be the first to die without cackling about it and penning clichés to hide an inner disquietude?

Without noticing it I had arrived at the little park on the Boulevard Haussmann, opposite the broadcasting station, where is located the tomb of that Louis and his Marie Antoinette who lost their heads under the guillotine's knife. I heard the rustle of the rain on the leaves of the plane trees. The roof of the curious elongated mortuary chapel, which the son of Philippe Égalité erected to the memory of the royal pair upon whom his father passed the death sentence, had turned a ghostly green under layers of fungi.

It looked for all the world like the castle of Schelluinen, which an uncle of mine took me to see in the dead of night when I was a boy of fifteen, because there were rumors that the place was haunted and that, by looking out of one of the upper-story windows toward the pond at the stroke of twelve, one could see medieval chevaliers riding out with banners and armor. I do not know from whom he obtained permission to spend the night in that deserted place, but I do remember the wind howling in the chimneys, a trapdoor in the roof battering all night long, and the fright I had when a regiment of rats with luminous pin-point eyes tripped over the bare floor of the room where we kept our vigil. Nothing else happened. I did not hear the rowdy cursing and carousing coming up from the moat, where a wing of the castle lay sunken in the mire, and which the fishermen of the neighborhood, coming home late at nights, said they had heard quite frequently.

There were redbreasts in the broken window with the peep of dawn. Curiosity had got the best of them, and they examined a little fearfully, I think, those two human beings there on a sack of straw in what was once a seigneurial bed. The boldest of those birds tried to understand what we were up to, and they craned their necks in a valiant effort to get to the root of the mystery. But the wind had calmed down, and not a leaf stirred in the abandoned garden upon which we looked while eating our bread and sausage.

Why not own up to it? We have all, at certain moments, skirted those unknown regions wherein the shades flutter and vanish, exhausted by the ecstasy of their own souve-nirs. Tell me, have you never on a mystic evening in the autumn, when the rain fell softly in the sand and rustled on the trees, come upon a house on the rim of a forest that immediately evoked the memory of other times and an-other life? You really believe you know that house—you would swear you had lived in it. The smell of a woodfire, the sight of a row of willows reflected in the water, or the presence of mushrooms or moss-covered rocks sets you sud-denly, impetuously, off on a trail and permits you to go back into your own past or into that of one of your ances-tors, who, without having lived in such a place, perhaps nourished the hope of living there some day.

How can I explain that on my first visit to London, as an immigrant boy in passage to Canada, I knew (and said so to my traveling companions with whom I was strolling about) that around the next corner we would see the Guildhall and, in that obscure passage in Threadneedle Street, we would find the Church of the Austin Friars in the English capital? Still, I had never been to the city before, nor had I ever studied its street plan.

And then, this small park with the royal mausoleum where I now paused a moment, why, of all the parks in Paris, had it always drawn me so ineluctably?

Why did it always bring back a vision of a patio where olive-skinned women with large golden earrings and necklaces of gold walked about exchanging confidences in a low voice? How often have I not looked up from a book or a newspaper in that garden, thinking I heard the sound of bare little feet pattering on cool paving stones, only to find that the hatched-faced keeper was merely making his rounds. Whence had come that silvery children's laughter I heard? . . .

I recited my little lesson at the broadcast station, listlessly and without interest, for I now knew why the average broadcast was so innocuous and meaningless. Formerly I had often silently reproached the speakers—the commentators and analysts I heard over the ether—for what seemed to me their abysmal ignorance and misconceptions, which, so I thought, they hid under fanfaronade and cocksure utterance. Now I knew that the broadcasting stations do not want speakers to say anything beyond the banal, the obvious, and the insignificant. Those voices whose tone seems to imply that they are about to announce momentous things, startling discoveries, and sensational developments are the camouflage that covers precisely nothing.

Those speakers bring to mind the pack of my grandfather's notebooks that I found after his death. They were

filled with sermon outlines. Lines were underscored with
red ink, and thick exclamation points appeared in the mar-
gins. At certain places in the text the old man had put
words of caution addressed to himself, such as: "Slowly
now, Pieter!" and: "Say the following quickly." At one
point in a sermon that tried to prove an impossibility—the
miracle of the five thousand loaves and fishes—by what
had apparently appeared to him an incomprehensible
mathematical formula, my grandfather had written in red
ink: "Wave arms violently, Pieter! Argument exceedingly
weak!" One can also use a violently agitated voice to hide
intellectual embarrassment. . . .

I felt exhausted by the wanderings of the night, especially by the last long walk to the railway station. I entered
the waiting room with the intention of resting a little before taking the first train out, whenever that should be. I
found the room darkened except for a solitary emergency
lamp that had been painted blue. The ghostly light colored the faces of the soldiers who were sleeping between
their bundles on the benches and on the floor with a
strange, unearthly light. I found a spot to sit down next to
a dragoon who had taken off his heavy boots and placed
them under his head for a pillow. He was lying on his
back so that the light shone full in his face. He was a mere
boy, perhaps nineteen or twenty, with light blond hair
and ruddy cheeks, his face as innocent as a cherub's. His
mouth was open, and he stirred uneasily in his sleep, rub-
bing his eyes and swallowing constantly in a quick audible
way as if he wanted to chase away some bad taste. On his
legs rested the head of another trooper who was sitting on
the floor. A trickle of saliva was running out of his mouth.
Soldiers were coming in and going out of the room.

A boy on my left suddenly awoke, sat up, pulled a bottle of red wine from his haversack, and took a swig. When he had drunk he wiped the mouth of the bottle with the flat of his hand and smacked his lips with satisfaction. Then catching sight of me for the first time, he said: "Would you like some?" I shook my head. Looking across to the bench in front, he noticed a priest and held the bottle up invitingly. The priest smiled and said: *"Je veux bien."* The boy stepped over and handed him the flask. The priest took a swallow and said: *"C'est du bon Médoc.* Very refreshing." The soldier smiled in a superior way and said: *"Oui, c'est le bon vin de chez nous,* that's the wine they make in our part of the country." The priest thanked him, and the soldier went back to his seat.

As he was stuffing the bottle back into his haversack, he looked over to the blond trooper who was lying on the other side of me. He watched him stir in his sleep and saw a fly buzzing around his face. Without a word he took a big red handkerchief from his pocket and spread it carefully over the sleeping man's face. I looked over at the priest who was watching the scene.

The priest presently got up and blew his nose. At the door of the waiting room I saw him wiping his eyes.

Just at that moment a man whose face was partly hidden by a heavy muffler and by a soft cap, which he had pulled over his eyes, walked by. He looked for a place to sit down and took the seat just vacated by the priest. When he sat down and removed his thick scarf, I saw that it was Jean Giono, the author, an old friend whom I had not seen for years. He recognized me and came over.

"What do you say to some coffee across the street?" he said. "Some of the cafés must be open by now."

We walked out of the station but had to wait before

crossing the street because of a troop of cavalry that was passing. The soldiers rode by silently, without looking either left or right. The street was filled with the metallic click of the horses' hoofs on the pavement. Presently an officer came galloping up alongside the procession. When he came near where we were standing, he reined in his prancing horse, stood up in the stirrups, and, looking backwards, waved his arm in the air. At this signal the hussars began to bend back and forth in their saddles, and the whole regiment broke into a trot.

"Are you writing anything at present?" I asked Giono.

"No," he said, "I can't write now. I'm choking. Tell me, is it going to start all over again?"

"I'm afraid it is," I said.

"Are you going?" he asked suddenly. "I mean, have you been called? You were in the last one, weren't you?"

"I was in the last war," I said. "But I am not *mobilisable* now. I was discharged as unfit for service. I do not think I would be called except in a last extremity. . . ."

"Would you go again?" he interrupted fiercely.

"I would," I said, "under the circumstances."

"What circumstances?"

"The present circumstances," I answered. "I believe that this war is not like any other. It is a war for an idea. I believe that if the Germans should win this war, the human race will be thrown back a thousand years, that all the advances will be wiped out, and that all the ideals and hopes of a new civilization and socialism and peace will vanish. We will go back into the night. . . ."

"Do the statesmen want peace and a new civilization and socialism?" he asked quizzically. "Is that what they're going to war for? Why didn't they bring peace and the other things, or at least try to bring them, while there was a chance without a holocaust? War brings no peace. War brings nothing but misery," he went on. "War settles nothing. Wars are not fought to change anything. They are fought to preserve the *status quo*. War does nothing but perpetuate itself. . . ."

"This war," I said, "will be fought to prevent the world from being turned into a huge slave camp. So long as Germany is not beaten there is no use in talking of human progress. We cannot even think of peace and of a better world so long as the menace of totalitarianism hangs over our heads. . . ."

"Do you realize that in defending yourself against that evil you must submit to it in your own house, in your own country? . . ."

"I realize that," I said. "But I'm willing to sacrifice my freedom temporarily and entrust it for safekeeping in the hands of Parliament or a committee of safety. That is what the English and the French and the American people did in the last war. That we must do again."

"So you accept dictatorship?" he asked again.

"Not at all," I said. "I believe that a measure of regimentation and of authoritarianism is inevitable in time of war. I would sooner submit to it temporarily, in a gesture of voluntary self-discipline, than have it imposed on me."

"Does that not come to the same thing?" he asked, shrugging his shoulders.

"No," I said, "it doesn't, for I know that after the emergency is over, I will have my rights back."

"Do you think the men who have been granted those extraordinary powers will surrender them voluntarily after the war?"

"That depends on whom I have trusted with the custody of my privileges and rights. I must see to it that they do not fall into the wrong hands...."

"Are there any men who can be trusted with power? Does not power corrupt and absolute power corrupt absolutely?"

"It does unquestionably. That is why there must be provisions to make the delegation of power temporary and those who hold power subject to democratic control...."

"And if they nevertheless betray your hopes?" he arched his eyebrows.

"At the first sign of betrayal of the people's confidence, those in power must be thrown out."

"How are you going to do this when they have absolute power?" Giono asked.

"In that case I'd fight them as the peoples have always fought tyrants and usurpers, and fight them till they are beaten...."

"I won't wait that long," said Giono. "I start the fight right now. I am refusing to obey the mobilization order. I am not stirring. I won't help in the killing. I want to keep my hands clean. I want to keep clean. I refuse...."

"You will be alone," I said.

"I'll be alone, yes, but I'll be against," he replied vehemently.

We sat down in a café on the Place de Roubaix. "Look," said Giono, nodding his head towards a group of soldiers around one of the large tables, "there are some men from my old regiment, the 52nd Infantry. Verdun is their *dépôt*. They must be taking the six o'clock train.... My God, they will be holding the line one of these days again, I suppose, as we held it in 1916. Do you remember the glorious battle of Verdun and Pétain's saying: 'They shall not pass!' " He laughed bitterly. "Where were you when we were holding the line at Verdun?"

"I was helping to hold it at the other end," I said.

"Did you hold it because you wanted to or because the military police prevented you from quitting? I still shudder when I think of it. Heroism, it is called now. Filth, I call it, moral filth and cowardice and dirt. We fought the battle of Verdun because we could not do otherwise. We could not get out. There were detachments of police right in the midst of the battle, in the communication trenches, under the tunnel of Tavannes, everywhere. . . . If we wanted to get out, we had to have a ticket of leave. . . . Idiotic, isn't it? No, not idiotic," he growled. "It was terrible! At the start of the battle, when the rationing parties still succeeded in getting through the artillery barrage, they were halted by the police and frisked. They also had to show the ticket signed by the captain. Heroism was strictly controlled. There we were and there we stayed.

"But did we fight? We gave the impression, no doubt, of being fierce attackers. In reality, we were running away in all directions. We were posted between the battery of the hospital, which was a redoubt, and the Fort Vaux. We had been ordered to recapture the fort. There we were for ten days without stirring. . . . Every day, back at the battery of the hospital, between two rows of sandbags, the police were executing those who had moved from their places, executing them without trial or inquiry. . . . What could we do? When you cannot leave a battlefield, you hide in it, don't you? You dig a hole, you bury yourself in it, and you stay there. But the boys who were found in such a hole were dragged off to the battery of the hospital and were made to walk between two piles of sandbags, and then their brains were blown out. That's the way it went with us.

Pretty soon it became necessary for every soldier to be accompanied by a policeman. . . .

"In the meantime, General Pétain wrote in his communiqué: 'They are holding.' In Paris that fine refrain was taken up by the official war historians, who started to conjugate in all the tenses and in all the persons, including their own, the verb 'to hold'; 'they are holding, they will hold, they have held at Verdun,' etcetera, etcetera. . . . Sure, we were holding, but if I had been General Pétain I would not have dared to take the military police out of the field for one single minute or ask that colonel of the 52nd Regiment at the battery to be a little more indulgent. . . . We were holding. That's right. First ten, then fifteen days. For eight days the rationing parties had not returned. They left at the sinking of the sun and melted in the landscape like this lump of sugar in the black coffee," Giono said. "Not a single man returned. Every one of them was killed, absolutely every one, every time, every day, without an exception. Nobody went out after that for food, no matter how hungry and thirsty we were. . . ." He was bending forward over the marble-topped table. He talked in a monotonous tone of voice. His dark eyes flashed with a somber fire, and he gritted his teeth violently as he spoke.

"We could see one dead man lying out there in the field," he continued, "all putrified and covered with flies, but around his waist was a belt of water bottles and chunks of bread threaded on a piece of wire. We waited for the bombardment to subside. Then we crawled out to him. We detached the water bottles from his belt and dragged the wire with the bread to our hole. Some of the bottles had been perforated by bullets. They were empty. The bread was soft and soggy. But we only cut off the side that had touched the man's body. That is what we were doing

every day. That way we lived for twenty-five days. . . .
That's the way we were holding the line. . . . Of course, the
stock of those dead-men provision closets did not last very
long. But we had to eat just the same. I was chewing the
leather strap of a water bottle. Towards evening of the
twenty-fifth day, a friend caught a rat. When he had
skinned the animal, the flesh was beautifully white. Still, I
stood with my piece of rat in my hand till dusk before
eating it. . . .

"The next day we had a lucky break, the twenty-sixth
day. A machine-gun crew, which had advanced behind us,
was caught by the barrage and was annihilated. The crew
of four was killed. They were lying out there not twenty
yards away from us. In the evening we planned to go and
get their haversacks. They had come up from the battery.
Therefore they must have brought provisions with them.
But we had to be careful, for right around us were other
holes, filled with other men holding the line. They, too,
were hungry. They, too, must have been watching for the
haversacks of those four gunners. And, most important of
all, those gunners had to be really dead. Fortunately, they
were dead. . . . In this way we came to the thirtieth day of
the great battle of Verdun. The whole world had its eyes
on us. We were terribly worried. What were we to do:
conquer, resist, hold on, do our duty?

"No, the great trouble was how to relieve ourselves. Outside the hole rained a deluge of steel. It simply amounted
to this: one shell crashed on every square yard of ground
every single minute, for thirty days and thirty nights. That
was the battle of Verdun. Nine of us had survived in the
hole. It was not really a shelter but a hole about two yards
square, with a sheet of corrugated iron pulled over the
top and an opening in front to look at the horror. Noth-

ing in the world could have brought us out of that hole
at that time. But what we had eaten and what we were
eating was now beginning to tell on our stomachs and bow-
els several times a day.

"We had to relieve ourselves. The first man who went
out to do that was killed. He was lying out there, right in
front of us, dead, with his trousers down over his heels.
Thereafter we did what we had to do in paper and threw
the paper outside. We did it in old letters. . . .

"We were nine men in a place that could scarcely hold
three. We were cramped. Our legs and our arms were all
tangled up. If one of us merely wanted to bend his knee,
we were all obliged to do the same, or he wouldn't have had
room in which to bend it. The earth around our hole
trembled incessantly. Clods of earth, dust, pieces of metal,
and all kinds of putrid things were flying about uninterruptedly on the open side. The man nearest the opening
had his face scratched and pummeled by a million fragments of iron and caked mud. We no longer heard the
bursting of the shells. We only took in the concussion of
the explosions near by, the sudden burst of hot air into our
lungs. For five days not one of us dared to move outside.
Nobody had any more paper. We did what we had to do in
our haversacks and then threw them outside. First we had
to disentagle our arms and legs, then unfasten our trousers,
and then relieve ourselves in a haversack that was lying
on the chest of a comrade. When that was finished, the
dirt was passed from hand to hand until the last man finally
threw it outside. That was the battle of Verdun, every day
more and more heroic. . . .

"After the thirty-seventh day we no longer left our hole.
There were only eight of us then. The one nearest to the
opening had been killed by a piece of shrapnel that struck

him in the neck and cut his jugular vein. He bled to death. We tried to plug the hole in front with his body. We were wise in doing that. The enemy was sweeping the sector with incessant volleys of machine-gun fire. We heard the bullets strike the body propped up in the opening. Although the man had been bled white by the mortal wound he received, he still bled every time a bullet struck him after his death. . . .

"I forgot to say that for ten days none of us had a rifle, or a bayonet, or a knife—not a thing. . . . But we were all torn by horrible cramps, cramps that never stopped, cramps that seemed to tear out our intestines. The cramps were made worse, I presume, because we tried to swallow small pellets of clay to calm our hunger and also because at last, on the thirty-seventh day, it rained, and we had tried to lick up the drops of water that dripped from the sheet of corrugated iron and that dribbled past the corpse with which we had stuffed the opening of our hole.

"Thereafter we simply relieved ourselves in our hands. It was a dysentery that ran out between your fingers. You couldn't even throw it outside. Those in the rear simply wiped their hands on the earth beside them. The three in front wiped their hands on the dead man. That's how we discovered that we were losing blood. Thick blood it was—glazy, *émail*-like, very beautiful blood. The man in front thought at first that it was the dead man who had started to bleed again. But the beauty of the blood made us reflect. . . .

"After the fourth day that his corpse blocked the entrance to our hole—it was the ninth of August—we began to notice that the dead man was putrefying. The air in the hole was becoming unbreathable. The pain in our intestines was then unbearable. We were devoured by a thirst, a thirst that had dried up our tongues and was turning our mouth into leather pockets—a thirst of fire. We had nothing more left in the hole, no arms, no haversacks, nothing. We only had one water bottle. That water bottle we used. For on the fortieth day we began to drink our own urine. . . . That was the admirable and glorious battle of Verdun. . . ."

Giono was silent for a moment. He glanced at the soldiers of the 52nd Infantry, who quietly got up to leave. "I am telling you all this," he said suddenly, "so that you will know why I am not going again. I want to keep clean. I won't take part. I am writing a letter to Daladier. He ought to understand. He was at Verdun holding the line. He may go again if he wants to. I won't." He was silent again and drank his coffee.

"Jean," I said, "don't write that letter. It won't do any good. You will only trouble other minds. There is enough confusion. . . ."

"I must write that letter," came back Giono. "I must tell the truth. That is the only thing there is left to do: tell the truth at all times, especially in times like these. . . ."

"Jean," I said once more, "if you write that letter you will be sorry. You will get into worse trouble than at Verdun. Why don't you ask for a temporary exemption and come with me and think it all over and then write. . . ."

"I have thought it over," he said somberly. "My mind is made up. . . ."

"I understand you," I said. "I only wished you had expressed your indignation earlier, you and others and all of us. We should have filled the world with our clamor and protest after the last war. It might have helped to prevent this new one which is upon us. We should have roused the Germans and everybody. Now it's too late. Now we must fight, if only to be able to speak again later."

"I won't fight," said Giono, shaking his head. "I am writing Daladier that I refuse. . . ."

"Jean, you are heading for the firing squad," I said desperately.

"The firing squad? Fine! That's just what I want! That's what I want: to stand alone there, my hands tied to the stake. Good! Alone, alone against the whole world! But clean! Clean, you understand! . . ."

Five minutes after leaving the station the train stopped, and the conductor came through the coaches to say that there was an air-raid alarm. From afar came the scream of the Paris sirens. Every suburb and village took up the wail, near by, far off, and beyond us, so that soon all the world seemed in a screeching panic. But I saw no planes in the sky, except a lone English fighter flying helter-skelter in the direction of Montmorency.

"They'll never come over Paris," the conductor assured us. "If ever a Boche plane gets that far, it will be that the pilot has lost his bearings. It stands to reason, *d'ailleurs,*" he went on, "our airmen are experts at interception. They will watch for the raiders at the border and force them down long before they reach the capital or make them unload their bombs in the fields before driving them back."

"*T'es fou?* Are you crazy?" spoke up a railroad worker testily. "Don't you know that our planes are all going to Morocco?"

"Why to Morocco? Is Abd el-Krim in revolt again? If that is true, I must say he's picked the right moment for an uprising," came back the conductor laughingly.

"I don't know why they're going to Morocco," said the

railroader. "But that's where they're going. I know because I work on the freights that haul the oil. . . ."

"Shows we have nothing to fear here. The war will be fought in Morocco," judged the conductor.

"It isn't that," returned the railroad man. *Il y a quelque chose de louche dans tout ça*—there's something crooked going on. Think of the tanks, for instance, too. . . ."

"*Eh bien,* what about the tanks? We have plenty of them. I read an article only this afternoon in *Paris-Midi* where a general by the name of Mordacq wrote that we have twice as many tanks as Hitler. He described the coming battles of the tanks, that general did, and he said that ours can crush the guts out of the German machines, which are of bad manufacture. They have not got the right kind of steel, the Boche, see!"

"*T'es fou!*" the railroader now said emphatically. "That general's article is just *bourrage du cran*—stuff and nonsense. . . . Most of the tanks are not going to the front at all, *mon vieux!*"

"Don't tell me," shot back the conductor tauntingly, "that the tanks are also going to Morocco!"

"Not to Morocco, no, they are being distributed over the length and breadth of the country, mostly to the big cities."

"Why is that?"

"Against us!" said the railroad man.

"Against us? What do you mean?"

"I mean against the people," came the railroadman sullenly.

"But what have the people done to deserve such mistrust?" asked the conductor in surprise.

"*Tu n'y comprends rien!*" came back the railroader. "Don't you understand anything at all? It is not a question of what the people have done, but what they may do.

The people may, for instance, insist on its rights, and bring back the Popular Front and put in a government that will insist on beating the Fascists."

"Then this government does not want to beat the Fascists?" asked the conductor again. "Still, Daladier said only last night that we are ready. . . ."

"Daladier is a scoundrel. Didn't he sell out to the reaction? Oh, it's the same crowd, if you must know; Hitler over there, Daladier right here. They have the same ideas, crush the people. They are both going to war for the same purpose: to get rid of the French people. We are too bothersome. We have to be tamed. Our government is as much an enemy of the French people, and worse, than Hitler. . . ."

"They want to make Germans out of us then? Is that what you mean?" came back the conductor again.

"No, they are going to make Fascists of us," said the railroader. "That's what they need this war for. They're going to slip the collar around our necks while we aren't looking. That's why Daladier sent the Chamber on vacation."

"*Les salauds!*" burst out the conductor. "But that's high treason what they're doing!"

"Call it what you will, I spit on it. France is rotten. *La France est pourrie, voilà!*"

When I left the train at Bourg-en-Forêt, it had stopped raining. The wind, too, had died down. But the sun had not been able to pierce the clouds. It had spread a pale reddish hue over the eastern horizon and was without form that morning. Only one small ray of direct sunlight, a narrow bundle of beams, had slipped through the low ceiling of bulging woolsacks in the sky. It stood like a slender pillar between heaven and earth and touched the village somewhere between the forest and the river. At that point shimmered a brilliant patch of gold. It was like a halo of light around the thatch-roofed farmhouse of Antoine Cerisy, the madman, who came to the door with a loaded rifle whenever anybody called. Except for that one bright spot, the village appeared to me suddenly so miserable and sordid that the realization of it came like a shock. The wet mist hung over the roofs like a dirty shroud, smoking and dripping.

There was nobody about in the street, though the hour was now quite advanced. I could hear the cattle coughing and lowing in the soaking meadows, but the smithy, where there was a good deal of activity in normal times, was closed. Gerbaud had a reputation of being the best horseshoer in the district. That's why they had taken him so quickly for the army, I figured. I looked in through the grimy window of his workshop and saw that the fire was out. All the fires were out in Bourg. Not the fires on the hearthstones, but the fires in the hearts of the people. The spirit had departed. The people had lost their courage before Hitler had struck his first blows. Bourg-en-Forêt lay there, like tens of thousands of other villages in France, waiting for something—but without much hope—waiting in the mud and the fog for someone with a mighty hand to lift them, to lead them towards an improbable, unimaginable destiny.

I know full well that this is folly and that no one will take me seriously when I say that the village sat waiting for a call. Villagers are not schoolboys who come running on the trot when the teacher rings the bell or claps his hands. But if they do not leap forward and come running, it is because of the immense lassitude that has come over them and over all the peoples of Europe since the termination of the last war. Their disillusion is too great for them to be roused, the abyss into which their hope has fallen too deep. And their lassitude and weariness are not the results of decadence and of some natural law according to which peoples and cultures rise and flourish and then disintegrate and go under. It is simply that the call to advance toward the ideal has been stilled, because the goal has been intentionally obscured. The First World War had made the world safe for democracy. But no sooner had that been done than those who had accomplished the task washed their hands of democracy itself. Democracy remained suspended in mid-air, as it were. It was not allowed to function. It was not permitted to evolve and grow from the embryo to adolescence. Its evolution was frustrated, its virility emasculated; the mobilization and assembly of its moral powers were inhibited and paralyzed. The word was there, but the word did not become flesh.

History is sometimes the shadow of a great man. It is the great individual, Carlyle said, who through his faith, his courage, his loyalty, his endurance, and his heroism creates all the things that have value and grandeur in the human being. But in our time the individual was to be replaced, as the creator of history, by the mass. History had become democratized, the world had been made safe for democracy. Making history was henceforth to be a democratic process, which meant that the great inarticulate suffering mass was to have a voice, a say, in the running of things. It meant also that the material circumstances of the masses were to change, for material circumstances are half the reality. The other half is the ideal.

History moves by ideals and sacrifice. The appeal to those ideals is what stirs the human heart most profoundly. There is no greater lie than the opinion of demagogues that the appeal to selfish interests exercises the greatest attraction on the masses. It has undeniably a certain effect, but stronger is the appeal and the call to sacrifice, to struggle, to blood, sweat, and tears, to poverty and hard labor. That is the heroic in human nature and is its strongest motive power, if an appeal is made to it.

This truth has been indefatigably preached by Carlyle. And do not the great facts of history justify him? Have not multitudes of martyrs come forward joyfully? Did not millions gird on the sword for the Crusades, and were not entire peoples, in the time of the Reformation, stirred by an idea? Was not Woodrow Wilson's call to make the world safe for democracy answered by millions who never gave their material welfare a second's thought, who disdained the dangers of the submarine and the battlefield, who volunteered precisely because the task involved the risk of peril and pain and death?

It is slandering the human spirit, Carlyle exclaimed, when it is said that it can be roused to heroism by promises of comfort and ease, recompense of sweets in this world or hereafter. In the lowest creature lies something nobler. Not to taste delicacies, but to do something manly and noble and to show himself under God's heaven a God-created human being—that is to what the humblest son of Adam aspires. Show the poorest roustabout that road, and he will change into a hero!

The peoples of Europe, including the German people, were just as ready to sacrifice and sweat and labor for the ideal of peace, democracy, and life as they had been for the holocaust of death. Their spirit was pitched to the highest tension when the new era dawned for the advent of which they had bled and fought four interminable years of heroism and courage and suffering. But the call to the new effort never came. Democracy, they were told, just meant a return to the old, to the *status quo ante*.

In his book, *Das Ende des Kapitalismus,* which was published in 1931, Ferdinand Fried investigated the ages of leading personalities in the political and economic spheres. The result of his studies showed that the average age of Reichstag members was fifty-six, while that of the most prominent industrial captains and magnates was sixty-eight. Fried confined his research to Germany, but others, taking up where he had left off, have established that in other western European countries the average ages of comparable personages were about the same. In startling contrast, Klaus Mehnert in his *Young Generation in the Soviet Union,* Maurice Hindus in his *Humanity Uprooted,* and Ella Winter in her *Red Virtue,* have made it clear that in Russia it is youth that occupies the leading positions both in economy and politics. Fried interpreted his findings as one of the indications of capitalism's decline. Without either denying or assenting to Fried's thesis, Dr. Jan Romeyn, a Dutch historian, concluded from Fried's observations that the leading personalities in the economic and political life of Europe in the after-war years—that is, the so-called reconstruction period—belonged to that generation which had learned to consider the era from 1870-1914 *as the normal one.*

What matters age? it may be objected. But those of us who belong to the generation that is now forty or thereabouts should take the age factor definitely into account when the question of the reconstruction of Europe in the after-war years and the ghastly dénouement of a new war is considered. *A priori* those periods do not have the slightest significance to persons who have but vague memories of the First World War and of the preceding era none at all. Only from conversations with their elders and from books can they form a picture of the past. But if they do that, they will see two things clearly: (1) the First World War produced such profound changes that, strictly speaking, one cannot speak of liquidation and reconstruction; (2) one of the real causes of the failure to settle the problems which arose after the war is that leading figures in politics and economy made an effort to reconstruct society on the model of what had been to them a normal world in the past.

The only real solution of those problems, on the other hand, could have been reached if a beginning had been made by recognizing that the world which had led to the upheaval of 1914-18 was not the normal or the ideal one. The past should not have been taken as a criterion. An effort should have been made to find the causes of the First World War and not to construct an ideal society on the basis of that discovery (for that would have been a wasted effort), but to search for present-day forces that would prevent the reconstruction of prewar society.

The object of all the reconstruction conferences—there were nearly one hundred of them in the years that elapsed between the First and Second World Wars—should not have been to liquidate the First World War (for it is impossible to liquidate anything that is past). It was the germs of a new world war—that is to say, the world which already had once led to war—that should have been liquidated.

This was the crime of the old men of Europe: the hankering for the past, its comforts, its privileges, and its relative tranquillity; their inability or unwillingness to see in the First World War, and in the depressions and crises which followed, the crisis of their world, the crisis of the capitalistic system itself. The world entered upon a permanent crisis with the First World War. Limited and temporary reforms, no doubt, were possible and were also achieved. But it requires no demonstration that it is impossible to speak of permanent reconstruction in a situation of permanent crisis and that, in the presence of a permanently dwindled consumption capacity of the masses, reconstruction can be only of short duration and must inevitably be followed by new, more acute crises.

For a real dynamic reconstruction, which can mean only the institution of a new social order to do away with the causes of the calamities that have overwhelmed mankind in the past, the experts, with their attempts at static reconstruction, were—and are—of no help or value.

The people's four-year effort to make the world safe for democracy had been vain and futile, because there had followed nothing but empty words and phrases. Slowly, from the pinnacles of hope, the peoples sank into despair. Disillusionment paralyzed their will. Inactivity produced lassitude.

There is an element of profound truth in the remark of the young officer I met in Amiens that wars are necessary because they save the peoples from mortal ennui. Georges Bernanos, in the maturity of his literary creativeness, abandoned his home in France to take up his abode on the pampas of Brazil, because he could not bear to see his country devoured by ennui. He told me once that the universal boredom was like a poisonous dust that you eat and drink and inhale with every breath. If a man does not fight it a single moment, it covers his face and his hands. Man must remain constantly on the move to avoid being covered by that rain of choking ashes. But where those philosophers err is in their conception of war as the sole escape from ennui. If the peoples can be stirred to war, which is, in the final analysis, but a sterile ideal, they can surely, and much more easily, be roused to life, to peace, to the fertile ideal of democracy. For that, no less sacrifice and struggle and heroism are necessary.

Were the French people not stirred by the formation of the Popular Front? What a resurgence there was of the national spirit, what splendid enthusiasm was evoked throughout the land! It was as if a new life had started: sordid environment was forgotten while the ideal that they were marching toward the sun dominated the French people. The era of the Popular Front was the last flourishing of the democratic spirit in Europe. It came near to attaining the heroic. No obstacles seemed insuperable, no sacrifices too great. Had war broken out during the régime of the Popular Front, the French people would have thrown themselves into battle with fervor and a will to conquer, and the French Republic would not have been the victim of Fascist violence. The banners of the people would have gone forward into the thunderstorm and the armies of France been imbued with the messianic zeal of liberators. France would have appealed to the heart of Europe, to the liberty-loving heart of the German people, and the ground on which they stood would have melted under the tyrants' feet. The peoples would have triumphed together, and on the ruins of the old world they together would have built a new society of fraternal collaboration.

This was not to be. The defenders of the old order prevented the emergence of the new, because the new menaced their privileged position in the old. Rather than entrust the destinies of France, of Europe, and of the world to the hands of the democratic forces, they broke the instrument of democracy, which was the Popular Front, and called in Hitler, in the foolish belief that Germany's National Socialism represented the wave of the future and in the vain hope that Hitler would safeguard their interests. But Nazism no more saves capitalism than Stalin's Communism. Nazism is state capitalism and dooms to death private capitalism and all hopes of rugged individualism.

These thoughts, which I kept to myself in those tumultuous and anxious days, although I was not ashamed of them, were forced on me by the things I saw around me. There is no other explanation for the debacle of France than the bourgeoisie's fear of victory. All the tortuous explanations about inner division, laxity of discipline, sabotage of the defense program, and the radicalism of the masses are false pretenses to cover up the crime of the rulers, which placed its own class interests before the national cause. It is they who lacked patriotism, not the people. It is they who used the state, and who employed the machinery of the state, to perpetuate their own dominant position in society. And it is to the knowledge that one class would do all it could to prevent the emergence of a genuine democracy that the people's lassitude and lack of enthusiasm for the war when it did come must be attributed. Only if the war had been made a revolutionary war, only if the people had been allowed to follow their ideal, could victory over German Fascism have been assured. As it was, the war was lost before a single shot was fired. Nay, worse, the French people were sacrificed in a war that was intended—beforehand, intentionally and deliberately—to be lost.

At the garden gate I found a policeman waiting for me.

"You'll have to come with me to the station," he said brusquely.

"What's up?" I asked. "Has the dog bitten someone?"

"I am not permitted to talk," said the man. *"Monsieur le commissaire* will no doubt explain."

I went off with him without having had a chance to go in my house. On the way to the police station we ran into the Abbé de la Roudaire accompanied by one of his choir-boys, who was carrying the holy oil. The priest had been administering the last sacraments to one of his dying par-ishioners. He looked worn and tired, and I noticed that his step lacked the old resiliency. We stopped and shook hands. I asked from whose bedside he had come, and the Abbé was just on the point of telling me when the police-man intervened. *"Monsieur l'abbé,"* said he to the priest, "this man is my prisoner. I'm not permitted to let him speak with anyone."

"Your prisoner?" the Abbé looked in amazement from the policeman's face to mine. "Your prisoner? But what has he done? What does this mean?"

"I don't owe you any explanations," replied the officer contemptuously, "I only need to say that France is at war and that we must be on the alert."

"France is not at war yet, *mon ami,"* came back the priest.

"Allons," the policeman turned to me, *"au poste,* to the station!"

"In that case," said the priest, "I will come along too." And he dismissed the choirboy.

"Monsieur," said the policeman to M. de la Roudaire, "your presence is not desired at the station!"

"Mon ami," came back the priest firmly, "I do not care

whether my presence is desired or not, I am coming along. I have my duty as well as you have yours."

"I caution you not to speak to the prisoner," shot back the policeman.

We arrived at the police station, where my guard turned me over to one of his colleagues, while he himself went into the commissary's office, presumably to notify that dignitary of my arrival.

The priest and I sat on a bench in the waiting room, where many other individuals, some of them manacled together, stood or sat around. Policemen went in and out, but one of them kept so close to me that I had no opportunity of speaking with my old friend.

After an hour's wait my name was called, and the policeman motioned me to get up and follow him. The Abbé rose too and walked with me to the door of the chief's office. As the policeman flung open the door to let me pass into the room, the Abbé began to walk in with me.

"Monsieur," said the policeman to him, "you must wait outside."

"Stand away!" retorted M. de la Roudaire fiercely.

The policeman shrank back, as if frightened by the priest's resolute words. We both walked inside.

Behind the table sat a man in a military uniform. He wore a pince-nez, and his tunic bore three rows of medal ribbons. He was a puny, anemic-looking individual with a bald head and dark mustache.

"Who are you?" he snapped at the priest.

"Arsène de la Roudaire," came back the Abbé, "officer of the Legion of Honor, curé of Bourg-en-Forêt!"

The officer sniffed and, turning to me, barked: "Where were you all night?"

"I was in Paris for a radio broadcast."

"How is it that you speak German?"

"I learned it at school, the same as French and English," I said.

"You were born in Holland, were you not?"

"That's right!"

"You were born in Holland, you broadcast to America, you speak German, you are in possession of a Canadian passport," he read from a sheet of paper before him. Then looking up, he said: "It's a strange combination, quite a salad! How did you obtain that Canadian passport anyway?"

"It was given to me by the Canadian authorities because I am a citizen of their country."

"How did you become a citizen of that country? Canada is not Holland or a Dutch protectorate, is it?" he asked, with a now-I-have-you-trapped sneer on his face.

"I was a visitor in Canada when the war broke out, and I joined the Canadian army as a volunteer. . . ."

"He became a soldier," interrupted the Abbé, "because he wanted to fight for France."

"For France? How good of him!" sneered the little man behind the desk.

"A Hollander in the Canadian army. How droll! I did not know the Canadians had a foreign legion," he went on.

"Politically I was no longer a Hollander when I entered the Canadian army, nor a foreigner, but a citizen of Canada."

"Ah, politically! I see your point!" he smiled. "In your heart you remained a Hollander though!"

"In my heart I felt that I was fighting for freedom . . . and for France!" I said.

"But you were a Hollander—that is to say, a Teuton, *un Germain*," he said.

"Racially I am a Teuton, I suppose, yes!"

"That is what I wanted to know," beamed the little man. "You admit you are a German, *un Allemand!*"

"I admit nothing of the sort," I retorted. "The Danes are Teutons; so are the Norwegians and the Swedes and the English. The Normans in France are Teutons, and so are the Alsatians. That does not make them Germans, does it?"

"You are giving me a lesson in racialism, monsieur?" he asked, raising his eyebrows quizzically.

"I am answering your questions," I said. "But," I went on, "I must also tell you that I am losing my patience. There is nothing to disavow or to be ashamed of in my past or in my race. What do you want to know of me? Speak to me frankly and openly, and I will answer you that way!"

"Don't get on your high horse now," warned the little man. "We know you have been to Berlin."

"Fine," I said. "What of it? I have been in Timbuktu also. Did you know that, too?"

"Monsieur," he said, "do not forget to whom you are speaking. Do not forget that you are a guest in this country and that you must not abuse our hospitality. You have on many occasions criticized France in your writings." He was again reading from a sheet of paper he had taken from the file that lay in front of him.

"I have only criticized certain French individuals, certain of their doings, certain French institutions. I have not criticized France. I have defended France. I have defended France not only in my writings, but on the field of battle."

"Monsieur," he said with sudden finality. "You published some sharp things about the French army, about the French foreign legion, about some of the most glorious of our generals. You run around at night in Paris looking in at railway stations, talking to people here and there. You are known to have German friends and Italian friends. Your house is full of German books. It all looks very strange indeed. . . . I must inform you that you are not to leave the commune of Bourg-en-Forêt any more on pain of detention. You must, moreover, report regularly once every three days to this police bureau. If you fail, sharp measures will be taken. That is all for today. You may go!"

"That is all very well," spoke up the Abbé de la Roudaire suddenly, "but I have not had my say yet."

"I am not interested in what you have to say, Mister Priest," shot back the little man. "You had no business here in the first place. Nobody sent for you. . . ."

"I do not need to be sent for," said the Abbé. "I go wherever I feel it my duty to go. . . . No man can tell me where to go and where not to go. Least of all, you, *monsieur le procurateur militaire.* I am going to speak to you, though I would prefer to speak to your superiors. I do not know them. But it is clear to me that you have been sent to our village of Bourg-en-Forêt to do something very sordid.

"I have known this man," he pointed to me, "for fifteen years. He has lived amongst us and he has been one of us. He has shared our tears and our joys. We never inquired whether he was born in Holland or in Tierra del Fuego. It does not matter in the slightest. An individual may be born in a chicken coop and still be a man. This man has been a citizen of France, in the higher sense, you understand, in the sense that he understood and was one with the soul of our people. That he speaks German is not a crime. That is a very worth-while accomplishment. He has defended France in word and in deed, in the press and on the battlefield. You cannot come here and insinuate that there is anything wrong with him. You ought to be ashamed of yourself to have been chosen for the execution of a task that is beneath contempt.

"You may tell your superiors, sir, that I, Arsène de la Roudaire, officer of the Legion of Honor, parish priest of Bourg-en-Forêt, and, if you must know, Vicomte de la Rochejacquelein, I say, that for the kind of procedure I witnessed here this morning I send them the expression of my utmost contempt."

The officer had taken off his pince-nez. He stared at the old priest with eyes that betokened alternately amazement and fury. But he was too taken aback to utter a word, and we left, *monsieur l'abbé* slamming the door most unceremoniously.

In the days that followed, Bourg-en-Forêt became the headquarters of a division of African troops. Unlike the units of the metropolitan army, who were dressed in the usual horizon blue, these colonials wore khaki uniforms and red fezzes. Most of their regiments were dispersed throughout the neighboring villages, but their commanding general installed himself in the château at Bourg and with him came, of course, the entire administrative staff, a corps of military police, the medical companies, two or three mechanized units, and the band. The band took possession of the park and practiced there from early morning till late in the afternoon, when its members repaired to the fair grounds just outside our commune, where they participated, along with thousands of other soldiers, in the evening prayer, according to the Mohammedan custom. After prayer the troops invaded the cafés and the six brothels in the Rue Danès de Montardart, and the citizens of Bourg withdrew in their houses. Every night the still-ness of our old streets was broken by the shouts and screams of these sons of Africa carousing and fighting amongst themselves.

We had three noncommissioned officers quartered upon us in the house, while twenty more men had taken up resi-dence in an abandoned shed at the foot of the garden. They were all away before daylight, when the trumpets blared for assembly in the streets, and they did not return until evening. But then we had our hands full. Among other things, it was impossible to make it clear to these soldiers, that, because of the black-out regulations, they must either keep the blue-papered windows closed or else turn off the electric lights. I would go out to the shed to explain the situation to them and persuade them to close the windows, but I was hardly back in the house before the air-raid warden in our neighborhood would come pounding on the door to tell me that lights were showing again in the garden.

This air-raid warden was a cantankerous individual, anyway—a neighbor of mine with whom I had had many a run-in about the repair of fences and walls and about dogs or chickens trespassing on his precious wilderness of a domain, but who, now that he was vested with a certain nocturnal authority and a brassard around his arm, en-joyed the welcome opportunity of harassing me to his heart's content. "If I see one more light on your place," he said to me one evening, just after I had been telling my soldier-guests for the twentieth time to obey the law, "just once more, *je vous assure,* I will denounce you to the mili-tary police as a suspect!"

"A suspect of what?" I asked in amazement.

"Suspect of signaling to enemy aircraft!" he came back.

I should have struck the scoundrel over the head right then and there, of course, but I controlled myself and merely closed the door in his face. But that was not the last I saw of him.

Within a week we took in three more military men. Two of them were underofficers of a Breton regiment that also had made Bourg its headquarters. They were two very grave and taciturn young men, blond of hair and with those peculiar blue eyes of seafaring people, eyes that are accustomed to look a long distance.

With them was the *aumônier,* or chaplain, of the regiment, a giant of a man with powerful hands, but a little unctious and sugary of speech, obviously an aspirant prelate. He began by tearing the colored pictures off the walls in the rooms where the Algerian noncoms slept—pictures of nude women they had clipped from *La Vie parisienne* and posted or pinned up above their beds. To this I made no objection, figuring that he had a certain spiritual authority, by virtue of his office, even over those Muslim warriors. But when he told me that a large lithograph of a secret Huguenot assembly (in the days of the revocation of the Edict of Nantes) and a photograph of Ernest Renan, which hung in the library where he had his couch, constituted an insult to a priest, I thought that he had gone too far, and told him so. He never spoke another word to me after that, nor did his two Breton parishioners, though they all ate with us at the same table in the evening. Among themselves they spoke the Breton language, of which, I regret to say, I do not understand one word. . . .

Our quiet world of Bourg-en-Forêt, wherein we had spent the better part of two decades, assumed a more unfamiliar aspect every day. Our village had become a military compound. Uniforms of all colors swarmed in and out of the garden gates, where formerly one had seen the lone figures of men and women move with the tranquillity and grace of bygone days. At dawn the bugles rent the air with their strident and metallic discords. The tintinnabulation of the Angelus at twilight was now followed by the gurgling yell of the Algerian muezzins. The nights were filled with the screams of the sirens, howling with sinister, bone-chilling insistence their announcement that the swastika-branded birds of death were hovering above our heads in the dark. At times you could hear the droning whir of their propellers, and it made you think of those flocks of giant vultures which follow the exhausted traveler in the desert with their cruel eyes, watching for signs of collapse before tearing at his flesh. By the light of the full moon the old cemetery, which we could see from the upstairs windows, with its crop of wooden crosses and thin white columns of marble, took on a frightening aspect. You felt the mystic relationship of death and what was going on around you. The cemetery had always been a friendly place, a garden where many an old friend slept between the rosebushes and the cypress alleys. Now it suddenly seemed to yawn like some eerie prehistoric monster waiting to be fed on carrion.

The suspense of the months and years of the so-called "war of nerves," that carefully calculated psychological device of the enemy to shatter the *sang-froid*, the vigilance, and the determination of the French nation, had been broken at last by the attack on Poland. Men breathed a little easier, because the uncertainty had at last been removed. But their nerves were still raw and frazzled, ready to snap. Now you understood something about the events at Dead Man's Hill in the last war, where the German can-

nonade battered away for three long months on one narrow
area of no man's land without lifting its barrage, causing
the onlookers to go insane by the hundreds each day and
compelling officers to stand revolver in hand—not to drive
their men into the inferno of steel—but to keep them from
throwing themselves forward spontaneously into the an-
nihilating fire. A hundred times you had felt like the villagers of Bourg when they said: *"Qu'ils viennent, nom de
Dieu!* Let them come, and we will see what happens."
Let us only come to grips with the enemy, get our fingers
into his throat or his in ours, one way or the other, as long
as this agonizing suspense comes to an end. . . .

Being restricted in my movements to the village of
Bourg, I wandered around in the daytime, dropping in
here and there to chat and to pass the time of day, or looking at the African soldiers drilling in the forest, carrying
out make-believe bayonet charges as we had done years
before in Camp Borden in Canada and later at Camp Pur-
fleet in England, laughing and shouting and swearing
when they drove their long "pins" into straw sacks dangling
from the tree branches.

The drill sergeants were showing them how to pierce
the objective: give a quick twist and withdraw the knife
rapidly before rushing over to a second bag of straw and
repeating the performance.

"When the enemy comes at you this way," I heard one
officer shout, imitating a man advancing with rifle poised,
"run right up to him, give him a violent blow with the
butt of your rifle in the groin, and at the same time turn
your gun around with a lightning gesture and stab him
through the throat. . . . That was the way I dealt with them
at Neuve-Chapelle back in 'sixteen. . . . That is the lesson
of the last war. . . ."

He had dealt with them that way? And with how many of them? I wondered. And what were "they" doing all that time? Just waiting to be stabbed like sandbags by *monsieur l'officier?* . . . Would those African boys remember all the fine points of instruction in actual combat? And what would they do if the enemy turned out to be a bearded little individual, of the kind I once saw advancing upon me not so far from that same town of Neuve-Chapelle? He looked very unsoldierlike, a clerk, perhaps, in civil life or a professor of biochemistry, whose coal-scuttle helmet was bobbing up and down ludicrously as he shook with the palsy of fear and whose eyes, through a pair of horn-rimmed glasses, looked as big as a cow's, wide open with horror, and who shouted: *"Drei Kinder, drei Kinder, drei Kinder!"* He kept on shouting those words with an insane frenzy until he plopped on the ground and began stuffing his mouth with mud. . . . What do you do in a case like that? Or what do you do when a mob of them come rushing up, howling like possessed souls, hurling hand grenades, and spouting liquid fire at you? What good is your bayonet in a case like that? Of what use are a whole belt of cartridges and all the fine lessons with the straw sacks? Why didn't he tell the Africans something about that? Lessons of the last war, my God! . . .

At the church of Saint-Louis des Français Masses were being said all morning. Besides the women of our community, the Breton soldiers now filled the nave. Grave-visaged lads, intensely pious and loyal to the Church, as were all Bretons. Their own chaplain, my house guest, was conducting the service. I noticed with pleasure that he had retained the old Latin pronunciation and had not fallen in with the fashion of making every word with a *u* sound like a long German *oo.* It seemed that some troops were about to leave for the front, for the celebrant announced, as Communion approached, that "by special dispensation" those who had partaken of food that morning could nevertheless receive the body of Our Lord. Hearing this, nearly all those present rose from their knees and walked up to the altar rail, their hands folded and their heads bent in prayer.

The air-raid warden called on me again that night. This time, he said, he would surely denounce me. The barn in the rear of the garden was blazing with lights. The Algerians were carousing and singing to the accompaniment of a clarinet played by one of the bandsmen. The tune, curiously enough, was the Polish national anthem, which the band had been practicing for weeks on end.

I suggested to the warden that he go himself to warn the lads about the danger to which they exposed us all and, if he failed to obtain compliance with his instructions, to threaten them with the military police. But of this he would not hear. He argued that I was responsible for the condition of the lights on my property and that I must enforce the law. "But I have told those men a hundred times," I said. "They won't listen to me. It is now up to you to enforce the law."

"Very well," he replied, "consider yourself under arrest."

While we stood talking the Breton noncommissioned officers returned home. My neighbor explained the matter of the lights to them, and it was they who volunteered to go to the rear of the garden to see how matters stood.

They had scarcely reached the barn when a sharp crash was heard, followed by the rattle of breaking glass and the shouts and curses of the Sidis. When I ran back I saw that a battle royal was going on between the Bretons and the

Algerians. One infuriated African was yelling: "You would put our lights out, would you? Now see how we are going to put yours out." With these words he came dashing up, swinging a curved knife. . . . Before any more damage was done the air warden had whistled for the police, who now came up in full force. To my astonishment I heard myself accused as the inciter of the trouble by the air warden and ordered by the commander of the police patrol to accompany him and four of the Algerians to the station. There I spent several hours explaining and arguing until the sirens began to wail, which was the signal for all and sundry to run outside the station to seek shelter in the cellars of the château. Instead of going to the cellar, I quietly returned home. . . .

The following Sunday morning I was awakened by two gentlemen who had walked into the garden without ringing the bell. At the gate stood the big limousine in which they had arrived.

"Is this your house?" one of them asked me.

"I do not own the house," I replied. "I rent it."

"Well," he said, "we think we need this house. . . . We are from the Turkish consulate in Paris. The consulate is to be evacuated this week. We are coming to Bourg-en-Forêt."

"There is little room left in this house," I said. "We are filled up with soldiers."

"That's nothing," said the Turk with an offhand smile. "The soldiers will go elsewhere, and you too!"

"I? But I have no intention of getting out," I said. "I have rented this house. I have a lease. . . ."

"Monsieur," the man with the heavy mustache interrupted me, "do not forget Turkey is an ally. . . ."

"An ally of whom?" I asked.

"Of France!" he shot back. "Of France, *évidemment!*"

"I am happy to hear it," I said. "In the last war Turkey was on the other side."

"Monsieur," he said, "you may omit the sarcasm. We are going now, but we will come back and we will not be alone."

And right he was. Two days later he returned in the company of a French army officer who announced that the house had been requisitioned. "I give you twenty-four hours to evacuate," he said. "The Turkish consulate will be installed here. . . ."

"Twenty-four hours is not a long time to move the furniture out and the books, *mon lieutenant!*"

"Oh, I forgot to say," he came back, "the furniture is also requisitioned. As to the books, you may move them out, if you wish. I do not think the Turks require any books. . . ."

The books stayed behind, nevertheless. There was not a truck or a cart or a wheelbarrow available in the whole of Bourg-en-Forêt to move them out. And there being no lodgings available anywhere, we decided to move to England.

The Abbé de la Roudaire accompanied us to the railway station. As we stood on the darkened platform a long troop train went by. We looked at the endless procession of coaches and freightcars crowded with the *matériel humain*. "You are not only leaving France," said the Abbé quietly. "You are leaving a world behind. What we have seen, we will never see again. This is the hour when the past is cut off from the future. Here is the dividing line. . . . Germany sits in the middle of Europe like a suffering and dangerous animal, the more dangerous because she is wounded and hungry. We can no longer still that hunger. That is the tragedy of our generation. . . . We should have helped Germany to live. That would have prevented her from turning into the ferocious beast she now is. Our statesmen did not see this. To have believed that it would be possible to keep a great and fertile people down and economically prostrated merely through a legal instrument was an error which may have been pardonable in the universal upheaval we had twenty years ago. That belief should have been abandoned upon ten minutes' serious reflection after the last shot had been fired. . . . If our statesmen had no regard for the elementary humane and Christian sentiment of human solidarity, they should have been led by simple political prudence, which says that one does not leave a neighboring nation to the bad advice of despair. . . .

"*Mais voilà*," he continued, shrugging his shoulders, "the evil is done. The beast we have made ferocious is out of its cage. Germany is now imposing on us the morality of violence because we did not exercise our duty as Christians. It is our own fault. . . . The law of God, *je veux dire* the law of cause and effect, works with inexorable precision: we face the consequences of our own sins of omission and commission. The universe is about to be thrown into convulsions such as we or our ancestors have never seen before. Perhaps we will learn to revise our conception of civilization in the years that lie ahead. . . . Perhaps we will learn that cannons, no matter who has them, never guarantee peace. . . ."

The train came hissing and thundering into the station. "When will we meet again?" I said to the priest, speaking close to his ear to overcome the roar of the stamping engine.

"Not in this world, *mon ami,*" he said, shaking his fine head. "Not in this world, I am afraid. But there, certainly," he pointed to heaven. "There certainly, in the fatherland of all Christians," and then, with a malicious twinkle in his eyes, he added: "But only if you wish it so, *bien entendu!*"

II

As Time One Day . . .

AN HOUR after weighing anchor in Ostend that Sunday morning, the small steamer on which I had taken passage ran into trouble. It seems that the man in the crow's-nest had spotted the periscope of a submarine to the south of us. Not only was the instrument's eye turned in our direction, but the raider was rapidly overtaking us. The skipper let me have a look through his spyglass, but I was a long time locating the small object in the choppy sea. Upon discovering of our danger, we had immediately veered sharply to the north, and the ship was now thrown into a zigzag course while the radio telegraphist, in his cabin behind the bridge, tapped out a call to the British Channel patrol, giving our location and the approximate position of the submarine. A quarter of an hour went by before the British crackled back their reply advising us to turn west from our new course and run into the harbor of Zeebrugge. But since that would have meant exposing the full starboard side of the ship to the submarine's torpedo tubes, our skipper judged it more prudent to keep on steaming due north in the hope of reaching the safety of Dutch territorial waters before the German could send one of his torpedoes after us. Accordingly, we were in sight of the town of Breskens, at the mouth of the Scheldt River, at four in the afternoon, and at six o'clock, when the church bells were ringing for the evening service, I set foot ashore in that Zeeland-Flemish town where, a few months later, the broken remnants of the Dutch army were to make their last and most heroic stand.

I walked into the principal church and looked up at the high pulpit wherein both my great-grandfather and grandfather had preached their first sermons as young men, and I ran my fingers over the Gothic letters of their names, which were carved in a stone pillar with those of all the ministers who had served the church of Breskens since the Reformation. Then I strolled back to the ship through the narrow streets with their one-story houses of red brick, which are built low and squat, as if they would clamp themselves to the earth and resist the impact of the storms of winter. I did not want to come under the spell of Holland and again have to go through the pain of tearing myself away from dear and sacred associations. But when I asked a boy the shortest way to the quay, he began to laugh and said that anyone who lost himself in Breskens must be the greatest *Domkop* in existence.

There was a smell of tobacco in the air and of dried fish and of nets boiling in the round stone ovens by the waterside. Young men and girls, some of them dressed in the colorful costume of the province of Zeeland, walked in the general direction of the shore, holding each other by their little fingers. Their speech was soft and turned to shy whispers when their round, light-blue eyes met the stranger's. In passing I glanced furtively through the crystal-clear windowpanes and saw families gathered around the linen-covered tables. I could see the furniture, the dishes, the mirrors, and the clocks, everything gleaming spotlessly as if brand-new. Here and there a man or a woman moved aside a snow-white curtain to peer out. But when I nodded my head their faces grew

suddenly harsh and severe. The children in the street
stared at me in frank amazement, and I heard one boy
say to his companion: "His shoes are English, but his
face is Dutch." When I called back: "How could it be
otherwise?" the boy returned. "Then why do you strut
with the air of a foreigner?"

Twilight was coming on when I crossed the gangplank
and sat down with the skipper to wait the fall of night
and a signal from the Channel patrol before proceeding
with our journey. Across the river, far away, we could
see the lights of Flushing dip and blink and the cool
moon coming up as a silver benediction over the island
of Walcheren. The tide was running swiftly. Its rolling
swell set the bells on the buoys tolling with irregular
strokes. The people of Breskens were going to sleep.
You could hear the footsteps of the lovers, who had spent
the twilight hour in dreaming on the quay, die away
in the distance. At the same moment someone turned on
dance music on the radio in the cabin. Another switch
of the dial brought the peasant voice of Daladier saying
that the French fatherland was thinking with tenderness
that Sunday evening of its children in the defense positions. There was more eloquence in that one word "tenderness" than in the hundreds of appeals for unity and
steadfastness sent out by the propaganda office. Then the
invisible voice slowly pronounced the words "justice,
liberty, and right," those terrible words which, in the
ears of the peoples, have in our day become the har-
bingers of disaster and holocausts. The shadows were
deepening on the water. The skipper and I were leaning over the railing and followed with our eyes a cloud
of phosphorescence which illuminated the depths with
a pale green glow. "They're jellyfish," he said. "They're

out of their course. They belong in the Baltic. They're not created for this". . . .

Not created for this! Weren't we all out of our course, the whole world? Was man created for the darkness into which Europe was about to enter? Now that the hour for the unification of Europe had dawned at last, the Continent was divided against itself and was getting ready to tear itself asunder. But not only the Continent: every man is innerly divided against himself, a victim of indignation, anger, and shame. How many are there who can still say with Rimbaud: "The world is good . . . I bless life"? How can we speak and laugh and dance when we know that somewhere a brother lies face downward in Gethsemane and that the cup of suffering is passed from one nation to another? How disengage oneself from the crowd of phantoms that press in from all sides? One has scarcely created a zone of silence around oneself ere the phantoms invade that small area of security. They unmask in the center of our lives, in the middle of our days and evenings and nights, to ask questions with questioning eyes. The tumult of the world pursues us into no matter what hiding place. The echo of its anguish prolongs itself in our own hearts. At every turn in the destiny of the world a thousand voices begin to speak in us, the voices of the questioners: the miners in the Borinage, the Okies in California, the slaves behind the looms and spindles in Manchester, the coolies in China, the soldiers of Japan, the muzhiks of the Ural, the hungry children in the gates of Calcutta, the immured prisoners in Franco's Spain, and the lost men in the concentration camps of Central Europe—souls rotting everywhere in the shadow of palaces and cathedrals.

Still stands the statue in the valley of Dura as in the

days of Nebuchadnezzar, its iron jaws wide open to receive the endless procession of the victims of the heca-
tomb. . . .

The boat began to move. We slid into the green-black
night. The signal lights of a destroyer snapped on and
off in the darkness. All at once the moon broke through
the clouds again, and the coast of Holland became visible
as far as the mouths of the Rhine and Meuse. A world
of dark miniatures emerged from the gloom. A lone sail,
ghostly in its whiteness, stood off for the north. It moved
over the black mirror of the sea like an image in a dream.
Time passed by, ages and centuries imperceptibly
blended into one day. My own life rolled by. . . .

Gorcum is a small town like perhaps a score of others
in Holland; sleepy, somewhat dilapidated in appearance,
without a single flourishing industry or one notable
monument. For one could hardly have called the fountain in the public square a monument, that baroque
monstrosity which had been erected by the municipality
to commemorate the departure of Napoleon's soldiers.
This dreary object, which rose to the height of the Burgomaster's chambers on the first floor of the town hall, consisted of a square-cut pillar of red granite with the statue
of a winged angel perched on its summit. Once the angel
had held an outstretched sword in her hand, but she
had lost both the sword and her right arm in a particularly violent thunderstorm I well remember, because,
during the night in which it raged, the lightning also
struck a chimney on my father's house. Reclining against
the sides of the obelisk in various attitudes of undesign-
ing charm lay four rusty cast-iron nymphs from whose
bulging breasts there trickled once a year—on the sover-

eign's birthday—a sleazy stream of bottle-green, evil-smelling water. This work of art stood in the middle of a round basin half filled with a thick fluid in which the boys of the town had introduced an assortment of frogs, salamanders, long-legged water spiders, and even some small fishes.

An inscription on the obelisk proclaimed in poetic language that "the jets of crystal-clear water here seen symbolize the gladsome flow of the Dutch people's liberty." I often thought, as I stood reading those words, that one could scarcely have held it against a stranger, if alternately contemplating the solemn words of the inscription and the moisture oozing forth from the iron ladies' mammillae, he should have reached the conclusion that freedom was in a bad way in Holland. For never, to my knowledge, did those nymphs send forth a gush really puissant and bright enough to gladden the heart of the onlooker. When the festive day of the Queen's anniversary came around, there was always something wrong with the hydraulic mechanism inside the bosoms of those metal maidens.

Gorcum had indeed little to boast of. Now, there are Dutch towns justly famous for their products: Delft, for instance, has its blue faïence, Gouda its clay pipes and its candles, Deventer its cake and ale; the fame of Schiedam's gin has spread far beyond the national borders. Gorcum has no such renown. True, there was the leaning tower, a massive, pre-Gothic structure that bore the official name of Sint-Jan, but the inhabitants had nicknamed it "the widower" because fire had deprived it of the companionship of the original church built by its side in the tenth century. The new church, erected just before the Reformation, was a grotesque, barnlike edi-

fice without any pretense to style at all. Of the tower, the
municipal archivists proudly affirmed that it had once
been seen and admired by no less a personage than
Charlemagne. Wherever the man had gleaned that bit
of historical information, I do not know. Charlemagne
did indeed reside in the Netherlands for a short time, but
the site of his castle was far away, near Nijmegen. That
he came as far east as Gorcum may be doubted and is,
on second thought, perhaps rather a fortunate circumstance. For, in spite of the celebrated company of learned
monks that accompanied him on all his travels, the King
of the Franks was by no means a gentle ruler. And then,
whether it must be accounted a matter of glory for Gorcum to have been visited by the conqueror of Widukind
has become a doubly moot question since the advent of
German National Socialism, which has relegated him,
whom it denounces as the butcher of the Saxons, to a
back seat in the Teutonic pantheon.

Who were the original inhabitants of Gorcum, our
ancestors? That was a highly controversial subject, which,
although it figured each year on the agenda of the
rederijkerskamer, or local debating society, had never
been settled quite satisfactorily, not even with the aid of
certain archaeological and historical experts who came
down especially from some university town or other to
enlighten us on the subject. There were a few citizens,
members of some of the oldest families, who held stubbornly to the tradition that there had been a Teutonic
settlement, back in the days of Julius Caesar, on the site
of our town. They explained that in the eternal wars
which raged in the Hercynian Forest, before the Christian missionaries somewhat tamed the martial instincts
of the Germanic tribes, one group of knights had been

driven out. The reason for their ostracism was obscure. These fugitive outlaws had come drifting down the Rhine in hollowed-out treetrunks and had finally settled in our precinct. Once ashore, they had given that part of the Rhine which flowed past our town the name of Merwede (or Merwe), had built a castle, or *steyn*, there, and had called that strong place Merwesteyn. If that story were true, some of our citizens must of course have been of noble blood, an assumption that they sought to impress on the masses by an appropriately superior bearing.

Now, although all this about the town origins may have been quite true, I think our amateur historians went a little too far when they embroidered an even more ambitious design on that simple legendary pattern. They boasted that one of the Roman Empire's finest legions, the one that served in Judea under Pontius Pilate, had been recruited in our neighborhood. I rejected that story instinctively, because, if substantiated, it might conceivably have landed us into no end of trouble—and still may. In our time, when punitive laws are made retroactive and when even the alleged sins of the fathers are visited on the children, it would not be difficult to blame the natives of Gorcum, of which I am one, for part of the terrible happenings on the mount of Calvary.

In the most ancient chronicles extant—for instance, in certain historical documents from the hand of Vincent van Microp, the town's treasurer, who flourished in the fifteenth century—the name Gorcum is sometimes interchanged with that of Van Arkel's Oude Veste, which means roughly, the Old Fortress of the Lords of Arkel. These lords of Arkel were feudal seigneurs who fought innumerable wars with the counts of Holland, the sons of both parties taking up where the fathers had left off—and so on for centuries. The Arkels seem to have been a valiant and rebellious lot who considered themselves as important as their liege lords at The Hague. Like other old Dutch noble families, such as the Brederodes, the Egmonds, and Yselsteins, the lords of Arkel claimed descent from the Trojans. On the tomb of one of these gentlemen, Jan XI, who ruled over the town and its environs from 1321 till 1359, it is expressly stated that his ancestors fought under Hector against the Greeks in the famous Trojan War. These Trojans were supposed to have come to Holland via Hungary in the person of one Heinemannus in the tenth century.

Quite fittingly, the last seigneur of Arkel died fighting in the streets of Gorcum against the troops of Jacqueline of Bavaria, Countess of Holland, in the fifteenth century. He was that famous Jan van Arkel of whom it is recorded that he once lifted his horse from the ground by seizing hold of a beam above his head in the town gate and then hoisting the animal up between his knees. The account of that performance, incredible as it may seem to our weak-kneed age and generation, must yet be considered more trustworthy than that of my Lord of Arkel's Trojan descent. In fact, seventeenth-century historians, such as Hadrian Junius and Abraham Kemp, have lightly dismissed that otherwise not uninteresting claim. Hadrian Junius, who, besides being a chronicler of note, was a renowned physician, wrote: "Troy was a sow with many little pigs, but that one of those little pigs roamed away from good King Priamus as far as Gorcum is said for a lark."

The truth is, of course, that nothing was known about the town's origins, for the good reason that no records existed from the first nine centuries of the Christian era.

Teutonic Knights may or may not have built a strong
place there against their feudal chiefs or to exact toll from
the river commerce, but it may also very well be that
Gorcum was the site of a penal colony, a place where
robbers and bandits foregathered, or, what is more likely,
a simple settlement of fishers and huntsmen.

If you asked my Uncle Kees the question: "From whom
do you think we descend anyway, from noblemen and
warriors or tradesmen and fishers?" he would reply: "We?
We don't descend at all! At least, we should not. We
should be ascending, not descending. It is far better when
you can take pride in your children than to go boasting
about your ancestors." And then he added these words,
which, I learned a good many years later, were Nietzsche's: "Not whence you came, O man, shall henceforth redound to your honor, but whither you go! Your
will and your feet, which always want to run ahead of
you, they will be your new glory!"

Still and all, in the Middle Ages the town must have
been a busy spot. You could tell that from the size of the
principal church, which had a seating capacity of seven
thousand, more than half the number of the whole town's
population in my youth. There had also been three great
monasteries in Gorcum and one convent. The ruins of
these still existed, but scores of dwellings had been erected
from the bricks and stones of the demolished wings of
these institutions, which the Reformation had closed.
Under the streets still ran the crypts and tunnels through
which the monks and nuns had reached the cathedral
in the center of the town. When the municipality
changed the lighting system of the streets from oil to gas,
and a gas main had to be installed, sections of that sub-

terranean labyrinth were laid open to the light of day,
and I, along with other little boys, walked in those mildewed subways until we were stopped by the police. We
were stopped, I should say, not because of any danger involved. There was little danger, for the masonry was in
perfect condition, but because of a gruesome discovery
made by the engineers in one of the underground chambers. At the north end of the town, beneath a street
known as the Broerensteeg, or Alley of the Brothers,
where a monastery of the Black Friars had once stood,
the workmen had come upon an iron door in one of the
tunnels. When the bolts of that door had been removed
and the door opened, the torches revealed a narrow stairway, almost a hundred feet high. On the steps of that
stairway lay or sat seventy skeletons.

The news of that ghastly find spread through the town
like wildfire, and an investigation was started immediately to determine the identity of those seventy men and
the manner in which they had perished. I do not remember who solved the riddle, but I do recall that some
Catholic historians from out of town positively identified
those skeletons as belonging to the friars who had lived
in the monastery that had once stood on the site above.
How those men died turned out an even more horrible
revelation. They had been locked up in that narrow passage without food or light and had been left to die. By
whom had that been done? you will ask. I am ashamed
to say that that piece of barbarism had been the work
of one of Holland's national heroes, Admiral de Lumey,
Seigneur of Treslong, the commander of the Water Beggars. He was one of the leaders in the revolt against Spain
in the sixteenth century, a fanatical Calvinist who had

made the Mohammedan crescent the emblem of the wild
freebooters he led and whose device was *"Liever den
Turk dan den Paap*: Rather Turkish than popish."

The skeletons were removed at the expense of the
Catholic hierarchy and the bones quietly interred in another city. I recall that the otherwise quite voluble
Protestant ministers in Gorcum had but little to say about
this particular incident beyond evoking extenuating circumstances for the authors of the ghastly entombment.
They reminded their hearers that, after all, Lumey had
been a child of his times and that the Catholics had dealt
no less severely with the Protestants, which was true
enough. For in Gorcum alone the Inquisition burned no
less than three hundred heretics at the stake. Their
names were written down in a register that was kept in
the consistory chambers. Once a year, on Reformation
Day, October 31, these names were read aloud in church
by one of the catechumens.

Even so, Uncle Kees did not let the matter of the
monks' skeletons rest. He and some other freethinkers
published a letter in the local newspaper calling for an
open and public act of contrition and expiation. Even
as the Protestants of Geneva had erected a monument to
Michael Servetus on the spot where Calvin had him
burned at the stake, so, in some street near the ruins of the
monastery, the inhabitants of Gorcum were, in self-re-
spect and in tribute to the spirit of tolerance, bound to
erect a monument or, at least, to affix a commemorative
plaque to the martyrs of Protestant fury. Nothing came
of that pious project, but certain precious altar vessels,
which had also been recovered in the deserted crypts,
found their way back to the church to which they be-

longed and did not remain in the Rijksmuseum at Amsterdam, where they had been sent provisionally.

Those were momentous days for us boys, but they were soon forgotten in the flow of everyday life. The gas pipes were installed. The oil lamps in the homes gradually disappeared, and the town assumed a brighter aspect in the evening. It took some time, though, before the church was equipped with the new means of illumination. Until I was ten years old we worshiped by candle light. In addition to immense candelabra suspended from the ceilings, each holding five hundred candles that burned down in the precise number of minutes it took the pastor to deliver his sermon of one hour and a half, we had individual candles in front of us in the pews. The pews were really boxes of the kind still found in King's Chapel in Boston. You entered the box through a small door and took a seat on the wooden bench. Your father and uncles sat on chairs that were also inside the box. The women sat in another part of the church, separated from the men.

The Dutch remain seated during congregational singing. It would tax the strength of a giant to remain standing during the singing, let us say, of the 119th Psalm, with its eighty-eight stanzas. But it was one of our delights as boys to watch the candles as the singing began. The breaths of the worshipers would suddenly strike the flames and send them flickering and throwing spooky shadows on the walls. Several candles were suddenly extinguished by the first fervent onset of particularly stentorian singers.

The huge Bibles were fastened to the sloping desks by means of long silver or iron chains. The difference in the metal reflected the social standing of the occupants of the pews. For each family had its own private box in permanent leasehold, with its name and, in the case of the nobility, its crest painted on the door. Those Bibles were printed in Gothic characters and contained the famous translation of the Scriptures ordered by the States-General in 1617. On the flyleaf it was stated that the translation was a true one from the original Hebrew and Greek "into our own Nether-German language." Nether-German Reformed was also the official name of the state church. Of late years such references to the Germanic origin of the Dutch people and language have been carefully removed. Everything has become Netherlandish or *Dietsch,* even the words in the national anthem referring to the German blood of the Orange family. In spite of these superficial emendations, neither the character of the people nor the language has undergone any startling transformation. The Dutch remain what they have always been: a Teutonic people speaking a Teutonic language. In saying this, I may perhaps be accused of providing ammunition for the Pan-Germans, who are trying to convince the Dutch people, whom they have conquered, that their future lies with the New Order instituted by Berlin and that, if they only will co-operate loyally, they will be regarded and treated as coequal with the Bavarians, Prussians, Saxons and Scandinavians. In other words, they will be recognized as Nordics and may hope, in times to come, to be integrated into the ranks of the *Herrenvolk,* the master people.

The fact of the matter is that the Dutch are Nordics and Aryans and all that and that recognition of this by the Slavic Prussians makes very little difference one way or the other. Because the Academy of Racial Science in Berlin has recognized an elementary ethnological fact, I am not going to repudiate it.

Since there were no industries to speak of and since the pleasant miracle of bread raining down from heaven has occurred but once in the course of history (and that in the faraway Arabian desert), the question may well be asked: how did the inhabitants of Gorcum make their living? And the rather astonishing answer must be that these inoffensive people, who intended nobody in the whole wide world any harm, actually lived by and off the deadly institution of militarism.

The garrison was the principal source of the town's income. It counted in normal times a few thousand men, all artillerists, and almost double that number in the early autumn, when old levies came back for a few weeks of training. For quarters the troops had a set of medieval barracks or armories located on an island in the middle of the town. One reached the cobblestoned parade square, which on three of its sides was hemmed in by the buildings that housed the troops, by means of a bridge. It was on that side of the square, too, where the bridge was located, but separated from the parade ground by a deep moat, that the townspeople gathered on August 31 to watch the annual parade in honor of the Queen.

That was indeed a glorious day. From early morn every house, the mansions of the rich as well as the dwellings of the poor, was adorned with the national tricolor. We boys were up early, for that day Mother took the silken orange-colored sashes from the cedar chest and fastened them around our waists with a fine bow so that the tassels hung on the left side about the level of the knee. Grown-up men wore orange ribbons in their lapels, and women had a small bow of orange silk on their dresses.

The officers of the garrison came out in gala uniform that day, with a plume of black feathers in their shakos and an orange sash around their shoulders. They were about early in the narrow streets, those gentlemen, saluting left and right with more than ordinary flourish. I say they saluted because it was a custom amongst the citizens to greet a man wearing the national uniform first.

There were, in fact, two categories of citizens you greeted on sight by uncovering the head, whether you knew them personally or not: an officer of the national army and a clergyman. Of course, you greeted many others and quite deferentially—the rector of the Latin School, for instance, and the Burgomaster, although in your heart you despised that squint-eyed snooper most profoundly.

But then you really did not greet the man at all, you rather paid your respects to the high office he occupied. To us in Gorcum there was nothing higher than the Burgomaster. He symbolized the supreme authority, the state, the top notch in the social order. When he passed by while you were at play near the church or in the square in front of the town hall, off came all the caps, and they stayed off till he was out of sight. All this does not alter the fact that on one occasion my brother and I subjected him and his ridiculous silk topper to an unmerciful bombardment with snowballs. He had it coming to him for refusing to proclaim an extra half holiday a week for skating, in spite of the fact that the river was frozen over —a rare enough occurrence.

I must add, for truth's sake, that it was quite dark at the time and that we had waited near his house with a large store of ammunition for an hour or so in a stinging snowstorm. There was no escape for him, and his hat went rolling down the square while he bellowed like a bull of Bashan all sorts of imprecations and dire threats. But the louder he shouted the faster our snowballs went raining on his chest and shoulders.

The parade started promptly at eleven o'clock. The regiment was drawn up along three sides of the square, with the band in the middle of the parade ground. At the moment that the colonel commanding the garrison, accompanied by his adjutant, came riding through the gate, the bugles blared forth. When they were silent, the command rang out to fix bayonets and present arms. That was a most solemn minute. While the troops stood at attention and the officers drew their swords, the majestic tones of the national anthem rolled out.

Many people wept unashamedly at the sound of the mighty old hymn. Not that they were stirred by its words. That would have been almost impossible. The national anthem of Holland is grand orchestral music, but its fifteen stanzas, beginning with the story of a prince of German blood whose domains lie somewhere in southern France, who professes loyalty to the King of Spain who had him assassinated and who, on top of that, is busy defending the Netherlands, constitute a tissue of incomprehensible absurdities to the modern man unversed in the historical details of the life of William of Orange. The author of this piece of archaic poetry, which is the longest of all the national anthems in the world, except the Chinese, was a nobleman by the name of Philips van Marnix,

Heer van Sint-Aldegonde, whose descendants are amongst the most bitter antagonists of the Dutch (Flemish) language and culture in Belgium.

I once had the honor to interview one of the Counts of Saint-Aldegonde. The name had become De Saint-Aldegonde instead of Van Sint-Aldegonde. That interview took place in the days when I was working as a newspaper correspondent in Paris and I had become interested in the cause of Flemish nationalism and the Pan-Dutch movement, which aimed at a reunion of all the Dutch-speaking tribes in the world—the Boers of South Africa and the farmers of Michigan included, under the aegis and protection, if necessary, of our big brothers, the Germans. Those were my nationalistic, imperialistic days. I look back upon them without shame or remorse, but with just a little self-pity.

The Count of Saint-Aldegonde, as the descendant of the composer of that noble hymn, seemed to me the ideal person to lead the great movement, which published a small newspaper in Holland. That newspaper was edited by a monsignor, a papal prothonotary by the name of Robrecht de Smet, a man slated to become the first Roman Catholic bishop in Scandinavia if ever the one and only Church should gain sufficient adherents in the domains of Gustavus Adolphus. Each week a thousand copies of the paper were smuggled into Belgium. I did it a few times myself. For it was the Flemings we wanted to reach. Across the front page, by way of banner, ran these words—in Dutch, of course: "Flemings never forget: Belgium is not your fatherland!"

When I showed this to the Count, he almost burst with

indignation. He ordered me off the premises, a fine old Dutch house in Brussels, and threatened to denounce me to the police. In fact, he picked up the telephone and actually spoke to M. Adolphe Max, the Burgomaster of Brussels, about my mission. He referred to me and my mission in such terms that I judged it most prudent to execute without delay a strategic retreat to prepared positions, as the war communiqués would say.

That would have been the extent of my acquaintance with the scions of the Aldegonde family and all their works had I not once, in a moment of embarrassment, used their name to my advantage. It came about this way.

One day—on January 21, 1926, to be exact—a solemn Mass of requiem was to be chanted in the church of Saint-Germain l'Auxerrois in Paris for the repose of the souls of Louis XVI and Marie Antoinette. This is an annual affair, I understand, and takes the form of a political demonstration by the royalists. In *l'Action française*, the monarchist newspaper, I had read that all the descendants of the House of France and the real nobility, as opposed to the Bonapartist crop, would be present. I wanted to see them, so I went to the service. At the door of the church was quite a concourse of prominent ladies and gentlemen. As they slowly filed inside I noticed that they produced cards. Of course, I had no card, but I did not give up hope. Slowly making my way forward in the queue, I heard the man in front of me say to the usher: "Oh, I am sorry. I have left my card behind, but I am the Duc de Talleyrand. You know me, of course." "Of course, monseigneur," said the usher. "Please to enter, monseigneur!" Then my turn came, and I said: "It is quite unfortunate, but I have also left my card behind. I am the Count de Saint-Aldegonde, you know me, of course!"

"Of course, *monsieur le comte*," said the beadle, making a bow. "Please turn to the left and sign the register." This I did. Talleyrand, who had preceded me in signing the register, handed me the pen after dipping it into the ink for me. He waited for me to sign. I could not think of any other noble name, so I simply stuck to my original story: Marnix de Saint-Aldegonde. I was given a front seat by another usher and sat between Charles Maurras and Admiral Scherer, two great monarchists, and behind a lady whom they addressed as Majesty. She was the wife of the pretender to the throne, the Duc de Guise. At the close of the service I made myself as scarce as coin in the Chicago city treasury.

If a good deal of the town's income was derived from the military establishment, some of it also came from the agricultural environs. There must have been a score of villages, some with populations as numerous as ten thousand, to whose inhabitants Gorcum was the chief trading center. I knew them all, those villages and hamlets, for I frequently visited them with my uncle, who was a landscape painter of some repute. I would not say that agriculture in our district was exactly in a flourishing—that is to say, a highly remunerative state. It could not be. Although there were no latifundia or large estates, such as existed in czarist Russia and even today in Spain, a circumstance which reduces the peasantry to a state little above that of serfs, with us it was the other way around: the land was fragmentarized into such extremely small parcels that really profitable exploitation was out of the question. The overgreat majority of the farmers barely eked out a living. They were poor. They walked on wooden shoes and probably had one new suit of clothes after reaching maturity, the black, heavy cloth costume in which they were married. I knew families in which one and the same suit of clothes had served at the weddings of both father and son with an interval of twenty or twenty-five years between the two celebrations.

Potatoes were the chief staple, potatoes and black rye bread. A dish of steaming potatoes would be placed in the middle of the bare table, and each member of the family and each guest would pick whatever he could consume, but piecemeal. You did not transfer the potatoes to your plate. Individual plates were not in use. These peasants kept their hats on while they ate. They uncovered only while they asked the blessing, which they did by muttering something behind their hats with which they covered their faces while praying.

If you wanted to see a village in Holland, or a city for that matter, the best day was a Sunday. You placed yourself before the door of the church shortly after the noon hour. Then you could see the entire population streaming out of the house of worship. Before going home for the midday meal, the inhabitants would stand around for a while, or go for a stroll, the elder men gravely discussing the fine points of the sermon and the younger talking what young people the world over talk about on a Sunday afternoon. My uncle was not so much concerned with looking at the costumes as with observing the faces of his countrymen. Often he would say when we sat in some village church waiting for the service to start or waiting at the door to see the congregation disperse: "If I did not know that this village is Hoornaar, I would say we were near the sea in Brittany somewhere or in the land of the Basques. You feel as if you were amongst sailors." For this feeling there was indeed no rational foundation; but the faces of the men, the quiet and dignified manner in which they moved, the self-conscious strength and the inner freedom—all these things probably made Uncle think of the sea, of fishing boats and harbors.

Of course, the Dutch are seafaring people, even if thousands of them have never seen the ocean. The great majority have sea eyes, pale blue, the color of steel, with a peculiar faraway stare in them, not of the dreamy kind, but of eyes that are accustomed to gaze on a vast expanse and see a long way.

Family life was established on a patriarchal basis in those rural regions. The paterfamilias had and exercised dictatorial powers; the woman served, but not in a slavish or oppressed manner. The right of corporal punishment was exercised, aye, with the rod, until the children had reached majority. One may wonder whether the boys of these rural Dutch families who served their term with the military in different cities, some of them in the great metropolises of The Hague and Amsterdam, were not taught by their contact with the big world to reject this almost medieval and surely ultraconservative exercise of family authority. But such was not the case. Paternal authority was reasserted the moment they returned home from their term of service.

Now that I have seen the peasants of other lands, those of France and Spain and Italy and Rumania and Russia, and then think back to the rural regions of Holland, to one of those Sundays spent in the neighborhood of Gorcum, I am struck with the inconceivable, deadening dullness of life in the Dutch villages. Not a single form of amusement was permitted. Football and other sports were proscribed on the Sabbath, a visit to the tavern or to a clubhouse was frowned upon. An occasional burst of children's laughter was hastily reprimanded as unbecoming young Christians on the Lord's day. At least, so it was in the Protestant villages. Across the river in Brabant, where the population is predominantly Catholic, the atmosphere was by contrast one of perpetual jollification.

There the boys played football of a Sunday afternoon, and the priests looked on or actually participated in the games as supervisors and referees. There a cinema opened on Sunday afternoon or a bowling alley, and in the evening there was dancing in the coffeehouse or in the market place. For us, as for those Calvinist peasants, there was just another sermon, another portion from the Heidelberg Catechism to meditate and inwardly digest, or just plain Bible-reading by some solemn elder without pastoral expositions or exhortations, preferably from the Book of Kings or Chronicles: King So-and-So reigned for so many years in Jerusalem and did what was evil in the sight of the Lord and was gathered unto his fathers. Can you recite the names of the Kings of Judah and those of Israel? I can, I can even do it backwards. But I wish I couldn't. I wish I had spent the time wasted in the acquisition of all that sterile knowledge in the pursuit of something more useful.

As in New England, so in Holland, although a few decades later in point of time, the motorcar and the motion picture have almost entirely effaced the originality and the individuality of the small provincial town and the rural community. I could hardly believe my own eyes when, after an absence of fifteen years, I watched the arrival of the seven o'clock train on a Monday morn-

ing, which was still market day in Gorcum, and saw how
the peasant girls were now wearing silk stockings and
short skirts and colored blouses and fancy store-bought
hats, instead of the lace caps and the laced bodices and
the six or seven superimposed long embroidered skirts
their mothers and grandmothers used to wear. Few of
the older women too, I noticed, still affected the quaint
medieval coifs with the golden corkscrewlike adornments
on the side of their heads. Men in peasant garb—a short
black jacket of cloth, baggy trousers, low shoes with silver
buckles or black clogs with bright green and yellow
flowers painted over the instep, golden earrings and necklaces of blood-red coral beads with golden clasps pro-
truding from the collar of their jackets—were rare curios-
ities in that crowd.

At the market there were now booths where you could
dress up in one of those peasant outfits for a price and
be photographed in it and be immortalized on a picture
postcard, which indicated plainly enough that the old
costumes would soon be relegated to the museums. Only
the oldest peasants still clung to that distinctive garb as
to something precious and really their own.

At the turn of the century Uncle Kees would occasionally take me across the river into one of the Brabant villages, on Ascension Day, for instance, or on the Monday
following Easter or Whitsun, which were holidays, to see
the Catholic peasants dance in the squares and taverns,
festively illuminated for the occasion with Chinese lanterns or colored glass cups filled with oil, on the surface
of which floated burning wicks. That was a sight. Then
they danced their own graceful native dances and great
majestic *rondes*. Now, after market, the boys and girls

from out of town crowded into the cafés and bars of
Gorcum to dance foxtrots and two-steps in the same stolid,
insipid, and joyless way you see it done in the dancing
palaces of the Dorotheenstrasse and in Hollywood. Their
heavy feet stamped awkwardly on the floor, and their
grace was that of young calves. It was horrible. But now
they were no longer peasants either. They were workers
from the suburbs pretending to be "American," for so the
modernization of life was called. It had taken everything
from them and given them nothing in return, except the
cigarette and a taste for cocktails.

In the town itself, on stiller days, when the outsiders
had left, I missed those singular types which in the past
had contributed, by their appearance and their independent, nonconformist behavior, to the richness, the
animation, and the diversity of life. A dapper young man,
his hair pomaded in the style of the late Rudolph Valen-
tino, his nose disdainfully in the air above an imitation
rhinestone pin in his cravat, advanced to serve me in the
remodeled shop of Willem Bos, which I entered ostensibly to buy a pencil, but in reality to see what, if anything, remained of the old atmosphere. "Can I help
you?" he said in a supercilious tone of voice, eyeing my
clothes the while and apparently not finding them quite
to his taste.

Shades of old Willem! How differently he would have
acted! In the first place, he would not have come forward with such obsequious alacrity. He would have remained in that dark and mysterious cavern in the rear,
which had now been replaced by a spruce little office
furnished with rows of steel filing cabinets and lighted
from above by a new skylight. He would have waited till
you had browsed around and made up your mind what

you wanted or whether you wanted anything at all, which made not the slightest difference to him.

Willem Bos' shop (it had a sign outside on which Uncle Kees had once painted a copy of Holbein's head of Erasmus, which had faded into an undistinguishable blur when I knew it) was located near the college, in a narrow street of old houses literally leaning against the walls of the cathedral. It was a dark shop, and smelled of glue and mice and old paper, and was seldom swept; never were the windows washed, but that shop contained fully fifty thousand books, and I honestly think that Willem had read them all.

For he never did anything but read and make notations with a stubby pencil in a huge ledgerlike book. In the course of the years he had been filling countless similar tomes. They stood on a shelf above his cot, behind a partition in the back of the shop. Willem ate and slept and had his being in that world of books. He cooked on a small stove and ate his meals from his desk, first spreading a newspaper over the table by way of napkin and then transferring the frying pan from the fire to the paper. He used no plates, but he drank wine, which was a rare thing in Gorcum in my youth. The meal finished, he resumed his eternal reading. That man read morn, afternoon, and night. When you passed by late at night you could see him under an oil lamp, deep in the rear of his shop, with his nose buried in some tome.

Willem had an immense beard, fast graying and not always clean, for he spilled snuff most carelessly. His deep black eyes stabbed you like darts of lightning when he was angry, something that happened not infrequently, for he was a man of irascible temper, impatient and impetuous. When I come to think of it, I never saw him uncover his

head, except once. Even when he ate his meals or when
a distinguished citizen called on him, he kept on his head
that outlandish, peekless fur bonnet which was more a
Turkish tarboosh than any other headgear I ever saw in
the Low Countries. For clothing he invariably wore a
black, double-breasted redingote. When going out he
threw a big cape over his shoulders, and he wore that
mantle winter and summer, heat, cold, or rain.

Willem's fiery temper was attributed to Spanish an-
cestry. For he hailed, so it was said, from the village of
Asperen, which is an hour's walk, or perhaps a little more,
from Gorcum. In Asperen nearly all the inhabitants were
swarthy or olive-hued. They were descended from Spanish soldiers who had been quartered there in the far-off
days of the Duke of Alva's campaign of extermination.
Instead of killing the people, whom he had been ordered
to lock up in the church and then to burn wholesale,
which was the lovely old Spanish way of dealing with
heretics, the commander of the troops in Asperen fell
in love with a village girl and married her. To prove his
good faith to the girl's father, who feared that his daughter would merely be taken to Spain upon the termination of the campaign in the Netherlands, the commander
promptly executed the local priests in an unusual way,
tying their legs to the clappers of the bells in the church
tower and setting his soldiers to toll the bells for all they
were worth. Having done this, the commander and his
men embraced the Protestant religion. They all remained
in Holland when Alva returned to Madrid, probably to
escape the vengeance of the man in the Escorial and his
Inquisition.

One of these soldiers of Philip the Tyrant, perhaps the
captain himself, was said to be Mijnheer Bos' ancestor.

It was a romantic story that fitted the man perfectly. But my Uncle Kees did not believe a word of it. I once heard him tell old Willem point-blank that he suspected him of being a Jew from Amsterdam, a descendant of Spanish and Portuguese refugees, who settled in the Netherlands after their expulsion by Ferdinand and Isabella in 1492. When Uncle Kees said this, Willem looked sharply back for a moment, took a pinch of snuff, but did not utter a word.

Willem never went to church, though I do not think he was altogether an unbeliever. Sunday was for him a day of "quiet" reading. Nobody and nothing could interfere with him that day, for he kept the door of his shop locked. All the eighteen years I knew him, and for so long as Uncle Kees had known him before me, Willem Bos had been engaged on a work which would prove, so he said, on the rare occasions when he deigned to speak of it, the close affinity of the Dutch people with the . . . Russians. I remember him telling me once that the Tolstoy family originally hailed from the Netherlands—a theory that has found some support in more recent years. But that was only an incidental matter with Willem. He was out to demonstrate something of far greater significance, namely, that the ancestors of the Dutch had not come floating down the Rhine at all, as the popular history books had it, but that they had drifted through the Baltic and North Seas straight from the plains of Muscovy.

This was not, I must admit, an altogether unpleasant supposition, and more than once Uncle Kees, on his walks with me, allowed his imagination to run riot on the subject. In such moments the Reverend Dr. van Toorenbergen, if we happened to meet that worthy dominie, was whisperingly designated from afar as the Archimandrate Toorenofskikoff and Willem van den Oever, the policeman, as Vladimir Poopopdenoeverovitch, the chief of the bearded Don Cossacks, who must have thought us both bereft of sense when we greeted him, muzhiklike with a snatch from the tune "Song of the Volga Boatmen": "Yo heave ho! Yo heave ho!"

In front of his shop, near the entrance, Willem Bos kept the current best sellers, the popular literature of the day. Some people never advanced beyond those tables and shelves. They were the casual customers who kept him alive. Beyond, in a second room, which was reached through a low door that seemed to be cut out of a wall of books, sat Willem himself, usually surrounded by friends and acquaintances, all up to their ears in politics. Uncle Kees would be there, and a silversmith named Meyer, a tall and anemic-looking individual; the organist of the cathedral, Frans Peer, who habitually wore a silk hat; an English instructor from the local college, who passed for an eccentric because he never wore a collar and tie, but a jersey; then an agronome by the name of Zandman, who had once been a Catholic priest, but who now served as the local correspondent of an irregularly appearing periodical called *The Dawn*, the official organ of the atheists; and various other men, all of them rebels, at least verbally—nonconformists, republicans, radicals, and followers of Bakunin. Domela Nieuwenhuis was their prophet and Barthélemy de Ligt, when he was in town to lecture, their coming Messiah.

Sometimes the debates in the back of the shop grew hot and furious, for the disputants often did not agree with each other about the ways of remedying the social and political evils they discussed. In fact, I believe they

had agreed to disagree. The Queen's and the Prime Minister's ears must have been ringing over in The Hague at
such moments, and the ears of Czar Nicholas and King
Edward and Joseph Chamberlain and all the other real or
imagined tyrants in the world no less.

In the heat of the conflict, I would sometimes slip away
to the outer room and place the ladder against the shelves
so that I could look over the intriguing rows near the
ceiling. It was as if Willem's intuition had told him what
I was up to, for he would come marching out of his den
and, looking up, call out: "If you're looking for erotica,
don't trouble yourself: I put them away a long time ago.
Come down from that ladder!"

Of course, I blushed scarlet, for I had been found out.
Fortunately, nobody could see my face distinctly in the
semiobscurity of the upper tiers. I would come slowly
down the ladder, but stop halfway, take out a yellow-
covered French novel, with some such title as *La Femme
fatale* or *Nuit d'amour,* and inquire innocently: "Is this
any good?" Whereupon Willem would say: "Take it and
find out! But don't let your father see it. Here, put it in
this cover," and he'd hand me a leather jacket with a title
like Bossuet's *Oraisons funèbres* or Jean de Labadie's
Sermons stamped on the back.

In saying that the crowd which foregathered of a winter
evening in the rear of Willem Bos' bookshop were radicals and rebels, I do not wish to intimate that these men
were hatching revolutionary conspiracies or plotting
against the security of the state. There was nothing furtive or secretive about their meetings. They dropped in
casually, one by one, without any prearranged signal or
word, quite as innocently as the cracker-barrel sages of
the American village stroll into a grocery store and then

sit down to dispense homely wisdom or just engage in plain gossip while whittling away at a stick.

Those men in Bos' place may be said to have been—*in parvo*, of course—what encyclopedists and philosophers like Bayle and Voltaire and Rousseau were to the Revolution; they were the forerunners, the trail blazers, of a new dispensation. In that sense, they may perhaps be called unconscious revolutionaries. For of this there is no doubt; they were dissatisfied, their sense of justice was outraged, and more than once I heard them unhesitatingly challenge and condemn the sacrosanctity of what the police, the politicians, and the official chroniclers were charged to defend. It is in the back of smelly little bookshops like that and in shabby garrets and amidst the jars of molasses and sacks of flour of rural grocery stores that the republics of tomorrow are born.

Of course, I was but a youthful bystander, and would not have dared to open my mouth in the presence of my weighty elders. Most times when taken there by Uncle Kees I promptly found myself a corner in which to look at a bound collection of illustrated periodicals and forgot all thoughts of politics, but I remember enough of their conversation to say that I am sure these men had no program of action. Nor did they harbor the slightest intention of formulating one or of launching some movement or other.

What they said on momentous questions of the day was not the expression of opinion of a board of safe, sound, and sensible men constituted to back the government and governmental authority. They spoke as individuals who felt strongly. They were the unrecognized and unnamed vigilantes of democracy. A suggestion that they constitute themselves a party, a league, or that they launch some movement or other would have been received with uncomprehending silence. They were individualists with all the faults of individuals, one of which was faultiness and intemperance of language. But their influence was none the less felt in the community. The very faults of individuals excite attention, Cardinal Newman, who knew whereof he spoke, once remarked, but whereas the individual loses, his cause gains. "This is the way of things; we promote truth by a self-sacrifice."

They were the perpetual antis of our community, the persistent conscientious objectors. Except at those irregular intervals in the back of the bookshop or on the benches by the river shore when they sought each other's company to talk things over, they did not join in the gatherings of any group or party. For parties were by them regarded, without saying so in so many words, as something like straitjackets. They refused to wear anybody's uniform. They did not nourish any ideology borrowed from the moment's fashion or from man's traditions, nor did they recognize any barriers of custom or discipline. But they revealed the same compassion in the presence of a little child in tears or of an animal in distress.

Their whole-hearted charity did not make any distinctions. Dogmatists would have called them irreligious, and as a rule the pastors and the prominently pious in our community of Gorcum gave them a wide berth. Still, I would say that they were animated by a sort of secular quietism: the inner voice played a major rôle in their lives. I can imagine old Willem Bos in an attitude of prayer before a divinity unknown to him, rendering thanks for having been born imperfect, restless, and rebellious, but always subject to the intoxication of goodness and praising that nameless God for having permitted the divine logic of sentiment to trouble forever the logic of our interests and our clans. Those men, humble in their worldly station, considered reprobates, eccentrics, and nuisances by the prominent and the conformers, represented an element that, I think, we need as badly as bread in a civilized community—spoilsports, challengers of established procedure, living reminders that the needs of the people can never be encompassed within the formulas of the official programs.

Even so, whether unconsciously or consciously, they did somewhat undermine the social order. For at least in my case, and in the cases of several other boys of my acquaintance, they did forever disturb our belief in the divine institution and therefore in the inviolability of the existing socioeconomic structure. Moreover, they destroyed our desire to see it perpetuated indefinitely.

And what were the things they grew so excited about? For there were times when the bearded giant's den, far from seeming like a peaceful after-dinner retreat for our home-grown philosophers, was turned into a bedlam of shouting voices and violently gesticulating middle-aged gentlemen. Well, there was, for instance, the case of a young officer, a man bearing a high-sounding aristocratic name, who had seduced the daughter of a fruit dealer in Gorcum and whose legal agents sought to exculpate their client by blackening the girl's character. In this they succeeded well enough, for the officer was merely transferred to another garrison and thus escaped the consequences of his misdeed.

It was this particular phase of the *cause célèbre* which infuriated Willem Bos and his cronies more than anything else. They called it class justice, in which they were right. They wanted to make an issue of it and stir the nation to demand a law compelling men, especially aristocrats, you may be sure, to contribute toward the support of their illegitimate offspring. I do not know if such a law was ever written on the statute books of Holland, but the girl in question became a sensation throughout the country. After her child was born she went, at old Willem's instigation, on the lecture platform and traveled up and down the land telling the story of her betrayal. Willem had written out the lecture for her. The halls and meetinghouses where she spoke, however, were barred to persons under twenty-one, and therefore I never learned the fine details of the affair.

And there was the incident of the editor of some free-thinkers' journal over in England, who had been imprisoned for publishing a picture in his periodical of Samuel anointing Saul, the first king of the Israelites. In this picture, it seemed (for I never saw the print), the costumes and accessories were those of a modern hairdresser's shop, its walls hung with posters that advertised certain ointments and pomades. The Prophet Samuel's silk hat was seen hanging on a peg and his umbrella hanging on the hall tree. Bos, Uncle Kees, and the church organist, Professor Peer, wrote a scathing letter to the King of England anent the editor's imprisonment, asking Edward VII whether he took his title of Defender of the Faith to mean that he must engage in such petty persecution as that to which the editor had been subjected. They wound up with a whole string of sarcasms about Saul the son of Kish, who went looking for donkeys and found a throne, and finally told Edward to stick to his throne, not to make a donkey of himself, and to set the editor free at once.

Nobody expected an answer, of course. But, strange to say, the English government, instead of ignoring the scurrilous epistle, rose to the bait and made a double ass of itself by lodging a diplomatic complaint at The Hague. Our townsmen were officially reprimanded, but they, knowing their rights and enjoying a triumph beyond expectation, immediately set to work composing a circular letter, which they sent to all the crowned heads of Europe, calling upon them to resign forthwith. They actually evoked a considerable response via the mails. I still recall the hilarity with which Wilhelm Hohenzollern's reply was received in the bookshop. The Kaiser, of course, never saw or heard of the original letter from Gorcum, but one of his *Obergerichtsräte* or *Ministerialdirektoren*—I forget the exact title of that Prussian doctor —had taken it upon himself to correct our townsmen's notions of the Brandenburg robber monarchy—*bei Gottes Gnade.*

Then came the dismal story of the arrest and execution of Francisco Ferrer in Barcelona. Ferrer was an educationalist and a philanthropist with strong anticlerical leanings. It was but natural that he should therefore have been regarded as something like an incarnation of Beelzebub by the monks and obscurantists of the Spanish peninsula. The man was a threat to their fat and lazy living and to their ruthless exploitation of the peasantry. In order to get rid of him, he was handed over for trial to a court-martial by Spanish officers, men of the mentality and intellectual standing of a Francisco Franco—that is to say, sly but ignorant, utterly immoral, cruel, and fanatical. He was charged with being an anarchist by a prosecutor who admitted that he had never heard of Bakunin, Kropotkin, Tolstoy, Élisée Reclus, or Étienne de la

Boétie. But that was enough for his judges and for the Bourbon who sat on the throne of Spain at the time. Ferrer was shamefully ill-used while in custody and was finally shot. It was "a monstrous case of class ignorance and vindictive bigotry," and Ferrer's martyrdom—for that it was—is as such described in all decent biographical dictionaries and encyclopedias referring to the case.

The ignominious trial and execution of Ferrer did not create as much of a commotion as the Dreyfus affair had done, chiefly because, I think, the world outside of that somber prison of the human spirit, which was and is still Spain, had no opportunity to become acquainted with the merits of the case. The clerical executioners of Montjuich were in a great hurry to dispatch their victim before the civilized world should become aware of the fact that the man whom they denounced as a diabolical mischiefmaker had committed no worse crime than to have advocated a secular system of education and a republican form of government for Spain. The idealist was dead and buried before the news of his martyrdom reached Gorcum.

But when it did reach there, the members of the bookshop collegium took prompt action. They called the citizenry to a protest meeting where, one after the other, they expressed their indignation and anger and sorrow. Not many people attended that meeting; the sly allegation that Ferrer had been an anarchist had done its work in Gorcum as effectively as "the smear" of Communism compels many Protestants and liberals in our time to withhold their sympathy and support from men who are singled out for destruction by the foes of democracy. Some opposition to the meeting manifested itself even in the town council, and that evening the police took the names of all the participants at the door of the badly lit, badly ventilated hall which served in the daytime as an auctioneer's shop.

Opposition or no, Willem Bos said: "Let them come to us here in Holland, those who are driven along the world's highways, the outcasts and the weary ones. . . . They tell us that this man [Ferrer] trampled on the Christian faith. . . . Perhaps he did, but do not forget that his feet and the feet of his companions were bare. . . . All tears have the same taste, and all hungers are twins—our eyes cannot distinguish between them and see whether the oppressed are Spaniards or Russians. . . ." And then all those present stood up and sang "This friend has fallen as a martyr," and I saw Uncle Kees and Frans Peer, the organist, holding each other's hands as they sang, the tears coursing down their cheeks. That was also the only time I saw Willem Bos uncover his head.

I saw Willem occasionally in later years, when I had returned to Europe as a newspaper correspondent. But he had grown rheumatic. The disease, he complained, had stiffened the joints of his fingers so that he no longer could hold the pencil stub. He had stopped making notations in those huge, ledgerlike volumes and talked of sending me the whole collection in France. When I told him that I had been assigned to go to Russia, he gave me a letter which it took him more than an hour to write. It was addressed to Pierre Degeyter, the composer of the *International,* whom I found in Moscow in a home for aged revolutionaries located in the Ulitza Rakova. I brought back greetings from the old musician, and it was then that I had my last conversation with Willem. I told him about conditions in the land of the Soviets and mentioned that all outer manifestations of religion were fast disappearing. He smiled at this. "Well," I said, "religion was but a superficial thing in Russia at any time!"

"Who told you that?" shot back Willem.

"They all tell you that. Maurice Hindus who knew Russia as a boy and who has been back there frequently since the Revolution, says the same thing. I saw him in the Hotel Moskowskaya in Moscow but two weeks ago."

"Hindus, the author of *Ontredderde Menschheid*," he quoted the Dutch title of the book *Humanity Uprooted*.

"Yes, that's the man."

"I have read that book," said Willem. "Mr. Hindus has no right to say that religion was artificial and superficial in Russia. Neither he nor the little commissars you saw there have a right to speak on that subject. But the Russian intellectuals have and they—Tolstoy, Dostoevski, Turgenev, Gogol, and Chekhov—they tell us differently. They were great religious souls themselves and they spoke for the Russian people."

"But then," I objected, "what are we to make of the antireligious movement in that country and of the closing of the churches and the banishment of priests?"

"When a student has learned his lesson, the teacher closes the book," said Willem Bos. "Humanity has been learning from the Gospel for two thousand years. It is time to close the book now and see if men will now translate the lessons they have been learning from it into reality—that is, make the lessons come to life in new social institutions, new human relationships, and a new covenant."

That was Willem's hopeful view of the socialistic experiment in Soviet Russia. He did not live to hear of

government-manufactured famines, of the merciless up-
rooting of the peasantry, and of the slow death for tens
of thousands in the frozen camps of the Sokolniki Islands.
He died before the treason trials. . . .

Willem, so that smoothly pomaded young clerk in the
renovated shop told me with the relish of a sensation-
monger, one day took some books from the shelves above
his cot and threw them into the stove. He forgot to put
the lid back or, what is more likely, he intentionally left
the lid off. The flames soon leaped up, but he still kept
on feeding them with paper. Neighbors and passers-by
saw the red glow through the glass in the doorway of the
old shop and tried to enter to help the old man extin-
guish the fire that was clearly getting beyond his control.
But he had locked and bolted the door and that morning
had not removed the night shutters in front of the single
window. He must have been aware of their efforts to
force the door, for his face appeared behind the narrow
glass aperture in the door that they had smashed. He
laughed at his neighbors in a raucous, bone-chilling guf-
faw and bade them be off. It was noticed that his beard
had been so singed by the fire that little of it remained.
Then they saw him go back toward the fire, which had
spread to the floor and to the shelves. He was dancing
around, throwing more and more books into the fire
and at the same time yelling at the top of his voice until
the smoke crept into his lungs.

So perished Willem Bos.

There were other types and eccentrics in Gorcum but
of a different, far less intelligent kind than Bos and his
cronies. They all had some sort of a queer streak. Peo-

ple said that they had been struck by a wing of the wind-mill, which was meant to convey that their mental condition was half-wittedness rather than idiocy.

The outright idiots were called "innocents." We had as large a number of them as any corresponding small Russian town or village.

All such individuals enjoyed a peculiar status; they were treated with the utmost kindness and solicitude by everybody. It looked at times as if they had been ordained by a suspicious divinity to roam the streets of Gorcum to see who would and who would not exercise charity toward them: a sort of quiet way of building up good and bad records for the Day of Judgment.

You were told never to pass those imbeciles without a kind word or a friendly pat on the arm, no matter how repulsive and unprepossessing they looked. If you had a coin to spare, it was a sin to keep it in your pocket, for one was not to forget well-doing and sharing one's wealth, as God loved the cheerful giver. So you always gave, whether you could really afford it or not. Sometimes, when you saw one of those beloved of the Lord come down the street and you felt sure he was going to make a touch, you hastily slipped into a side street or into a shop to avoid meeting him. But then remorse smote you until you met him again and you handed him a double portion. In that way those brethren had you coming and going. The vision of that awful Day of Judgment when the recording angel is to open the book and read your sentence was so deeply ingrained in your mind that you preferred to impoverish yourself and miss a sweet or lolly-pop now and then rather than gnash your teeth all eternity long in that place of outer darkness where the worm and the fire do not die.

Still and all, I thought I could draw the line when it came to the two Jewish "innocents" we had in Gorcum. As Jews they were destined for hell anyway, according to the interpretations of that Good Friday, two thousand years ago. So you passed them by and stuck your tongue out at them in the bargain.

This I did to a man who was colloquially known as Manus the Rhymer. He had a black beard and strange luminous eyes that followed you when you passed him in the street. I don't think he was as "innocent" as he was reputed to be, for his nickname had been given to him because of his ability to recite spontaneously some little rhyme that fitted your name or the first word you mentioned upon meeting him. "Ah," he'd say: "Pieter, the nephew of the painter *baas* [master]—how would you like a roll with sweet milk *kaas* [cheese]?" You would say: "It's a fine *dag* [day]," and Manus would take you up at once with the rejoinder: "That is why I can afford a *lach* [laugh]," things of that sort.

One day Manus passed us while we were at play near the church, and some of the boys spoke to him about the Crucifixion. Manus grew violently angry and first cursed and then spat at us. This only excited the boys the more, and they twitted him about circumcision. It ended up with us pelting him with pebbles and driving him home, weeping and sobbing.

A few days later I accompanied my mother as far as her sewing circle, and we met Manus on the street. He stood still and turned as pale as a ghost, it seemed to me, and pointed an accusing finger at me. But he did not utter a word. I stood as if petrified, and my mother, too, was horror-struck. I had to tell her all the details of the scandalous torment that we had inflicted on the old man.

She then warned me that to hurt a Jew is one of the worst offenses that can be imagined, for, said she, God guards them as jealously as the apple of His eye. They are still God's people, and it is written that whosoever curses Israel shall be cursed.

I had to go and apologize to Manus, a journey of expiation on which Uncle Kees accompanied me, for the man lived rather far away. We found him in his hut outside the Arkel Gate and chatted with him till eventide. Thereafter we were, if not fast friends, at least on speaking terms. But he never again rhymed for my benefit. He collected without any effort at all.

It is impossible for a stranger to see Holland with the same eyes as a native son. I have sometimes watched visitors from abroad, amongst them some of those phenomenally busy creatures who "do Holland in a day," in accordance with the schedule set by the tourist agencies, shake their heads with commiserating and condescending smiles over the comparative unpicturesqueness and lack of exoticism in the Dutch landscape and then have seen them run off in order not to upset the routine, which called for France and Italy in a week. They would arrive with the ferry in Gorcum, cast a rapid glance at the old tower, pronounce it "not too bad," then run over to the bulwarks and perhaps be seized with a fit of laughter over the tar-smeared old muzzle-loading guns on the ramparts, turn a pair of binoculars in the direction of the stunted tower of Woercum across the river and the twin spires of Loevestein Castle, and then be off in search of . . . I don't know what.

It pained me not a little as a boy to see them so obviously disdainful of our sights, and when Uncle Kees

translated some of their disparaging or downright contemptuous remarks, I would say heatedly: "But why don't
you tell them that we have a museum too, or that over
there, in Loevestein, Grotius was once imprisoned and
other great Dutch republicans?" And he would answer:
"There is little use, my boy! They only come to see what
their Baedeker tells them to see. They are in search of
eccentricities. To us Holland is a living creature, warm,
a being of flesh and blood. When I look at that river
and those fields, it is as if my mother embraces me. But
you must not expect strangers to feel that way. . . .They
have their own mother!"

A living creature, breathing, palpitating with life!
The steeples projecting from the verdure across the river
in Brabant were like the faces of brothers, the cracked
roofs and crumpling walls of the houses and churches in
our town like so many shells left behind by successive
tides of generations whose blood ran in my veins. When
the trees in front of the house suddenly rustled in the
night under a sharp gust of wind, you listened as to the
whisper of mysterious voices. They did not speak of the
future, though there were times in the autumn, as the
storms bent them with fierce impact, when it seemed that
they lamented the sadness of days to come.

They spoke of the past. They remembered. They did
not judge or condemn. They spoke of what they had seen.
They knew and they communicated what they knew to
your heart without words or letters. In those hours when
you ventured out in answer to a mysterious inaudible
call, the dead met you at every darkened corner, walking
in the rain.

Oh, there was no fear of the dead then! Those spirits
stopped to talk and joke. Their secret history, inscribed

on the stones of the old buildings that had been touched by their hands, became an open book, but that book was indecipherable to the noninitiated. Communication in this case was a matter of blood. The dead became alive again in your thoughts. The atmosphere was saturated with their presence. You may not have known their names, the faces of some were too far effaced for them to be recognizable, but you felt their breathing in the leaves on which the raindrops tapped and you saw their outline in the interlocking branches that swayed to and fro by the light of a flickering lantern.

Have you ever come into an old garden whose paths were almost obliterated by weeds and moss and have you felt your breath suddenly stop, as if someone clutched your throat, at the sight, for a fleeting instant, of a familiar figure hastily scurrying away behind a clump of bushes or a ruined wall? Have you never wandered alone in an old house and stood still to listen? To listen for what? Was it not as if you heard a call, the voice of your mother, since long turned to dust, with the same intonation and the same tenderness that stopped you in your tracks when a child?

There was one house in Gorcum, old and uninhabited, which stood alone at the end of a street near one of the town gates. At a certain hour, about twilight, it was said that the face of a woman appeared before one of the windows. On her head was a bonnet of the kind worn by Dutch women of a hundred years before. How came she there in that deserted house, which had stood still and abandoned, with all the doors securely locked for decades?

Uncle Kees knew. "That woman," he said, "was Anneke, the wife of our great-great-grandfather. He was a

wigmaker by trade. They were married in 1812, just
a century ago. Their names are in the parish register:
Reinier and Anneke. Two months after their wedding,
he, Reinier, was conscripted for Napoleon's army and
marched off to Russia. He wrote but two letters. I have
those letters in a cupboard upstairs. But after that not
another word came from him. He must have died in the
snows of Poland or at the Beresina, along with a hundred
thousand other Dutch boys. But Anneke never tired of
waiting for him. She was a bride of twenty when he left.
She was eighty when she died. Every day of her life she
spent at that window looking for her lover and husband
to come home through the town gate. In the course of
time her features imprinted themselves on the window-
pane. That's what we see there now, that hazy white
shape. Look, there she is!"

But I would not look. I closed my eyes, and a shiver
ran down my spine. I waved my hand at Anneke with
my eyes shut, as so many townspeople did, by force of
habit, I imagine, because their mothers and grandmothers
had done so in passing the house. Young lovers touched
the walls of that house by way of pledging their troth
because that gesture was supposed to assure steadfastness,
even deathlessness in love. . . .

Frequenting that collegium of freethinkers, or, as they
should perhaps more justly be called *"libres croyants,"* in
the rear of Willem Bos' bookshop, as I did for years,
albeit as a silent and, as was often the case, uncomprehending bystander, and most of the time unknown to my
parents, who would probably have removed me from
Uncle Kees' influence had they known that it was he
who tolerated and even encouraged my presence in that

strange company, produced in me a restlessness that has haunted me all my life. I am aware through various criticisms leveled at an earlier book (*Days of Our Years*) that a mere journalist is not expected—in fact, it is considered rather bad taste—to inject matters so intimate and personal as his spiritual evolution, his doubts and beliefs, into "an objective account" of his experiences, especially if the storm and stress of life and the sight of great injustice and much inhumanity have failed to turn him into a cynic. I must say, in passing, that I never intended to write objectively and that I spew it out, that objectivity which masquerades under the name of impartiality and which goes out of its way to present, as the saying goes, both sides of the question. There are no two sides to truth, and there are no two sides to a lie. It is either yes or no. If you want to be sincere, you must be partial.

I was writing of my own life, and I fully agree with Lacordaire when he said that the exterior life is nothing without the interior. That intimate life is the dialogue man engages in from the moment he is able to think until he falls to sleep forever. The inner life is the real life. The rest of it—the wanderings to and fro over the earth, the sojourn in unfamiliar places, and the company of prominent and distinguished men—was, at least in my case, purely incidental. I do not mean that I despise great men. It is good to be in the company of those who have not allowed bitterness and loneliness and jealousy to gain the upper hand over them. They are those who have gone through the arid land and who have created their own wells of living water, new sources of life, and who offer others freely to drink. But I feel at rest only when I find solitude to think, whether in a railway train rumbling through the Danakil desert or in the forest of

Montmorency. Yes, I make no bones about it, to think of salvation and of eternal life and of the question where we are going and what is the sense and what is to be the end of all our striving. Perhaps I have not come to a solution. But to say, as some of my critics did, that such questions are no longer timely or actual and that they had best be left to die with the theologians and the metaphysicians in the forgetfulness of the inner chamber, is not borne out by the reality.

Mazzini found that there was not a single great victory of the human spirit on record and not a single important advance of human society without that victory and that step being rooted in religious faith. Any doctrine whatever, he said, which does not take into account man's need of faith and his need to solve the eternal questions of human destiny and origin, has always been and will always remain impotent to create a new social order. It may for a time succeed in setting up beautiful forms, to be sure. But those forms will lack the eternal fire that Prometheus brought from heaven.

The spiritual questions will continue to haunt man, whether churches and clergy disappear or survive in the apocalyptic era into which we have entered. My attention was pointed to Russia, and I was told to notice how those naïve doubts and disquietudes of mankind's infancy have disappeared in the clear sunlight of Soviet life, how they no longer trouble the human conscience. I answer: what do you know about it? Are you sure? Can you say with certainty what a peasant sitting at eventide under the cool elms, in front of the collective farmhouse, thinks of? Or, as he lays himself down to sleep in his crowded room, half hungry or at best stuffed with sour bread, what the city worker secretly wonders about? Is that the *sum-*

mum bonum—the commissar and his girl drinking vodka cocktails in the Hotel Metropole, while listening to a gypsy orchestra playing American jazz? Is that the all-highest and eternal good?

Even if Russia or humanity as a whole ever reaches the blessed estate of a material millennium in a classless society, even then, and then only, in a more ineluctable manner than ever, these questions of whence and whither will be posed as they have never been posed before. Then, not the economically purified and superfluous church, not that old instrument of domination, but a new educational system will extract and remove the poison from that question of where we are going which troubles even emancipated human beings after the daily task is done. The more well-being is assured and the farther away the fear of old age is removed, the more questionable becomes the subject of death, which breaks into life at the most unexpected moments, blasting its hopes and obscuring its goal.

At home and in the church the "eternal, unassailable truths" of the Christian religion, according to the Calvinist conception, were hammered into my head by dint of constant repetition. Uncle Kees and his friends shrugged their shoulders about the whole business. When the dominies and catechism masters proclaimed with pitiless consistency that man was fundamentally bad, inclined to do evil in his heart, not worthy of God's mercy, and that therefore but a few were predestined to be transferred from this vale of tears to eternal glory, those men in the bookshop only smiled and said what was absolutely the contrary: man is good and it is through his goodness that he shall not only inherit the earth but will make a paradise out of his earthly home. Whom was I to believe?

Heir of a religious tradition on the one hand and later in life a humble disciple of scientific methods, I have lived in a state of inner contradiction which started with the awakening of my conscience. Between my heart and my mind the dialogue never ceased. Only very slowly and gradually did the reconciliation between the two take place.

I had to go out in the world and discover the truth for myself. I think I found the truth. But I will not let that allow me to condemn the piety of my ancestors and teachers. For they were deeply sincere in their beliefs. With them it was not a mere case of pulling a sanctimonious face and speaking in a subdued tone of voice. With them it was a case of ascetic zeal having been turned into moral rigorism. With their teachers Calvin and Knox, they rejected the idea of sanctification by good works alone. They had sunk into a quietistic piety, almost mystical, wherein they sought an understanding of the divine by meditation, since it was not possible to acquire merit through the work of their hands or through learned discourses. There was a good deal of dogmatic piety, too, which consisted in strict observance of divine ordinances and prescriptions of what Luther called *"Herzens Frommigkeit."* Their love of God motivated all their actions. Their religion was one of confidence, and, since confidence is psychologically a question of cessation of will, the love of God was a matter of sentiment and piety and warming of the heart. But this piety could not assert itself fully without the will also being active, on the one hand as confidence and on the other as a practical exercise of the love of one's neighbor.

What they all had in common was that intense and intentional Calvinistic joylessness. If our dominies had had their way, we would forthwith have returned to the state of affairs that prevailed in Geneva when the great Reformer exercised his spiritual dictatorship in that city. There, and in many cities of Holland just after the Reformation, life was a collective cell of penitence, a spiritual concentration camp, where there was only room for consciousness of sin and humiliation.

Even at weddings, in my youth in Gorcum, dancing and music were still proscribed, because John Calvin, four hundred years earlier, had willed it so. An unbearable censorship reigned over all cultural activity: one was not allowed to read a "worldly" book or visit a theater. I do not know what form of divine punishment was held out for a peek at a troupe of visiting actors, who came to Gorcum from time to time, but the apprehension of dire consequences sank so deeply into my bones, that I, until this day, experience a moment of uneasiness when I enter a place of amusement.

It may well be that this is a subconscious remembrance of that time when the members of the Royal Theater of Amsterdam or The Hague stopped in Gorcum for a one-night performance of *Hamlet*. There was, of course, no chance that I would be permitted to be present. Not even Uncle Kees had the courage to brave the censure of the fundamentalists by going into the meetinghouse with a ticket in his hand. That would have damned him irrevocably and forever. Not that he cared a great deal, but he had to consider, he said, the sensibilities of other members of the family, who would have been damned with him. And so he did the next best thing, for he was determined to see *Hamlet*. He bribed one of the stagehands to bring him a ladder. We both stood on the top of that ladder looking on to the stage from the side, through an opening in the wings, when one of the performers, a man in the costume of a medieval knight, suddenly caught sight of me and poked the lance he held in his hands into my shoulder. I lost my balance and fell backwards. Uncle Kees caught me, but my weight threw him off his balance in turn, and we both went down for the count, with the ladder on top of us, with a crash louder than the "Anvil Chorus."

The noise stopped the players, while the stagehands, the police, and the director rushed backstage to ascertain the cause of the disturbance and the extent of the damage. Uncle Kees was so badly hurt that he could only limp away, but not before the director had seen him. This gentleman thereupon went before the footlights and explained the incident that had caused the interruption of the play, naming, to the vast amusement of the audience, Uncle Kees and myself as the culprits. For weeks · we did not dare to show our faces on the streets.

One would only have to look into the works of the Genevan historian, J. P. Galiffe, to find in what direction our dominies would have driven us, for they never tired of lauding the epoch of Calvin as the nearest man had ever come to seeing the Kingdom of God established on earth. Not only did they never, by so much as a word, condemn the horrible inhumanity of Calvin, which caused his contemporaries to call him the Genevan Torquemada, but they told us that his rule by censorship and the executioner's block for the slightest misdemeanor—Calvin had a child burned at the stake because it had lifted its hand against its mother—was "worthy of emulation in every respect." It was theocracy, the highest form of social organization we can attain. The fact was that Calvin's was as ruthless a dictatorship as that of the Communists and the perfect model of what came to be known in our time as totalitarianism. Barthelémy de Ligt was not wrong when he stopped me in front of the monument to the heroes of the Reformation on the Promenade des Bastions at Geneva one day and, after pointing to the statue of Calvin and his associates, Farel, Beza, and Knox, and to their faces bereft of the slightest trace of human compassion and mercy, said: "Look, there you have the real fathers of Bolshevism!" Paul Birokoff, Tolstoy's onetime secretary, who was with us, gravely assented.

Human feelings and sentiments were almost entirely pushed aside by religious dogmas and rules. Man was corrupt from birth and could do naught but evil if he followed his own natural inclinations. Hence, he had to be ruled by an iron hand; his life and his activities had to be hemmed in by ordinances, regulations, and the fear of terror and torment if he was not to behave as a raging beast. That was the fundamental notion of our Calvinistic leaders.

In the course of a life that has not been altogether devoid of adventure, I have, under the most diversified conditions, come in contact with men of all classes and races, including primitive tribesmen and the socially disinherited, and I have from those experiences reached one conclusion: in order to tame the beast in man, it is infinitely more desirable to accord him complete confidence than to appear before him armed from top to toe either with weapons or with threats. I have learned that the Father of the Church who said that the human heart is Christian by nature was not wrong. But I have become convinced that the old Roman saying—"*Homo homini lupus*"—is a fallacy.

Man is not by nature or inborn sentiment inclined to look upon his fellow as a ferocious animal. It is true that demoralization by hunger may very well turn him into a wolf, which proves one thing only: he must be protected against hunger in order that he may learn to regard his fellow as his equal. Man, once said Henri de Man, is not entirely egoistical and he is not entirely altruistic, but his altruism is in a quite different way part of his nature than is his egoism; his egoism leads to altruism in the measure that he obeys the dictates of his own nature.

This I have not learned from priests or moralists. On the contrary, they would have caused me to lose the faith entirely and would have led me to despair. I have learned that from men who had never dealt with priests or professors of morality. And it is for that reason, too, it may be said in passing, that I am convinced of the fundamental error of those who maintain that socialism must necessarily lead to failure because of human nature.

The most striking incident that showed the innate goodness of the human heart came to my youthful ears in that dark room in the rear of Willem Bos' bookshop in Gorcum, when my Uncle Kees recounted a story that had come to him through some of Tolstoy's friends in Geneva.

It appears that Tolstoy was in the habit of receiving a certain peasant, a member of one of Russia's thousand and one religious sects, who, because of his convictions, was singled out for all sorts of petty persecutions on the part of his landlord. Not only did that boyar, who was one of Tolstoy's neighbors, insist that the peasant in question do more than his share of the work on the estate than anyone else, but he frequently beat the man un-

mercifully. Now, the peasant was a believer in nonviolence. He was not a follower of Leo Tolstoy, for the sage
of Yasnaya Polyana had not himself come to those evan-
gelic views about overcoming evil with goodness.

One night the peasant was telling the great man the
story of his life. He told of the hardships he had suffered
and of the cruelty of his master. "He beat me and beat
me," said the muzhik, "and the pain he inflicted was
sometimes more than I could bear. That went on for a
long time. But I never reproached him by as much as
a word for his inhumanity and even less did I allow any
thought of resistance or revenge to enter my mind. One
night, as I was led toward the shed, where my master
usually administered the beatings to his serfs, he came
to me with outstretched arms and begged my forgiveness
on bended knee."

Upon hearing the end of the peasant's story, Uncle
Kees said, Tolstoy got up in great emotion and walked
around the room a few times and then burst into tears,
but they were not tears of sorrow. They were tears of
gladness.

I had a most convincing experience myself along these
lines when, in the fall of 1935, I walked across half the
width of the Ethiopia, through the darkest part of Africa.

Having been assigned by *The Toronto Daily Star* and
the *Bourse égyptienne* of Alexandria to "cover" the campaign in Ethiopia and finding that no news of the actual
progress of the Italian advance could be obtained in the
capital city Addis Ababa and yet disliking to march with
the conquerors from Eritrea under Ciano and that old
castor-oil expert and hero of numerous wrecking exploits
in the newspaper offices of Milan, General de Bono, I
left for Egypt and from there flew back to Ethiopia. With

a Galla tribesman as my guide and some Amaric boys and a couple of mules, I walked from Gallabat in the Sudan to the front lines occupied by the Ethiopian army under Ras Seyoum.

I had not a single weapon of any kind on me. The two revolvers I had bought in Cairo were confiscated at the border station of Gallabat by the British, who were playing the noninterventionist game for all they were worth in anticipation of bigger exploits to come in Spain. I traversed a hostile, primitive, and what has been even called a "barbaric" country from one end to the other, covering a route over which a scientific expedition, for whose safety the Emperor Haile Selassie had delegated two thousand soldiers, had preceded me two years earlier. That expedition and its guard, I learned later, had run into some fierce fighting and had actually fought its way through.

The boys in my two-by-four caravan were members of a tribe that is generally considered the most rapacious in the whole Ethiopian Empire. They were poor as church mice and had probably never been tempted as they must have been by the sight of my wealth of sacks of millet, beans, and other provisions. They were seven, and I was one. They could have murdered me a hundred times over on that trip, and nobody would have been the wiser. Moreover, we traversed a country that was at war. We passed through villages where the Disparata Circus of the Italian Flying Corps, in which Ciano and his two brothers-in-law, Vittorio and Bruno Mussolini, had done their noblest work, dropping bombs on crowded market squares and sprinkling mustard gas in the grass so that hundreds of barefooted black children lay writhing in agony.

Unable to distinguish between an Italian and another white man, those people might have been expected to pounce on me at first sight and tear me to pieces. After all, was I not just another member of that white race which was engaged in bringing them civilization. Yet, not a hair on my head was touched. I was received with the greatest kindness everywhere. I was received with honor by village chiefs and was the guest in the primitive homes of Coptic priests. The best was not good enough for me. Why?

Because my boys told the villagers: "This man is unarmed!"

Conscience plays a much greater part in life than most people suspect or admit. Their skepticism, however, is justified in so far as it directs itself against the morality which decides the "thou shalt" and the "thou shalt not" according to commandments and interdictions carefully indexed and paragraphed. This morality so restricts the activity of conscience to the sphere of ideas learned by rote that it is quite incapable of confronting the reality. Moreover, we know by experience that, however carefully it has been constructed, this morality becomes useless under the stress of a strongly felt animal instinct or a powerful economic interest.

We now know too well that the root of all our acts goes back to our instincts to have much confidence in a moral tribunal completely separated from the world of intuition. And the same experimental sciences, as Henri de Man has pointed out, which have laid bare the dependence of our entire spiritual life and the process of conscience on the instinct, have also made it known that man's most powerful force is his moral instinct.

The argument of the Marxists that everything in life is determined by economic considerations and interests is therefore but partially true. No one will deny that economic interests play a part, and even an important part, in the determination of man's actions, but they play by no means an exclusive or dominant role. It is the force of conscience, rooted in that subconscious Christian soul of man of which the Church Fathers spoke, to which must be attributed most of the great reforms of history and most of the revolts against the existing order.

It was the bad conscience of the Christianized and humanized *bourgeoisie* that led it to make more and more concessions to the proletariat. Will anyone seriously defend the notion that the threatening revolt of the American working class was responsible for the social legislation of the New Deal? The working class had no power, it was a weak and unorganized minority in 1932. It is the social consciousness of Franklin D. Roosevelt and of other men who share love of humanity, philanthropists, if you will, that is responsible for the immense forward movement of the socially underprivileged.

It was the Christian conscience working as a leaven in contemporary society, the sense of responsibility toward God translating itself into a responsibility toward the brother in distress.

The notion that there has always been a bitter struggle between the *bourgeoisie* and the upcoming working class is not borne out by the facts of history. Jaurès himself admitted that the *bourgeoisie* desired to be just to the working classes when it gave them the school and intellectual recreation. If the Protestant *bourgeoisie* had entertained any misgivings on the subject of granting the people too much enlightenment and rights, it might have followed the example of the old Church and kept them in ignorance.

"The essential contribution of the Protestant Reformation is that it desired every man to read," Henri de Man once said. But read what? The Bible! The Book in which the prophets cry out passionately for a future wherein no man shall build and another inhabit, no man sow and another reap, no man seek to gain great advantages at the expense of another man; the Book that launched anathemas against the rich and the usurpers and that called for the fulfillment of the messianic dream of a universal brotherhood!

That Book with its uncompromising demand for justice, for social justice and peace, the bourgeois Reformation placed in men's hands, and said: "Here, take and read for yourselves! Do not take anyone's word for it. Here are set forth your rights. This is the charter of your freedom. Do not trust intermediaries. See with your own eyes, see the light that is yours."

If the *bourgeoisie* had trembled for the future, said Jaurès, she would have acted like a thief in the night and hidden the Book, as Rome had hidden it.

It is true that since the Reformation there has come into Protestantism an immense lassitude, a flight from consequences, a deterioration of ideology, a time of dissimulation and softening. Luther was the first bourgeois to desert the banner of a militant, on-justice-bent Christianity. He had given the Bible to the people, had himself translated it into their idiom. He had told the people that they were the free children of God, that they were brothers. The people understood that their new-found spiritual freedom also applied to their economic condition and they formed great leagues. The peasants of

Germany marched in great processions under banners on which they had inscribed a loaf of bread as the symbol of their right to live, and a cross as a symbol of the religious motivating force of their revolt.

Oliver Cromwell said once: "When the cause of Christ and the cause of the people coincide, then only will both prosper." Leonhard Ragaz has called the breach between these two the tragedy of Western civilization. That breach occurred in the year 1525.

With his Bible translation and his ninety-six theses nailed to the wall of Wittenberg's church, Luther had thrown wide open the doors of the new freedom. But when the peasants came to him, whom they regarded as their father in God, and asked him to demand with and for them some of the most elementary human rights, the simplest, most self-evident social privileges, in the name of the new freedom he had himself proclaimed, in that moment Luther, from whose merits I will not detract, first hesitated and then refused.

He, the renovator of Christianity, had nothing but cold words. And when thereupon, also as a result of Luther's lack of sympathy for the people's cause, it came to civil war, he, the representative of the Christ of whom it is written that "when He saw the multitudes He was moved with compassion on them because they fainted and were scattered abroad as sheep having no shepherd," in that hour Luther flung forth his blood-soaked writings into the world, calling upon the princes to beat down the peasants as mad dogs. He declared that instead of using prayer as an instrument men could now gain heaven by killing and incendiarism.

The princes heard these words, and the people heard these words; they flew at each other's throats, and for

half a century central Europe was turned into a hell.
Tens of thousands of villages were destroyed, hundreds
of thousands of farmhouses went up in smoke, and the
German land was turned into a slaughterhouse of its own
children. From the burning dwellings of the peasantry
a cry of despair went up and a river of blood issued.

It is that river which separates the cause of Christ
from the cause of the people to this very day. Rome has
not crossed it but has only widened the breach by sup-
porting and blessing all the people's butchers, from Philip
II and Charles IX to Dollfuss and Francisco Franco, but
Protestantism has not crossed it either. And it is because
of "that red, red thing over there," that splash of blood,
the *dmai achicha*, "the blood of Abel your brother," that
the world has been plunged into chaos and misery.

Not until that breach is closed can peace return to
this world!

We had one individual in Gorcum who, while being
the source of undying wonder to many women, my
mother included, at the same time caused more irritation
and controversy than any other citizen I can remember.
His name was Joris de Pater, and he had once been the
public notary, which in Holland is a position of social
eminence only second to that of burgomaster. He had
retired early in life and lived in one of the most preten-
tious houses in the community. How he had come by
his fortune was a riddle over which many never ceased
to wonder and gossip. The usual explanation was that
in drawing up her last will and testament for an extremely
rich woman he had inserted his own name in the instrument for a sizable sum and that he had repeated this

profitable performance half a dozen times when other clients had made him their testamentary executive.

Joris de Pater had in his youth been a cripple, at least so everyone said who had known him as a young man. But when I knew him, and as long as I can remember him, he was a physical giant in perfect health. He claimed that he had been healed on a pilgrimage to Lourdes. That may have been possible, of course. The only drawback to the alleged miracle was that he was not a Roman Catholic—in fact, he was an elder in the Reformed Church. And so the question was: how could a non-Catholic have been healed in that place in southern France where the one and only requisite is precisely to have an abundance of faith? That was the great mystery about Joris de Pater.

As I said, he was always looked upon with a kind of wonder, which in some people amounted to awe. Moreover, everybody knew that he had made the trip against the explicit advice of his doctor. For some time he had been dying on his feet, his physician had warned him that he would never be able to accomplish the pilgrimage. Still he had gone. And this man, who had been carried to the train as a hopeless invalid, had returned to Gorcum walking as straight as a candle. In my day people still stopped in the street to watch him as he went by, though the miraculous healing had occurred twenty years before. They still could not get over it, especially those who had known him as a miserable cripple, who dragged his legs slowly and painfully with the aid of a pair of crutches. But the strangest part of it all was that Joris de Pater, instead of being a model Christian after his health had been supernaturally restored, had become one of the most notorious, though secret, libertines in the community. There was no end to the stories circulated about his scandalous behavior.

I can see him yet, tall and white-haired, of truly gigantic proportions, not without a certain dignity. He was always dressed in a frock coat and top hat and carried a black cane with a golden knob. But his face was as pale as death, cadaverous and spotted with large brown moles. He was a bachelor and had no relatives in Gorcum and more enemies than friends.

Of course, to my Uncle Kees, who had gone to school with him, there was nothing miraculous or prominent about Joris de Pater. He had always, he said, known him for the fraud he was.

"But isn't it possible that he was healed?" I would argue. "You yourself knew him when he was a pitiful paralytic. Why deny the evidence? Here is a miracle if ever there was one. Doesn't that prove the truth and validity of the Catholic faith?"

"A miracle!" Uncle Kees would snort. "I do not deny that healings take place, though I do not see why we in Gorcum should be saddled with the one and only case that seems to be genuine. Why," he exclaimed, "over in Paris they laugh about Lourdes. Oh, no, I do not deny it," he would continue. "I have to abide by the evidence. I do not deny even that the miracles in Lourdes emanate from a being called the Virgin Mary, though I do not see why She would have any truck or trade with that scoundrel of a De Pater.

"But what does it all prove? Miracles are no proof of the validity of an ethical system. Suppose a Dyak came to Gorcum and said: 'Boohoohoo, our God, is a great God. He turns away the poisoned arrows from our enemies in the jungle. He makes the sick walk again and makes the sun rise on our crops and the next day he sends the rain. I tell you, he sure is a great God. Our Dyak God alone does wonders.' What would we say to that? We would examine the foundations of that Dyak's faith and his metaphysics. We would inquire into his doctrine and his moral character, would we not? Well then, if we did that and found that if that Dyak had received good counsel from his God but had betrayed that deity by favoring the rich and sending the poor back into their misery with empty consolations, if we found that he was unmerciful to animals, and that his religion was smart rather than pious, sly rather than wise, more political than true, that his religion had killed the good pagan qualities in him and that it carefully watched the oppressed so that they had no chance to rise, if I heard that in the Dyak temples or sacred huts they hung up battle flags and that the priests blessed those who go out to kill, if I found those things, I would simply spit on all their miracles and I would send the man back to his jungle."

That's the way Uncle Kees talked. He always turned everything into a dissertation. But I knew from his words that he did not entertain much respect for his old school companion.

Even so, as I was saying about this man Joris de Pater: he was an elder in the Reformed Church and a member of the board of supervisors of the local almshouse and of the orphan asylum; I seem to recollect that for a time he even served as the town's delegate to the provincial council, a position that usually went only to the most prominent citizens. All these things did not take away the fact that in his private life he was far from blameless. If truth be told, Mijnheer de Pater was a most immoral old codger.

Under that solemn, dignified exterior of his and that almost feverish interest in eleemosynary institutions and causes, he hid a truly vile and lecherous character, as became quite apparent on and after that dreadful morning when the news ran through the town that he had been found with his throat slashed and lying in a pool of his own blood.

But that was much later, after he had become thoroughly discredited and nobody had any more use for him. All that was known of his private life when I was a boy was that he engaged one pretty maid after another in his household service. Now, why did he do that? Could he not, like any other old bachelor, have taken a middle-aged housekeeper and avoided all the unsavory rumors that were current on his account? Must men not guard even against the semblance of evil? It can easily be imagined to what tongue-wagging such conduct gave rise in a small community like ours.

After a few days in his service, those girls would leave and disappear from town altogether. The strangest stories circulated as to what had happened to them while in old man De Pater's house, why they had left him, and where they had gone to hide their shame. I am not writing a *chronique scandaleuse* about Gorcum, but I must tell of those incidents and rumors because they throw a revealing light on the final dénouement in Joris de Pater's life and also because the life and death of a man like that absorbed the interest of our citizens as much as the clash of nations and ideologies casts a spell of horror and anticipation over the men and women of our time. Society in Gorcum was a miniature world. Life moved on a scale restricted by a near-by horizon, but its loves and hatreds, its pettiness and jealousies, were no less real and affected us no less. It was all we had.

Two weeks after De Pater's death, when his house was put up for sale, I visited the place in the company of some other boys—anyone could go in during certain hours of the day, always under the watchful eye of the bailiff and his assistants, to inspect the furniture and the table-ware that was to be auctioned off. With the other boys I wandered through the rooms, ostensibly very much interested in the paintings, the bric-à-brac, and the art objects, but in reality edging up to the stairway in order to dash upstairs over the thick rugs as soon as Mijnheer Jacquemijn (that was the bailiff's name) turned his back and take a peek at the mysterious attic that had figured so much in the gossip about the goings-on in the old notary's house while he was still alive.

And to be sure, there it was: all the floor space in the top story of the house had been turned into a vast chamber with solid rows of mirrors along the walls and a great, thronelike bed built in the center. This bed, which was really more a huge couch, lay piled high with fantastically colored silken cushions and velvet covers. With its three white marble steps leading up to it, too, and the heavy brass chandelier overhead, it looked more like an altar to Venus Lubentina than anything else I have ever seen, except when, much later in life, I paid a visit to Constantinople and saw the deserted harem of Abdul-Hamid in Yildiz Kiosk. De Pater's attic made you think that you had entered a seraglio. How a grim-faced old Dutchman, who never smiled and who in public gave the impression of respectability personified, could have engaged in such sensual Oriental fantasies is more than I can explain. Everybody went in to see the show, and for weeks on end De Pater's harem was the subject of conversation in Gorcum with much giggling and snickering and whispering, of course.

How did he come to his gruesome death? Was it revenge on the part of one of the girls he had ruined. Or was there a question of money involved? He had always been drawing up last wills and testaments: could it not be that some disinherited nephew of one of his old-lady clients, enraged at what he considered old De Pater's villainy in the matter, had committed the crime? That sounded reasonable enough. It was surely a clue for the police to investigate. The old notary had made plenty of enemies and potential enemies in his lifetime.

At one time, in fact, half the town was not only bitterly disposed to him, but in mortal dread of him. It came about this way: De Pater's house stood on the corner of the Arkelstraat, a street inhabited by rather well-to-do burghers, and a narrow alley in which there was a brothel. This house of ill fame disappeared when the government discontinued the practice of licensing houses of prostitution, but in my youth it functioned full blast. You never entered that alley, of course, but you could not help seeing the big red lantern that hung halfway down the alley and the number 31 painted in black letters on the glass when you went through the Arkelstraat after nightfall. Now, as has been said, Joris de Pater lived on the corner. On that corner was also a lantern, an ordinary street lamp, which was fastened to the notary's house by means of a wrought-iron arch.

By dousing the lights in his own front room, the old notary could therefore, quite unobserved, watch anyone going by in the street slip into the forbidden alley. And

this he did. In fact, he spent half his evenings and his
nights quietly sitting in an armchair before his darkened
window, like a cat watching for a mouse. When anyone
he knew passed by, and this person, after a hasty glance
around to be sure that he was unobserved, furtively
walked into the alley, the hidden De Pater had a clear
view of the features of the brothel's prospective client.
If he recognized the person, he would jump from his
seat, suddenly part the curtains in his room, and tap on
the panes. In the stillness of the evening that tap would
sound like a pistol shot to the man in the street, whose
conscience, under the circumstances, would not be too
serene anyway. He would look up, startled and upset,
on being discovered. When their eyes met, Joris de Pater
would simply nod and perhaps wave his hand in recognition; then he would step back and vanish from sight.

Now, on the surface there was nothing wrong in all
this: a man may greet an acquaintance, may he not? A
wave of the hand like that is, after all, just an act of
elementary politeness. You may even say that it was a
kind and friendly gesture and that to be recognized in
so amicable a manner by Mijnheer de Pater, who was
a man of influence and standing, was not something to
be disdained. Or else, it may be said in extenuation, that
Joris de Pater, in thus shocking some guilty conscience
or other now and then. was really a guardian of public
morality. And, in truth, it must be said that by that
abrupt signal on the windowpane he caused many a
burgher suddenly to change his mind. There can be no
doubt of that. But only one wholly ignorant of the
notary's corrupt mind and character would attribute his
gestures at the darkened window to a kind, paternal and
moral solicitude. For what did he do, Joris de Pater?

He let it be known in the conservative club, where he dropped in occasionally, that he was keeping close tabs on the persons who dodged into the alley, that he had a register in which he had entered the names, and that on that register he marked the hour and the number of visits they paid to the erotic establishment. In other words, he talked about his discoveries. He not only talked, he lied about the matter.

On the day following one of those nocturnal incidents, if he met the man whom he had seen the night before, he would exclaim: "Ah, good afternoon my dear Heer van der Velde, I am glad to see you. You look quite well, I must say. Ahem, ahem! . . . By the way, that was rather a late hour to be up and about when you passed my house last night. I trust it was not on account of your esteemed mother-in-law: I hear she's been ailing?"

The man thus accosted (Joris made sure that his victim was with a friend or even with one of his children) would blush with shame or become flustered and agitated and would not know what to answer. De Pater would laugh his metallic, diabolical laugh and pass on his way.

Or he would say: "A fine morning, Mijnheer van Duffelen, a fine morning indeed! We had a little rain last night, though. Ah, yes, but it did the gardens a lot of good, you may be sure. The farmers will not grumble about a few showers like that. Oh, no, ha, ha! Still, one should be careful. It's not a healthy thing to walk out at nights in the rain, Mijnheer van Duffelen. Not healthy at all, you may take my word for it. Did you see that new girl Madam has imported from The Hague? Ha, ha, she is a *Française*, I am told. I see her walking by my house occasionally. A most charming young lady! What do you say, Mijnheer van Duffelen? Ha, ha!" And on his way he would go, leaving Van Duffelen in a state of guilty agitation and remorse.

That was the way this man De Pater aroused enmity against himself, but that was only the beginning of it. He got into the habit of stopping persons on the streets and addressing them with remarks of that type even when they were wholly innocent. He spoke to men in whose mind there had been no thought of ever visiting the alley in question. If he took a dislike to anyone, and I think he hated every human being except himself, he would try to connect him with immoral practices by a more or less sly reference to a visit to the brothel. A man might seek to disinculpate himself by saying politely: "You must be mistaken, Mijnheer de Pater. I was not out of my house at all last night. It certainly was not I you saw passing your house at the late hour you say." Upon hearing such a remonstrance, De Pater would only feign surprise and say: "Now, it is quite possible that I was mistaken, my dear sir! Please forgive me, in that case. But still, I am not blind and I still do recognize my friends when I see them. You are Mijnheer de Boer, are you not? See, see, I was not mistaken this time." And off he would walk with that devilish grin on his face; and the damage would have been done: another citizen's peace of mind would be destroyed and I don't know what family quarrels set in motion.

Men began to avoid Joris de Pater. That was only natural. Upon seeing him coming down the street swinging his cane (he was a conspicuous figure), they would quickly turn up a side street or walk into a shop or hastily engage in animated and deep conversation so that they could pretend not to notice him in passing, anything to prevent meeting him face to face. He became the most execrated individual in the community, a man avoided as if he were afflicted with leprosy.

Of the manner of his death I can only recount what came out at the trial of his nephew, a young man who was a stranger in our town, but who visited him quite frequently and who generally stayed with him during the summer school holidays. This young man was his heir, the son of De Pater's only sister, who had married a poor broker's clerk in Amsterdam. Strange to say, this boy—Marcus was his name—was a frank and open-hearted lad, jolly, a good and welcome companion on excursions when he went swimming and boating in the summertime. His talk was somewhat strange and unfamiliar, for the Gorcum dialect differs a good deal from the language spoken in Amsterdam, but that only made him more interesting.

Often we laughed about his peculiarities of speech, but he took it as good fun and laughed with us. He must have been fourteen or fifteen when I first knew him, almost as tall as his uncle, with curly blond hair and a friendly disposition. It was this boy Marcus who killed the notary and who confessed to the crime, but then he was fully eighteen years of age.

Being De Pater's only heir, so he testified before the tribunal in Dordrecht, where the trial was held, from his earliest youth he had been coached by his parents to venerate his uncle and to please him in every way possible. Whenever the boy came to Gorcum, he was loaded down with small presents and with plenty of advice on how to ingratiate himself with the old notary. For though it was most likely that Joris de Pater would leave the greatest part of his not inconsiderable fortune to his nephew, one could never be quite certain until the terms of the will were made known. And that could not happen until he had died. Marcus' parents had to take into consideration that it was not a law of the Medes and the Persians that made their son De Pater's probable heir. Moreover, the old notary was streaked with a queer and perverse twist, and it was not beyond the realm of possibility that he would leave his relatives in happy expectation during his lifetime, only to disappoint them at his death by letting them discover that he had bequeathed the money to some charitable institution or other or to the church. Marcus was to behave so as to prevent the perpetration of any such meanness.

The whole boy's life became a course of training in amiability. He was never to do or say anything that would in the slightest call forth his uncle's disapprobation or arouse his anger. This was an almost superhuman task, to be sure, for old Joris was an irritable person, intolerant of the least gaiety or lightness of heart such as a boy of sixteen might display. Marcus had to toe the line while on those lengthy summer visits to his uncle and subdue his animal spirits and his natural loquacity to the point where he must have resembled a novice in a Trappist monastery.

Joris fetched him from the station at the beginning of the summer holidays, asked him a few questions about his parents and about his progress in school, and took him back again to the station when the time for departure came around. For the rest of the time the notary only saw him at mealtimes and then enjoined strict silence on him. The boy was left to roam the streets at will and go wherever he liked so long as he was back in the notary's house for dinner and supper. That is how it came that he frequently accompanied us on the excursions across the river and even on boat trips to Rotterdam to see the Zoological Garden and the picture galleries and museums under the pleasant and expert guidance of my Uncle Kees.

In the course of his last stay with Joris de Pater, when Marcus was eighteen years of age and had been graduated from college, the notary had in his employ a maid of ravishing beauty. She was a girl of about twenty, with titian hair and a figure that often made the officers of the garrison, and others besides, stand still in the street to watch her pass by. Dina was her name, Dina Tempelman. Her father filled the position of combination gravedigger, bell ringer, and beadle in a small Reformed parish in a Brabant village across the river. The position in De Pater's house was not Dina's first job. It was said that she had previously been employed in the home of a young pastor in some near-by hamlet but had been dismissed by the pastor's wife upon the discovery that she was carrying on a liaison with the lady's husband.

How Joris de Pater had subsequently got hold of her, I do not know, but I surmise that it was merely a case of the old lecher having let his instincts guide him. At any rate, she was in the notary's house when Marcus visited there that summer. The old man guarded her as the apple of his eye. He never allowed her to go out after dark or stroll in the park where other young people went of an evening. For the first time in his life he was as generous as a Maecenas. Dina was dressed in the height of fashion: jewels, hats, finery, everything was imported for her without regard to cost. The expensive clothes and other adornments naturally heightened the allure of this girl who had formerly been a mere peasant. She became more and more indispensable to Joris in his old age. Marcus must have written his parents in Amster-

dam about his uncle's infatuation for his servant girl,
complaining, no doubt, that he was having a miserable
time as an unwilling witness of the billing and cooing
that was going on between Joris and Dina.

This much is certain: Marcus' parents came to Gorcum
to size up the situation with their own eyes. There they
could not fail to observe that dear Uncle Joris had progressed far beyond the stage where his liaison with the
green-eyed Dina could be dismissed as one of his habitual
passing whims. Of course, they could not argue or plead
with the old man. That would only have made matters
worse: in a fit of contrariness he might have married the
girl forthwith and blasted all their hopes. The notary
was perfectly well aware, of course, why his sister and
brother-in-law had come to Gorcum and he point-blank
refused an invitation to go back with them to Amsterdam
for a short stay during which, it was suggested, he should
close his house and dismiss the servants to save expense.
He knew what they were up to. No, he was too old to
go traveling now. Moreover, he was set in his ways and,
except for an occasional fit of dizziness, was quite comfortable in his own house. His dear Dina, he said, was
taking excellent care of him.

Marcus' parents were at their wits' end. The hopes
and expectations and efforts of a lifetime seemed about
to go up in smoke. There was this girl, a lithe, voluptu-
ous creature, eating at the table with them, fluttering her
long lashes in a meaningful and truly scandalous manner
whenever Uncle Joris looked in her direction. She was
pouring his liqueur for him and lighting his cigar and
then sliding onto his lap with a sensuous feline gesture.
It was almost more than they could bear. And then,
when he went upstairs (for he had got into the habit of

retiring early) , she, too, slipped away—just to see for a minute, she would say, if her baby was all right and to tuck him in and give him his nightcap. It was all too brazen and calculated for words; the hussy, that snotty peasant with her unsavory reputation. She would rob decent, law-abiding people of their comfort in life, would she? Well, they would see! Did Marcus' parents make certain suggestions to their boy? I cannot say. Anyhow, when they returned to Amsterdam, Marcus stayed behind for a few more weeks and he, too, fell in love with the girl. And what is worse, after the old man had been put to bed, the two young people found that the night was theirs. . . .

Two weeks after Marcus left Gorcum to enter the university, his parents received a notification from Uncle Joris that he had married Dina. Nine months later less two weeks they were notified that a son had been born to Dina. Marcus was not told of these happenings until much later, but when he learned of them he left the university town where he was studying and came to his parents. He confessed to them that he was almost certainly the father of Dina's child. With that confession the boy sealed his own doom.

In the first place, his parents denounced him as the destroyer of his own and their happiness. They withdrew their support, going to the extent of closing their doors to him.

Marcus was alone in the world, without money or friends, unable to find a position and consumed by remorse. He tramped the length and breadth of the country, grew a beard, and lived the life of a vagabond. One day his wanderings brought him to Gorcum. He took lodgings in one of the cheapest hostelries, a veritable beggars' hotel, located in the worst slum, a mere flop-house for transients and prostitutes, and went from house to house selling picture postcards and pencils.

Gorcum is not so large that he could long avoid meeting his uncle in the streets. They did meet. But although Joris de Pater did not recognize his nephew at first and roughly ordered him to be gone, Marcus revealed his identity and was told to come to the house in the Arkel-straat at nine in the evening.

What happened there in Joris de Pater's parlor was disclosed the next morning when Dina came downstairs and saw her husband lying on the floor in a pool of blood. The notary clutched a linen money sack in his rigid hands, but it was empty. His throat had been slashed with a razor, apparently while he was counting out coin to Marcus, and he had toppled backward dead.

Marcus was soon caught. He confessed and received a life-sentence. Dina was permitted by the court to change her name and moved away from Gorcum. The murderer's son became a prominent politician in The Hague. I saw him there when I last visited Holland, but he declined to be interviewed on the Nazi menace. There wasn't any Nazi menace, he said. That menace only existed in the fantasymongering brains of American news-papermen!

That part of my youth which I spent in Holland was overshadowed by an event of the utmost significance in the religious and political life of the Dutch nation. A split known as the Separation had occurred in the Protes-tant body shortly after the end of the Napoleonic era. A second split took place in the eighties. It was known as the Doleancy, from the Latin verb *dolere*, which means to be afflicted, to suffer, or to mourn. Tens of thousands of Calvinists left the state church in protest against conditions in the official body, where modernism and latitudinarianism had not only made an appearance but had become virtually dominant.

Although this second split had occurred almost two decades before I was born, its implications and consequences were still keeping the minds of men in turmoil and agitation. The Doleancy had been the protest of the small people against liberalism and against the doctrinal skepticism of the majority of the ministers, who had come under the influence of the German school of Biblical criticism and who had set up their own schools at the Dutch universities, introducing a state of mind even more radical than that of their neighbors. They called themselves reformers and claimed to be working for a renewal of religious life. But instead of fortifying religion, they had opened the door to free thought.

When these renovators ventured to proclaim from the pulpits that the Bible did not contain the whole religious truth, they came in direct conflict with the Calvinist thesis. When, moreover, they denied the divinity of Christ and rejected such doctrines as predestination and justification by faith, they found that the people would not follow them. Bitter controversies raged. But since the provincial synods and even the national synod were chiefly made up of modernists and indifferents, and since there was therefore no authority to repress and banish the new heresy, there was only one thing to do if men were not to be contaminated by what was called the Enlightenment: follow the example of the Hebrews of antiquity and go into exile.

The impetus to this evacuation of the state church

by the Calvinists was given by a young minister, Dr. Abraham Kuyper, when he preached a sermon from the text "Get thee out of thy country, and from thy kindred, and from thy father's house." Kuyper called the state church the Egyptian house of bondage and showered on the official Protestant organization epithets that had formerly been reserved for the Church of Rome. The Reformed Church now became Babylon, the great harlot, a temple of idolatry where science and rationalism had taken the place of papist veneration of the saints and of the Virgin Mary. The people were called upon to leave that abomination, where men ordained to the preaching of the Word of God had fallen back upon the ethical precepts of paganism.

These accusations were not altogether undeserved, judging by what occurred in Gorcum itself. In our town one of the ministers of the official church refused to have the Creed read during the services at which he presided. Another confined prayers to a mere recital of the Our Father. This man never preached from the Bible, a book that he dismissed as "a marvelous record indeed of the spiritual evolution of an Oriental tribe," but hardly a guide for sober-minded Europeans. He reviewed books from the pulpit and recited the poetry of contemporary artists. In politics he was, quite consistently perhaps, an anarchist.

One of his colleagues, in a parish across the Merwe, went so far as to make sport in his sermons of the sacrifices held of old in the Hebrew Temple. "What a blood bath for Jehovah!" he would exclaim. "What a putrid smell must have been the burning of the fat of ten thousand sheep in one day! What odors in the Holy City!" He called the Levites who prepared the sacrificial animals for the altars the boys of the skinners' guild. In one sermon he imagined a cantankerous labor dispute between them and the laundrymen's union in Jerusalem over the removal of the bloodstains from the priestly garments. When he reached that point in his homily, that pastor's entire congregation rose and left; much to his own amusement, let it be said. His name was Dr. Talma, and he later entered politics and ended up with a position in the cabinet.

I recall this Dr. Talma in later life visiting our home and going to church on Sunday to hear one of my uncles preach. The sermon contained some rather mild references to hell and hell-fire. Talma heard it in silence, of course, but when he was eating lunch at some prominent citizen's table, and the lady of the house brought in her baby, he took the child in his arms and walked around the room with it, singing a lullaby, the words of which were inspired by the morning's sermon. It went something like this: "This baby's going to hell, this baby's going to hell. Hi ho, the pastor says: 'This baby's going to hell.'"

It was as if a bombshell had suddenly fallen into the room. My uncle and the elders looked as if they had seen a ghost. Everybody left without finishing the meal.

Another of the radical dominies, a great friend of our family, was Dr. Louis Baehler, the son of an orthodox pastor and the brother of a famous organist. This gentleman, who became one of the most renowned Sanskrit scholars of his time, had embraced Buddhism and preached the doctrine of the Enlightened One of the East from his pulpit in a Protestant church. Fine dissertations, no doubt (I still have them in book form), but hardly calculated to appeal to the religious sentiments

of Frisian farmers who had been brought up on the Heidelberg Catechism. Louis Baehler was tried for heresy,
but the provincial synod, which was made up for the
most part of modernists, was so impressed with his defense
that he did not even incur a reprimand. Only the spokesman of the fundamentalist minority uttered the objection
that the Dutch Reformed Church was, after all, a Chris-
tion institution and that a minister who was officially
charged to preach the Gospel of Christ but who preferred
Buddhism should perhaps be invited to go elsewhere.
The protesting member was informed in polite language
that if the Almighty wanted the Calvinist doctrine to be
preached exclusively, He could be counted upon to do so.

The masses turned away from the Reformed Church
and founded their own religious organization, the Church
of the Doleancy. In many localities, the new dissenters
joined those congregations of the Separation which had
seceded half a century before.

What this meant can be imagined only with difficulty
in an age of religious indifference, when Protestantism,
if not actually dead, trails docilely in the wake of Rome.
The Doleancy was an upheaval of the first magnitude.
It was as if the world stood still. Business houses suspended operations as partners first passionately debated
the issues involved in the breach in the church and then
broke off their association to go in opposite directions.
The controversy raged from one end of the land to the
other. The smallest community was not immune. In
some towns martial law had to be proclaimed as the
sectaries seemed about to come to blows. Political parties
were suddenly split into fragments as their members
took sides with one or the other religious groups. In
Gorcum the dissenting Calvinists affixed a large poster

to the doors of the Protestant cathedral on which was painted in letters of red: "This is not the House of God. This is the abode of the Devil!" In other places far more drastic denunciations were hurled at the state church.

Old friendships were dissolved with great bitterness. Uncle Kees used to tell how one dissenter, a lifelong friend of his father's, came to the house to ask my grandfather to join the exodus from the state church. When Grandfather refused, saying that though he remained a Calvinist, he had no intention of retreating and leaving the field to the Amalekites (a term he used habitually when he referred to the modernists), the dissenter rose from his seat and said: "Anthony, I hate thee in Christ as once I loved thee in Christ. If thou must stay, forget not that thou stayest in a brothel. Thou wilt repent for this in all eternity with gnashing of teeth and a worm gnawing at thy perverse heart."

Our family was rent in twain, too, by the Doleancy. On my mother's side nearly all our relatives went to the new church. Some went so far as to leave Holland entirely and settled in Michigan. Men and women, who had formerly been on terms of intimate friendship, passed each other without a glance of recognition in the streets. And still it was not that they differed on religious grounds. The controversy raged between fellow Calvinists: those who left the state church and those who remained. I seem to recall that there was little bitterness against the modernists, who were responsible for the whole turmoil. Nobody begrudged them their dominant position in the official church body. They were much more an object of pity, for they were men, who, though they had known the light, had nevertheless turned their backs on it. Since the Calvinists could scarcely bring in the Inquisition, they left it to God to take care of the modernists, firmly believing that the Almighty would not take half measures with those infidels.

I was acquainted with an old woman, Vrouw Monshouwer, who was known as a "Mother in Israel"—that is to say, a matriarch who exercised an unofficial influence on congregational affairs and who discussed theology with the pastor as if she had been a full-fledged elder. Vrouw Monshouwer had been a widow for ten years. Her husband had not followed her into the Doleancy movement. He had died without repenting of his refusal to leave the state church where he had been a deacon and a firm supporter of the Calvinist fraction.

"Every afternoon at four o'clock," she said to me once, "I hear Wynant [her dead husband] screaming in the pains of hell." When I ventured to express the hope that Wynant's suffering would soon end and no longer trouble her with his terrible moans, she replied: "His sufferings will never end, my boy. God is just, and my Wynant must find out that God is not mocked. He will burn forever and ever, and when I go to heaven," she added as casually as if she had the railroad ticket in her purse, "I expect to hear his cries from down below there in the pit." She said it as blithely as one who is looking forward to hearing Hans Kindler execute Handel's "Largo."

When I was a youngster, fifteen or twenty years had elapsed since the fatal breach, and still the "mourning" went on. That is, the controversy raged. But by that time the dissenters had organized their own schools, their own clubs, their own debating and choral societies, their merchant associations, labor unions, picnic groups, sewing circles, newspapers, brass bands, and beer breweries.

They had their own butchers, grocers, and candy shops. It would never have entered a dissenting housewife's head to buy even five cents' worth of meat in a shop run by a man who had the sinful misfortune of having a brother-in-law or a second cousin who took up the collection in the state church of a Sunday.

How deep an impression the religious upheaval made on the minds of the people and how devastating an effect it sometimes had on the social life we could see with our own eyes in the case of a local merchant who lived right across the street from us. This man's name was Adriaan van der Werf. He was a descendant of the famous burgomaster of Leiden who had defended that city victoriously against the Spaniards in 1573 and who had been instrumental, through his heroic conduct, in obtaining the charter for the founding of a university in his town. This Van der Werf and his family had gone over to the new church at the time when Dr. Kuyper sounded his call for the great "exodus from Egypt." That had been quite a few years before I was born. When I knew the man to the extent of being able to talk to him with some understanding of such weighty matters as religion, he expressed some doubt as to the wisdom of his having left the church of the fathers. He said that the thought had troubled him ever since he had made a study of events in England, where, instead of creating a new split, certain eminent divines had boldly taken the only step that could lead to "the healing of the torn body of Christ." He referred, of course, to certain leaders of the Oxford movement, such as John Henry Newman, later a cardinal. "That," said Van der Werf, "is the road we should travel: back to authority, back to the Apostolic Church. This eternal splitting and fragmentarizing of the Christian body is a sin. Moreover, Rome is no longer what it was in the days of the Reformation. There is a Pope now [we were speaking in the days of Leo XIII] who is well disposed toward all Christians, a saintly man and a wise man, who prays for us and who would welcome us back with kindness and without recrimination."

These were strange words coming from an elder in an ultra-Calvinist church, and I listened to him both with horror and fascination. But worse was soon to come. Now, though this man Van der Werf, as has been said, was a merchant dealing in rugs and carpets and curtains, he was also somewhat of a scholar. He had attended the Latin School in his youth and had read the Fathers in the original. In his house there was a considerable library, for he was wealthy. Not wealthy in the American sense, but well-to-do in a town made up chiefly of lower middle-class people. A man like that may have been worth a hundred thousand gulden. He served the best people in town—the military officers, the mayor, and the councilmen—as well as the good families in neighboring villages. When there was a wedding among the prominenti in the vicinity, it was always Van der Werf who was called in to furnish the house for the newlyweds. He had inherited the business from his father, who had been master of the merchants' guild for a lifetime. A man like Van der Werf had no reason to worry. He had all his heart desired. He was perhaps the only one in our community, except my Uncle Kees, who had been abroad. That is to say, he had once undertaken a pilgrimage to Geneva to see with his own eyes the pulpit in St. Pierre's and the hall next door where Calvin, Knox, Farel, and Beza had preached and taught.

"When you had gone that far," Uncle Kees said to him

once in my hearing, "why didn't you continue on your way and see Rome and Florence and Naples and Paris." Van der Werf looked at Kees in wide-eyed surprise: "Rome?" he said. "God forbid! Suppose something should have happened to me in that city, an accident or something, or if I had been laid up in a hospital. Heavens, what a terrible thought: to go and meet your Maker from Rome." Uncle Kees only laughed at this. But this same Van der Werf was now speaking of the Rome he had once detested in quite different terms.

I see him yet: very tall, with a black mustache and a slight stoop. He walked with a careful measured step and always wore a black suit and a silk hat on Sunday. He was not only an elder, he was one of the ornaments of the dissenting church, one of its pillars. I think he had paid almost half the cost of their building and of the belfry they had constructed after the "exodus."

One Monday morning word went around that Van der Werf, "that man of God," had been absent from his pew on the previous Lord's day. Yet, he had not been ill or ailing, and everybody in his family was quite well. His sons and his wife had been present at the service, but not the elder. Now, what could one make of that? One could say that he had been indisposed perhaps or that he had preferred to read to himself at home from a book of sermons. Or else that a relative from out of town had been visiting him. You could think of a variety of good and sufficient reasons for Van der Werf to have remained away from church. But then he had not turned up for the evening service either. And what is more, he did not appear the next Sunday and for weeks and weeks on end.

People would say to him: "I didn't see you in church

last Sunday. Were you not feeling well?" And he would reply: "I am feeling quite well physically. But I am worried!"

"Worried about what?"

"About the state of Christendom. I begin to feel that we're on the wrong track in our church."

"Ah, ah," people would nod their heads understandingly, "that's it, is it? You think we made a mistake then in leaving Babylon and that we ought to return to the bosom of that harlot. So that's what you are thinking!"

"I am not thinking anything of the kind," he would retort. "The state church isn't a Christian's home. That is obvious. It is a temple of paganism. Never will I return there. Yet return somewhere we should. I am convinced that it is God's will. I am convinced that it was all a ghastly mistake."

Now, what was a ghastly mistake? What was the man talking about? Was he not contradicting himself? He considered the state church a temple of paganism and said that he would never return there. Then what mistake had he and others committed in leaving it? What could he mean? Could it be? . . . But no, for that Van der Werf was too sensible a man. Go back to Rome? To that abomination? Impossible! Does a man turn around when he is on the road to heaven and deliberately throw himself into the arms of Antichrist and Satan? That is the way the townspeople talked about the rug merchant's inexplicable behavior.

But then—could it be true?—someone had seen Van der Werf leaving the house of the Roman priest one evening. It could not be that he had gone there to take measurements for curtains or rugs, for there was a Catholic rug merchant in town, and the Catholics, as well as the members of the various Protestant sects, patronized exclusively those who, as it was said, were of the household of the faith. Then what had Van der Werf been doing at the priest's house, like Nicodemus, in the secrecy of night? Had anyone an explanation for that?

If no one had, the consistory, at least, was not going to stand for it. It was bound to go to the bottom of those rumors. To that body Van der Werf, too, surely owed an explanation. And that body duly sent a delegation to the man's house, the pastor in the lead, with five of the elders accompanying him.

I saw the small procession come down the street and stop in front of the Van der Werf home. I do not know if any event in later life made so sinister an impression on me as that small group of silent, hard-faced men dressed in black, solemnly walking down the street. I had a feeling as if something terrible was about to happen, the same feeling I had when later in life I was sent to watch the execution of criminals in Fulton Tower, Atlanta.

That was the way Calvin's bailiffs must have walked down the Rue de l'Archevêché when they went to fetch a heretic, or the helpers of Titelman when they made ready to apply the slow fire to the feet of someone who had mocked the Mass. What passed in Van der Werf's house I do not know, of course. But what I know is that next Sunday his name was read out in church as that of one relapsed.

The man became an outcast. He may just as well have closed his business, for no one went to shop there any more. His wife died, and he took it as a sign from God. But whether it was a sign to arrest him in his headlong course for perdition or to urge him to continue on his way and resume his talks with the Roman priest, he could not tell. I asked him one day, for I saw him almost as frequently as I saw my uncle. "I do not know," he said. "I miss every indication of the *testimonium spiritus sancti.*" He meant the testimony of the inner voice by which Calvinists, as well as Quakers, set great store. His hair grew long, and he, who had once been a model of sartorial perfection, began to look distinctly unkempt and scabrous.

After a time he closed both his shop and his warehouses. His children, of whom there were five, were one after the other removed from his home by relatives and friends who feared that their father's erratic religious views would contaminate them. He never protested by so much as a word against this interference with his parental authority. In fact, he was indifferent to everything that went on around him. He could be seen wandering about the streets at all times of the day and night, always immersed in deepest thought.

One day, as Uncle Kees and I were returning from a long walk by way of a narrow path alongside a canal, we met Van der Werf going in the opposite direction. Kees saluted him by uncovering and said: "How are you, Mijnheer van der Werf?" The poor man, looking up in bewilderment from his meditations, replied: "Oh, it's you, *mijnheer de schilder,* my compliments, my compliments!" He then made as if he would be off, but he presently retraced his steps and said: "By the way, it is absolutely untrue, mijnheer, that the Bible is the sole Word of God. There is, after all, such a thing as tradition. We deal altogether too lightly with the apostolic succession. . . ." And then dropping his voice almost to a whisper, he continued: "Mijnheer, we are orphans,

orphans we are, miserable waifs, but willful orphans, for we have a mother, and that mother is the Roman Catholic Church!" With these words he turned and went off muttering to himself.

"That man is out of his senses," I said to Uncle Kees.

"No," said he, "he is not out of his senses. But he soon will be if he doesn't come to a decision one way or the other. He is afraid to take the great step. He should go where his conscience tells him to go, even if it be the Church of Rome. I don't know what he is afraid of. He doesn't need to be afraid that he will lose customers. For he has none left. His business is ruined. It must be the fear of shocking his fellow citizens that keeps him from becoming a convert to Catholicism."

But Van der Werf never entered the Roman fold. One day he had a revelation, as he put it, to reopen his shop. He went to the barber and had his hair and his beard trimmed. On Sunday he donned a new black suit and once more wore a silk hat, which he had previously discarded for a peasant's cap. He sat in the last pew, a pew officially marked "for the poor." When the pastor began to pray, Van der Werf knelt down. In doing so he caused a minor disturbance, for Calvinists do not kneel at prayer. They stand up. During the week that followed, the windows of his shop were cleaned for the first time in nine years and brand-new rugs put on display in the show-rooms. The official reopening was scheduled for a Saturday evening.

On Saturday afternoon, as an employee of the gas company was fitting the lamps in the shop with new sockets, it was noticed that the lamps would not burn.

"There must be water in the pipes," said the fitter to

Van der Werf who was standing near by. "The gas is not coming through!"

"It's God's hand," returned Van der Werf, without a moment's hesitation. "You had better come down from that ladder," he told the fitter. "God has sent me a warning. I have no right to reopen my shop and pretend that everything is well with my soul. I am a miserable sinner. How can I be sure that my name is in the book of life when it is written: 'Many are called but few are chosen,' and when it is further written: 'Two from a city and one from a house.' "

The shop was not opened that night or at any time thereafter. It soon fell back into its old grime and dilapidation. Van der Werf again took up his wandering about the streets. In the end he became an object of repulsion. His hair had fallen down his shoulders, and his beard was a mass of vermin. Sometimes he could be seen with a loaf of bread under his arm, breaking off small pieces, but when you came near, you could hear him mutter in endless repetition: "Church of Rome . . . Church of Dordt, Church of Rome . . . Church of Dordt, Church of Rome . . . Church of Dordt . . ." Dordt (or Dordrecht, as it is known in English) is the city in Holland where the first synod was held after the Reformation.

Van der Werf's body was found when neighbors, having missed him for weeks, notified the police, who broke down the door. The dead man was seated in an armchair bent over the *Confessions* of Saint Augustine.

Oh, we had our troubles in Gorcum. Never think we did not. There was, for instance, that man Jan Bronkhorst, too, the shoemaker on the corner of our street.

I saw him every morning when I went to school. In the summertime the window of his workshop was open and when I passed by he would stop his eternal tapping on the last and call me over. We would talk for a few moments until the bells of the carillon started to play the hymn that preceded the stroke of the hour. By running fast I could make it to the door of the schoolhouse before the clock had struck its nine blows.

"I don't know what they are teaching in that school of yours," Jan would say. "Probably a whole lot of things that pass my understanding. But if perchance the teachers say anything about America, please let me know . . . tell me about it. Or, if you happen to see a book in the library that deals with America, you could perhaps borrow it for me, could you now? I won't soil it, I promise you, and I will return it in the shortest possible time." And that promise he would keep. In order to learn something more about America, Jan Bronkhorst would drop any work he had on hand and take time off to improve his mind, as he would say. America was an *idée fixe* with him. Nothing else mattered in this world. He was filled with America and spoke of it night and day.

"When I go to America," he would begin, "I'll say to them over there. . . ."

"Just a minute," people would interrupt him, "just a minute now, you are going to say this and you are going to say that. Are you aware that they won't understand a word you say? They don't talk Dutch in America. They speak English."

"Listen to me," Jan would reply, "there were Dutchmen in America hundreds of years ago. They were amongst the first there. Don't you think they will remember at least a few words of their mother tongue, just enough to understand me? I'll say to them: 'Here I am, Jan Bronkhorst, a shoemaker. . . .' "

Everybody would laugh at this and someone would say: "They won't understand even that. They'll shrug their shoulders at you and go their way. Do you think they have time in America to listen to your propositions? I should say not. Moreover, they have all the shoemakers they need over there."

"Ah," Jan would come back, "but a good Dutch shoe-maker, have they such a one, can you tell me that?"

"Man, don't be a fool," someone would reply. "Don't you know that they make shoes with machines in America? Do you think they have time there to be measured and to come back two or three times to be fitted and then at last, after a couple of weeks, to see you come in your Sunday best to deliver a pair of shoes? Do you think that's the way life is run in America?"

"Machine-made shoes can never take the place of hand-work," Jan would retort a little angrily. "If it were only for that, to impress that fact on the minds of Americans, I want to go there. . . ."

"Oh, yes, they are waiting for you in America. They're going to welcome you with open arms. People are going to say: 'Here comes Jan Bronkhorst, thank God! Now at last we'll have real fine shoes.' You'll be like another Columbus when you reach the shores of America. You will be met with a brass band, and the Burgomaster will say: 'Welcome, Jan Bronkhorst! Welcome, dear fellow! Thank you for coming here. We suffered for ages, those corns and bunions, you know, that you get in store-bought shoes. But now all is well. . . . Jan Bronkhorst is here. Long live Jan Bronkhorst! Thank you, Jan, for discovering us. . . .' "

"Don't be too sure," Jan would reply. "I'll find my way over there. They bake bread in Gorcum, they bake bread in Amsterdam, and I think they bake bread in America too."

"If it's bread you want," they'd tell him, "why move away at all? You have your bread here, haven't you?"

"I don't want bread alone. I want freedom," Jan would say.

But the question of the language worried him just the same. He would say to me: "Now, in going by in the morning, could you not just tell me a word or two of the American tongue or write it on a piece of paper, and when you return at twelve you could stop a moment and see if I had learned to say those words correctly. If you'd do that, I'd be speaking American in no time. I'm sure I have a natural gift to pick up foreign languages. I'm not like those ignoramuses, Piet Esvelt and Servaas de Bruyn and Gerrit Vos and all those other nincompoops who stand around here. They're stagnating in their own ignorance. They wouldn't move a foot to improve their lot. Of course, it's true that they have no chance here in Holland. Here everything is set for all eternity. One man's a shoemaker, and his son'll be a shoemaker after him. . . . It's like a law. . . . The other's a grocer, and his son'll be a grocer after him. Klaas de Jong opens a cask of margarine tomorrow morning to poison his clients, and young Klaas is learning the trade from his father, and so it'll go on and on till the end of time. Now, in America, there's opportunity. When I come to America, I'm going to. . . ."

I taught him a few words, such words as I learned myself from the schoolbooks: "Good morning, sir, have you seen the sailor? No, but the knife of the teacher has fallen under the chair!"

"What does it mean?" asked Jan. I told him: *"Goeden dag, mijnheer, heeft U ook den zeeman gezien? Neen, maar het mes van den onderwijzer is onder den stoel gevallen."*

"Is that what it means?" Jan would ask. "God Almighty, it does look strange! You're not fooling me, are you? Say it again, will you?"

I would repeat the sentence, but at noon when passing by he would recite something like this: "Goat morrning, sear, half iauw sane tehe saeelor? No, but tehe caneefe of tehe tayaasher haas vallen onder tehe sjaaeer!"

"You had better teach me something useful," he would say. "What in hell do I care where the sailor is gone or whether the teacher's knife is under the chair or in the river. You'd better teach me to say: 'How much is that loaf of bread in the window? Please give me my change. What kind of leather would you want for the soles?' Words of that kind, you know, useful words, words that would help me get around in America."

It was not the language alone that worried Jan Bronkhorst. The money question also perturbed him. Emigration to America for himself, his wife, and three children would come to a sizable sum of money. It was all good and well to talk about America and dream about it and read about it and even try to learn the language. But how was one ever to get there? How could one raise the funds? That was a most perplexing problem. . . .

One morning, I had just turned the corner on my way to school, when I saw a crowd of people, both men and women, standing in front of the shoemaker's shop. Some

peered through the dark window. Others talked excitedly; still others went in and out of the shop.

"What's going on, Ryer?" I asked the son of the taproom keeper.

"Jan Bronkhorst has hanged himself. They're in there
cutting him down!" came the answer.

I ran into the shop, dropped my parcel of books, and
made my way into the rear room, where most of the
people were standing.

Jan was sitting on the floor, his gnarled, pitch-black-
ened hands lay limp in his lap. His head rested on his
breast, and he was breathing heavily. "Give him air,"
Servaas de Bruyn of the hardware store was saying. "Give
the man air. Stand aside. Can't you see he must have
air?"

I kneeled down by my old friend's side.

"What's the matter, Jan?" I asked him. He looked
up at the sound of my voice and gave me his hand. Tears
were coming in his eyes. Someone gave him a glass of
water. When he had drunk a few sips, he said to me:
"*Pieter, jongen,* I suddenly realized this morning that
I'll never see America. . . . I'll never have the money
to pay for the train and the boat. Never! Every time I
have saved up a hundred florins or so, something happens to make me lose it. I had one hundred and twenty-
six gulden the day before yesterday. Yesterday I paid
sixty-nine florins in taxes. It's always the same. I have
to start saving all over again. . . ."

And then they lifted him to his feet, and he sat on his
stool by the last. He picked up a dilapidated old shoe
and contemplated the holes in the top, saying: "Well, I
had better put a nice strip over this so that nobody can
see that it's patched. That's the way Mijnheer Polvliet

wants it." And with those words he went back to work.

But he was never the same again. He would still talk about America and actually describe to you how people lived there and how much more free they were and, above all, what opportunities men had there, but he would fall into a morose silence when he reached that point in his monologues. A cloud would pass over his face, and he would be silent. The question of the money was troubling him again.

Three months or so later, the same scene awaited me one morning when I went to school: the same crowd in front of the shoemaker's window and the same individuals rushing into the shop and out, all agitated and excited.

"Has he hanged himself again?" I asked as I came running up.

"Not yet," said Servaas de Bruyn, "but he's going to. Someone looked in while he was fastening the rope and called for help. He hasn't jumped yet. They're talking to him now. You had better go in, too!"

I went inside. There was Jan sitting on his knees on top of a high cupboard with a rope around his neck. The other end of the rope was fastened to a sort of rafter on which usually hung some sheets of leather. He was saying: "If anyone goes to warn my wife, I will jump at once. Stand aside, everybody, so you won't get hurt. I'm going to jump. I've had enough of it."

"Jan," pleaded one citizen, "don't make a fool of yourself. . . . What will become of your children? Think of them! Think, Jan! Your wife can't sew shoe leather. Your family will go to the poorhouse instead of to America. Your children will go around in rags and hungry, and people will say: 'There go the children of Jan Bronk-

horst . . . their father hanged himself.' Will that not
be a shame forever?"

Another man said: "Who is going to make shoes for
us when you are gone?"

To this the man on the cupboard replied in a sudden
burst of anger: "Make shoes for you? You, lousy paupers,
you haven't worn a decent pair of shoes in all your lives.
Do you think I want to go on patching your miserable
chunks of leather all my life? Get away, get out of here,
do you hear?" He was yelling at the top of his voice.
"Let a man die if he wants to. What in hell is it of your
business what I do?"

"Jan," spoke up Servaas de Bruyn again, "that rafter'll
never hold you. It'll break when you jump and you will
fall here on this table and hurt yourself, but you won't
break your neck. You'll be laid up with a broken leg
for weeks, that's all you will accomplish."

More and more persons crowded into the room. Jan
looked at the faces staring up at him with contempt. All
at once Willem van den Oever, the policeman, entered.
He sized up the situation at a glance and walked over to
the cupboard. "Get down," he ordered. "Get down at
once. You have no right to cause a disturbance of the
peace like this. I could arrest you for it, but I won't
if you come down at once."

For answer Jan Bronkhorst spat at the policeman and
called out: *"Diender,* servant [of the law], I have the
right to die when I want, have I not?"

Willem calmly wiped the saliva from his uniform and
said: "All right then! Everybody step back now. He
wants to jump. Let him jump. Come on," he called up
to Jan. "Come on, jump! We're waiting for you. It's
Wednesday today. Your funeral will be on Saturday.

Be a man, jump down and you'll hear your neck crack, you damned fool. That's the last thing you will hear in this world, too. You'll wake up in hell where you belong. Come on, jump, you damned coward!"

"If you order me to jump, I won't," said Jan. "I won't take orders from a cop!"

He unfastened the noose and down he climbed.

It was suggested to Jan that he could perhaps leave alone for America, try to earn some money, and send for his wife and children later. This idea seemed to cheer him up for a time, but soon he fell back into the same morbid state of brooding. "I couldn't leave them here alone," he told me. "How will they live when I'm gone? I may not be able to find work so quickly." He was beginning to lose his faith in America, too, and it became clear that the end was near.

A few weeks later Jan jumped into the river and was drowned. His body was never recovered. But he left a note addressed to the local newspaper, which was never published, of course, and in which he had written: "Respected fellow citizens. I wish to apologize for the trouble I have caused you. I have worked hard, but I have been like a dog that hopes and hopes that somebody will throw him a bone. Nobody has thrown me a bone. Farewell. Your fellow citizen, Jan Bronkhorst."

Until far into the nineteenth century one may distinguish two classes among the people of The Netherlands: "reliefers" and *rentiers*. Up until 1830 more than half the population of the capital city of Amsterdam was "on the dole"; in other cities conditions corresponded to this norm in ratio to their population. On the other hand, investment in bonds provided all the enjoyment that go with the possession of capital without exertion or responsibility. One of the ablest economists summed up the socioeconomic condition of the country in the first half of the last century in these words: "The Netherlands remained long a product of disintegration and economic stagnation, rotten to the very core; a nation of monopolists, *rentiers,* and 'reliefers,' a land of social contrasts without opposition."

Only the petty *bourgeoisie,* the so-called *kleine luyden,* small people, the lower middle class, slowly came into opposition. At first their protest directed itself chiefly against the church, against the Kantian influence, the spirit of Enlightenment, and against the reorganization on liberalistic principles of that institution after the withdrawal of the French garrisons from Holland. It led to the Separation.

Out of the Separation grew a political movement that later crystallized in a political party known as the Antirevolutionaries. In this party the nobility and the owners of large estates formed a common front with the lower middle class against the up-and-coming liberal *bourgeoisie.* Religiously and socially, the Separatists and the antirevolutionary party were directed against the individualistic, atomistic principles of the French Revolution.

The first battle between antirevolutionaries and liberals was waged on the subject of education. It lasted nearly half a century and ended with the liberals giving in. They accepted the "school with the Bible." But they did not surrender because they were persuaded of the desirability of an educational system based on religious principles, but because they came to see, in the religious school, an instrument of social defense against the growing Social Democratic movement.

Although 1848 had been a year of revolutions all over
Europe, The Netherlands had remained quiet. The occasional tumults and rebellions in the cities were the outcome of the unbearable poverty in which the mass of the
people found themselves.

After the critical years of 1848-60 came a period of
economic amelioration. England became the workshop
of the world. The world's markets expanded as fast as
production. The idea of free trade triumphed. From this
general improvement Dutch agriculture profited. But
commercial capital also grew stronger. Holland stepped
into the ranks of the modern capitalistic countries. Questions of private initiative and state control made their
appearance. In those years, certain political and theological tendencies began to be marked more clearly. The
antirevolutionary alliance between orthodox aristocrats
and the small people grew firmer. The ethical Protestants
became more conservative, and the liberals moved, in a
theological sense, farther toward modernism. Two great
popular leaders arose: Abraham Kuyper and Domela
Nieuwenhuis. It lay in the line of Dutch tradition that
these two men, who gave the people political schooling
and organization, should both have been clergymen.

Kuyper fortified the antirevolutionary movement until
it became a neo-Calvinistic party, wherein the "small
people" completely dominated "the men with the double
names," the aristocrats. Many of these last remnants of
feudalism thereupon grouped themselves around a bar-
onet by the name of De Savornin Lohman and formed the
Christian-Historical party. Kuyper and his party of
"small people" took a radical-democratic direction.

Domela Nieuwenhuis, on the other hand, organized
the first socialistically tinted labor movements into a

Social Democratic party. The nucleus of the Socialist movement lay in the large cities but soon reached out into the newly born industrial regions, penetrating even into the solidly Catholic south.

The first Socialists in Holland had an almost impossible task before them. The extremely low standard of life of the laboring class, the total absence of social legislation, the long hours, the inconceivably bad housing conditions, the low wages, the neglect of children, and insufficient education placed them before a wall of apathy and ignorance that seemed almost insuperable. Holland still lacked a great industrial apparatus such as had grown up in England and in France.

Only after the year 1870 did modern capitalism begin to deploy its full force. The colonies in the Far East and in South America were opened to private capital. The Prussian victory of 1871 had set German capitalism on its feet and introduced an era of unprecedented prosperity. For Holland this meant a vast increase in the transport of goods and enormous profits. In this way developed colonial-commercial and maritime capitalism. Great industries and companies were formed and new industries rose, as it were, from the ground. Imports and exports quadrupled within thirty years. From the middle of the nineties a period of unknown prosperity prevailed. This lasted until 1914. But in the meantime a sharp battle developed for new markets. Prices went up, and wages fell behind. Militarism asked for constantly greater expenditure. Trustification set in, and imperialism was born.

This material prosperity naturally produced an artistic and humanistic renaissance. Whereas poetry had been dominated by theology in the first part of the nineteenth century, it now liberated itself. New names were heard. Multatuli fought a passionate struggle against the petty-bourgeois spirit. More than any other writer, Multatuli contributed to the awakening of Holland. Also, a new science and a new philosophy made their appearance. Painters were struck by the beauty of an entire country seized by the fever of construction: Van Gogh, Breitner, Witsen, Toorop. Ruskin and Tolstoy gained a wider influence. A feminist movement came into existence. The cities were modernized. Young poets, Frederik van Eeden, Van Deyssel, Frank van der Goes, Gorter, wanted to "push Holland into the stream of the nations."

But now the political and social contradictions also grew more marked. Abraham Kuyper, the leader of the neo-Calvinist party, had founded a university of his own and had led a second great exodus of dissenters out of the state church. For a moment this neo-Calvinism hovered on the brink of radical-democratic republicanism.

The "God-given Leader," as he was called by his followers among the "small people," saw a danger in the growth of the state. "All our independent democratic institutions," he explained, "are disappearing before the magic slogan of the one and indivisible state. What will become of us if the process of centralization, now scarcely begun, will have run its full course? Where will we find the power to fight back if the apotheosized state continues to brand every resistance as sacrilege? What becomes of personal initiative and individual freedom if this Caesarism of the modern state keeps on growing and if modern imperialism transforms its *panem et circenses* into economic regulations, and if material prosperity permits itself everything, while there is nobody to resist, because nobody can resist? I know this process," he said, "has not reached our borders yet: But it will come!"

Kuyper thought that there still lay a creative impulse in Calvinism. Calvinism, he prophesied, would produce new leaders from amongst the people to withstand the encroachments of the state. "And if the state commands anything that is contrary to the law of God, you must resist the state, refuse obedience, and suffer rather than obey," he told his followers. For a moment neo-Calvinism seemed on the verge of taking a clear socialist direction. "Every true Christian aspiration must condemn the actual condition of our society;" said the leader. "The world is loosening its bonds with Christ. . . . Society lies kneeling in the dust before mammon. . . . I see improvement, I do not hesitate to use the word, only in a socialist direction."

But it was only for a moment that Calvinism seemed to be moving to the Left. Kuyper himself became in time the most devoted servant and protector of nascent Dutch imperialism. He broke a railway strike in 1903 in which the modern state for the first time used the expedient of drafting the workers into the army, thereby placing them under martial law. Democracy ceased to make concessions to the working classes the moment it involved sacrifice and sharing with the upper classes.

The general economic decline set in with the outbreak of the First World War. The enormous profits that Holland extracted from the bloody upheaval did not reach the people. Wages fell far behind commercial and industrial expansion. The military apparatus and especially the navy required greater and greater sums as it became clear that the First World War of 1914-18 had been but a prelude to a world-wide struggle for the redistribution of markets and that in the second phase of this conflict

Holland and its Indian possessions would inevitably be drawn into the maelstrom.

In those years preceding the Second World War, Holland virtually lost its independence to the British Empire. England did not look upon Holland any longer as an independent state: Britain's frontiers were pushed eastward to the Rhine.

In modern times, Britain has fought four wars: against Spain, against the France of Louis XIV, against Napoleon, and against the German Empire. The goal and object of these four wars was in each case the same: to prevent a Continental power from gaining control of the North Sea shores—that is to say, The Netherlands—and to maintain the balance of power in Europe.

Whereas Holland's geopolitical situation had saved it from being drawn into the war of 1914 even as, reversely, Belgium's geopolitical situation had caused that country to be drawn into the Great War, in spite of its status of neutrality and its military preparedness, because both the Allies and the Central Powers had included the violation of Belgium neutrality in their war plans, any future conflict in Europe was not likely to spare The Netherlands. The technical evolution of aerial warfare had made of the territories across the Channel and the North Sea a matter of vital importance to Great Britain. England could no longer leave Holland its freedom of action. That the Dutch government took the same view of the situation appears from its declaration in the Second Chamber in 1934, when it was said that the new Dutch army was not organized in the expectation of fighting an independent action of defense, a localized conflict between Holland and a western European Power being unthinkable.

The happy days of neutrality and war profits were past. Holland's independence became so much a matter of appearance alone that even if it had been free to make a choice in Europe, its Asiatic possessions, long threatened by Japan, forced it to slant its policy entirely in the direction of Great Britain.

Thus, just before the outbreak of the Second World War, Holland's international policy was closely bound up with that of Great Britain. Its neutrality and independence were mere phrases. Its insignificant military forces were unable to defend the country. In effect, it had become a mere adjunct of the British Empire.

Why, then, did the Dutch government spend enormous sums on armament programs and ruin still further the prosperity of the country by draining it of whatever wealth remained? Because, as Vice-Admiral Fuerstner, the gentleman who was to become Minister of Marine in the government-in-exile, expressed it: "If Holland should show a willingness to defend itself, the world would be able to speak of 'brave little Holland' in an eventual conflict of the future, as it had spoken of 'brave little Belgium' in the previous war." In less sentimental language, this meant that Holland was prepared to do its share in the imperialistic sphere of interests to which it belonged. Fuerstner had his eyes chiefly on the Far East. "The Dutch people will have to make sacrifices," he said. "We will have to take our place in the sphere of power politics which is developing in the Far East. This means for the Dutch people: safety first! First: national security and guarantees of imperial unity (with India) by placing adequate means of defense in the hands of our peace-loving government! Only then better schools, only then social security, only then other great civic works such as the filling in of the Zuider Zee. . . ."

In other words: first and foremost, the maintenance of the existing politicoeconomic system—a system which, though it included an immensely rich colonial empire, has reduced certain sections of the Dutch Indies to the same abject poverty as the rural regions of British India and which caused the Dutch people themselves to suffer not less from the depression than the people of Denmark, who have no colonies. That was the sum and substance of the Dutch "national idea" as propounded by the statesmen who were to stand at the head of the nation when the German attack came.

It was a question of the national idea and the national safety-deposit box being synonymous!

It is a curious fact that those who think themselves the bearers of the national idea, in nearly all countries of the world, are the bitterest enemies of the purest cultural traditions of the peoples. Freedom, justice, and humanity are words and concepts which do not go with a mentality that, instead of having its roots in the past, springs from the politicoeconomic demands of the moment. The rearmament campaign and the psychological atmosphere created by it were interpreted as a national reveille by the imperialistic school of statesmen in whose hands lay the reins of government when the Second World War broke out. In reality, it was an attack on the physical and spiritual health of the Dutch nation, in that it sought to create a morality which aims at the destruction of the human personality and which has for its purpose the production of subhuman creatures.

The demands of Dutch national culture, at the moment

of the German invasion, were diametrically at variance with the basis of the political-economic life and with the consequences of it. No hostile power or conqueror has ever been able to eradicate what is most characteristic in a people, its culture, which is the real basis of its independence. However, the demands of modern imperialism, Dutch imperialism not excluded, are: Fascism, the concentration of the means of production in one hand, concentration of political power, dictatorship; and death, psychologically, to culture, so that there is a docile mass to deal with instead of a nation. . . .

The invasion itself showed up the deceptive character, the flimsiness, and the inefficacity of the imperialist game played by the Dutch government. In the years 1933-40, in the course of which the German danger on the borders grew constantly more acute, the Dutch government sought to deflect the people's and the world's attention, by periodically reiterated and increasingly vociferous declarations of neutrality, from the close organic relationship that existed between British imperialism and its adjunct, Dutch imperialism, and from the political function that Holland fulfilled on the Continent as one of Great Britain's chief instruments for the maintenance of the balance of power.

In order to give a semblance of authenticity to this attitude, which was contradicted by the very nature and facts of the international conjuncture and which it assumed for the purpose of diverting the Dutch people's attention from the fact that Holland, instead of being a small European nation, was in reality a great Asiatic Power that played the game of imperialist power politics as recklessly as Japan, Britain, and France, the Dutch government purposely refrained from working out a plan of co-ordinated defense with Belgium, France, and England, who were equally threatened by the resurgent imperialism of Germany.

This course of action, or rather this neglect of taking elementary precautions, which, in the light of events, turns out to have been the height of folly and, as a matter of fact, downright suicide, still found defenders after the Queen of The Netherlands had become an exile in London and the King of the Belgians a prisoner in German hands, their countries battered to pieces, and the peoples of Holland and Belgium helplessly caught in the strait-jacket of German Fascism.

Instead of admitting, in a spirit of contrition and repentance, the illusionary policy of neutrality, which was fundamentally a mere trick to appease Adolf Hitler, and instead of confessing a lamentable lack of foresight and a constant misreading of the signs of the times on his part, Eelco van Kleffens, chief of the diplomatic section of the Department of Foreign Affairs of the Dutch government-in-exile, wrote a book in justification of that policy which had contributed so effectively to Holland's undoing.

Although the lessons of the war of 1914-18 were still fresh in everybody's memory, particularly the fact that Germany had not paid the slightest heed to Belgium's protests of neutrality when the German High Command considered the violation of Belgium territory a question of ineluctable "military necessity," the governments of Holland and Belgium hid again behind that brittle bulwark when Germany's armies started on the rampage once more. The Dutch government persisted in proclaiming its neutrality (though it was involved up to its ears in the issues that were at stake) after the Nazi Reich had openly declared itself and had proved itself far more contemptuous of considerations of international morale than Kaiser Wilhelm's First World War régime.

Because it had worked so well during the war of 1914-18, when Germany had avoided Dutch territory in her drive to the Channel ports, the same policy of neutrality, to the effectiveness of which Holland's salvation in the previous war was now erroneously attributed, was taken up again. It deceived nobody—except the "realistic" statesmen at The Hague.

Had the German armies skirted Dutch territory for the second time in twenty-five years, the world would never have heard of Van Kleffens and his colleagues as defenders of democracy. These gentlemen would have allowed Holland to be encircled by the Axis armies, as Sweden was, and still have prided themselves, as did Sweden, on their country's national independence.

In an hour when the political sky darkened progressively and when the thunderbolts were striking right and left, Dutch statesmanship placed its trust in what Von Bethmann-Hollweg had once sneeringly dismissed as a scrap of paper. It embarked on and persisted in that fantastic course after the League of Nations had turned to ashes, after the maxim of collective security had been universally abandoned, after Poland and Czechoslovakia had been conquered, and after two neutral Scandinavian countries had been overrun by the German armies. Until the last minute—until it was too late—the governments of Holland and Belgium refused to have their military staffs enter into discussions with the French and British.

Ruat coelum, fiat neutropassiva!

This policy may now well be lauded by the authors themselves as a sample of prudent and consistent statesmanship, but men of common sense have another word for it.

But the Dutch people, who are a good people and who are the victims and martyrs of the imperialist policy pursued by their several governments, will, in a common effort with the other conquered nations of Europe, throw off the Nazi yoke. And they will also want to know what led to their enslavement.

Holland will rise again! But not the Holland of the men of guile and blood. It will be a Holland that has clean hands and a pure heart, a Holland that shall have wiped off the stains of the oppression of the Indonesian people and have freed herself of all imperialistic connections—a truly neutral Holland in a free Europe.

It is that Holland which will intone the seventh and last hymn which Uilenspiegel prophesied at Veere, the hymn of independence and freedom and eternal peace! . . .

We had our troubles in Gorcum. True, they were not great, world-shaking events, problems of a magnitude to require the solicitude of statesmen and crowned heads. They were just the mean, little troubles of small people, troubles resulting from carefully hidden destitution, inarticulate sorrow, and what may be called decent poverty. There was a good deal of that in Gorcum, just as there was in the whole of Holland. Those who would have the world believe that Holland before the German invasion of 1941 was a sort of Cockaigne, a terrestrial paradise, a democratic ne plus ultra, with milk and honey flowing freely for everybody, are misleaders and prevaricators. Holland hid its misery. A native pride caused the people to be silent about their trials. The mass of the Dutch people had no share in the riches of India and in the wealth that flowed from petroleum wells. I recall peasant recruits telling my father and Uncle Kees that they were overjoyed to be in the army for a few months, for there they could at least eat their fill and have meat more often than once a week.

The school children were made to sing that they lived happily and freely on Holland's dear soil and that, broken free from slavery, they were now, through unity and courage, members of a great and free nation. Young as I was, the words used to stick in my throat when I looked around me and saw the boys and girls who were singing that. Will I be believed when I say that I knew children who never saw a glass of milk; that at home we never ate butter, only margarine, in that land of famous dairy farms; that meat was a luxury, reserved for Sundays in that country swarming with the choicest cattle in the universe; that we had one egg each year at Eastertime in that land where chickens are more plentiful than anywhere else on earth; that we had but a few sacks of coal to last us through a sharp winter; that my mother went years without a new dress, and that in the house across the street four children perished of malnutrition, one after another?

Holland's soil was dear to me. How could it have been otherwise? Twenty-eight generations of my ancestors lay buried in that ground. I was an integral part of it, and it was part of me. The rain and the wind and the storms that swept over it were the elementary gods that belonged there as much as I and as much as the polders and the dikes and the wet grass and the churches. Something of myself was deposited in that soggy land and in the gray stone of the buildings. I was that swallow chirping under the eaves of my father's house. When the flowers on the meadow's borders swayed to and fro under the magic touch of the breeze, it was by a prearranged signal of greeting between us. Dear was the land of Holland. But dearer yet the people. In order to love them and defend them, it was not necessary to await the arrival of a foreign enemy. They needed defense then, defense and air and light and food and clothing and music and art and culture!

Did they not have these things? Have we not been told over and again that in Holland the people lived in affluence and well-being? Is there not a saying about being as rich as a Dutchman? Is that not a pretty good criterion by which to judge social conditions in Holland?

What did it avail the people that they had fought themselves free from Spain and from France as they were always made to sing and shout, when they were the slaves of the selfishness and the greed of a small coterie of bourgeois who owned all the wealth, who enjoyed all the art, all the privileges. The good life in Holland? Yes, for the crew that sat on top, that owned the shares in the East India Company, that sent donations of money and vegetable crops to Hitler and his party, that had the army at its beck and call and the church to feed the masses St. Paul's narcotic: "Be subject to your masters with all fear."

Not long ago I was talking with my father about the citizens that dwelled on our street thirty-odd years ago, when we still lived in Gorcum, a short street, no longer than five city blocks. We counted nine suicides in two minutes. "And what ailed all those people who were sitting out in front of their houses in the sun in the summertime?" I asked. "Tuberculosis," he said. "All tuberculosis and malnutrition. Let's forget about it!"

We may forget about it. But the dead do not forget. The dead do not so lightly resign themselves. They encircle you. They beleaguer you. There is a day when they come to ask for a reckoning. Do you think that was just a cosmic accident, that which occurred in the spring of 1940?

III

The New Order Comes to Gorcum

THE RAIN had stopped. A strong wind, blowing to the south, had come up with saltant gusts and was rapidly drying the streets. Under the feeble rays of the street lamps, the puddles of water between the uneven cobblestones were rapidly shrinking in size as if they had been miniature lakes whose bottom had dropped out. It had been the first rain of an unusually dry spring, and the long drought had given rise to much uneasiness. But for two hours that afternoon and once more after supper it had poured in steady, swishing torrent. And just before sunset, when there had been a break in the clouds, the farmers and the gardeners, whose money is the rain water, had been fully reassured. The fading light of day had just allowed them time to see that a miracle had occurred in the fields: the late trees had suddenly caught up with the early verdure, and in the orchards and pastures all was once again in bloom and growth. Now the evening was far advanced. The carillon in St. John's tower was playing the hymn that preceded the stroke of ten: "The Lord is great, His Name is great, the wonder of His works is great, endlessly great His love!" The silvery tinkle of the bells traveled through the deserted streets with the melancholic sweetness of a music box, a little sadly, as if the great tower, whose face looked over the town's walls into the meadows, expressed its regret over the descent of darkness, which would deprive it of the sight of the pleasant scene beyond. Between the elms around the cathedral church, the golden mask of the moon had made its appearance; a philosopher, you would have said, with a crooked, somewhat amused smile contemplating the sleeping town.

The night watch had begun to make his rounds. With a pocket torch he was busy verifying the locks on the shop doors along the main street. A boy, his wooden shoes striking the paving blocks with a rhythmic click-clack, whistled a shrill marching tune. He stopped whistling as he passed the *doelen,* or meetinghouse, whose door suddenly swung open, letting a yellow beam of light fall across his path. A group of men darkened the doorway. Their voices suddenly caused the silence to recede in the quiet street, and their laughter sounded hollow with its far-traveling echo.

There had been a lecture in the *doelen* that evening. About fifty citizens had turned out to hear a professor from the University of Utrecht discourse, as objectively as he could, he had said, upon the merits and demerits of the different social philosophies that were contending for mastery in the great countries of Europe. The lecturer had spoken from firsthand observation, for he had traveled far and wide. He had told of the great experiment in Russia, of collective farms, of popular clinics, and of the miles upon miles of brand-new factories he had visited near the Dnieperstroy, of the bustle and activity and generally of the new life in the cities of that old Muscovy which had lain torpid for so many centuries. But he had also spoken of what he called the amazing reorganization of German life that had come since Adolf Hitler had taken over the reins of power from the faltering hands of tired and aimless democrats. He had praised the neatness and the cleanliness of the German cities and the methodical planning of the new régime; he had compared it with the apparent chaos and confusion and the immense wastefulness he said he had observed in America.

The doctor had interspersed his lecture with many amusing anecdotes. It was that one about Mussolini telling Hitler that some day they would share the mastery of the world: "You Asia and Europe, and I Africa," after which Hitler, tapping the Duce on the shoulder, says: "Sure, Benito, but now shine my other boot," which had brought the greatest laugh.

The collector of internal revenue, Mijnheer van der Plank, was still chuckling about it as he stepped out of the *doelen* into the silent High Street. He shook hands with several other gentlemen, who were lighting a last cigar before retiring.

"Yes, the rain is over, I can smell it," Van der Plank was saying. "I think I will do a turn around the park and have a sniff of this good air by the river before I turn in."

He was about to move away when they heard the nervous chug of a motorcycle becoming louder and louder. Before they could utter a word, a soldier with a short carbine flung over his shoulder and a steel helmet on his head roared by. He went on to the next intersection and there brought his machine to a stop with a sharp grating of brakes. He was seen speaking to someone for a moment, his motor roared again, and he vanished. Mijnheer van der Plank and his friends walked over to the man to whom the soldier had spoken and asked him: "Well, what did that boy want so late, Mijnheer van Sas?"

"The soldier was looking for the military bureau. I

told him the barracks are right at the end of the next street, if that was what he wanted," came back Mijnheer van Sas.

"Did he say anything else?" asked the tax collector, blowing out thick clouds of cigar smoke. "He didn't say another word," Van Sas shook his head, "but he seemed in a desperate hurry. There must be something serious brewing."

"Nonsense," broke in another man, the principal of the high school, "nonsense, they've got to invent something urgent from time to time in the army to keep all those boys from growing too fat and lazy. I remember when I served with the infantry in Breda—let us see now, that must be a full twenty-five years ago—we were on maneuvers and the division had hit the hay at nine, when all at once at midnight, toot-toot-toot, all the bugles go blaring, and we are roused out of bed. Mind you, twenty thousand men! Packs on! Every company falling in! The wagon trains wheeling in position! A general alarm! And what do you think had happened? Ha, ha," the principal laughed at the thought of that night. "I tell you what had happened: a farmer's wife had tripped over a rat in the dark in the back yard of her home and had broken her leg. That's what all that fuss was about. The soldier quartered in her house was a bugler, and he had sounded the alarm. Twenty thousand men rushed to arms. Even the officers of the general staff came galloping along the dike. Man alive, was that a night! We were made to march and countermarch till dawn."

All the gentlemen smiled at the principal's story and started to stroll down the street.

"Eh, what's that?" called out Mijnheer van Sas. "Lights in the town hall at half-past ten in the evening! Now

surely the world is coming to an end. And in the Burgomaster's chambers, too! I wonder if it could be a burglar.
No," he corrected himself at once, "it is not a burglar,
for here goes the good Burgomaster himself. . . ."

"Good evening, Mijnheer Verwey!" someone called
out to the Mayor. "What brings you out so late? Nothing serious, I hope?"

"Gentlemen," said the Burgomaster, as he stopped to
wipe the perspiration from his forehead, "gentlemen, the
situation is very serious. It is grave. It has not been so
grave in a hundred years." With these words he rushed
up the steps of the town hall and disappeared inside,
leaving the small group of lecturegoers speechless with
amazement.

Again the sound of a roaring motor was coming up the
street. Another dispatch rider whizzed by. And now
the call of bugles could be heard from the direction of the
barracks.

"That's the reveille and the fall-in signal," said Van
der Plank. Lights began to appear in many windows.
Citizens peered out into the darkened streets. Others
appeared in the doorways of their homes. One of the
town councilors, Dr. Tiegel, came riding down High
Street on his bicycle.

"What is it, Doctor? Where are you heading for?" the
principal called out.

"I am joining the Burgomaster. The Germans are
moving at dawn. Holland will have to fight!"

"That Jew," said Mijnheer van der Plank, "always
exaggerates. I'm going to bed. *Het zal wel losloopen met
die Duitschers.* It won't be that bad with those Germans.
Hitler knows full well, as the Queen once told Kaiser
Wilhelm, that we have seven feet of water for Prussia's

six-foot grenadiers. Just think of it, what can they do with their heavy tanks in our mud? It stands to reason that they'll get stuck after the first hundred yards, with this rain we had this afternoon, too. No, Adolf Hitler will think twice before he sends his *Wehrmacht* into our polders. It would mean disaster. Our soldiers would take them under fire the moment they get bogged down. Then what? The English would be landing in Rotterdam and Flushing and IJmuiden and at a dozen other points before we were twenty-four hours older. The French would come marching up through Belgium, and Mijnheer Hitler's bluff would have been called effectively—yes, most effectively." He laughed a little nervously, for none of his companions replied.

"You forget the German air fleet," remarked Mijnheer van Sas after a while.

"The German air fleet?" resumed Mijnheer van der Plank, as if he heard the word for the first time. "No, I do not forget the German air fleet. But let me tell you, Van Sas: no country can be conquered from the air. It is the infantry that has to do the trick, today as in the days of Napoleon. There is nothing new under the sun. Why," he said, assuming a tone of authoritative finality, "what could the bombers of General Franco do against those Red ragamuffins in Madrid? Do you remember? Nothing, I tell you," he went on answering his own question, "absolutely nothing. For two years Franco hurled against Madrid everything Mussolini and Hitler could pass on to him. But it was the infantry, the Moors, if you please, who had to go in there with the cold steel in the end and put an end to the Bolshevik masquerade."

"You forget Guernica," interrupted Mijnheer van Sas again.

"Guernica? Guernica?" Mijnheer van der Plank returned with evident irritation. "Why do you always speak of Guernica? What did happen in Guernica? Permit me to tell you what happened there: the Reds bombed their own people. That's what happened at Guernica. I have that on the authority of that German lecturer we had here two or three years ago."

"And Warsaw then?" came back Mijnheer van Sas. "Wasn't that leveled to the ground?"

"You are now talking of a less than half-civilized country," Mijnheer van der Plank returned. "Of course, the Germans dealt vigorously with the Poles. But please, do not overlook the fact that the Poles are Slavs and that there is an undying hatred between Teutons and Slavs. Here in Holland it's quite different. We are a kindred people. The Germans would not dare to proceed against us in the way they dealt with the Poles. It would outrage the conscience of the world. America and Roosevelt would never stand for it. And Hitler knows it. . . . No, I'm not in the least perturbed," he chuckled. "What's going on tonight is just another movement of troops near our borders to exercise some pressure on the British and French. That's all there is to it. I'm going to bed. It's late enough. Tomorrow is the tenth of May, and I will have a busy time sending out tax notices. . . ."

At six o'clock in the morning the Borgstorm began to toll. The Borgstorm is the thundering peal that is tolled by Roelant, which is the heaviest bell in St. John's tower. It is rung only when the country is in danger. Other, lighter bells ring out when there is a fire or a ship in distress on the river in a winter tempest. None of the living had ever heard the Borgstorm toll before. It had not rung since the Belgian uprising in 1830. Not a little perturbed, the bell ringer had asked the Burgomaster that morning if he really should start the twenty-ton bell in motion. The man was afraid that the old tower would not support the vibrations.

"Let Roelant ring the Borgstorm!" said the Burgomaster imperatively, "and keep ringing him until all the villages in the neighborhood have taken up the tolling." And so the Borgstrom tolled, dolefully, with heavy basso voice, which woke up the little children and brought the entire population into the streets. The Burgomaster spoke from the steps of the town hall at seven. "Burghers," he said, "the Germans have crossed the frontiers of our country. They are streaming into the provinces of Groningen, Overijssel, Drenthe, Gelderland, Brabant, and Limburg. Two days ago they gave us a solemn assurance that they would respect the neutrality of these Netherlands. This morning they broke that pledge. . . . Fighting has started. Our men are resisting heroically. . . . The government will keep us informed by radio. The English are surely coming to our help. . . . May God protect Holland! . . ."

Some truck farmers left the town in the early morning to go to their accustomed task in the fields outside the walls, but for the rest all business in Gorcum came to an abrupt standstill. The schools were open, but very few of the children turned up. Most of the families who owned radio receiving sets remained indoors, clustered around their instruments, listening to the government's news broadcasts, which came at half-hour intervals. At the town hall the council had gone into permanent session.

Burgomaster Verwey was expecting word from The

Hague before giving the order for the town's evacuation. Ever since the war of 1914-18, a plan lay ready in the secret archives whereby the inhabitants of Gorcum were to be evacuated en masse to the province of Zeeland. For Gorcum, with its antiquated earthen walls and moats and with its outlying circle of forts, was one of the key positions in the so-called Water Line defense. When news came in the early morning of May 10 that after the violation of the German borders the Dutch troops had immediately begun to fall back, this did come not altogether as a surprise to the people. Every schoolboy knew that the field army stationed in the outlying provinces was merely to fight a delaying action of a few days until the dikes could be opened and the defense of the important inner provinces brought in readiness. As soon as that was done, the people knew there would be an inundated area some forty miles wide in front of Gorcum, Utrecht, and Amsterdam, confronting the invader and baffling his advance as effectively as the flooded areas on the Yser had held back the Kaiser's armies in 1914 in their drive through Belgium toward the Channel ports. An invasion would therefore become, so most people thought, a race between the German armies and the Dutch engineering units charged with blowing up the dikes. On the other hand, if the Germans could advance fast enough to prevent the demolition of the dike system, then it was all up with Holland. This they also knew.

At ten o'clock, that morning of the tenth, the people of Gorcum knew that their country's air force no longer existed. The first concern of the Germans had been to destroy the airdromes and to blast the machines on the ground. The first blow had been successfully carried out during the early hours after dawn. Even so, the Dutch army was still intact and it was now, so the government radio announced, resisting every inch of the ground.

By eleven o'clock the town of Gorcum, itself over a hundred miles from the nearest fighting, was thrown into confusion. A boy by the name of Hendrik Wats was walking along the canal that bisects the city when he saw the hatches of two of the flat-bottomed river ships tied up there open and several helmeted figures emerge. At first he took the men to be Dutch soldiers, but as he listened to the commands of an officer who, revolver in hand, took up a position near the gangplank, the boy realized that they were Germans. He started to run away, but the officer called him back. Hendrik turned around, taking cover behind one of the thick oak trees that line the quay. The officer called again and then fired his revolver. Then Hendrik Wats ran for all he was worth. He ran two or three blocks and then bumped into old Hootse, a retired cake baker, who was leisurely pacing up and down before his house taking the morning air.

"Mijnheer Hootse," the boy cried, out of breath, "I've seen the Germans. They're over there," he pointed backward, "coming out of those ships.

"Don't be silly, boy," said Hootse, "the Germans are still far away. . . ."

"But, Mijnheer Hootse, I heard them talk, and one of them fired a shot at me. . . ."

"Boy, don't stand there lying to me," said the cake baker severely. "There is a place for liars in hell. . . ."

"See," said the boy, "they're coming this way. Those men walking between the trees," he pointed in the direction whence he had run. "They're German soldiers. I'm afraid!"

"They're not soldiers, boy," Hootse said again reassuringly. "I see two girls, but no soldiers. You are wrong. Look, those girls are not afraid. You ought to be ashamed of yourself. A Dutch boy afraid! What would Michel de Ruyter say of you now, or the Prince of Orange. . . ." But Hendrik Wats was gone.

Two girls walked by. Mijnheer Hootse knew them well by sight. He had often seen them pass his house. They were maids, he knew: one served in the household of Mijnheer van Andel, the grain merchant; the other was in the service of Mevrouw Fernhout, the lawyer's wife. Both were fine girls, blonde and lithe, well made, good to look at. The cake baker allowed his eyes to follow the two maids with evident relish. He had an eye for such things. . . .

But what was this? What? Was that a soldier coming there, walking along the quay? And what was the man carrying? Was that a machine gun? Mijnheer Hootse had never seen such things in his life. When he had served in the army, they did not have machine guns. "Yes, that is a soldier," he muttered to himself. "No mistake about that. By God, there is another one, and a third, and a fourth." Suddenly a young man darted from behind a tree, revolver in hand. Hootse was standing on the stoop of his house.

"Get into your house," the boy snapped at Hootse. "*Schnell!* Quick!" The cake baker almost fell backward. He jumped inside, slammed the door, and drew the bolts. He stood behind the door and opened the spyhole. There he was: the man with the revolver. No doubt about it. The Wats boy had been right. "What now?" Hootse had his eyes glued to the spyhole. "Well, I will be damned," he muttered again. "Those two maids! There they stand, at the bridge. They've something to do with those soldiers. Look," he said to himself, "one of the girls is waving her hand to that scoundrel who pointed his gun at me. Those damned bitches! But they're German, too, of course. Every well-to-do family has a German maid. *Donders nog toe,* Dutch girls were not good enough!" He took one more look. "My God, the quay is full of German soldiers," he called out. "What is that rogue doing now standing on the other fellow's shoulder? My God in heaven, they're cutting the telephone lines! Heavens above! I wish I had my old rifle now. . . ."

Mijnheer Hootse walked rapidly through his house into the garden. He crossed the small plot of land, opened a door in the stone wall, stole into an alley between two rows of small gardens, and then ran. In five minutes he was panting up the steps of the town hall. He burst into the council chamber. "Burgomaster!" he blurted out. "Where is the Burgomaster?"

"His worship is having a cup of coffee at the club," said the Councilman Hakkert to him. "Why are you so excited?"

"My God, man!" panted Hootse. "The Germans are in town!"

"In which town?" asked Hakkert.

"In this town, by God, here in Gorcum!"

"Hootse, dear fellow, if I did not know you to be a teetotaler, I would say that you are drunk. Go home, my good man. You were up too early this morning. The events of the last few days have upset your nerves. Go home and have a good sleep. Go now, we're too busy here. . . ."

"But I can't go home, my street is full of Germans," protested Hootse.

While they were speaking, another citizen burst into the doorway. "Town is full of Germans," he cried. "They're coming out of the ships moored at the quays. German maidservants are directing them. They have taken the River Shipping Exchange Building. Others are hammering at the prison gates. A whole company is on the way to the guardhouse right opposite this town hall. Give me a gun. Let me get at them!"

"Now, what's all this? Why this commotion?" came the voice of the Burgomaster, who had just returned from his cup of coffee.

"These citizens say," explained Councilman Hakkert, "that the streets are full of Germans."

"Full of Germans? Why, the Germans are miles and miles away," shouted the Mayor. "You are the victims of optical illusions, or of drink, citizens."

"The Germans are in Gorcum!" screamed Hootse.

"The Germans don't drop from the sky!" roared the Mayor. . . .

But here was Cornelius Meurs, the policeman. He saluted the Burgomaster humbly. "It's true, Mijnheer the Burgomaster," he said. "They are here. They are in the streets. My colleague Van Pelt has been killed. Others have fallen. There is severe fighting going on at the prison. The fishermen of the Visschersdyk [one of the slum quarters of Gorcum] went at the Germans with knives. . . ."

"My God," exclaimed the Burgomaster, "telephone the military."

"The lines are cut all over town," the policeman said. "There are Germans at the town gates."

"But how did they get there?" asked the Mayor.

"They are dropping from the sky in parachutes," said

the policeman. "The sky is full of floating parachutes above the road to Dordrecht. . . ."

Another citizen came in. "Burgomaster," he said calmly, "two German airplanes have landed on the parade ground."

"On the parade ground, right between the army barracks?" asked the Mayor in amazement.

"Right there!"

"But, but . . ." faltered the Mayor, "the troops, our soldiers, what?"

"Our soldiers rushed the airplanes but were cut down by machine-gun fire. That's the first who approached the planes. . . . Then the Germans came out of the planes and tried to enter the barracks. But by that time the general alarm had been sounded. Hundreds of our boys stormed the Germans with the bayonet. . . . The Germans . . ."

"Yes," gasped the Mayor, "what then?"

"Our men would have killed them all, had it not been . . ."

"Had it not been for what?"

"Had it not been," continued the citizen quietly, "that the Germans received reinforcements. A whole battalion of them came riding through the back streets on sidecars."

"On sidecars? How did they get through the gates?" asked the Mayor again.

"They did not come through the gates," resumed the citizen. "They found those sidecars ready for them in the River Shipping Exchange Building!"

"Schaeffer!" exclaimed the Burgomaster. "My God, that's Hans Schaeffer's work! He has been president of the Shipping Exchange for years. He's a member of the

Chamber of Commerce. A Dutch citizen, member of this council. . . . His brother Friedrich is director of the Rural Loan Bank. . . . I played whist with him at my house only last night. . . . My God! What next?" He sank down on a chair, clasping his hands before his eyes.

"Friedrich Schaeffer, the banker, was out early this morning," said one citizen. "I saw him strolling by the river. He returned by way of Toll Street. His house, as your worship knows, has a garden abutting on the arsenal."

"Yes!" screamed the Burgomaster.

"The arsenal is on fire," said the citizen.

The Burgomaster jumped up and rushed over to the window. He turned the curtain aside and looked in the direction of Toll Street. A thick pillar of black smoke rose from that district.

Dr. Tiegel, the councilman, came into the room. "It's the same everywhere," he said. "In Rotterdam German soldiers poured out of ships moored in the harbor at dawn this morning and occupied the Meuse Station and the Wittehuis [the only skyscraper in Holland]," he said with a wry smile. "They found the top stories of the Wittehuis stocked with machine guns. They were guided to those places by German residents of Rotterdam. I just heard over the radio that the head of the German Chamber of Commerce in Rotterdam has been arrested. He seems to have been in charge of guiding the invaders to the hidden stocks of armaments. . . ."

Dutch soldiers interrupted the councilors and citizens. They had entered the town hall by the rear door. One of their officers requested the Burgomaster to evacuate his chambers and all the rooms looking on the square at once.

"They are in the guardhouse," he said curtly, referring to a medieval building that stood opposite the town hall. "And," added the soldier, "we are going to blast them out!" Infantrymen were now pouring into all the rooms. The clatter of breaking glass was heard and soon every window had its machine-gun nozzle pointed in the direction of the guardhouse.

The firing lasted all afternoon and through the night. In the morning the Dutch troops stormed the guardhouse and took it at the point of the bayonet. Good news came also from near-by villages. The squads of parachutists who had dropped at Hardinxvelt and Werkendam, near the great railway bridge of Sliedrecht, had been rounded up or destroyed. Those who had landed by airplane in Gorcum's barracks square had been annihilated, while the enemy detachment that had seized the prison had also been overpowered.

Gorcum was free of Germans, but elsewhere in Holland the night had favored the enemy. In Rotterdam they had occupied the island in the Meuse and had crossed to the right bank. In Dordrecht and its vicinity heavy fighting was taking place between Dutch troops hastily brought back from the front lines and airborne German detachments. In the border regions, the Dutch army was falling back steadily under the onslaught of the Panzer divisions. The pride with which the first reports of the army's resistance were received soon changed to anguish as it became clear that the greatest heroism was of no avail against the avalanche of fire and steel that bore down on the outer provinces. In eastern Utrecht the Royal Guard had thrown itself into a counter-attack and had forced the Germans back twelve miles. Two hours later the brigade had left eighty per cent of its effectives on the field when subjected to a merciless bombardment by the *Luftwaffe*. Six infantry regiments in Gelderland, rather than retreat an inch, had preferred annihilation on the spot. From every corner of the kingdom came word of resistance that astonished even the Germans. But what was the good of it? The reinforcements did not come. The British fleet remained out of sight. Near Maastricht, in the southernmost part of the kingdom, the Germans had crossed the Meuse and were rushing their mechanized columns into Belgium to drive a wedge between the Belgian and Dutch armies, or rather, to prevent them from effecting a juncture.

There was no more sleep for the Gorcummers. Word had come that towns far behind the actual firing line, such as near-by Zalt-Bommel and Gouda, after cleaning up the first wave of parachutists, had nevertheless fallen to the enemy in a second attack, which had taken place in the dead of night. Because the troops of the garrison were urgently needed at the front and even raw recruits were being thrown into battle in an attempt to stem the enemy's lightning advance, the watch for new waves of parachutists had to be entrusted to a hastily improvised civic guard. These men, who were drawn from all classes of the population, took up positions on the town walls, on the roofs of the churches, on the post office, at the waterworks, and in what remained of the arsenal. To prevent an eventual charge from being preferred by the Germans that these vigilantes had operated as snipers, it was decided to leave them unarmed. And although it was realized that this measure would place the men in an embarrassing predicament if they actually should come face to face with heavily armed parachutists, each member of the civilian watch was carefully instructed where to report and how to signal the first reappearance of danger.

The first night passed without an incident in Gorcum itself, but the news from the front and from The Hague and Rotterdam continued to grow steadily worse. Reports that German airplanes were systematically machine-gunning the streets of The Hague caused less anxiety than information about the battle raging in the streets of Rotterdam. There the entire Marine Corps was hurling itself in futile attacks against the positions occupied by the Germans. Reinforcements for the Nazis were continually arriving by air and the area of German occupation was extending slowly.

The radio announced that while a battalion of marines and a company of sappers were being drawn up in one of the city's parks on the shore of one of Rotterdam's many inner waterways, and just when the men were receiving final instructions from their officers, they had been raked by a burst of machine-gun fire from a Swedish steamer quietly riding at anchor a short way from the shore. Suddenly the ship's portholes had opened, and from a dozen apertures the *rattlers* had started to spew death.

When news of this treacherous incident reached Gorcum, the indignation of the citizens knew no bounds. "This isn't war they're waging on us," said Ary Stam, a giant fisherman, sometimes called Ary the Devil by his neighbors because of his habit of terrorizing the whole neighborhood when on a drinking-bout. "This is not war, this is vile trickery! Who can guarantee that there are no German sharpshooters hidden in those fine houses on High Street. There are Germans in Gorcum. One of them is that banker Schaeffer, who set the arsenal on fire and then flew the coop. Another one is that Baron who runs a life-insurance agency, Von Krass is his name. There are German engineers at the ship wharf near town. Let's get them and put them in security before they start more damage here."

Ary was speaking to his neighbors, all of them fishermen or fishmongers who lived in a quarter of the town, a veritable slum ghetto, near the Dalem Gate. He may have been drinking heavily, as was his wont, and was probably in that phenomenal fighting mood which had so often landed him in jail. "Ary," said his neighbors, who tried to calm him, "Ary, those Germans in Gorcum are protected persons. They sit in the club and hobnob with the rich, we can't do anything against them. It will get us into trouble with the authorities. Moreover, they are naturalized citizens. Before the law they are as Dutch as you are. It would be cowardly to go and get them. They are unarmed and helpless. . . ."

"That's just what I want to see," Ary shouted. "I want to see if they are unarmed. I don't trust any German after this. I won't trust them, do you hear me," he cried out angrily, "no matter how highly placed and respectable they are. There are Germans in The Hague, too, whom I don't trust!"

"Ary," called out his wife, who stood in the crowd that had gathered around the fisherman. "Ary, shut your big mouth! Don't you dare say anything more. We know whom you mean when you talk about the Germans in The Hague. Shut up, I tell you, or I will . . ."

"Every German should be investigated," Ary Stam shouted, not paying any attention to his wife's threats. "I say, let's go and get them before they get us," he declared, drawing a bottle from his pocket and taking a big swallow of raw gin.

"You'll get a bullet in your backside from the police if you do anything rash," Piet de Bot, another notorious member of the neighborhood's gang, shouted at Ary. "You aren't the law. You can't do what you like. Go and try it, get those Germans, and you will see what happens."

But Ary would not listen to reason. "I have my knife," he said, drawing a wicked-looking curved blade from his pocket. "I've sliced open thousands of salmons and sturgeons in my day. I'd just like to try it on one German. I just want to see if their blood is red, that's all."

With those words he walked off, followed by a crowd of his cronies, the gang that always stood by his side in street battles with fishers from another street and with the police.

On the way to Baron von Krass' residence, those men must have forgotten the errand upon which they set out. They must have stopped at one of the numerous drinking dives in the neighborhood and changed their plans, for they were found half an hour later battering in the door of a man named Otto Glatzker, a barber, who had settled in Gorcum at the time of the inflation in Germany. After entering the house, they found Glatzker crouched in a cupboard, alternately weeping and whimpering that he had been naturalized, that he was a loyal subject of the Queen.

But Ary Stam cut him short: "Where were you the day before yesterday when those umbrella bastards dropped into Gorcum to murder us? I did not see you with us when we butchered them at the prison! Come on, where were you, Glatzker?" While he spoke Ary was caressing that ugly knife of his. Others held the frightened barber. Then Ary gave the order to take Glatzker to the Dalem Gate, a dilapidated and half ruined relic of the Middle Ages, the upstairs part of which the fishers used for drying their nets.

"We're going to round them all up," Ary said, "and at the sight of the first umbrella bastard coming down into our streets, it's going to be the night of the long knife for you, Glatzker."

But on the way to the Dalem Gate, the fishermen and their prisoner ran into Kees Boon and Jan Trouw. Kees Boon was a smith, a giant as big as Ary Stam, who walked with a springing step and an inner fortitude. He always went bareheaded. He was a most singular person: though the son of extremely poor parents (his father had been employed at a livery stable), he had acquired a liberal education by omniverous reading. He wrote pieces for such radical newspapers as *Bevrijding* (Liberation) and *De Wapens Neer* (Down Your Arms). From time to time he also sent a contribution of poetry to the local press. Everybody remembered his piece about the lonesomeness of the swans just outside the Arkel Gate, whose pond had been filled up with sand and mud so that a cement factory could be built on the site. Or that piece about the widowed young mother who sewed clothes at night in the feeble gleam of a poor oil lamp and who had thrown herself out of the window because she had no money with which to buy cherries for her sick child, when a vendor passed by outside calling out his wares. That was Kees Boon, a poet and a Socialist.

Jan Trouw was Kees Boon's friend. Trouw was a lay preacher for a sect known as the Darbists, but he was a follower of Tolstoy and a proponent of nonviolence as well. Trouw worked as a house painter on weekdays. On Saturday nights and on Sundays he preached in a small hall located in the worst part of town. When I say the worst part, I mean the poorest, a district inhabited by fishers and their families, who had never worn leather shoes in their lives, who died like rats of tuberculosis, and who always bred more starvelings. It was to those people that Jan Trouw preached the Gospel. I knew him well, for he had been employed by my Uncle Kees, when we were both young, to mix his paints and to keep his studio in order. I do not think I have ever met a more gentle and sweet soul. Uncle Kees used to say of Jan Trouw with a Biblical quotation: "Behold an Israelite indeed, in whom is no guile!"

Boon and Trouw seemed to have learnt that day what was up, for they met the crowd of fishers, most of them staggering drunk, with Ary Stam at their head, near the Dalem Gate.

The two friends stood still in the middle of Dalem Street, facing the oncoming crowd of shouting, knife-brandishing fishers. Ary Stam was in the lead, singing with a mighty bellow that song about the Water Beggars, who in 1572 had captured the town of Brill from the Spaniards. Behind him came two fishers, who held between them the captive German, who was bleeding from the nose and mouth.

"Stop!" cried Kees Boon. "What do you men intend to do?"

"Get out of our way, poet," sneered the drunken Ary. "This is nothing of your damn business. You stick to your books and your smithy and see if you can make a living for your brats."

"I demand an answer," said Boon. "What are you doing with this man?" he pointed at the German barber, whose torn shirt was covered with blood and dirt.

"If you must know, *mijnheer de dichter,*" said Ary in a whining voice, "we're going to string him up in the Dalem Gate and when he hangs I am going to cut his. . . ."

"Coward!" said Boon. "You are all cowards," he turned to the fishers, "you are not worthy of the name of men."

"We are Dutchmen," screamed back Ary Stam. "We are defending our country against these German traitors."

"You are Dutch cowards then," came back Boon. "You are not men!"

"If you say that again, I will stick my knife into your guts!"

For answer the smith knocked the fisher down with one blow of his iron fist. Ary's knife went flying onto the cobblestones. Boon picked it up. But the infuriated fisher, taking off his wooden shoes, rose quickly and came for the smith with a lump of wood held over his fists like a pair of awkward, clumsy boxing gloves.

But now it was the turn of Jan Trouw to intervene. "Brothers, brothers," he called out. "Let's not fight each other. We don't know what hangs over our heads. . . . Rotterdam has just been bombed. Thirty thousand men and women and children of our people have died this afternoon in one terrible half-hour. Think of it, Ary, brother, human beings are being slaughtered like animals. For what? For markets! For the sake of profits in the coffers of the rich! Shall we do the same? To kill is so easy, Ary! To make men live and love and laugh in the sun, that is what Jesus wanted. To see little children grow up. . . ."

"Shut up about your Jesus!" cried out Piet de Bot,

who was one of the men holding the captive Glatzker. "We've heard enough of him."

"Shut up yourself," Ary turned around in sudden anger. "Jesus is one of us. Leave Jesus out of this. . . ."

"That's right, Ary, He is one of us," said Trouw. "He is our friend, the friend of fishers and . . ."

"But these Germans are murdering our kind," Ary interrupted.

"Does that mean that we should do the same to them? Let us show them that we are Christians, Ary, the friends of Jesus. Would Jesus approve of it if we hanged this man? Let him go home to his wife and children. Let one man go home to his children. Thousands of others will not go home any more. . . . Let us not stain our hands with blood."

The fishers let Glatzker go. But as the barber scampered off, he called back in his vilely accented Dutch: "I'll lodge complaint against all of you!" At which the whole crowd laughed heartily.

In the night that followed, Gorcum was occupied.

Although the German authorities had appealed to the people in the occupied areas to co-operate with them in trying to restore order as quickly as possible, not a single one of Gorcum's inhabitants had ventured outdoors during the first forty-eight hours after the town's investment. Many had hid in attics and in cellars, fearfully listening to the rumble of the wheels of war, the steady, almost endless rhythmic tramp of heavily shod feet in the streets and the roar of propellers in the sky. The rumor had flown about that the invader was sure to retaliate in a most cruel fashion for the Dutch army's stubborn resistance and that he would show himself especially severe in cases where civilians had impetuously rushed into the fray, as had occurred in Gorcum. It was held more than likely that the ghastly fate of Rotterdam was to be meted out to several other communities in the Netherlands.

Assurances coming over the German-controlled radio that the Dutch people had nothing more to fear, now that the danger of British intervention was forever removed, were not taken at their face value. The inhabitants of Gorcum fully expected the army of occupation to launch a systematic campaign of destruction and terror as soon as actual fighting stopped in that last corner of Zeeland Province, where the army held out so heroically and so long.

It was through the children that the inhabitants first regained something of their composure and peace of mind. The youngsters would walk out of the houses, quite shy, of course, and even turning their eyes away from the strangers they saw in the streets. But finally some of them would stand still, fascinated by all the unwonted bustle and the color and the animation in the streets, which was as interesting to see as the moving in of the heavy circus vans that came once a year to Gorcum at the time of the kermis. German soldiers would make friendly gestures to the youngsters, call them over, ask them their names, or give them candy. Soon the shyness would vanish and in the end the soldiers and the children would make friends. Then the parents, too, would take a peep outdoors. Father would stand in the doorway or saunter up the street a short way, his hands in his pockets, as if he were not concerned about anything in the world, looking at the sky or casually filling his pipe. Then, perhaps, he would cast a glance at a piece of artillery and at the German soldiers cleaning it. And one of the soldiers

would run forward and hold a match for him, and Father
would say: *"Nein, danke schön,"* at first, but the soldiers
would not grow angry in the least. I mean they would
not take Father's refusal as an insult, but go about their
work as if nothing had happened. In this and similar
ways, one citizen after another would be reassured that
no immediate danger was threatening and that it was
quite safe to walk about. People would say that you
could not blame those soldiers for anything, that they
had merely carried out orders, that they were quite
human and did not even behave arrogantly, as victors
are expected to do. The news got around that the strange
soldiers were behaving quite correctly, in friendly fashion
even.

One heard, for instance, that a German soldier had
politely rung the doorbell and had asked for a pail of
water. Again, another boy had come to ask if he could
warm some coffee on the stove in the kitchen and had told
the lady of the house that his father was a grocer over in
Düsseldorf, even showing her photographs of his father,
his mother, and his little sister, quite decent-looking
"burgher"-people too, they had seemed to be, judging by
the pictures. His father's grocery store looked exactly
like Van Maaren's store, nothing strange or outlandish
about it. And then the German boy had played with the
dog, and when the lady had given him some sugar for his
coffee, he had thanked her most profusely—poor boy,
he probably had not tasted sugar for years—and had offered in return a metal cigarette case that he had made
himself from a Polish shellcase.

It was soon remarked that those German boys greeted
elderly folks first with a deferential salute and kindly
wished them the time of day. All that was astonishing

really, and a great relief, too. The people had expected
an entirely different attitude on the part of the invader,
far more stern and harsh and irreconcilable. Before long
the streets crowded with citizens watching the goings-on
and inspecting the monstrous tanks and the other war
material parked in the squares, in front of the town hall,
by the side of the cathedral church, near the railway
station, and in a dozen other spots. The soldiers would
hold the door of a tank open or beckon a passing citizen
who showed interest to step up on the machine and look
inside. They were just like little children, those German
soldiers, proud of new toys. And then every German soldier seemed to have a camera and to be taking snapshots
of everything in sight, buildings, queer old shop signs,
children; some even took pictures of the fountain in the
main square, as if those rusty old nymphs at its base, with
their green mildewed eyes, were worth looking at, let
alone being photographed.

In the taverns and the taprooms, which had been the
first places to reopen, the German soldiers were no longer
sitting or standing alone in small isolated groups. They
would ask some loitering fisherman to sit down and have
a drink with them, and if he acepted they would say:
"Gesundheit!" and the Dutchman would answer: *"Ge-
zondheid!"* or he would say *"Prozit!"* to show that he
was not altogether ignorant of the world and that he knew
a word or two of German himself. And then all would
laugh and have another drink.

And so contact between the invaders and the townspeople was gradually established, so that on the ninth or
tenth day of the occupation, when a German regimental
band gave a concert in the market square, there were not
only German soldiers listening, but demobilized Dutch

soldiers as well, besides many civilians. And if you had looked about sharp on that occasion, you would have noticed, too, that some of the Dutch girls had begun to smile back at those yellow-haired Bavarian or Saxon farm boys in uniform, who strolled about in pairs and who looked for all the world like lads from the neighboring villages of Gelderland. And in the restaurants and other public places, men were getting into conversation with German officers, quite unintentionally sometimes, to be sure, for instance when they watched them play at billiards or at cards. And some went around saying that they had talked with the Germans about the war and about the Fuehrer and about the frightful things their *Luftwaffe* had done to Rotterdam, and the Gorcummers boasted that they had dared to rub it in about the coming invasion of England.

Yes, it was not long before you could hear some people say that it made very little difference to them who was sitting in The Hague, the former ministers or Seyss-Inquart, the new German Governor-General, adding that they had not seen or expected to see either the one or the other at any time. They said: "Well, why make so much fuss about the invasion? We were the weaker of the two—weren't we?—and England and France left us in the lurch. What else could you expect? We may be glad that no worse has befallen us. Holland isn't a paradise under the Germans, far from it. But they do pay for everything they buy, don't they? They behave in an exemplary fashion. What more can we expect? They've given orders that no man may be discharged from his position. Wasn't that a good measure? Was it so wonderful before the invasion? Come, own up to the truth now! Wasn't there a great deal of misery in Holland before the invasion? Wasn't everything run for the benefit and in the interest of a small clique of ladies and gentlemen with double names, the barons, counts and *jonkers* who ruled the roost from The Hague. Wasn't it about time that those people were shoved to a back seat? No, surely, it isn't a paradise yet. True enough, but do you find it worse than before?" That's the way some began to talk.

Others said: "If the Germans remain for fifty years, our people will be so thoroughly Germanized that they will feel insulted if you refer to them by their old nationality. Provided, that is, the Germans keep on behaving as they do at present."

The newspapers also began to sing a different tune. The Germans had not come to oppress the Dutch. On the contrary, the Dutch were Aryan brothers who were destined to play a high rôle in the new Europe. They would take their place by the side of their kinsmen of Germany and rule the world. It all depended on the Dutch themselves. If they co-operated and showed an understanding of what Germany was trying to accomplish in Europe, all would be well. If, on the other hand, the Dutch people kept on paying heed to the foolish messages that came through the air from England, if they really believed that poor battered England would some day send an army to chase the Germans away from the North Sea coast, they would be chasing a chimera. If they listened to the pleas from abroad to stage a revolt, they would be contributing to their own doom.

And then, the newspapers said, the people only needed to open their eyes to see what the Germans were doing. Did it augur ill, for instance, that a commission of civilian experts had arrived in Gorcum from somewhere in the Reich and was holding conferences with the president of

the Chamber of Commerce and that the small steel plant
of De Vries-Robbé outside the Arkel Gate was to be
greatly enlarged, that three thousand new men were to
find employment there, and that Looyen's wharf outside
the Chancellory Gate had received a big order for river
speedboats? Did not that mean that there would be jobs
for all, and to spare? Was it not a pleasant prospect to go
and see Berlin under the new scheme of cheap railway
fares, which allowed at least fifty persons per week from
Gorcum to travel to the Reich capital? How many of
those slum dwellers near the Dalem Gate and the Melk-
pad had ever seen The Hague, their own country's capital, in former days? How many? Except to some men
who had served their turn in the army in or around The
Hague, that city was almost a mythical, far away region
of glory and splendor. They had never seen it, nor had
they the hope or the means ever to see it.

Then the German military authorities turned the
doelen into a motion-picture theater, and so Gorcum had
at last a cinema house of its own, for the old hall was not
transformed only to entertain German soldiers. It was
thrown open to the general public. And strangest of all,
the Germans asked permission to use the old church of
the Huguenots in the Arkel Street, that fine building
with the sharp steeple which had slowly been falling to
ruins. It was to be repaired and refurnished, and Lutheran services were to be held in it. And the Gorcum people could scarcely believe their own ears when, passing
by on a Sunday morning, they heard a men's chorus in
that church sing Luther's old hymn: "A safe stronghold
our God is still," the hymn they themselves knew so well.
Now, what was wrong with all that?

In the course of the fighting in and around the prison,

where the German troops from the river barges had bar-
ricaded themselves and whence they were promptly dis-
lodged by the resolute action of the townsmen, there had
been killed a policeman by the name of Cornelius Meurs.
This Meurs had a brother named Gyse, a feeble-minded
individual who earned his livelihood by beating carpets
and begging pennies at the church door. Gyse was not
taller than the average boy of nine or ten, as I remember
well, but he had the torso and chest expansion of a giant,
while the strength of his hands was such that it had almost
become a byword in the community. I knew both the
Meurs boys well in my youth, for Cornelius had visited
the Bible school where I was a pupil myself for the better
part of seven years. Their family was extremely poor,
but at one time it had been among the best known in
all Holland. The ancestors of those two boys had been
bell casters, and till this day you can find the name of
one or the other of the Meurs artisans inscribed on the
bells of dozens of towns and villages in the southern part
of Holland.

Although the dwarflike Gyse did not go to school, it
must not be supposed that he was absent from our games.
Gyse followed his brother Cornelius wherever he went.
He accompanied him as far as the school door in the
morning and was waiting for him again when classes
were dismissed in the afternoon, winter or summer, rain
or shine. The two were inseparable. And this, I think,
for the very good reason that Cornelius was the only
human being who could understand his brother's speech,
which consisted of a variety of animal-like grunts and
groans pitched in different tones to express different
emotions.

In the sham battles that we waged in the forests of

reed along the Merwe River's edge far outside Gorcum's walls, Gyse Meurs served as our one-man supply column. He carried whatever you gave him to carry. But you could communicate to Gyse only through his brother Cornelius. If it became necessary to drag over some pieces of water-soaked driftwood from the shore to reinforce some castle or other we were building in that jungle of reed, Gyse was the man to go and bring it over. No load was too heavy for him. We would simply say to Cornelius: "Cor, tell Gyse to go and get that log we saw away back there by the water. Tell him now, for we need it." Then Cornelius would put his hand on his brother's shoulder, would look into his eyes, and would order him by means of the same kind of low growls his brother habitually emitted.

When Gyse was sixteen or so, just about the time when I left Gorcum, he was put to work as a lamplighter. He could be seen going through the streets towards sundown and carrying a long pole over his shoulder, and you could see him again around dawn going from post to post extinguishing the gas lamps. I do not know how he had come to lose this position, but at the time of the invasion he was no longer employed by the municipality. He seems to have been roaming the streets more or less idly, but never far, it appears, from his brother Cornelius the policeman.

The relationship between the two brothers had become even closer since the death of their parents and with the passage of years. They occupied a small cottage in some back alley. Of an evening Gyse could be seen sitting on the stone threshold, patiently waiting for his brother to come off duty. When he saw the familiar figure swing round the corner, Gyse would jump up, run as fast as his short legs could carry him, and happily throw his arms around his brother. Cornelius would stoop down to kiss the dwarf. Then, with Cornelius' hand resting on Gyse's shoulders and Gyse holding on to Cornelius' coat, the two would walk the rest of the way home together.

On the afternoon of the invasion, some neighbors brought the body of Cornelius Meurs back home on a pushcart. The dwarf was not in at the time, so the neighbors placed the body in the *bedstee,* a sort of cupboard in the wall that served the brothers as a sleeping place.

I do not think that anyone intended Gyse to go in there unwarned of his brother's death. But that is the way it happened. He came home, stumbled into the front room of the cottage, but was back in the alley in a minute, screaming out his grief in a frightened and pitiful voice. The neighbors tried to quiet him by patting him on the head and speaking kind and reassuring words to him, but nobody could really make it clear to the dwarf what had happened to his brother. He wailed like a possessed soul and kept it up for days. Only after the body had been removed and the funeral had taken place did he grow quiet again. He sat on the doorstep staring straight ahead or paced back and forth in front of the cottage, his hands clasped behind his back and his head bent on his chest, as if immersed in deep thought. By and by, however, he walked abroad again and once more made his appearance at the back doors of the homes where he had formerly been given small jobs to do.

As he resumed his wanderings through the town and saw the changes that had occurred—the blackened ruins of the arsenal were not far from his alley—and saw, above all, the many strangers in uniform, it must have dawned slowly upon him that there was some connection between these newcomers and the death of his brother.

I have a letter from Gorcum written since the German occupation, wherein the writer remarks that the only person to be annoyed unmistakably by the presence of the Germans was Gyse Meurs. He would walk up to a German soldier or officer, stand boldly in his path, shake his huge fists, and emit those strange, incomprehensible growls until he was frothing at the mouth. Some would be amused by the comical little man and simply pass on their way. Others, taking Gyse's actions perhaps as an affront to the dignity of the Third Prussian Regiment of Death's-Head Hussars, lately mechanized, would order him gruffly to be gone and perhaps administer a well-directed kick at the shuffling dwarf's posterior.

As these incidents grew more frequent, the burghers of Gorcum grew rather alarmed at Gyse's behavior and were on the alert to watch his movements. When they saw him advance toward a party of Germans, they would hastily intervene to divert his attention or kindly lead him off, lest in the end worse than a kick from a Prussian jack boot be his lot. There was no way of warning Gyse of the dangers he incurred by those manifestations of hatred for the conqueror. Appeals to reason would not have penetrated that somberly disturbed mind. Words made no impression on him. At the sight of a German uniform Gyse's eyes (I can well imagine from having seen him grow angry more than once as a boy) would first narrow down to mere slits and then open wide with the frenzied light of immense hatred. It was clear that the man would commit an outrage sooner or later, throw himself like a tiger on a German soldier if he would catch one alone and tear him to pieces with his amazingly strong hands. It became therefore imperative to watch Gyse constantly or to have him removed to some institution where he would be kept out of harm's way. If that had been done, a great calamity would have been avoided. It is also true that nobody could have predicted the horrible way the halfwit was to avenge his brother's death and the sorrow he was to bring on the community.

At one end of Gyse's alley, separated from the rows of humble cottages that made up the neighborhood and towering over it like some mighty castle, stood an old windmill. This structure was the equivalent of three stories high. It stood near a section of the town's earthen defense works. The wooden gallery that encircled its octagonal shape was about where the second story of an ordinary house would end. From that gallery one could look over the town and see the river to the point where it bends around Loevestein Castle. In my youth, I recall, the wings of this mill had become unsafe and had been removed. But it remained in use. When the doors of the mill stood open, you could see how it was operated by a blindfolded horse. The horse walked around in a circle of sawdust on the outside of a complicated system of creaking beams and crossbeams. These beams met prismlike in the center of the ground floor and there turned on a thick metal point as in the old-fashioned merry-go-rounds that were to be seen until a few years ago at the fairs of Flanders and Holland. But the millstones, which ground the corn, were invisible. You could hear them rolling about with thunderous rumble on the oaken floor above. It was a breath-taking experience to watch the mill in motion, and I, along with other boys, must have spent hours in fascinated observation of those wondrous and somewhat mysterious wheels within wheels.

For some reason, probably because the mill's outer gallery projected above the city walls and could be used as a military observation post, the Germans, a day or so after the occupation of Gorcum, requisitioned the building. Troops were quartered in it, and some of the men even slept between the giant millstones on that first story.

For days on end Gyse Meurs could be seen sitting on the grass of the earthen wall and watching the activities at the mill, the soldiers coming and going, the bread and supplies being delivered and all that. Nobody disturbed the half-witted dwarf. He did not come near enough to be in anybody's way, and the Germans soon grew accustomed to seeing him there, his knees drawn up level with his chin and staring at them as if mesmerized.

Curfew was at nine in the evening, and at ten the town was plunged in complete darkness. Civilian air-raid patrols and detachments of German soldiers thereafter walked through the streets and saw to it that no infractions of the black-out rules occurred. But none of these patrols visited the neighborhood of the old windmill. Had they done so and had they turned their electric torches in the direction of the grassy knolls of the defense works, they would have seen there a crouching figure cautiously moving about or just lying motionless for hours, his eyes glued on the door of the mill. For three weeks, night and day, Gyse Meurs never left his observation post. He was thoroughly familiarizing himself with the habits of the soldiers quartered in the place.

On the night of June 12 he struck, and his vengeance was something like Samson's last performance in the temple of Dagon of the Philistines. Around ten o'clock he saw the soldiers returning from the taverns in town and noticed that they were accompanied by women. He could hear their subdued, secret laughter as they walked up the cobblestoned pathway which led to the mill. No sooner did he hear the heavy oaken door slam shut than he crawled out of his hiding place. He then approached the mill with a long ladder, which he placed against the gallery. He climbed the ladder, scaled the railing of the gallery, and, moving stealthily forward, lifted himself to one of those narrow slits which served to admit the daylight in the upper story. What he saw inside apparently steeled him to carry out the rest of his design. Like a cat he slit down the ladder once more and raced for the door. He tried the latch. It opened. Gyse Meurs was inside the mill. It seemed that his eyes could penetrate the Stygian darkness of the wide room, for he ran with unfailing step around the machinery toward the small door that gave access to the narrow stairway leading upstairs. Noiselessly he slipped the heavy iron bolts into their locks—the German soldiers were locked in, except for the door upstairs that opened on the gallery. Again Gyse ran through the darkened mill room, went outside, and sped up the ladder.

On the gallery he took hold of the great metal wheel which, when the mill was still equipped with wings, had been used to set the hood or roof of the mill to the wind. With an effort that made him gasp, Gyse lifted the wheel and carried it to the side where the door was located and then wedged it tightly between the door and the railing of the narrow gallery. The wood creaked, but the dwarf worked on as if he had not heard anything. When he had the wheel in place, he lifted himself once more to one of the windows and looked inside. Almost at once he dropped back. One of the soldiers had seen something move against the glass of the ten-inch aperture in the wall and had walked over to look out. But Gyse was gone. He slid down the ladder and entered the dark mill room once more. For a moment he stood still to listen. He could hear footsteps upstairs and voices. One man was coming down the stairs. His feet could be heard stumbling uncertainly on the narrow wooden stairway.

Then Gyse seized hold of the wooden beams at the place where the horse used to be harnessed to the machinery and, planting his feet in the sawdust, heaved with all his might. It was as if the whole structure was about to crack. The machinery grated and creaked, but slowly it came into motion. Gyse kept on walking and pushing. Above his head he could hear the millstones go into motion and, above their rumble, the cries and shouts of the trapped soldiers. Faster and faster he walked, knowing perhaps that if he could come to a trot—that is, exceed the normal pace of a horse—the millstones would be torn loose from their moorings and go careening over the floor above. Whether he knew that this would happen or not, it did occur.

But what Gyse could not see was that an oil lamp was upset upstairs and that the burning oil was spreading over the floor, which was as dry as tinder. In five minutes the mill was a huge flaming torch that threw a ruddy glare on the water of the river and could be seen for miles around. By then the alarm had been given, and the volunteer fire department of Gorcum was on the way. Soldiers were hacking at the door with axes and picks but could not break it down. Burning timbers were falling from the gallery onto the fire fighters below. Finally, a hole was chopped in the door large enough to push one man through. Gyse saw him by the light of the burning woodwork of the ceiling and rushed forward. Before the dwarf's impact the German soldier went down like a sack with Gyse on top of him, throttling the life out of him with his strong fingers. Then the building crashed.

The bodies of thirteen German soldiers were removed from the ruins the next day, also the charred remains of two unrecognizable females. The German High Command, after a thorough examination of the building, reached the conclusion that the dwarf found with his fingers buried deep in the throat of the dead German soldier was responsible, but that he must have plotted with others. It was announced, therefore, that unless the citizens of Gorcum would come forward voluntarily and denounce the accomplices of Gyse Meurs, three citizens would have to pay with their lives for the crime committed against the German army.

Herr Hauptmann Baron Waldemar von Schwabenfels of the Third Prussian Regiment of Death's-Head Hussars, lately mechanized, was sitting in the board room of the orphan asylum. He had personally selected the stately old mansion, with its marble stairway and its high windows, to serve as military headquarters for the occupational forces in the fortress of Gorcum and its environs until the town hall, where everything was still upside down because of the fighting that had taken place there, could be repaired and put in order. On the large oaken table in front of Herr von Schwabenfels stood a gold-framed photograph of Adolf Hitler and a silver coffee set. He had lit a cigar and as he leaned back in a broad red-leather armchair, he raised his brightly polished boots to the table.

The new commander of Gorcum was no longer a young man. Upon first glance one would have put him down as fifty, though he must have been older. He wore the Iron Cross and some other decorations which showed that he had served under the Kaiser in the previous World War. He carried himself well. The recent campaign in Poland had reduced the corpulence that had come upon him in the years he had spent on his estate in East Prussia. The sun had bronzed his features and heightened the vividness of his blue eyes. A close-cropped mustache did not wholly hide his souvenir of Verdun— a livid scar across his upper lip where a piece of shrapnel had struck him. His men said of the *Hauptmann* that he was a good sort. He had a fatherly way with them, a circumstance attested by his kindly, slightly wrinkled face. His first word to Burgomaster Verwey of Gorcum, when he informed that gentleman of his deposition, had been rather in the way of a humble apology. "I beg your worship," he had said, "not to blame me for this rather violent irruption into your community. . . . I am only obeying orders. I assure you that I'd much rather be seeing how the peaches and plums are doing on my farm in Oels."

As he slumped back that June morning and blew out rings of smoke, Baron von Schwabenfels allowed his eyes to travel back and forth along a row of paintings on the wall before him. They were portraits of past regents and donors of the institution in which he had now taken up his abode; full-faced gentlemen in black cloth blouses with high ruff collars, wig-wearing dignitaries of the eighteenth century, and, finally, men in side whiskers and stiff black suits—a procession of Dutch faces and costumes representing four centuries both of change and continuity. He surveyed the pictures casually, but his eyes returned again and again to a Directoire water clock on the mantelpiece. On top of that clock were two metal figures in the costumes of Napoleonic grenadiers, with uplifted mallets in their hands. The Baron was waiting for the hour of ten, when the two mechanical grenadiers would beat out a tune on the musical bells and then, with a curious gesture of uplifted mallets that made them appear to be saluting the onlooker, switch around and beat out the strokes of the hour on a deeper-toned gong.

As he was anticipating the mechanical play, there was a knock on the door and in strode Herr Stantarttruppenfuehrer Erich Schwartz of the S.S., one of Himmler's Gestapo agents, who had been sent to Gorcum to reorganize civilian life. The Gestapo man saluted him with outstretched arm and said: *"Heil Hitler!"* Baron von Schwabenfels brought his right arm forward in response and sighed.

"Well, what is it, Schwartz?" he asked.

"I beg to report, *Herr Hauptmann,* that the shops will all be open this morning. The workers have returned to the wharf. The Jews have been assembled in their synagogue. But the schools remain closed until we have examined the teachers. I have ordered the confiscation of all the sugar in the town. We'll need an entire train for it. There are a thousand sacks of flour, too, and several carloads of canned fruit and vegetables and a good stock of cocoa. . . . And then, eh, *Herr Hauptmann,* Gestapo headquarters have ordered that fifty men are to be deported for the outrage at the mill and three to be executed. The execution will be at three this afternoon.

We think it best to have a public execution in order to set an example."

"Have it your own way, Schwartz," said the Baron. "You know what's best. By the way, has Lieutenant Schmidt come in? . . . Oh, there you are, Schmidt," the Baron exclaimed, jumping up from his chair, as a young officer came into the room. "I was just asking for you. You may go now, Schwartz," he added, turning to the Gestapo man. When Schwartz had left, Baron von Schwabenfels fell back into his chair.

"That cursed swine with his Jews and executions gives me the creeps, Manfred," he said. "I was just sizing up that clock on the mantelpiece when he came in. It's mine. I'm shipping it to Silesia. Did you say you wanted the chandelier in the hall? You'd better hurry and get it down. There is apt to be a Gestapo inspector here this afternoon. We're going to have an execution. Get everything packed before that bird arrives. By the way, did you get some good pictures?"

"Yes," laughed Lieutenant Schmidt, reaching for the cigarettes, "I think I have a line of ancestors down to the fourteenth century now. I picked them up in the museum."

"Good, good," beamed the Captain. "I hope you covered up your—ah—little loan."

"Oh, yes," came back the Lieutenant. "I had the vacant spots covered with photographs of him," he pointed to the Fuehrer's photograph on the table, "of him, and Clubfoot, and the Flying Pig."

"Excellent!" returned Captain von Schwabenfels. "Have the pictures put together with your lamp and my clocks, and we'll ship them all out this afternoon before those thieves of the Gestapo arrive. . . . By the way, any news from the front?"

"He went to France this morning!" replied the Lieutenant. "That means it will soon be over, I suppose," Captain von Schwabenfels said. "At least, let us hope so!"

Baron von Schwabenfels dreaded the hours that were to elapse before the execution. Not that he was plagued by any qualms of conscience. A crime had been committed against the German authority and the German army, and that crime was to be punished. If the Dutch would not indicate who the culprit was, that was their affair. In such cases the innocent had to suffer for the guilty. But he looked forward with nervous apprehension to what was to come before the actual shooting, which Lieutenant Schmidt was to supervise. That was all arranged.

The Baron knew from experience in Poland that, as military governor of a newly occupied community, he had to listen to the supplications for reprieve on the part of the relatives of the condemned men.

Why should he have to go through all that torture? It was the most futile gesture of this whole insane business of war, for it was decreed beforehand that, though advocates and relatives of the condemned were permitted to make representations, no mercy was to be shown. But maybe these Dutchmen won't ask for pity. Maybe they won't come whining and weeping like those horrible Polish priests and women he had been forced to hear in Kalisz last fall. He hoped the Dutch would not make him go through the same ordeal again. He hoped they would let the condemned go to their deaths without a whimper. Then Lieutenant Schmidt would have the pleasure alone. He could have it.

That boy Schmidt had a strong stomach. He came out of the S.A. ranks and had served as supervisor of a concentration camp. He had seen a thing or two. He would not weaken. Schmidt, the Baron thought, actually takes a delight in executions. Had he not finished off those Jews in Kattowitz with his own revolver? *Herr Gott Kreuz noch 'mal!* He had simply waded in their blood!

An orderly, who came to take the water clock away, informed Baron von Schwabenfels that a deputation of burghers was waiting in the antechamber.

"Men only?" asked the Captain.

"At your service, men only, *Herr Hauptmann!*" answered the man.

"Show them in!" he added. "I may as well go through with it!"

The delegation consisted of the pastors of the various Reformed churches and three Catholic priests. It was the first time that these men had ever appeared together anywhere. They filed in slowly. Baron von Schwabenfels noticed that not one of them bowed or clicked his heels. Suddenly the thought flashed through his mind that they might have come to murder him. Should he take out his revolver? That would look childish. But still, suppose they intended him harm? You could never be sure. These men were patriots, outraged patriots. They might be desperate. He was alone. The Baron rang the bell. An orderly appeared.

"Let the guard fall in here," he ordered, "and leave the door open. *Heil Hitler,*" he said, turning to the delegation. "What is it?" They did not answer his salutation. A hard crowd, he thought. It will be a long time before we make Germans and Nazis out of these brethren. They will be hard to break. But that is work for the Gestapo.

"These men are innocent," began the pastor who stood in front, without any preamble. "Is it part of your code to execute innocent men?"

"I do not owe you any explanation, *Herr Pfarrer*," said the Baron testily. "German soldiers have been killed in your community in a most atrocious, barbaric manner. There is to be punishment for that. If you can name the murderers, we may consent to a revision of the trial. I do not guarantee absolution for those now condemned. There is a bad spirit in your community, a spirit of opposition to the German army, most disgraceful and ungrateful. We came as brothers and liberators, and you received us as enemies. The Fuehrer had the best intentions toward Holland. He gave the German word of honor that no harm would come to your country if there were no resistance. You disregarded the German word. He guaranteed the safety of the dynasty. The dynasty fled. He came to bring you freedom from the English yoke, and what do we find: resistance everywhere, resistance with deadly weapons."

"I never saw an Englishman in all my life," said the pastor curtly.

"That may be true, *Herr Pfarrer*, but the English exercised an occult control over The Netherlands, the English and the Jews. The Fuehrer could no longer permit that." The Baron looked at the gold-framed photograph of Adolf Hitler and wondered if he was saying the right thing. "No man or woman of the German race in this whole world is going to remain in the power of Jews. Neither here, nor in England, nor anywhere in the world. That is Germany's mission. The last century has been the age of the Jews. The next thousand years will be the German epoch. Germany is at last coming into its own. For hundreds of years we Europeans—*was sage ich?*—we Germanic brother peoples, have been kept fighting each other by England. That is the greatest scandal of history. But it is now ended. . . ."

"When did we ever fight before?" asked the pastor dryly. "We, the Dutch and the Germans, or the Germans and the Scandinavians, except at the time of the Reformation, which surely had nothing to do with England?"

"*Herr Pfarrer,* let us not quibble," came back the Baron. "Germany is victorious, and Germany's will is to rule the Continent now!"

"Quite right," replied the pastor. "But if we are to be brothers, Germanic brothers, as you say, why not deal with us in a more brotherly fashion. Why not spare the lives of the three unfortunate men, who are as blameless of the outrage as I myself or you, *Herr Hauptmann.* . . ."

"You only have to name the culprit's accomplices, and we will surely reconsider our decision."

"We cannot name accomplices when there weren't any," said the pastor. "There are no accomplices, and the men you condemned are surely innocent. We give you our sacred word as Dutchmen," the pastor pleaded.

"*Meine Herren,* the condemned men must die for the good of Holland.

"For the Holland of the future, *Herr Hauptmann.*"

"As you wish, *Herr Pfarrer,*" returned the Baron. "I do not quarrel about words. Facts alone count with us."

The selection of the persons to be executed in retaliation for the dwarf's insensate revenge had been left to the discretion of the Gestapo's representative in Gorcum, Parteigenosse Erich Schwartz. This individual, a tall cadaverous type who had earned his spurs in the early days of the Nazi régime by his iron nerve in administering the most atrocious tortures in the concentration camp of Oranienburg, had not been long in making up his mind as to who should expiate Gyse Meurs' crime. From the moment of his arrival in the town, simultaneously with the troops of the Third Prussian Regiment of Death's-Head Hussars, he had quietly proceeded with the arrest of those Dutch citizens whose names figured on the lists supplied him by the *Ausland Amt,* that branch of the German Secret Police which keeps on file the names, addresses, past activities, and business and family relationships of every individual in every city, town, and village of the whole world who is either an active or a potential opponent of German Fascism.

With the aid of certain sympathizers of the Nazi cause in Gorcum—half a dozen men who made up the local membership of the National Socialist Bund—Schwartz had not experienced any difficulty in locating those individuals whom Berlin considered more dangerous than armed troops. He had not arrested them in a single wholesale raid. He had these men placed in custody one by one. So as not to arouse popular indignation or to cause a sensation, they had been quietly removed from their homes in the dead of the night. In this way few in Gorcum were aware of the number of those arrested; fewer still knew where the vanished ones had been taken. The usual commentary on these nocturnal disappearances was that such and such a person had been moved to Germany for a more or less lengthy period of "political education." Relatives who went to inquire about them at the Toll Barracks, a very old building—the remnant of a huge castle—where the Gestapo had established its headquarters, were told that they would soon have their loved ones back. They had merely been sent away, along with intellectuals and radicals from other countries occupied by the German armies, to receive instruction in the duties of the new type of European citizen.

What the relatives were not told, however, was that their husbands, fathers, and brothers were chained up to the walls of the old dungeons of the Toll Barracks and that day after day they were subjected to the brutality and mistreatment of the Gestapo men. It was curious, too, that in rounding up the so-called "dangerous" elements, Schwartz had paid very slight attention to the types who might have been expected to fear Fascist conquest most. So it was, for instance, that the only Communist member of the town council of Gorcum, who had also been the organizer of the local ironworkers' union, not only had not been molested, but had been placed in charge of the newly established section of the *Arbeitsfront*. His employer wrote me: "Things have changed little. Jaap van Nunnik [the Communist in question] still comes to do the collective bargaining for the workers, only today he wears a brown shirt and greets you with a hearty *'Heil Hitler.'*" None of the men who in the past had been classed as rabble rousers or agitators had been disturbed by the Gestapo.

The men arrested were persons like Kees Boon, the smith and local poet, and his friend Jan Trouw, the house painter, who preached of a Sunday in the chapel of the Darbists. These two men, on whom even the most

conservative and reactionary Gorcummers had looked in
the past as harmless idealists, incapable of the least
act or thought of violence, had been among the first to
be taken into custody by the Gestapo. This leads one to
think that the Germans entertained different notions on
the subject of their innocence and harmlessness. As a
matter of fact, not the most vociferously patriotic citizens,
those who had called for a fight to the death against the
invader and who had always been in the forefront of
nationalistic and patriotic endeavor, were regarded by the
Germans as their most determined opponents, but rather,
strange as it may seem, the men of peace at any price, the
conscientious objectors, the followers of Tolstoy, the believers in nonviolence. The first to join Boon and Trouw
in the dungeon of the Toll Barracks had been the president and officers of the district organization of Kerk en
Vrede (Church and Peace), a young pastor from the
near-by village of Dalem and his colleagues from the
small fortified town of Woercum, across the Merwe River.
These men, the fundamental idea of whose preaching
had been spiritual defense alone, would have had Holland disarm completely, strip herself of army and navy
and face the world as naked as Isaiah of yore, in an attitude of absolute defenselessness. They were willing to
face occupation of their country and subjugation of their
people without offering the slightest opposition, in the
belief that in so doing they carried out Christ's command
not to resist evil. Now they were indicted as Germany's
worst enemies. Their ideas had not had a wide following, but to the extent that their influence had made itself
felt, one might have expected that the Germans would
have hailed them as comrades and collaborators in that
they had contributed something toward disrupting unani-

mity on the subject of national defense and so had helped
to assure Hitler's victory. These were the men who had
been thrown into jail. And it was out of their midst that
Parteigenosse Schwartz selected the three who were to pay
with their lives for the burning of the mill and its soldier
occupants.

But at the last moment, the Gestapo agent changed his
plans about having the execution take place in public.
He could not keep up the pretense that his prisoners had
been sent to Germany for political re-education and yet
produce them at so short a notice before the firing squad
in the town square or on the bowling green. Moreover,
the military commander of Gorcum, Baron von Schwabenfels, had caused the announcement of the forthcoming execution of the three condemned men to be affixed
to the billboards as soon as he had learned the names
of those selected by Schwartz.

The *Parteigenosse* had decided that the execution was
to take place on the rifle range behind the Toll Barracks,
an area that was closed to the public. The three men he
selected were Sylvan de Wit, a plumber; Jan Trouw, the
preacher and painter, and a schoolmaster named Gerrit
Jan Strang. The three were informed of their fate at
noon, three hours before their death. A request to see
their wives and children for a last time, which Baron
von Schwabenfels had granted, was later countermanded
by Schwartz. The Gestapo man had taken all details of
the execution in hand and had even told Lieutenant
Schmidt that his presence would not be required. The
only witnesses of the execution were the inhabitants of
those houses whose rear garden walls touched on the rifle
range. Some of them watched the strange procession that
came out of the iron cellar door of the Toll Barracks that

afternoon. I have it from one of the spectators, who stood behind the Venetian blinds in his room, looking across his small garden through a pair of binoculars, that his attention was drawn to the scene by the voices of the condemned.

The three men looked grimy and unkempt. Their faces could be seen plainly. My old friend, Jan Trouw, was almost unrecognizable. His left eye was swollen horribly, and the lower part of his face was covered with a heavy growth of beard. . . . They were chained together. Sylvan de Wit was weeping and had to be assisted by one of the soldiers as the party climbed the stone steps that lead to the rifle range. There were twelve soldiers in the squad. An officer preceded them, while the Gestapo agent, Schwartz, followed behind. The three were placed under an elm tree. Schwartz advanced to read something to them in German, of which, of course, they did not understand a word. The Gestapo man read quickly and in a monotonous tone of voice. Suddenly the sound of the carillon in St. John's tower disturbed the summer afternoon's stillness. Instinctively the three men looked toward the tower. And then, without paying any more attention to Schwartz reading the verdict, the three of them fell in with the tune, singing the words with broken voices: "The Lord is great. His Name is great, the wonder of His works is great, endlessly great His love! . . ."

When the three condemned men began to sing, Schwartz looked at them in surprise and ran back quickly toward the firing squad. . . . At the same moment, the command rang out: "Fire!" When the smoke had cleared away, the secret onlookers saw that De Wit and Strang had fallen flat on their faces, but Jan Trouw was on his knees, trying to raise himself. Blood was coloring his shirt in dark red blotches. . . . Schwartz walked over swiftly to where Trouw was kneeling. He held a revolver in his right hand. Trouw had almost raised himself, but Schwartz fired, and he fell. Yet again the painter rose to his knees. This time Schwartz kicked him in the face with full force. Sinking back, Jan Trouw pointed a finger at the Gestapo man and called out: *"Toch zijn jullie ook menschen!* And yet you too are human beings!"

For answer Schwartz bent over and, steadying his revolver in the crook of his elbow, fired once more. . . .

The new order had been established in Gorcum!

IV

In the Steps of the Sun

1. *Sunrise in Manchuria*

KOSTYA AND TAGO had been together ever since that morning when it seemed as if a thunderstorm had struck Vladivostok and a shower of screaming shells came crashing into the Ulitza Petrova. Tago lived in the Ulitza Petrova, which was really not a street at all but a narrow mud alley flanked by huts put together out of castoff lumber and covered with sheets of corrugated iron. Japanese fishers lived in that alley, Chinese dock workers, Korean street peddlers, and a swarming mass of Russian *Lumpen* proletarians.

How Kostya had come to be in that alley on the morning of the bombardment must always remain a matter of conjecture. He was the only son of a White Russian officer who had been imprisoned by the Red partisans. It may very well be that the child had escaped the attention of his nurse, had found the garden gate unlocked, and had wandered off. The garden of the colonel's house touched here and there on that populous alley. All Kostya remembered later about the day of the bombardment was that a shell splinter had cut him just above the knee and that he had run in the direction of the Peter and Paul Square,

AUTHOR'S NOTE: In this chapter, in which I have followed in the steps of the sun, I have telescoped the stories of persons and events which are part of my physical and intellectual experience. I have tried to recapture and interpret the impact of the times in which we live on people I know. P.v.P.

where some men in uniform had caught hold of him and had bandaged his leg.

Of what happened after that he remembered little. The fire had continued to rain from heaven. Great clouds of smoke had hung over the city. Dead men and women had lain about in the streets side by side with the swollen bodies of horses, whose legs were extended stiffly into the air, broken carts, thrown-away rifles, and the pulverized masonry of buildings. In the evening Kostya had found himself with a crowd of women and children herded into a church, where he had fallen asleep by the light of candles whose flames dipped and fluttered each time the muffled sound of an explosion was heard and then returned to their former quiet brilliance. He remembered the play of the candles and also that he had slept next to a boy who had given him a piece of bread in the morning. He had not been able to understand the boy's speech, for he was a Japanese. Still, he had followed him around all that day, and in the evening they had gone back together to sleep in the church.

Only once had Kostya recognized his former home as he wandered with the Japanese boy through the streets in the days that followed. He had recognized the house because of the dog that had come jumping at him from the garden, barking, whining, and wagging its tail. He and Tago had looked into the garden, and Kostya had made signs to his little Japanese friend to follow him. He had pulled Tago by the hand up the path to the white villa, where he thought his mother would still be waiting for him. But when they had entered the house, they found every room filled with sleeping cots and straw sacks and Red soldiers lying and sitting about, even on the stairway and in the kitchen. The soldiers gave the children some food and then sent them away with the admonition not to come back.

So they had started their wanderings together and their life together, Kostya and Tago. The Japanese boy had never been able to identify the hut on the Ulitza Petrova where he had once lived. The whole neighborhood had been smashed and burnt beyond recognition by the bombardment. Many years later, when Tago had learned to speak Russian fluently, he told Kostya how he had seen his mother and baby brother killed before his eyes on the morning of the bombardment and how he then had run away as fast as he could and had continued running until, toward nightfall, he had been pushed into that church by a policeman. Tago's father had been away with the fishing fleet on the day of the disaster.

The first winter was a frightful ordeal for the two children. How they survived when hundreds of adults froze to death is almost a miracle. But they came through. They had joined a band of street urchins, waifs, like themselves, of the great storm that raged in those years in all the Russias. Their shelter at nights had been the cellars of a ruined government building; the gang sneaked in after dark and decamped before daylight. On the coldest nights the bigger boys built a fire there from the wood and debris that lay about in heaps all over Vladivostok.

In the daytime the boys scattered to roam and to gather up what food they could lay their hands on. They learned to dig scraps from garbage cans and to pilfer from freight cars in the yards of the Trans-Siberian Railway. That was dangerous work, for the Red soldiers on guard had strict orders to shoot the Besprezorni on sight. In order to make the militiamen obey that order and show no mercy, the sentinels were themselves held accountable for cars broken

into and charged with counterrevolutionary weakness if
any goods were missing.

It therefore became a struggle of life and death between
the Besprezorni and the soldiers, in which the children
pitted their wits against the vigilance of the Red army.
Occasionally there were pitched battles in which the children did not always come off worst. Swarms of Besprezorni
would move up stealthily through the yards and simply
overwhelm the sentinels before the men could make use
of their arms. Then the soldiers had their eyes gouged out
or their throats cut with pieces of glass or with crude knives
or even with their own bayonets. For it was the law of the
jungle that had returned to Russia in those years of chaos
and famine, and many of the neglected children grew up
into fierce young tigers, themselves hunted of men, but
taking revenge with amazing ingenuity and frightful
cruelty. .

Only in the spring had there been fish and fruit enough
for the youthful desperadoes, and they did not need to fight
and kill for their food. They went out foraging in the
country, robbing farms and barns and orchards. By the
autumn of the second year, when the Soviets had overcome
most of the interventionist expeditions and could devote
more attention to social problems, the Besprezorni were
being rounded up in Vladivostok. Tago and Kostya were
sent to an institution, which was housed in the former
country home of a Vladivostok merchant, fifty miles up the
Pacific coast. There they spent the winter.

But in the following spring they ran away and rode the
huge freights that steamed past Lake Baikal and over the
Siberian prairies. From time to time the two boys joined
a gang of other lads for a short time, only to break the

new partnership soon thereafter and move on with another gang. In this way they roamed all over Asia. . . .

For ten years they made Tashkent their home. Tashkent was the city of abundance, where the best of fruit was for the picking, where the mild and even climate relieved you of the trouble of searching for a roof over your head, and where every man did what he liked. It was an ideal place for vagabonds like Tago and Kostya. The police was of the easygoing Oriental type; the Beluchistan militia paid more attention to checker games in the coffeehouses than to strategy and ballistics and watching for pilferers in the bazaars. The merchants of Tashkent, grown generous and lazy through long years of prosperity, followed the anarchistic policy of live and let live.

In Tashkent the boys grew up. In time they were taken in hand by the Communist party. They joined the Youth Pioneers, learned to read and write, and even came as far as the people's university. Their friendship never waned. They were inseparable. Kostya had grown up into a slim tall lad with blue eyes and yellow hair. He was no longer dressed in rags but wore a white peasant blouse and a pair of high boots. Tago was short and squat, but with powerful arms and slightly round legs. This startling contrast in physique sometimes made people stand still in the streets and shake their heads smilingly. One saw such strange and wondrous things in the new Russia!

The first brief parting between the boys came when Kostya fell in love with a girl who was studying economics and social science at the university. Her name was Tatya, and she was staying at the same boardinghouse as the boys. Tago thought that the girl, with her endless questioning and lectures, was merely using Kostya as a subject for experimentation, a willing listener on whose patience she could unload her newly acquired knowledge. But he was wrong: Kostya was seriously in love. He talked of spring flowers and the perfume of a woman's hair. He even wrote verses and was morose and silent when Tatya went to classes in the evening and could not see him.

Then Tatya suddenly turned her back on Kostya and went to live with a Red army soldier, a Lett, whose regiment was stationed in Tashkent. Then the trouble began.

Kostya was so depressed over the jilting that he went around alone for weeks. He seldom returned to the house in the evening and even spoke of life as no longer worth living. Whatever Tago did to console him and to talk him out of his despondency was of no avail. Kostya wanted his Tatya back. Nothing else would do.

Tago, who had begun to fear for his comrade's reason, had a talk with the girl. When, in the course of the conversation, she remarked casually that she still loved Kostya best after the militiaman, Tago's mind was made up at once. If that was all that stood in the way of Kostya's happiness, he reasoned, he would merely have to eliminate the obstacle. It seemed very simple. Tago therefore sought out the Lett, treated him at the seltzer bar, and one night went strolling with him in the Lenin forest, where the soldier was found next morning with a knife between his ribs.

Upon being taken to the hospital, the Lett hovered between life and death for weeks, and when he finally recovered it was quite natural that he should tell Tatya who his assailant had been. She in turn confronted the two friends with the facts and threatened to denounce them to the police. The boys knew full well that an act of bodily aggression against a member of the armed forces would fall under the heading of political crimes and would bring them up against the GPU. They therefore thought it wiser to leave Tashkent as far away as possible.

But now they found also that times had changed. Railway stations were watched; there were gatemen and conductors who verified identity cards and tickets before allowing would-be travelers on the platform. The boys could not just rush through a station with a crowd, climb to the roof of a passenger coach or a freight car, and remain there undisturbed until hunger or sleep drove them down for food or rest, to continue their journey a few hours later on another train. That was the way they had traveled west ten years before. Now that sort of free and easy vagabondage had become fraught with difficulties of an unexpected kind. . . .

They nevertheless managed to go as far east as Novo-Sibirsk. In that city, which was being turned into an industrial center under the Five-Year Plan, they had figured to remain and get jobs. But they were promptly arrested the first day they set foot in the town. Upon their statement to the police that they both hailed originally from Vladivostok they were ordered deported to the Maritime Government of the Far Eastern Soviet Republic. There was no escaping this time, and in Vladivostok they were lodged in jail and held for disposition by the military authorities. Because Tago could not prove that he had been born on Russian territory, he was ordered deported to Japan, while Kostya was held as a deserter from the army for having failed to register at the proper time and was sent to a disciplinary battalion in Tikhonkaya.

So the two friends were at last separated. But they could not forget each other. There were, to be sure, no means of communication. In the first place, each had no notion of where the other was, and then relations between Russia and Japan grew so strained after the occupation of Manchuria and the incursions into China that mail service between the two countries stopped altogether.

During the tension over Japanese violations of the borders of Outer-Mongolia, Kostya's regiment was transferred to Krasny. He had served his term for desertion and had been attached to the corps of guides, a half-motorized, half-cavalry unit charged with watching Japanese troop movements in the region of Lake Urvonor.

Scarcely a day passed without some skirmish between border patrols, and once or twice pitched battles were fought with entire regiments and even divisions thrown into the fray on both sides. The Japanese seemed to be testing out Soviet defenses before turning on the Russians in full force.

One evening Kostya was sent ahead with four other troopers on a reconnoitering party. Soviet observation planes had signaled the presence of a considerable body of Japanese motorized infantry in the neighborhood of a wooded territory about three miles inside Soviet territory. The Russian scouting parties were not only to determine the disposition and strength of the Japanese units, but they were instructed to raid the opponent's advance posts with the object of capturing some prisoners and questioning them about the enemy's intentions.

It was at the head of one of these small raiding parties that Kostya set off about dusk in the direction of the Japanese lines. For two hours he marched his men through the forest without finding a single indication that the enemy was near. Not until they reached a vast patch of shrubbery did they slow their pace. In the clearing they advanced step by step, cautiously exploring every foot of ground and peering ahead to the dark mass of the oak forest, which the air force had indicated as the probable limit of the Japanese penetration. They were not fifty paces from the first trees, after having crossed the better part of the swampy clearing, when Kostya suddenly ordered his men to throw themselves flat on the ground. He had seen the flash of a torch amongst the trees. It was only the feeble ray of a pocket torch, and there was no reason to believe that the enemy had spotted them or was aware of their presence. But the fact that prowlers were near by had indubitably been established. Were they the advance patrols of the Japanese army or merely Mongolian hunters camped for the night on the edge of the forest? Kostya whispered to his companions to set up the machine gun they carried and to wait while he went on alone to investigate.

Revolver in hand, he stepped forward into the dark. His companions lost sight of him immediately. He had not gone fifty yards when he again saw a brief flash of the torch. He also heard voices. Men were coming in his direction. He strained his eyes in the darkness. Bending the branches of the shrubbery aside with one hand and holding his revolver in the other, he made one or two more steps forward, now tiptoeing and holding the branches so that they would not snap or rustle their leaves and so betray his presence. He was about to drop to his knees and try to move still a little closer when he stepped on a dry twig. The snapping of the dead twig sounded like a pistol shot in the stillness of the night. Kostya stopped at once to see what would happen. He held in his breath, and his jaw dropped with the tension of the moment. He did not have to wait long.

From a point no more than twenty yards distant he saw the fiery tongues of a machine gun suddenly leap into the dark. At the same instant he fell down, struck by a bullet in the thigh. As he rolled over into the undergrowth, he pulled his whistle from his tunic pocket and blew it for all he was worth. That was the signal for the companions he had left behind to open fire. In a moment machine guns were rattling from both sides, and Kostya hugged the ground as close as he could to escape the showers of bullets that raked the shrubbery.

When the fusillade subsided, Kostya tried to raise himself to his knees but he found that his leg would not support him. The pain was agonizing. It was not the sharp pain of a clean puncture, but a heavy, dull ache as if his leg were being twisted out of its socket. He could feel the warm blood streaming down his knee and along his calf. He tried to slit his trousers before setting a tourniquet, but his strength failed him. It was clear that the Japanese had used explosive bullets: an ordinary steel-jacketed projectile could not have caused the gaping wound Kostya felt in his thigh, nor would it have shattered the bone. He lay on his back. He took off his leather belt and tried to twist it around his injured leg. The effort cost him his last ounce of energy, and he sank back into semiconsciousness.

A heavy downpour of rain in the night brought him back to life. Or was it that sharp cry he thought he heard there, twenty feet away from him? Kostya raised himself on his elbows and listened. There it was again: first a cry and then the sound of a man moaning in distress. The effort of raising himself to his elbows exhausted Kostya. He sank back again and lay still. His leg did not hurt now, but his head pounded violently. He felt his wound. It was still bleeding, and he tried to tighten the belt around it, but his fingers felt strangely numb. They slipped powerlessly off the leather. The moaning in the shrubbery turned into a death rattle. He thought of firing a shot to draw the attention either of friend or foe. To fall a prisoner into Japanese hands would be better than slowly bleeding to death, he thought. His hands sought the revolver in the dark, but he could not find it. Well, then, if the gun was not there, he must try his whistle. He was fumbling for the whistle cord when the wounded man in the shrubbery near by started to scream. What? Kostya rose on his elbows again. Had he heard aright? His breath came in quick gasps. His brain cleared as if his head had been drenched by a shower of ice water. It could not be! Had he heard someone calling his name? He listened breathlessly. There it was again: "Kostya, Kostya, *bratushka!*"

No doubt of it now. That was Tago's voice. That wounded man in the clump of bushes was Tago, his friend Tago, and he was dying. Kostya tried to call back, but his voice was only a whisper: "Tago, little brother, I am here. I will bring you water!"

He started to crawl in the direction of the moaning man. His leg now felt like lead, like a dead weight that kept him fastened to the ground. He rolled over and dug his nails into the soil and pulled himself forward a few inches. But now there was the cry again: "Water!" first in Japanese, then in Russian. Kostya bit his lips and dragged himself another foot forward. His head was clear now. He could hear the other man's labored breathing. . . .

The sun was rising above the Manchurian plain and sent its first golden rays through the undergrowth when Kostya reached Tago's side. A bullet had passed through the Japanese's lungs. He was delirious with fever, but he turned his head toward the Russian soldier and whispered: "I knew it, *bratushka,* that you would come. . . ." Kostya, exhausted by the effort, dropped his head on his arms. His hand stole out and reached Tago's. Then they lay quietly waiting. . . .

2. *Usseen's Last Dream*

USSEEN HAD been in Singapore four years. It may have been five. He could not reckon the time precisely. For those years had passed as a dream. But it had been an evil dream, one of those dreams in which you are aware that you are dreaming and from which you hope subconsciously, as it unfolds itself, that you will soon be delivered. There were only three or four incidents in those four or five years that stood out clearly in his mind. He remembered the day when he had shipped from Canton and how he had been sick in the hold of the steamer, where hundreds of other young men, everyone as poor as he, had lain on the dirty floor for as long as it took for the journey to Singapore.

Had it been winter or was it summer when he had started out on that great adventure? He could not recall that any more. It must have been summer, for had not Kwan-Yin, his sweetheart, accompanied him to the big city? Had they not walked the three days it takes to go from Lungtang to Canton, and had they not slept at nights under the chemara trees by the side of the road, she with her head on his shoulder, so that by the light of the full moon he had lain watching the shadow of her lashes on her face? On the quay he had kissed her eyes before he walked up the gangplank, and she had given him the small wooden flute that her father had carved. Yes, it must have been summer, for he remembered the fetid smell of the durian fruit in the hold of the steamer and of the garlic and oil and dried fish. Then they had arrived in Singapore, and he and his fellow passengers had been locked up.

There are rice depots in Singapore and oil depots and horse depots, and there are also coolie depots. The horses are stabled with care, and there are guards over the oil, so that no one can come near it. The horses are groomed every morning. They are given fresh vegetables, and flannel bandages are wound around their legs. The coolies are dumped into windowless, unlighted sheds of corrugated iron on which the sun beats down all day. Coolies may be beaten at will and kicked and cast aside when they have become sick and feeble. The coolies are the animals in Singapore. There are too many of them. When one coolie dies, another coolie takes his place. There is never any lack of coolies. China has millions and millions of them and will always send more.

Always? No, not always. Usseen knew that too. Kwan-Yin had told him that. Kwan-Yin had been to school. She could read. In the books she had read, it was said that the time will come when coolies will no longer be bought and sold by the boatload and shipped far away. The time will come when everything will be different and lovers will remain together and marry and build a house in a garden. For that day when the great change is to come, she had told Usseen, you must watch, and you must always be ready. That he remembered well. She had said it with great earnestness and she had pressed his hand to her breast when she had told him that.

Then he had been put to work. That day he also remembered clearly. He had been put to work with a hundred other coolies unloading boxes and cases and crates from steamers that had come from China. All day long, from early morning, through the blistering heat of midday, until the sun started to go down, he had rolled a barrow, and he had pulled and dragged and hoisted the heavy merchandise until his joints had almost cracked. He had been too tired to eat and yet had not been able to sleep because of the pain in his muscles and his blistered hands, and because of the feeling of flaming coals on his shoulders and back, where the sun had scorched him. And the next day it had started all over again, the same toiling and moiling under the eyes of a *balanda* in a white coat, who screamed and yelled until he became blood-red in the face. Usseen had felt like laughing at him, for when the man grew angry like that, he looked for all the world like one of those red-painted devils in the masquerade at the fair at home in Lungtang. But his desire to laugh had been turned to bitterness when the man in the white coat had pulled a rubber truncheon from his pocket and had beaten him unmercifully on the head. Then he had thought again of the day of which Kwan-Yin had spoken, the day when lovers will no longer part, and the tears had come to his eyes.

He had expected his fellow workers to run to his side when the unmerited blows began to fall. But they had remained at work. They had no ear for his cries and no eye for his sorrow. They had only worked the harder. Then he knew that much would have to happen before the day would finally come and that the waiting would be long. And the next day it had been the same, lugging enormous bales and shouldering them and rolling them, with the overseer standing near-by and watching him, until it had seemed to Usseen that he was no longer a man, but an animal, a pack mule, a beast that does its work without thinking, without a will of its own and without a soul. And each night he had been locked up in the coolie depot with hundreds of others and had eaten his bowl of rice.

He could not remember how many nights he had spent in that dark hole, without a breath of air, almost suffocating in the fetid atmosphere amidst unwashed and sweating bodies. He had wanted to walk out of the cage, to have a swim in the sea, and to stroll over where he could see the lights, more brilliant than those of Canton, and speak to a letter writer in the bazaar about a message to Kwan-Yin telling her that he remembered her whimpers and her teeth and the walk under the *chemara* trees. But the overseer would not allow him out of the gate of the compound.

And then he had drawn his flute from his pack and had gone to sit behind the bunkhouse near the barbed-wire fence, and he had played the melancholy tunes of his village to express his sadness. But then his fellow workers had objected, for they wanted to sleep and dream and forget. His fellow workers took most of their wages in opium and at night, no sooner than the day's work was done, they stretched themselves on the wooden benches, the wooden blocks under their heads, to smoke. They had come running out of the bunkhouse when he started to play his flute to tell him to stop his music and to leave them in peace.

There had been some, too, who had noticed his sadness and who had urged him to buy opium from the overseer as they did and to forget his troubles in dreams. But each time Usseen had looked at the long rows of his fellow workers, stretched out on benches in that dull, heavy stupor, he had shuddered. He knew that he would never return to China, never again see Kwan-Yin if he were to fall before the temptation of the drug. Even when his fellow workers had told him of the delights of opium, of the glorious beauty in which their souls sailed away, of the inconceivable happiness that only a few puffs would bring, Usseen had not heeded them. Kwan-Yin had told him that opium was the curse of the people and that so long as they indulged in its wasting delight, the day of freedom could not come. He remembered Kwan-Yin's words. "We will remain what we are, the slaves of strangers," she had said. "It is to prevent us from thinking of our own condition that we are given the poppy seed."

Then one of the coolies with whom he worked, the old man who served as a water carrier, had warned Usseen that no coolie ever left the depot alive unless he was crippled in an accident or was too sick to work. Months and months had gone by after that, Usseen could not remember how many, but he had come to know that what the old man had said was true. He had seen it with his own eyes: no coolie ever left unless the last ounce of his strength had been dissipated by opium and he was no longer fit for work. When a man had reached that stage, he was simply dumped outside the compound and left to perish, and when the stock of human labor was depleted by many who could no longer carry on, a new gang of coolies was imported, and the process of using them up was renewed.

Usseen had pondered over this for weeks in his slow, patient way. He had thought of a plan to regain his freedom and had finally carried out that plan. One morning he had pretended to stumble and had allowed the barrow to overturn so that an immense packing case had broken loose. The case had crushed his foot. The pain had been excruciating, and the blows that the overseer rained on his head had made him lose consciousness for a moment. But he had been carried to the bunkhouse and had been given water to drink. His foot had swelled and throbbed, and no doubt some bones had been broken, for after weeks he still could not walk on it.

Then the overseer had come into the bunkhouse one

evening, accompanied by another *balanda,* and the other *balanda,* after examining Usseen's foot by the light of an electric torch, had shaken his head. A few minutes later Usseen had been dragged from his wooden bench, pushed through the alleys that ran between the dark dock buildings, and thrown on the roadway. He had had the presence of mind to call through the grilled gateway to ask the overseer for his wages. But the white man had only laughed and had told him that the long weeks of his inactivity had eaten up his wages. . . .

Usseen could not think now how long he had lain in the roadway. Several days it must have been, for he had seen the sun go down more than once. Then a ricksha driver had given him a bamboo stick, and slowly—it had taken him hours and hours—he had limped in the general direction of the rows of bright lights. But there a policeman had ordered him off the main street, and he had slunk into an alley, where he had sat down in a doorway and fallen asleep .

It was not until the sun stood high that he had awakened. A truck was moving through the alley. It was loaded with fruit and vegetables. The vehicle stopped quite near him, and as the men started to unload, he had stretched out his hands to them. They had thrown him some overripe melons and after a few hours he had recovered his strength sufficiently to pick up his stick and walk a few steps. But soon he was forced to sit down again.

He had lived in that alley for a long time and had come to know that the building where the fruit and the vegetables were delivered each morning, besides other victuals at other times of the day, was the Rumah Makan Europe, the hotel where the big white mandarins with the gold on their caps and the rich Chinese babas lived. One of the cooks had fed him on scraps and in the evening had often come to sit with him in the alley. Then his foot had slowly mended, and at last his friend had given him some old clothes and had set him to work sweeping the court-yard and mopping the kitchen. Then Usseen had eaten food such as he had never tasted, but rice, too, rich and tasty rice, with sauces and curries he had never dreamed of.

So Usseen had made his start in life. Thereafter he had walked freely, except for a slight limp, and had had the scribe in High Street compose many fine letters to Kwan-Yin, the beloved and gentle of heart. He had been saving a little money, too, and if he was careful, he had figured with his friend's help, if he was careful he would have money enough in five years to go back to Canton and buy a small truck farm in Lungtang and marry Kwan-Yin. He carried the money in a little sack. He had sown it care-fully together and at the end of the sachet had tied a strong silken cord. In this way he carried it suspended around his neck, over his heart and under his blouse.

Sometimes in the evenings he sat on the roof of the garage of the Hotel Europe and played the flute Kwan-Yin had given him. But they were not the quaintly sad tunes of his village that he played, but the songs they sing at weddings and festivals.

Sometimes, too, he wandered through the streets, to the Chinese quarter, where the houses are of cobalt-blue and the shop fronts are painted with gold and flames and fire. He stood outside the teahouses and looked into the flowery pavilions, where hung huge pictures of Chinese women. But the more he stared the more convinced he grew that none of the women on the pictures was as beautiful as his Kwan-Yin. The richly carved doors of the brothels stood wide open. He could see pretty children in silk and brocade move about inside. But he never entered those palaces. Never once did Usseen enter. Gently he pushed the doll-like girls aside who walked in the streets and who stopped him with high-pitched, tickling, singsong voices: *"Pigi di atas, pigi di atas!"*

Many evenings he spent walking on Banda Street and on Trengganu Street or on the other side of the city, across North Bridge Road, strolling along by the blue shops and through the shouting, pushing, gesticulating crowds, over dark bridges beneath which lay entire sampan villages asleep, past old Hindu temples that rose like secrets from the ground, and past white mosques that looked like stately veiled women. And then back again to the paradise of flowers in Sago Street, with its hanging gardens and thousands of superimposed verandas and balconies hung with colored lanterns, where thousands upon thousands of black men and white men and yellow men and brown men shoved and elbowed and pushed each other past the stalls heaped with food, the tables loaded with fish and meat and quivering intestines or piled high with fruit, yellow, green and red, and the booths with ducks and geese, fried and cooked and baked twenty-nine different ways.

And above the stalls were the windows lighted by silver candelabra, and in the rooms candles burned before lacquered altars and where young Canton women with red flowers in their hair, their yellow faces painted red, nodded and beckoned with sensuous, insistent gestures. He listened to the plaintive, lascivious tinkle of the samisens and saw the strange almond-eyed Japanese mousmees bow to him and show their incredibly white teeth. He met shouting English soldiers rolling by in rickshas and fat Chinese merchants whose hands lay on the edge of the cart, heavy with jeweled rings that sparkled in the red floodlight of the roaring dance halls and tea joints. . . .

And then the war had come to China. His friend the cook read from the newspaper about the fall of Peiping and Shanghai and of the Japanese armies marching southward, ever nearer Canton. He learned of the devastation and of the looting and burning and raping, and he had wondered anxiously what had become of his father and of Kwan-Yin.

And so the years had gone by, and the sack around his neck was bulging with money. Finally he had exchanged some of it for a boat ticket to Canton. He had not spent all his money: no, most of it was still in the sachet around his neck. That was the money he would use to buy a small farm and to marry Kwan-Yin.

And so the day finally approached on which he was to sail. He had given up his job, but his friend had allowed him to sleep in the small room above the garage until the day when the boat would depart. That night he felt very happy. He played his flute and as he played he thought of the trees and gardens of Lungtang and of Kwan-Yin and he imitated on his flute the laughter and the hand clapping of little children. But he could not sleep, so strong were his thoughts of the journey and of his home.

At the twelfth hour he walked out along the Esplanade and along High Street until he came to Sago Street. There he loitered until he saw a group of men standing around a storyteller. The man was a Chinese, and his listeners were for the most part coolies and street hucksters. The man was telling them of emperors and of heroes and of magicians who moved in brilliant golden garments and who played with fairies and princesses. Near by, a wajang

flamed up so like a palace of red and gold and silver that
the reality was broken, and the listeners saw everything as
in a dream.

White *balandas* passed by, stopped a moment to watch
the scene, shrugged their shoulders, and walked on. They
did not see what the listening coolies saw in the glorious
apotheosis of the night: women with the soft faces of
flowers smiling from boudoirs of celestial luxury. The
kong-ko was not only telling the story with his lips. He
spoke with his eyes, with his face, with his body, and with
his hands. His gestures expressed the finest soul things,
his eyes flamed with all the passion of the personages
of his story, and, with light, scarcely noticeable motions of
a finger, he would give a turn to his recital that made his
listeners gasp. The storyteller had that grace of gesture
which the greatest European or American actor would
envy him.

Usseen had stood still to listen too. When the storyteller
stopped talking, Usseen stealthily took a coin from the
sachet around his neck and dropped it into the man's tin
cup. He asked him to go on. The man bowed to Usseen
and began again: "One day," he said, "the sun-god was
in an irritated mood. The offerings on the altars had been
insultingly small. The sun-god therefore walked into a
deep cave and rolled a huge stone in front of his hiding
place and said to himself: 'I will punish the humans now
so that they will never forget me again.' When daytime
came and the light did not appear, and the cities remained
in darkness and the fields could not be distinguished, there
was lamentation throughout the whole land. The people
in their millions lit their lanterns and went to the temples
of the sun-god, and they burnt incense and fine sandalwood
to his honor, and they placed chickens and choice viands

on his altars, and they sprinkled his statues with wine and with the perfume of the sweetest flowers. But the god of light still remained in hiding.

"Then the Emperor, the Son of Heaven himself, went in search of the sun-god. He found the god's hiding place and he spoke to him through a crack in the rock that the angry deity had placed in front of the cave. But the sun-god refused to hear the Emperor nor would he come out to look at the treasures in gold and jewels that the Son of Heaven had placed as an offering before the cave. Then the wise men of the realm—the sages and the priests— were assembled before the cave and each in turn pleaded with the god. But he grew more angry and hid still deeper in the cave. And as they waited the people came with torches and lamps and sat in great multitudes before the cave, weeping and wailing and imploring the god to come out and give them back the light. And the people grew more and more disheartened, and they fasted many days and many nights, even the women and the little children.

"And when their despair was greatest, there came to the cave a dancing girl, and she painted on her abdomen the face of the sun-god and began to dance. And by the light of the torches the face of the sun-god shone red and violent with anger on the girl's belly. And when the girl turned her body now this way and then that way and placed her hands on her hips and squeezed the flesh of her abdomen in wrinkles, the sun-god's face was seen to be grinning and screwing up his nose and pulling such grimaces, now of anger and of comical mirth, that the Emperor and the sages and the people began to chuckle. First they laughed quietly as if they were but slightly amused, but as the girl danced on and her dance became wilder and faster and grew more passionate, the face of the sun-god appeared to

be sneezing and coughing and wrinkling his chin and closing his eyes and when she pushed her navel down, it was as
if the sun-god winked most obscenely. Then the Emperor
roared with laughter, and the sages shook with mirth, and
all the people clapped their hands in gladness. Then the
sun-god suddenly rolled away the stone from the cave and
peeped out to see what had caused all the mirth. And when
he saw the girl and the picture of himself on her belly, then
he, too, shook with laughter, and at once the light of day
returned."

The storyteller stopped. "Do you know," he said, turning to Usseen, "what that dancing girl's name was?"

"No," said Usseen, "I do not know."

"Her name is Kwan-Yin," said the man, "and I have her
here in my home. She will dance for you, too." And he
beckoned Usseen to follow him into the alley.

And Usseen went, for the mention of a girl who bore his
sweetheart's name had surprised him and had shaken him
deeply. And the storyteller took him into a small house
and left him in a curtained room to wait till he should go
and call the dancing girl. And, as Usseen waited, a maid
came in and served him tea. And he drank of the hot
beverage and inhaled the fragrance of the leaves. And he
grew weary with waiting, and his head nodded on his
breast, and he fell asleep. But when he woke, he was no
longer in the storyteller's house. He was lying on the sea-
shore, and his head was throbbing. He rubbed his hand
over his forehead and down his neck, and he missed the
silken cord that had been for years around his neck.

And when the sun rose, Usseen knew that the day of
freedom would never come.

3. *A Socialist Sentence*

THERE WERE three men in the train compartment when the American newspaperman entered at the Kharkov railway station. They were three Orientals: a Chinese, a Korean, and a Japanese, all three of them scholars, who had been delegated by their respective universities in the East to attend a scientific congress in a central European country. They had come by way of the Trans-Siberian Railway as far as Moscow. After spending some time sightseeing in the Soviet capital, they were now utilizing the month of time they had to spare in studying the *Völkerchaos* of the Union.

"We are most anxious," said the English-speaking Japanese member of the party, "to see the way the Bolshevik regime has dealt with the nationality question. While imposing a political unification on so vast and heterogeneous a collection of tribes and nationalities, Russia is at the same time encouraging the development of the individual national cultures of all these peoples by stimulating their native theaters and literatures, even creating alphabets for tribes that up to the present have had no written language and creating a native culture, where formerly nothing existed but the most primitive tribal relationships. We want to see how it is done, how it works, for we consider this of the utmost importance.

"Up till now," he went on, "colonizing states have contented themselves with exploiting the riches of Asiatic and African peoples while caring very little for their cultural welfare. Imperialist exploitation has in many parts of the earth caused native culture to wither and degenerate and, in some instances, to disappear altogether. Why is Russia proceeding in a different manner? Why is her objective not the economic exploitation of backward races but their cultural education as regional entities? And how does she do it? That is what we've come to find out. . . ."

The conversation in the railway compartment was interrupted time and again in the course of the night when the train came to a halt. Each halt brought a new upheaval in the even tenor of train life. Not only would hundreds of passengers stumble and push and elbow each other through the corridors, armed with jugs and tin cans and kettles, to go and get a supply of hot water from the locomotive for the purpose of making tea, but other hundreds of peasants would storm the train from the platform to get seats.

Hard experience had taught the three Orientals, who had suffered many similar innumerable halts and irruptions since leaving Vladivostok, that the only way to save their compartment from being swamped by newcomers and themselves from being crowded out of their seats was by creating an impression of overcrowdedness. They did this by jumping from their seats as soon as the sound of a new invasion made itself heard in the corridor, spreading all their belongings and baggage over the seats and then sitting down on the floor.

To the peasants who peered into the compartment, the sight of so many occupied seats and of three men on the floor was sufficient proof that there were other occupants who were temporarily absent to lay in a supply of hot water. Invariably they passed on, to try their luck at the next compartment door. The three Orientals were inordinately pleased with their little stratagem. Each time the train set in motion again after a halt and a new peasant attack, they celebrated their successful bid for privacy with a good laugh.

But their stratagem did not work in the case of the American newspaperman. He was too seasoned a traveler not to see through the *ruse de guerre* of the three Orientals. He moved some bundles aside and sat down in the corner seat. To the agitated signals from the men on the floor, he replied that if there were other passengers returning to their seat, he was prepared to argue it out with them. In the meantime he would remain where he was. A moment later when the train started up, the three Easterners laughingly admitted that they had been vanquished.

Their scheme received another jolt at a small station not far from Kiev. At that point another man entered the compartment, stepped over the baggage and the crouching Orientals, and planted himself near the window. The newcomer was a man of about fifty, with a greying mustache and dark hair. He wore a leather cap and a coat that was badly frayed at the sleeves. His only piece of baggage was a large leather briefcase, which he held on his lap. It was shortly after dawn when he entered, but it was not until an hour later, when he accepted a cup of tea from the American newspaperman, that he was drawn into the conversation. Besides Russian, he spoke only Yiddish, which the American newspaperman also understood, at least better than he spoke Russian—because of the similarity of Yiddish and German.

The conversation thereafter was carried on in the following manner. The Russian spoke in Yiddish, which the newspaperman translated into English. The Japanese thereupon translated the words spoken in English into Chinese, and the Chinese in turn translated them into Korean. It was an awkward and cumbersome procedure, but it worked out fairly well.

When the Russian citizen had learned the object of

the visit of the three Orientals to the USSR, he told them that he was a member of the state judiciary and that he was on his way to a small Ukrainian town to finish hearing the trial of a murderer and to impose sentence. He invited his fellow travelers to leave the train at the next station, which was but a few miles farther up the line, and witness a session of a rural Soviet court.

This invitation was accepted by all. Although it was necessary to obtain the train conductor's consent for this interruption of the journey and although this important personage, when he was finally located (fast asleep) in one of the baggage cars, strenuously objected to being a party to breaking the rules, one American dollar and the Soviet Judge's eloquence overcame his scruples in time to allow the travelers to leave the train at the next station. There they sat in the railway station while their host ran about for someone to look after their baggage during the trial.

It was early morning when the Judge and his four guests entered the court building. The halls and corridors were crowded with peasants who had come to witness the trial. In spite of the early hour, the temperature in the courtroom resembled that of a Turkish bath. The air was humid and soggy. Two hundred or more peasants must have been packed in that room. It was with the utmost difficulty that the Judge and his four guests made their way forward through the throng.

The courtroom looked more like a rural lecture hall or Puritan meetinghouse than a court of justice. The white-washed walls were devoid of adornments and symbols. There were a few benches, but most of the spectators stood up. Some sat on the floor in front, near a small rostrum on which stood a rough wooden table and two chairs. The

Judge sat down on one of the chairs, leaving the other for a young man in a white blouse, who took notes of the proceedings. A search of the building for more chairs having proved unavailing, the Judge was compelled to ask his four guests to sit on the edge of the stage. There also sat the two lawyers: the state's or prosecuting attorney and the advocate charged with the defense, who was also in the state's service.

The defendant turned out to be a peasant of about forty or forty-five with a violent red beard and clear blue eyes. He was extremely nervous when he was brought in by two militiamen, peasant boys who blushed self-consciously when ordered by the Judge to take a seat on the edge of the platform by the side of his guests and the lawyers. The trial began with a speech by the prosecuting attorney, who set forth the facts of the case, which were very simple.

It appeared that the defendant had killed his neighbor in a drunken brawl. There had been no provocation, the prosecuting attorney declared. The two muzhiks, after drinking together for the better part of a day, had suddenly and without apparent reason started to belabor each other with empty vodka bottles. It was in the course of this battle that the defendant had crushed his opponent's skull. Sobered by the sight of blood, he had thereupon run out into the forest to hide himself, but after a week he had returned to the village and had given himself up to the police.

From time to time, as the prosecuting attorney recited the story of the crime, the Judge would interrupt him and, addressing himself to the defendant, ask him if he had fully understood what was being said. The Judge spoke to the muzhik in the way a father might speak to his son.

If the defendant answered that he had understood, the Judge asked him kindly to repeat in his own words what the accuser had brought forward.

Then the defending advocate took the floor. He called several witnesses, who could do nothing but confirm what had been said by the prosecutor about the circumstances of the murder. Two hours went by in debate. Then the Judge, who had not donned any judicial robes, but who was dressed in an ordinary Ukrainian *roubashka,* or white blouse, refreshed himself from a pitcher of water and announced that he would deliver judgment forthwith.

Hearing this, the defendant broke into a violent fit of sobbing. He beat his breast and tore his hair until the two militiamen ran forward and tried to calm him. The Judge, too, rose and, reaching over from the platform, held out the pitcher of water and a glass to the wailing muzhik. The peasant stopped crying and seized the pitcher with both hands and drained it in one gulp.

Then the Judge went back to his chair and said, amidst the tense silence of that audience of peasants: "Defendant, you have committed a crime. You have killed your neighbor. That was a crime. You have killed a citizen of the Union of Soviet Socialist Republics. That makes yours a counterrevolutionary crime. You have injured the commonalty by depriving it of one of its members. You know as well as I do, as does everyone here present, that such an act is punishable by the supreme penalty. I have the right and the duty to sentence you to death. . . . But if I sentence you to death," he went on after a brief pause, "I, too, may be committing a crime against the commonalty in that I deprive a second family of its breadwinner. If I sentence you to death and the sentence is executed, your children will be as unfortunate as the children of the man you killed. . . . Therefore, I ask you: 'Defendant, are you genuinely and deeply sorry for what you have done?'"

The peasant stepped forward and crossed himself. "I am guilty, Citizen Judge," he said. "My crime is great. I do not deserve leniency. I have killed a man who was my best friend. . . ." He broke into sobs again.

"Defendant," said the Judge once more: "My verdict is that you are deprived of your civic rights for a period of ten years. But you are not to drink vodka again . . . at any time. I further sentence you to plant your neighbor's crop before you plant your own and to harvest his crop before you harvest your own for as many years as his own children shall not be able to do it. . . . Do you promise this?"

"I promise," said the peasant, and he walked away.

"That was a wise sentence," said the Chinese scholar, after the Judge's words had been translated to him.

"It was a Jewish sentence," said the American newspaperman to the Judge.

"No," answered the Judge with a flash of irritation. "That was a socialist sentence!"

4. *The Prepared Sermon*

HE HAD just eaten a small breakfast and sat watching the sun rays with golden feet step in and out of the bowl of goldfishes on the windowsill of his study when the bell rang. He stood still and heard his wife shuffle through the hall and open the door. Then he heard a sharp voice ask: "Is this the home of Rabbi Jacob Warner?"

What could anyone want of him at so early an hour, he wondered. Had some member of his congregation fallen sick? But if that were so, they would not be asking if this were his home. The members of his congregation knew that he lived here in the Weisbachstrasse and had lived here for thirty-seven years. They did not need to ask that question.

He could hear his wife saying that the Rabbi could not be disturbed, for this was the day he spent in preparing his sermon for the next Sabbath. No visitors could be received at all. She was asking if the gentlemen could perhaps not return. . . . But she did not finish the sentence, or else it was drowned out by the stamp of heavy hobnailed boots.

Rabbi Warner went to the door of his study and opened it. Before him stood an S.A. man. Behind the S.A. man were four other men in brown shirts.

"Warner," said the first S.A. man, glancing down at the Rabbi's slippered feet, "put your shoes on. You're coming with us!"

His wife came into the room that moment, but one of the brownshirts pushed her back into the hall and slammed the door shut behind her. The S.A. man ran his eyes over the books on the shelves. "Throw these books down," he commanded, "and let us see what the Jew is hiding behind them." The brownshirts obeyed the order, and the tomes clattered to the floor. The Rabbi looked as his precious volumes burst out of their bindings.

"I assure you, upon my word of honor," he said meekly, "that nothing is hidden here. . . ."

"Maul halten!" cried out the S.A. leader and, turning to the other troopers, he added: "See if there are not some garbage cans outside. Get the stinkingest offal you can and dump it over these books. The *Frau Rabbiner* will have something to do while we attend to her holy husband at the Brown House. . . ."

He wanted to kiss his wife and reached out his arms toward her as they marched him through the hallway, but one of the brownshirts struck him on the head from behind so that he staggered forward. They walked down the stairs. Although the heavy boots of the S.A. men made a loud noise on the wooden steps, the Rabbi noticed that none of his neighbors in the other apartments looked out to see what was going on. He was pushed into an automobile.

As he sat between the two soldiers in the rear seat, he stealthily felt the knots in the *tsitsis*, which is the sash pious Jews wear under their coats. He thought of his wife and mentally recited the words of the Twenty-third Psalm: "Yea, though I walk through the valley of the shadow of death."

He walked down the stairway into the cellar of the Brown House. His escort pushed him into a large room. The room was so brilliantly lit that it made him blink his eyes. He stood before a table at which an officer of the S.A. was seated.

"Undress yourself," the officer said to him. "Take off everything, your glasses, your garters, everything." He undressed as quickly as he could. Then he stood up. His clothes were lying behind him in a small pile on the seat. The S.A. officer looked him over.

"Why don't you obey, Jew?" he said to him.

"I did obey."

"Did I not tell you to take off everything? Why do you keep your wedding ring on."

The Rabbi tried to slip the ring off quickly. It did not go very easily. He told the S.A. officer, "It has been on so long. I don't know if I can get it off."

"Do you want us to take it off for you?" the officer asked icily and, turning to one of the brownshirts, he added: "Just come over here with your bayonet a moment, *Genosse*, the Jew cannot get his ring off."

The S.A. man who had been called walked over smilingly and, drawing his bayonet from its sheath, said: "Want some help, Jew?"

The Rabbi had his ring finger in his mouth and pulled so hard on the ring that his false set of teeth came away and fell to the ground. The officer put his boot on it and with a twist of his heel ground it to small fragments. The Rabbi handed him the ring, and the officer put it in his pocket.

"Now over the barrel with him," he said, "and let him have it, some for Abraham, some for Isaac, and some for Jacob."

Two men seized the naked Rabbi by the arms and led him to a barrel that was lying on its side in the middle of the room. They tied his hands and feet to rings in the floor on either side of the barrel and one began to beat him with a leather strap. The first blows stung with a frightful sharp pain, but soon a dull feeling crept into Rabbi Warner's brain so that he no longer felt the blows. He could still hear the strap striking his bare back, but it was as if the blows touched an object far, ever farther away from him. Then he felt a splash of water in his face, and he awakened as from a bad dream. He found himself lying on the floor. An S.A. man was kicking him in the side.

He rose to his feet with the greatest difficulty, but when he tried to move his wet hair from his eyes and his forehead, he found his arms so heavy that he could not lift them from his side. He noticed now that there were other prisoners in the room with him. One of them was a boy of sixteen or seventeen. He thought the boy's face looked familiar, but he could not recall where he had seen him before. If he had seen the boy come into his room, the Rabbi thought, he might have recognized him. Now, without his clothes, that was impossible. The S.A. officer was questioning the boy about a typewriter.

"I own a typewriter," said the lad, "but I did not type those leaflets."

"Does your sister type?" asked the officer.

"No," answered the boy curtly.

"*Todprügeln!*" the officer commanded. "Beat him to death!"

Two men tied the boy over the barrel and started to beat him with sticks. They struck at his head and the boy cried out a curse. "Harder!" said the S.A. officer, who was sitting behind the table. Rabbi Warner looked on aghast. He could see the blood running down the boy's face and falling on the cement floor in big drops. He felt sick. His knees began to tremble and sag. He hoped that the boy would lose consciousness quickly. But the S.A. officer ordered the men to stop the beating.

"For the last time I ask you," the officer said to the boy, "does your sister type, yes or no?"

"No," replied the boy again.

The S.A. officer lit a cigarette, wrote down something on a sheet lying in front of him on the table, and nodded to the two men who stood on either side of the barrel. At once they resumed their beating. Rabbi Warner closed his eyes. At the same moment he received a blow in the face from a brownshirt standing beside him.

"Keep your eyes open!" the man said.

The S.A. officer left the room. One of the executioners bent low to look at the boy's face. "He's still breathing," he said. "I think I'll have to take off my coat." He took off his tunic, hung it on a peg, and went back to the barrel. . . .

"Stand here together, you Jews, right here," one of the S.A. men commanded the prisoners. They obeyed him. The Rabbi was in front. "You've all had your beating. Now lift your right hands and say: '*Heil Herschel Gryznspan*, leader of the Jewish swine!' Keep on saying it until I tell you it's enough. The first of you to stop goes back to the barrel."

The Jews repeated the phrase in chorus, while the S.A. man walked out of the room. He returned presently and looked over the prisoners, who were still reciting the phrase he had told them to repeat. The commander came back into the room, accompanied by ten or twelve S.A. men. He pointed to Rabbi Warner and said: "There he is!"

The brownshirts ranged themselves in a semicircle around the table. One walked over and with a pair of scissors cut the left side of Rabbi Warner's hair away. Then he took hold of the Rabbi's beard and cut the right side of it away. Then he stepped back. The troopers laughed and slapped their sides.

"Say something in Hebrew," the S.A. captain ordered.

"Thou shalt love the Lord thy God with all thy heart,"

the Rabbi slowly pronounced the Hebrew words. But one
of the other officers interrupted him. "Were you not preparing your sermon this morning?" he asked him.

"Yes," said the Rabbi.

"Well, you can preach it here to us. You'll never again
see your synagogue, for we've just burnt it. Go ahead,
preach the sermon," he cried out. "All quiet now, everybody. Jacob is going to preach a sermon to us."

"Could I have my hat?" asked the Rabbi.

"Can't you preach without a hat?" the officer asked him.

"Give him his hat!" he commanded. Someone handed
the Rabbi his hat, and he put it on his head. The sight
made the S.A. men laugh the more. The man was naked
and he was shivering. Drops of water still clung to his
back. Then he spoke.

"God created man in His image and likeness," he said.
"That was to have been my text for the coming Sabbath."
And he continued: "When it is said that God created man
in His image and likeness, it means that man is both spirit
and body. Man was given the Spirit of God so that he
should be able to dominate and rule his body, so that he
could master over his every act and his passions and over
the whole of nature. . . ."

When he had spoken that far, some of the S.A. men interrupted him. "Let us cut out the nonsense," one of
them said. "No," others again insisted, "let the Jew finish.
He is interesting!" The Rabbi resumed his sermon.

"When we consider," he said, "that in creating man God
poured out His own Spirit into him, our bodies are the
temples of His holy Spirit. . . ." But that was enough for
the S.A. men. "Look at the temple of Jehovah," one of
them cried out, pointing to the naked Rabbi with half his
beard shorn away. "God's image and likeness, ha, ha!"

"Yes, and look at that fine temple on the barrel over there!" another man shouted laughingly as they all glanced at the dead boy.

"Tell me, Jacob," one of the men who had beaten the boy to death said to the Rabbi, "I am not a temple of God, am I?"

"Doch! Yes, you are indeed!" replied Rabbi Warner gravely, nodding his shorn head. For answer the man struck him in the face.

5. *The Trouble in Flanders*

IT WAS all because of the comet of the summer before. That had been the start of the troubles in Laag-Kapelle. For two whole nights everybody had seen it crawl through the sky with its red devil's tail trailing between the stars. It had come up in a wide curve from the direction of Holland, had crossed over the whole of the Flemish land, and then had gone out by way of the sea, to the French side. That was the area in which disasters and calamities were going to occur, from Holland to France. You could tell that by the comet's course. The *Pastoor* of Wiersbeke had been in Laag-Kapelle himself that evening. He had seen the comet and had shaken his head. "This is no laughing matter," he said gravely. Now, wasn't that enough to have made any man tremble? And then there was Aloysius, the cross-eyed magician. He had told some people that he had heard the comet bark.

That may have been exaggeration, of course. At least it is to be hoped it was an exaggeration, for a barking comet is the worst of all. It is a sure sign of a hundred years of war and famine and evil in general. Aloysius may have been mistaken. He may have heard that dog of Cyriel Gezelle about which the gentry of the château were always complaining. Indeed, Aloysius may have been wrong. Yes, but you could not deny that he had the second sight, that same Aloysius. Did not everybody in Laag-Kapelle remember how he had foretold the death of the King, aye, and the death of the young Queen Astrid in a foreign country? Wasn't that strange now?

There surely was something about that fellow Aloysius, something uncanny and weird. Could it not be that he had extra-sharp hearing, too? Who can tell these things? Oh, we all know that there are ladies and gentlemen over in Brussels and Ghent who laugh in your face when you speak of the Black Nun and of the evil eye and of comets and of the werewolf. They are so wise. They have seen so much. Only, they've never been to Laag-Kapelle in their lives. They've never even been as far as Wiersbeke, and God knows what queer things happened there. The *Pastoor* could tell them a strange tale of that if he wanted. But he would not, of course. "There's no use," the *Pastoor* was bound to say, "those people will only laugh and they will go to their death in ignorance, without ever having felt the presence of the elementary things."

Now, since that comet of the summer before last, you could simply count on your fingers the disasters that had come over Laag-Kapelle and over the entire land of Flanders. Has anyone ever seen or heard of such dreadful things? Take the home of Pol Teniers, the farmer who has the big pasture in lien from the château. That comet was not out of the sky before he burned himself while boiling the pigs' feed—burned his foot so cruelly that he had to sit still on a chair for six weeks. That was no pleasure, you may be sure, with the harvest standing before the door and his two boys, Palier and Baudouin, away to the regiment.

It was the same day that the Scheldt broke its dikes. All the fields were flooded. The chicken coop came floating into the yard in the night and bumped into the door, as if it wanted to say: "Here are your twenty-three dead chickens, Pol!"

That night, too, Pol's wife had given birth to twins. He had been alone in the house with her when the pains came on. He had brought the rabbits into the room, and the goats and the two calves, for fear that they would drown outside, for the river had turned into a boiling lake. He had been splashing about in the stable with his aching foot, tying up the horse and the cows, when he had heard her cry. "Pol," she had said, when he ran into the house, "it has come." He had waded up to the bed and had looked at her face. Jesus, Mary! He would never forget her face that night.

He could not remember how he had managed. Well, he would not have managed at all, that is the simple truth of it, had the *Pastoor* not come in. He had his cassock tied up around his waist and was wearing big fishermen's boots up to his hips. "I had a feeling I was needed here," the *Pastoor* had said. And then the two men had gone to work with the pots and pans floating on the floor and the rabbits blinking at them from the chimney shelf and the calves mooing. That is the way the two children were born.

One was dead, and the other was born blind, that was the little Miriam. But you had not been able to tell right then that she was blind. Fiene, Pol's wife, had noticed the blindness only the next day. But the *Pastoor* had seen it the first night. He had covered up his perplexity by saying: "Now if that child had been a boy, Pol, we would have had to call him Moses, for it is drawn out of the water. So we will call it Miriam, for Miriam was the sister of Moses." That is the way the good priest had spoken. But he had merely said those pleasant things to divert Pol's attention from Fiene's suffering and to hide his own uneasiness. He had confessed that much later, when they had stood together a moment in the gray dawn under that leaden sky. "I thought for a while there, she would not come through the night," the *Pastoor* had said. "Neither did I," Pol had answered, "such suffering!"

"God sends no more suffering that a human soul can bear," the *Pastoor* had added. "I think the water is somewhat lower!" And with those words he had splashed off to go and say the early Mass.

Then Pol had returned inside and had looked at his wife and the new child. It was not their first. It was their eighth. But it was the most beautiful child he had ever seen. Looking at its red little hands, he had forgotten to draw on his pipe and had become all weak until he had gone out to swear in order to feel a man once more. It was when he returned that Fiene told him that the child was blind.

And then, one evening a month later, it had died. "It's the comet," Fiene had said. But Pol said: "That God does this to us, I will not put up with without a word or two. When I go to heaven, that will be the first thing I will ask Him to account for. . . . I'll have to hear that from His own mouth. It's all very well to say that God has His reasons. But this time He will have to give me an explanation. Else I will never be able to sing the hallelujah with the angels!"

Pol had not been able to think of anything else but the dead child for days. He had climbed to the attic and had taken the older children's toys out of the box and had turned the wings of the little mill that he had made for Palier, his eldest, years ago: he had thought how little Miriam would have laughed to see the wings turn. Then he had gone downstairs, and they both had wept. Three months later, when Fiene and he had been at work in the fields pulling up sugar beets, he had seen her all in tears, and she, falling on her knees, said: "Now I no longer have a little Miriam!" And then he had run over to her, for his soul was full, too, and he had taken Fiene in his arms and had promised her another child, and then she had smiled at last. But to himself he had said: "God asks for children, and then He takes them away. Is that the way a Flemish farmer man would act?"

They had worked only the harder, Fiene and he, in order to forget little Miriam. Their land was good, after all. That, too, was a gift of God. A farmer is chained to his land. A farmer lives in order to work. Every morning the fields awaken him and call him. Of course, you can leave the land and go and find a job on the quays in Antwerp, in the mines of Hainaut, or go to a factory. Many abandon the land that way. But once you have put your finger on that soil, your soul is pulled down with a pulley, as it were. Then the land becomes your life. You rise before daylight. For a farmer sleeps with one eye open. One night he listens to see if the rain has stopped and another night he listens for the first drop of rain to fall. He knows, even in his sleep, what the plants need and the grass and the trees. When they are athirst for sunlight, he is athirst. When they complain and sigh because of too much water, the peasant sighs and groans and moans with them. He gets up in the middle of the night, looks at the moon, wets his finger to feel which way the wind blows, cocks his ear in the direction of the stable to hear if all is well there, and goes back to bed. That's the way it goes: day in, day out, in the rain, in the burning sun, bent over the soil, crawling over it, stamping on it, nursing it, sweating over it on hands and knees, until his frame becomes crooked and gnarled from looking down at the land. And still the land is a blessing. You feel the magic of the soil

in your blood when you look at a piece of untilled soil and
you stick the spade in the earth and you say: "God bless
us both, you land of Flanders, *heerlijk land,* and me, your
son, you fat old black wench!"

That is the way Pol worked and loved the land. He
would never get rich of it, he knew that. The chatelaine
would not let him. At New Year's he would have to lift
the heavy stone from the middle of the floor and take out
the bank notes from the tin box, the bank notes from the
last harvest, and carry them over with a smile to the château and drink one glass of the chatelaine's sour wine, so
sour that he would, upon going home, run right into the
estaminet for a good pint of malt beer with which to wash
his mouth. Poor again, he would mutter to himself, but a
clean mouth at least. And Fiene is home and waiting for
me with the children, and the pork and the potatoes are
on the table.

And then Fiene had become pregnant again. But the
two sons, Palier and Baudouin, had not come home from
the regiment, not even for a week's *congé* at Christmas.
That had been strange enough, strange, I mean, in a
vaguely disquieting and portentous way, about which Pol
would have preferred not to speak to anyone, least of all
to Fiene. How that woman would have worried if she
could have heard the *Pastoor* of Wiersbeke speak about
those things in Neighbor Verschaeve's stable, when he
had said that there was a grave danger of war. That you
could not say to a woman like Fiene, not in the condition
she was in.

"Oh, those boys," Pol had said casually, as if it had been
the first time that he had given the matter any thought at
all, "those boys. Why, of course they've found themselves
a sweetheart over in those Wallonian towns where they

are in garrison. What did Fiene expect? To keep them tied to her apron strings all her life?"

That is the way he had spoken to his wife. And the *Pastoor* had backed him up. What would you, the *Pastoor* had said, that they come to Laag-Kapelle in the wintertime when you cannot step outdoors without sinking into the mud up to your knees? Would they be doing that now when they might be strolling up and down the fine avenues of Liége or Hasselt and sit like kings in the mirrored and gilded taverns of the big town, with their buttons all shiny and their caps set to catch some Marieken or Amelieken with hair as the golden grain? Was it likely that they would come running home to Laag-Kapelle and go wading in the mud and help their father perhaps boil the pigs' feed or cut up the beets for the cattle?

Oh, no, they would let Pol shift for himself. They knew he was capable of getting along without them. "No, no," the *Pastoor* had said: "God has put man together in an altogether curious fashion. The one day he's Mother's little baby and the next he's blushing and sighing and stammering, and his heart is shaking and trembling like Pierre Verloot's piccolo when he plays the *Brabançonne*. Man hangs together in an altogether curious fashion, with hooks and eyes like a rich lady's dress. Even more mysterious. Once a boy like Palier hears a woman's laugh and gets that laugh stuck between his ribs, he's no longer a baby. You can't hold him, isn't that right, Pol?" the *Pastoor* had asked. And Pol had assented gladly enough.

But he had looked sideways at Fiene and had seen by her face that she believed neither him nor the *Pastoor*.

And so Christmas had been a lonesome and dreary time, not only at Pol's farm, but at most of the farms in Laag-Kapelle. That, too, had boded no good. For at Christmas, when the Child Jesus comes to Flanders, everybody ought to be home, everybody ought to be home to welcome Him. Then there is a glad expectancy in the air, a happy anticipation as for a feast or a wedding, so that even the fields grow still and the chickens and the cattle become aware that something good and beautiful is about to happen. Then there is beer on the table after Mass and fat meat and fine rice pudding cooked in milk for the angels that come to sing peace on earth in the snowy meadows. But because the angels don't eat the rice, the children have it, and the *Pastoor* comes to taste it, and then Pol takes his harmonica from the cupboard and they all go on the *ronde,* through the courtyard and into the stable, singing and dancing, the *Pastoor* too, the good and saintly man, holding the ends of his cassock in his hands, stepping high and fast like a little girl holding up her skirts, and his white hair flowing in the wind, all glad to welcome the new Lord, until the pigs stick their snouts out of the pen, and the calves look foolishly with big wide-open eyes at all the noise and commotion.

Happiness is not something that is thrown into a man's lap, the *Pastoor* had said only at last year's celebration. You have to do something for it, even drink an extra pint of beer, if necessary.

But this Christmas something dreadful had happened, something to spoil the day for the whole village. They could still not imagine how it had occurred, how the animal had broken loose. For that is what had taken place: the bull of *monsieur le baron* had escaped from his pen and had come roaring and snorting through the fields. Just as they were sitting down to the noonday meal, a dreary and strangely silent repast, anyway, without Palier and Baudouin, they had heard it, like thunder strokes storming into the stable. When Pol had run out to find out what was up, he had seen the bull coming out of the stable and tossing a little goat on his horns and then trampling it to death before coming for the house, his head low to the ground, throwing up the clods of snow and charging for Pol with bloodshot eyes. He had quickly slammed the door shut. But a moment later the whole house had shaken from top to bottom as if the lightning had struck. The door had cracked in splinters under the impact of the bull's charge. But he had not broken through. The angels of Bethlehem must have been on guard over Fiene and the children. It was as if the Devil had got into that bull. From Pol's yard, the animal had stormed into Cyriel Ge-zelle's plot, ripping the fence to pieces and tossing that yelping dog of Cyriel's high into the air, two, three, four times, before disappearing into the stable where it gored Cyriel's fine black mare. And then out again. It would have been easy to kill the bull with a shot, but the *garde champêtre* had come running along the road, shouting at everybody that it was the bull from the château, that *monsieur le baron* had ordered that no harm was to come to his bull, and that the farmers had to bring it back alive.

What were they to do under the circumstances? What is one to do with a wild bull that belongs to a man who can raise your rent overnight, who has a right to one third of your beet crop and your potatoes and cabbage, and who owns your house and can do with it what he likes? *Ach God*, it was good that someone had mastered that bull and brought it back to the château stables. But what a damage had been done, and on Christmas, too! It is all because of that comet, Fiene had said, who had grown pale with fright when the animal had crashed into their door.

And then in May it had come, the great calamity. Pol

had brought the news from the *mairie* in the neighboring commune, where he had gone to pay some taxes. That is why the bells had been ringing all morning: *den Duts* (the Germans) had attacked Belgium again. Oh, God, and the King so young, and his wife dead, and the old King dead. Who was there to give him counsel and advice?

On the fourth day those of Hoog-Kapelle, all the old men, the women, and the children, had taken to the roads. They had been streaming past since dawn, carrying sacks and baggage and furniture and bird cages. The Mayor, an old clock tied around his neck, was wheeling his wife on a wheelbarrow. And all the children were crying, and the women were saying to Fiene as they went by: "Better come, too, *den Duts,* he is burning the houses and slaughtering the cattle and shooting everyone he meets."

But Pol had said: "I won't go. Here is my place. Here I have lived and here I will die, if it pleases God." And always more people had passed. Where were they going? Into the land of the French, into the sea? Did they think they could escape that way? They're in Brussels, the *Pastoor* had told Pol at noon. At night he had said: "They have taken Antwerp. Louvain is in flames. All the villages of Brabent and East Flanders are burning. Tomorrow morning they will be in Ghent and in Bruges."

Above their heads roared the Stukas, like gray evil birds, dipping down to peck at the buildings. They had seen one dip low at the parish church. Before it had touched the spire, the building had seemed to leap into the air and had fallen back in a cloud of dust. And then the *mairie* had gone and the land-survey office and the château and the church of Hoog-Kapelle, between the elms on the hill. Buildings like that just leaped into the air and crashed back down to earth a pile of smoking ruins. "He has sharp eyes, *den Duts,"* said the *Pastoor* of Wiersbeke, when he stopped in for a moment in the evening. "All along the road he has picked out the shrines and blown them away. Look," he said, "this is a finger of the statue of Our Lady of Flanders. This is all that was left of it when I passed by the site this afternoon."

Upon hearing that, Fiene had moaned in a strange way and had fainted. Pol and the *Pastoor* had lifted her on the bed. The children could not be sent to the attic to sleep, for the sky outside was full of the droning Stukas.

"It's the army they're after," Pol said. And Fiene moaned again and asked where Palier and Baudouin could be.

And so a few days had passed. She had a high fever. But the doctor could not be found anywhere. The *Pastoor* was busy here and there amidst the ruins of the village, but in the evenings he dropped in.

"Where are my boys?" she had asked him. "Their regiment is safe," he lied. "They have passed the Nethe and will soon be in the French land." Outside, the rumble of cannon could be heard, now near, then far off. "It's a night of thunder, a bad night for the boys to be out. Go out a minute, Pol," she said, "and see if they're not coming."

"She's losing her mind," said the *Pastoor*. "Is everything in readiness?" But Pol only wept. "I will be back in the morning," the priest said.

That night the remnants of Palier's and Baudouin's regiment struggled through Laag-Kapelle. The King was with them and Prince Karel his brother. They stopped at the parsonage, and the *Pastoor* prepared a meal for his high guests. The King sat by the stove in the kitchen. Prince Karel stood in the doorway talking with some officers. The *Pastoor* of Wiersbeke was frying a big omelette for them on the fire. "It will be *oeufs sur le plat,* sire," said the priest. "There are no plates left." Leopold ate only a morsel, but he drank a little of the priest's wine. His uniform was covered with grime. His face was drawn and haggard. An officer came in.

"It's the twenty-second of the line, this time, sire, totally annihilated."

"We ordered them not to retreat," said Leopold sadly, "and they stayed at their posts. How did it happen?"

"Flame-throwing tanks, sire. Two companies were burned to a crisp."

"Which companies?" asked the *Pastoor* suddenly, looking up from the fire.

"The fifth and seventh," said the officer.

"They are the boys of Laag-Kapelle," said the priest. "They are the boys from the village in which you are now standing."

"There is a sergeant out there," the officer said. "He is of the fifth, he saw it all. He is the only survivor."

"If there is no help from the French or British at midnight," said Leopold, "I will surrender. This is not war. *C'est une boucherie!* My father would have done the same under the circumstances."

The priest had gone out. The sergeant was Pierre Verloot's son. "We were told to hold the farmhouses of Zoetekop," he told the *Pastoor.* "We held them until *den Duts* came up with fire wagons and spouted flames into the windows."

"Palier and Baudouin were there?" asked the priest.

"They are still there," said the sergeant. "They were burnt to death. I looked at Palier before I left. The flame caught him in the face and chest. His uniform was burnt off him. His neck was all green. . . ."

The *Pastoor* took the holy oil from his room and made ready to go. The King stood up out of respect to the Host. "I am taking Our Lord to a farmhouse," said the Pastoor.

When he neared Pol's house, the *Pastoor* sounded his bell. He had not been able to find a boy in the village to ring it for him. At the sound of the bell, Pol threw the door wide open to let Our Lord in.

"How are my boys?" asked the woman as the priest bent over her. He noticed that her eyes had become fixed and staring.

"You had better light the candle," the priest said to Pol, and to Fiene he said: "Your boys are well. Palier and Baudouin, they are in Hoog-Kapelle. They are with the King. All are well."

A Stuka roared overhead in the darkness and threw a flare. Suddenly a garish bright light shone through the window. For miles away the whole countryside became visible. Fiene stirred uneasily. The light had caught her eyes. All at once she raised herself on the pillow and said: "Why do you deceive me? You cannot deceive a mother! Look, look at the window! There are my boys! *Dag* Palier, come in, boy! Why do you stand at the window, Palier? Look, Pol, he has a wreath of green flowers around his neck! Look, there is Baudouin, too. He has flowers on his head! *Dag* Baudouin. . . . Come in, my boys! . . ."

The *Pastoor* of Wiersbeke said: *"Nunc dimitte, Domine. . . . Domine, miserere."*

Pol stepped over and closed his wife's eyes.

6. *On the Road to Baghdad*

A THIN, sharply pointed bundle of sun rays that since dawn had been trying to pierce the masses of bulging rain clouds over the eastern Mediterranean did not break through until the sixth hour of the day. But then it fell almost greedily upon the only object in sight on the hard, sandy beach north of Haifa. That object was a motorcycle with sidecar attachment racing at top speed in the direction of Akka, the old city with the Crusaders' ruins, under the walls of which Napoleon was stopped in his march "to throw the Turkish Empire upside down." The motorcycle was driven by a soldier, and the passenger in the sidecar was Major Frederick Saunders, of the British Intelligence Service.

The reason for Major Saunders' extraordinary speed was that he had instructions to liberate a Jewish prisoner in the dungeon at Akka and bring the man back to military headquarters in Jerusalem the same day. There was therefore no time to lose. All of Palestine was in a state of alarm. An insurrection, inspired by German agents, had broken out in Iraq. At the same time, information was filtering through that German transport planes were landing mechanics and small tanks on the airdromes of Syria and Lebanon. It looked as if Herr Hitler, finding the oil supplies from Rumania insufficient to keep up the daily aerial attacks on Great Britain, was going to make an attempt to seize the wells of Mosul.

General Sir Archibald Wavell, the conqueror of Libya, had arrived in Jerusalem to confer with Sir Harold Mac-Michael, the commander of the Palestine garrison. As a disciple of Allenby, in whose great campaign of 1917-18, he had learned the lessons of desert warfare, General Wavell had seen at once that the small force of regular troops at Britain's disposal in the Near East would not suffice if the Germans should launch a really determined drive for Mosul and the pipe lines running from the oil region to the seaboard of Palestine and Lebanon. England was far away, and the conquest of the island of Crete by German air-borne troops had shown that it would not be advisable to denude Britain of still more of its defenders. General Wavell had thought at once of Lawrence and his Arab irregulars, who had rolled back the Turkish left flank in the Revolt in the Desert twenty-four years before and who had thus enabled Allenby to strike at Palestine and beyond the Holy Land at Damascus.

But where look for irregulars now, men who would ride out into the desert and harass the enemy's lines of communication, blow up bridges, shatter munition dumps, and raid the airdromes? Many of the Iraqi Arabs were clearly on Germany's side. The network of intrigue woven by Raschid Galiani Bey of Iraq extended over the entire Near East.

Could Britain call on the Arabs in Palestine who were gathering in their mosques to hear the inflammatory messages from the fugitive Mufti of Jerusalem, Hameen el Husseini? The ex-Mufti was openly calling the Arab tribes, not to the support of Britain, but to revolt against the British authority.

Yet, auxiliaries had to be found. General Wavell could not remove any more troops from the Libyan front and expose Egypt to a new drive by the Italians, who since their shattering defeat in Libya had been reinforced by considerable contingents of the German *Luftwaffe*.

Why not call on the Jews? General Wavell wanted to

know. The Jews were not only willing, they were anxious to fight on Britain's side. One hundred thousand young Jews in Palestine were clamoring for arms, pleading with England on bended knee not to be left unarmed in the face of the German juggernaut. The Jews had not only transformed the Palestinian wilderness into a garden, but they had equipped the country with an industrial apparatus that was proving of the utmost value to the British defense forces in the Near East. Why not allow them to defend what they had themselves built up?

But the Jews, General Wavell was told, had no trained forces. What was the sense and the use of allowing masses of untrained men to hurl themselves in the path of the Panzer divisions if and when they should come?

Then, why had not the Jews been trained and armed, and why are they not being trained and armed now? No matter what happened in the immediate future, whether the Germans would undertake a drive for the Suez Canal then or later, before the war was over Britain would need every man she could get, Australians, Indians, Canadians, Jews. Even with all them she might still have to call on America for help.

Practical strategist that he was, General Wavell knew that a war cannot be won by speeches, by dropping leaflets, and by chalking the letter V on the walls, but that for fighting you need men and arms and still more men and arms.

That is why he did not understand, when he came to Palestine, why the tens of thousands of young Jews who volunteered to fight in Britain's cause were not being trained at a moment when the enemy was at the gates. The question he wanted answered was this: why does Britain dispense with the services of a nation which has shown itself loyal, which was eager to fight, and which possessed superb fighting qualities?

That is the reason, too, that General Wavell, upon learning that the Jews had built up a secret self-defense corps to guard the valuable Palestinian industries and farms during the periodic Arab riots, wanted to see the commander of that corps.

But its commander was in jail. He had not been tried yet, fortunately, for a trial automatically would have brought the death sentence, mere membership in the defense corps being punishable with death.

"Get that man out of jail," ordered General Wavell, "and ask him to come and see me here in Jerusalem!"

And so it was that the rays of the morning sun spotted Major Saunders driving helter-skelter along the Mediterranean shore for Akka and back again in the afternoon. But on the return trip he drove an automobile. And in the tonneau of the car with him was the commander of the Irgun, the illegal National Jewish Self-Defense Corps. The commander's name was Raziel, which in English stands for "Mystery of God."

There was nothing mysterious about Raziel's appearance or personality. He was short and stockily built, with broad shoulders and powerful arms. He hailed from the Russian Caucasus but had early in life moved to the land of Israel, like so many young Jews, in the belief that at last his people were to live within walls of their own, free of the fear of massacres and persecutions on one pretext or the other, able to begin rebuilding the national life after twenty centuries of dispersion among alien cults and cruel taskmasters. It was a legitimate desire that had been sanctioned as such by the civilized nations of the world.

When Great Britain, instead of carrying out the mandate entrusted to her by the League of Nations of facilitating the building of a National Home for the Jewish people in Palestine, and for dark and mysterious reasons of her own curtailed Jewish rights, sabotaged Jewish effort and placed every conceivable obstacle in the way of the builders of Zion, some young Jews banded themselves together in a self-defense corps. They did this when they saw, as all the world saw, that the periodic uprisings and murder expeditions of the Arabs were not repressed by the British in a way that would have made their recurrence an impossibility. Raziel, the passenger in Major Saunders' car, was the organizer and commander of this corps, which the British at once proscribed and subsequently tried to destroy.

Raziel had landed in jail shortly after a trip to Poland, where he had gone to visit the branch of the self-defense corps. In Poland the Jewish self-defense corps was not illegal. The Polish government sympathized with the aims of the Jewish nationalist movement, not for any altruistic reasons, but because the aim of that movement is to take Jews to Palestine and because a diminution of the large number of Jews in Poland must progressively render the Jewish problem in that country less acute.

Flying back from Poland, Raziel landed at the Lydda airdrome and there was recognized by an Arab custom officer as the commander of the illegal military organization. He was placed under arrest. While the military authorities were notified and a car was being sent from Jaffa to take the prisoner away, Raziel escaped his captors' attention at the airdrome and hid about the buildings for three days. He managed to convey the circumstances of his predicament to some night watchman, who smuggled him out concealed in a garbage can. Raziel reached open country, where he made himself known to some Jewish members of the regular rural police, who in turn ordered an airplane for him to fly to Haifa. This airplane made a forced landing at the same airdrome of Lydda Raziel had left but a few days previously. He was recognized again and was thereupon sent in chains to Jerusalem, being later transferred to the dungeon at Akka.

But even from prison he carried on as commander of the Irgun. Several of the guards were members of his illegal organization. They admitted friends and collaborators to Raziel's cell, saw to it that the visitors got safely away before daybreak, and in addition kept him informed daily about the situation in the country.

The Arabs were rioting again. Every day Jewish farmers were shot from ambush or killed by land mines placed by Arab insurrectionists but manufactured in Germany and Italy. The Jewish community had decided not to retaliate. With admirable self-restraint the Jews refrained from the slightest act of revenge, in the belief that the British would soon overcome the seditious movement and the Arab fury spend itself.

When Raziel learned, however, that the murder campaign was inspired by Axis agents, operating from Syria, he gave the word to the members of his organization to retaliate. "We cannot," he said, "allow ourselves to be slaughtered like lambs. Death is not a program for national regeneration. . . . We must learn to hit back."

Thereafter a dead Arab would be found on the spot where a Jew had been killed on the previous day. When this method of procedure did not diminish the frenzy of the Arab campaign of assassination, retaliation was doubled. In a month peace and tranquillity had returned to Palestine.

Over the heads of the British authorities, who had imported four or five regiments from Palestine, but who could not prevent the Jerusalem-Haifa railway from being bombed every day, who built an electric fence on the borders to keep marauders out but who did nothing to round up the terrorists inside the country, Raziel organized a secret security service that made an end to the depredations in a few weeks' time. His ten thousand resolute men jumped to action from any task upon which they were engaged, whenever danger threatened and before the British troops had left their barracks.

On the outbreak of the war in Europe, Raziel voluntarily disbanded his organization so that every member could have full freedom to enter military service, should Britain consent to the formation of a Jewish Legion.

"That's the man I want," said General Wavell shortly after he had arrived in Jerusalem and had heard the story of Jewish self-defense. Raziel was brought from prison. The charge of having organized an illegal corps of volunteers, which carried the death penalty, was torn up by the General himself, and the erstwhile commander of the Irgun, because of his fluent command of Arabic, was entrusted with a mission to the rebels in Irak.

Raziel took with him twenty-four of his most trusted colleagues from the old Irgun and went to Baghdad. There, in the guise of Bedouin, they mixed with the guests in the various native caravanserais. Before long Raziel learned that Raschid Galiani Bey had decided that, if he were forced out by the British before the Germans could send him reinforcements, he would blow up the wells and refineries at Mosul.

A special crew of a hundred and fifty German military mechanics was held in readiness on the outskirts of Baghdad to race to Mosul whenever Raschid Galiani should give the order to carry out the work of destruction. Upon learning of this plot, Raziel immediately sent whatever information he had to the British High Command. General Wavell sent word back through one of Raziel's partisans that he could not promise assistance: the British army had engaged the Iraqi but that it would take days, perhaps weeks, before he could break through to Baghdad.

This reply threw Raziel back on his own resources. But being determined to prevent the plot from being carried out, he took five of his men in an automobile and by a roundabout road raced back to British headquarters. There he obtained ten machine guns, twelve cases of hand grenades, and twenty-five revolvers. The material was loaded into five Fiat automobiles captured in Libya, and the caravan started back for the Irak capital. Twice the Jews were held up by Iraqi patrols, but they managed to elude their pursuers each time. On the third day Raziel was back in Baghdad. Right under the nose of the rebellious government he took up a position where he could watch the German mechanical outfit that had been selected to carry out the destruction in Mosul in the event of a British break-through.

The Jews did not have long to wait. A few hours before Raschid Galiani fled to Iran, he gave orders for the Germans to proceed with the demolition. But ten miles out of Baghdad the German crew ran into Raziel's ambush. He had distributed the ten machine guns in five sections of two along the road. It had been decided that ten of his men were to rush out of their hiding place and bring the German motor caravan to a standstill by hurling hand grenades at the trucks. If they survived, they were to return to the machine-gun emplacements. Four of Raziel's companions died in bringing the Germans to a halt. Thereafter the Germans alighted from their trucks and opened fire in the dark. Six more Jews crept forward and set the German trucks on fire by means of bottles filled with gasoline. The glare of the burning trucks silhouetted the surprised Germans as the Jewish machine guns mowed them down. Shortly before dawn, when their ammunition was exhausted, the Jews rushed the Germans with hand grenades and drove them off. Raziel was killed in that last dash. Only six of his companions survived. But the attempt on the oil refineries of Mosul had failed.

7. *Another Day Will Come!*

JEREZ IS A soft, amber-colored wine that contains the essence of early morning sunlight, dewdrops, and satin. The late Sir Henry Deterding of Royal Dutch Shell, who was a connoisseur, admired both its Latin clarity and its oily smoothness. It is also the favorite drink of physicians, philosophers, and the Holy Father, Pope Pius XII, whose eyes sparkled as brilliantly as the poor Fisherman's ring on his finger when I saw him drain a glass of it, in preference to the proffered champagne, at the prefecture of Lisieux back in 1938.

Jerez takes its name from a town in Spain. In that town's neighborhood are some of the richest landed estates in the whole country. Ilya Ehrenbourg, who was a frequent wanderer in Spain, thought that in Jerez originated the old Spanish boast that if Christ had looked over the Pyrenees he would not have been able to resist the tempter. The estates are owned by the families of Villamarta, Andez, Garvey, Queipo de Llano, Pared, and others. These owners have never seen their estates. Since the Gestapo has come to make life and the pursuit of happiness for the Spanish grandees once more secure, they live in Madrid. Before the Hitlerian deluge they spent most of their time in Paris, on the Riviera, on the Côte d'Argent, in Deauville, and in Arcachon-les-Bains.

The peasants around Jerez go barefooted. They eat water soup with a few drops of oil in it. They sleep on the bare earth between the cattle. But the monks have had their salaries restored by the state, and the civil guards have returned to see that the peasants do not steal a handful of straw from under the cows' hoofs.

That is the new order of General Francisco Franco.
Everything has its appointed place in the new Spain, and
property is as sacred as the Holy Trinity. The Nazi pagans
from Berlin own the mines, the railways, the factories, and
banks. Serano Suñer is in charge of political re-education.
In a little more than two years one million former Loyalists have been re-educated and are buried in mass graves.

The Andalusian *bourgeoisie* loves to be entertained
with sad songs, poetic tragedies, and idyllic stories. Enter-
tainment of that sort goes well with a glass of Jerez and
the flashing black eyes of some little Dolores. Because they
are somewhat sentimentally inclined, it should not be
thought that the estate owners are not excellent business-
men. Their capital is of respectable proportions and with
the aid of certain operations on the Stock Exchange their
vineyards are again and again transformed into purest
sugar. The civil guard and the major-domos assure the perpetual repetition of this sweet miracle. For Jerez means not
only golden wine and pesetas in the hundreds of millions
and naked, famine-stricken poverty, it also means battle.

Today there is a lull in the fight. To keep his promise
Franco must kill a million more former Loyalists. That
takes time. The men of the Gestapo sit in the Royal Palace at Madrid and in the government house at Barcelona
to assure tranquillity while the Caudillo puts the dots on
the *i*'s. Those dots take the form of garrotting, shooting,
hanging, burning alive, and mass starvation. Unable to
give prosperity to the richest land on earth, the Caudillo
kills to keep up the pretense that he is busy restoring the
order that he himself disturbed. The Pope counseled him
to be "merciful but just" and gave him his blessing in
anticipation. That is why anybody who at any time in

any way had anything to do with the Republic must pay the penalty of loyalty. Pablo Casals lies in the dungeon of Montjuich awaiting execution for having directed an orchestra under the Republic.

In Jerez there used to appear a four-paged newspaper. Its publisher was Sebastián Oliva, a day laborer who worked in Señor Pared's vineyards. He had given the paper the name of *Voz del Campesino,* which simply means Voice of the Farmer. Oliva was an old-time revolutionary who knew the inside of the prison of Jerez as well as those of Cordova and other Andalusian towns. He told me once that he had spent half of his life behind prison bars. He did not say this in any boastful way. He said it in the most natural way in the world, just as a man would say that he had been married twenty-five years. In 1936 Oliva was a man in his fifties, with hands as gnarled and broad as tree roots and with dry, burning eyes. He knew a little English, for he had in his youth been to Cuba, where he had worked in the plantations. There, too, he had made the acquaintance of the prisons.

His ideas were too naïve and confused for politics, incomprehensible to the landlords, but in his own mind they constituted the incontrovertible truth. He was a man without education, yet animated with strong feelings that burned in him like a fire. "I am for justice and truth," he was wont to say, "justice and truth, nothing else." Those words always came back in his conversation. "I do not care how many millions Señor Pared makes as long as he is just. . . ." In his room Oliva had two books: the Bible and Cervantes.

The monks of Jerez called him an anarchist, a Communist, a Red, an agitator, a destroyer of morale, a heretic,

an underminer of the family, and a libertine. He told me:
"I am only a farmer. They've hated us farmers ever since
the days of Cain and Abel. But why should Andalusia be
a paradise and the farmers live in pigsties? Is that justice?
My neighbor Mauro Bajettiero has four children, who
must remain in their hut because they have no clothes to
put on their backs. They cannot go to school. Yet Mauro
works from morn till night on Señor Pared's estate, and
he receives two and a half pesetas per day. Señor Pared
owns sixty thousand acres of the finest land and an oak
forest to hunt in. When one of Mauro's children died last
year, Señor Pared's major-domo refused my neighbor permission to cut the wood to make a coffin for the dead child.
He called him a damned anarchist for asking. Is that
right?" Oliva chuckled. "I was called a red tiger," he said,
"for having published the circumstances of the child's
death in the *Voz del Campesino*. Would you not have
published that in the newspaper you represent?" he asked.

He showed me the article in question. It was a sober
piece divided in two parts. In the first part Oliva had set
forth in the simplest words the details of the tragedy in the
Bajettiero family, how the breadwinner had to walk seven
miles to work and back at night, how the children ate
boiled acorns most of the time, how parents and children
slept on a heap of rags on the bare floor of their hut, how
Mauro had done time in the jail of Jerez for snaring a
pheasant on Señor Pared's estate, and how upon his return
the youngest child had died of the "blue sickness": hunger.

The second part of the article was subtitled: "But Another Day Will Come." In this part the editor had concluded with a somewhat naïve description of what life
could be like for men like Bajettiero and others if the

estates could be divided up into small parcels, if the monks would content themselves with teaching religion, if the government would abolish the civil guards—in short, if justice could be made to prevail in and around Jerez.

All this, it should be said, was not merely a dream with Sebastián Oliva. It was a program. He fully believed that the millennium could be dragged down from heaven. He also believed that the Republic would perform the miracle. With him the word Republic had an awesome mystical sense. He pronounced the word slowly, with a certain solemnity, as a mufti would say: "Allah is great, nothing is beyond Allah's power!" It would, Oliva admitted, take some time to make the change, but then: "We farmers are patient," he had wound up his article. "We can wait still a little time longer. . . . In the end the Republic will triumph, and the wealth of Spain will belong to the people of Spain."

That was his conviction. He did not say: we must hurl bombs at the major-domos and set their houses on fire or plunder the monasteries. He was convinced that drastic measures of that kind were not necessary and would be entirely superfluous. The Republic was in power, the next election would bring the friends of the farmers into the government, and the reign of heaven on earth would begin.

Oliva did not know that there were men in Berlin and Rome and Madrid who had for years been planning otherwise. Franco launched his revolt to prevent Oliva's millennial dream from materializing. To this end he brought in the Moors from Africa, the Condor legions from Germany, and the colored-arrow divisions from Italy. Do not all things work together for salvation to him who believeth? Junkers soon soared over the vineyards of Señor

Pared. Mauro's children were still eating acorns. In a month, maybe two, the Republic would begin parceling out land near Jerez. Until that time the farmers would have to be patient. But would there be a Republic in two months?

The region around Jerez is rich and generous: orange groves with large golden fruit, peaches, wine, endless fields with heavy Spanish onions, everywhere blossoms and gorgeous colors. It is as if nature has tried to reconstitute the paradise that was lost at Eden. There is a monastery on the hill with two hundred rooms. Crowds of beggars have sat before its doors since time immemorial. On the other side of the fields are the silk factory and the canning plant. The girls employed there receive two pesetas a day. The factories are the property of General Queipo de Llano, the drunken sot whose voice could be heard over Radio-Sevilla, boasting, bragging, telling the Moors to rape the women of the Reds first and then rip them up with the bayonet.

Oliva had been named *alcade* of Jerez. It was his task to stop the peasants of the neighborhood from seizing the land. They must wait till the agronomes and surveyors could arrive from Madrid to make a just division. Oliva was for justice. But the peasants said that a beginning must be made at last. They had waited long enough. Why delay, now that the major-domos and the civil guards had all disappeared?

Well, then a beginning was to be made. First, the church lands were to be divided. They were the richest estates in the district and belonged to God. At least, so the priests always said. They, the priests, merely served in the capacity of God's tenants. Six hundred peasants marched in a delegation to the monastery, a silent, hard-eyed crowd. But the doors were closed, and nobody answered the bell.

Could it be that the monks had gone the way of the civil guards?

So much the better! Well, then into the vineyards! Come Fernandez, come Mauro, where do we start to measure your plot? As the peasants entered the monastery gardens, a salvo rang out. The shots came from the monastery. Six men fell to the ground, three dead, three wounded. The first salvo was followed by a second and a third. But no, no one was hit. The peasants had taken cover. In an hour's time they were back in the village to deliberate and to consult with Oliva. He still counseled moderation, but he could no longer stem the tide.

The peasants equipped themselves with arms and gasoline cans and advanced to the assault. The monastery was set on fire, and the monks surrendered. They were put to work putting out the flames as the farmers carried away the furniture to their bare huts.

Mauro Bajettiero did not take any furniture. He had entered the chapel and espied the gold-stitched gowns with which the statue of the Mother of God was draped. He removed the clothes, thirty superimposed costumes, donations from the rich ladies of Jerez. Now his children and his wife would have something on their backs at last. They would also be covered in the night. They would not all die of the "blue sickness," which is caused by hunger and destitution.

When the rebels captured Jerez, Oliva had fled. He and other farmers, amongst whom was Mauro Bajettiero, managed to reach Cordova and joined one of the loyalist units. After the war they passed into France, where they were sent to the prison camp of Ceres. Two years they waited in weariness. Two years, while Europe went up in flames and Franco waded in blood.

Then they were repatriated. They crossed the border back into Spain just as the noonday sun stood highest. Their names figured on the list that Franco had sent to his old teacher Marshal Pétain. Behind Oliva's and Mauro's names appeared the words: "Accused of blasphemy."

8. *The Unsaid Prayer*

HIS HANDS trembled a little as he poured himself a cup of tea. There had been so much work that day. First there had been the evacuation of a hundred children from the village. That was in the morning. Then there had been a tedious delay at the railway station, when a last minute checkup revealed that two of the children were missing. Could it be that they were among the victims of last night's air raid? Perhaps the morrow would tell, when the wardens should have removed the debris above the shelter near the church. Then there had been a burial. That had taxed his strength to the utmost. He had been with the parents of William Gillespie, a pilot in the R.A.F., who had been shot down over Middlesex a few days before. What could one say to a father and mother of an only son? That he had died so that England might live? That sounded quite inspiring and touching in official orations, but Mr. and Mrs. Gillespie were amongst his dearest parishioners. He had to give them a ray of hope, something to cling to in their cruel bereavement. . . .

The Reverend Thomas Baxter heaved a deep sigh. He was no longer a young man. He was verging on sixty-three years, though he bore few of the signs of age; his hair was rather grizzled, but not grey; his eye was mild, but clear and bright. Mr. Baxter had come to Hampton Road forty years ago. It was his first parish; it would probably be his last. He had dreamed of retiring in a few years and devoting the remaining years of his life to some scholarly work from which the arduous duties of a rural dean of the Church of England had kept him thus far. But his wife had fallen ill, and then the war had come. Now there could be no thought of retiring, of course.

He drank his tea in silence and looked around the room. This was not his own home. His own home lay in ruins, next to the battered church. This was one of Sir Henry Matthews' cottages, which had been placed at his disposal after those first aerial onslaughts on East Anglia. His wife lay in the next room, a helpless invalid. His daughter was busy in the kitchen.

It was evening, and he was tired, but he dreaded the coming night. Would the Germans return as they had done on the previous ten nights? Would they again make Hampton Road one of their targets? The bombings had riddled Mr. Baxter with fear. But he had had to put a brave face on it and go out after the all-clear signal and speak to people and pretend that he was, if not unconcerned, at least not upset but calm and collected. In short, he had to set an example to others.

At William Gillespie's grave that afternoon he had spoken from the text: "Who for the joy that was set before Him endured the cross." He thought of it now. Was that the right word to have said? And then he thought of the government's announcement that it was framing its policy on the assumption that the war would last three years or more. That was the thing that had disturbed him most that day: three more years of war. He thought that there must have been few hearts in England that did not quail for a moment when that announcement came. It was all well and good to pretend to grin and say: "We are Englishmen: we can take it and hold our thumbs up in the air," but Englishmen were only human beings, too, after all.

Mr. Baxter wondered how much more his parishioners could stand of the sleepless nights and constant bombing.

And yet, more was to come apparently, for what else could the government's announcement mean? In his imagination, the prospects of the future tended to grow more and more terrifying. The calamities in store assumed almost monstrous proportions. . . .

His wife was calling from the other room, and he and his daughter reached her bedside simultaneously. "Have you heard from Gilbert?" the woman asked. She referred to their son, a lieutenant in the tank corps, now on duty in Europe. He had a letter from Gilbert, he reassured her, and the boy was doing well. He was going to read the letter more carefully as soon as he had washed up. He had only glanced at it in the afternoon when the mailman had pushed it in his hands. He asked his wife if she would like some tea, but she did not answer him.

As he spoke, the sirens began to wail. The woman on the bed stirred restlessly. "Who is that crying?" she said. "Someone is crying!"

Father and daughter exchanged a significant look. Mrs. Baxter's mind was wandering again; the weeks and weeks of fever had affected her brain. Mr. Baxter felt his wife's forehead and stooped down to kiss her. Then he walked back into the sitting room and took his son's letter from his pocket. He turned at once to the last page, the page that had disturbed him most when he had glanced at it in the afternoon. The boy's letters had been so optimistic in the past, so full of good cheer, that this latest message with its note of somber despair had upset him the more.

"It is your conviction, I know," his son had written him, "that what we are facing is the consequence of sin and that it is not for us to apportion the guilt. . . . But the consequences of sin fall upon the innocent and the guilty alike. Here in the first line, between two raids, two bombardments, two attempts to dig a hole in the night, with dead men all around me, what remains of life? Is not this punishment too great?"

Mr. Baxter looked up. The droning of airplanes filled the dark sky above. "Here they are again," he muttered. There was a muffled crash in the distance. He went back to the sickroom. "Isn't it early in the year for thunder, Thomas?" his wife asked him. There was another crash, nearer this time. "They are bombing the church again," said his daughter, as she stepped into the room. "But they are swinging to the north. Hear, that is the sound of our fighters. They are attacking them. . . ."

Mr. Baxter was holding his wife's hand in his. In the other hand he held his son's letter. He glanced at it involuntarily by the light of the bed lamp and read: "What else can I tell you? Life? What is it? What remains of it? It is something more than a phantom, a phantom which is itself so inconsistent that it fails to move us. I quit you on these words of Lawrence: 'When things get very bad, they pass beyond tragedy—and then the only thing we can do is to keep quite still—and guard the lost treasure of the soul, our sanity. . . . If we lose our sanity, nothing and nobody in the whole vast realm of space wants us, or can have anything to do with us. We can but howl the lugubrious howl of idiots, the howl of the utterly lost howling their nowhereness. . . .'" Mr. Baxter shuddered. He keenly felt the suffering his boy must have undergone when he wrote those words. And then he thought of the government's announcement again, three more years of war. . . .

It seemed an endless span of time if those years were to be charged with suffering and horror the like of which had never been experienced on earth before. Was it shameful to be afraid of the future? he wondered. He was not afraid of death for himself. What he feared was sudden death or, as he had often said, to be cut off in a flash and to pass to his judgment unshriven. He had always prayed to be spared from sudden death, to be granted at least a moment of recollection, that he could turn his heart again to God in penitence and faith before leaving this life. No, on the whole he was not afraid of death.

He was afraid for his people, his parishioners of Hampton Road, for England. What we are facing, he thought again, as he had written to his son: "What we are facing is the consequence of sin: sin of pride, sin of fatness, sin of self-righteousness. If there were only an acknowledgment of this, if there only would be contrition and penitence, then we could again pray for fortitude. . . ."

The rattle of machine-gun firing in the sky above shook him from his meditation. "They'll soon be coming back this way," said his daughter. "Our fighters are trying to intercept them. I hope they've dropped their bombs elsewhere, so that they will not be forced to unload again in our neighborhood."

He nodded his head. The firing grew heavier. In the distance were some heavy detonations. He thought of the sermon he was to preach the next Sunday. The fortitude for which we ought to pray, he thought, is not that the natural virtue of man which enables him to square his shoulders and determine his course, come what may? The fortitude for which we ought to pray is a gift from the Holy Spirit, a gift which enables us to face the evils we most dread, a gift which enables us to resist mere recklessness—that appearance of courage, which is not true courage. This Christian grace of fortitude would not, to be sure, banish fear. It was not a sort of Dutch courage; but it would enable men to control fear. With Christian fortitude we could, he thought, enter upon arduous tasks with the quiet and steady will that men would naturally bring to bear on relatively easy matters. Christian fortitude would enable men to keep their heads, whether in adversity or prosperity. . . .

There was a knock at the cottage door. Mr. Baxter rose to open. A farmer was standing before him. Could Mr. Baxter come with him quickly, the man was asking. They had just dug a woman out of the ruins, and she was seriously hurt, so seriously that she might die in the night. She had asked for the parson. But would he hurry, please, for there was not much time to lose.

Mr. Baxter went into the bedroom to see that his wife was comfortable. He kissed her on the forehead and tucked the blankets in at the sides. He said to his daughter, as he put on his hat, that he hoped he would not be gone for long. Then he went out with the farmer. The man carried an electric torch to guide their way. To the left, but far away, a house was burning fiercely. "That must be Mr. Mortlock's place," said Mr. Baxter. The farmer said it was. It had been burning for an hour. But in the village it was worse. A whole row of cottages had gone down. They just toppled over like houses of cards," the man said. "We can't tell how many dead there are. We had only begun to dig when I was sent to fetch you. . . ."

Suddenly the rumble of a bombing squadron was heard approaching from the northwest. "They are coming back from London," said the man. "Our fellows are on their tails." A Verey light illuminated the landscape. They could see the skeleton of the burnt-out church, starkly outlined on the knoll. "They are lighting their way home," said the farmer. The bombers were nearly overhead. They were looking for a target on which to unload before flying over the Channel. Fighting planes threw out Verey lights to show the oncoming bombers their targets. All at once the air was filled with the crash and thunder of exploding projectiles. The two men crouched behind the trees at the roadside. The bomb fragments whistled about their heads. Mr. Baxter covered his ears with his hands, but his eyes turned in the direction of his own cottage, above which another parachute light was slowly floating to earth. He could hear the whistle of the bombs as they rained down in the vicinity of his home. "Merciful heavens," he said, "if we are going to escape this, it will be a wonder."

There was a deafening series of explosions. By the flash of the striking bombs, he could see his cottage wrapped in flames and smoke. Then, just as suddenly, the flock of raiders passed, and all that could be heard was the rattle of machine guns from the British fighter planes chasing the invaders.

Mr. Baxter ran back to his cottage. He was breathing hard. The farmer was racing along behind him. The first glow of light had appeared in the east when they reached the place. The cottage was a heap of rubble. Mr. Baxter threw off his coat and started to pull at some of the cracked timbers. The two men worked in silence. But they were soon forced to give up. Then Mr. Baxter sat down on the stone bench in front of what had been his house and stared at what had become the tomb of his wife and daughter. It was daylight when the village people came up. The parson was just pulling a sheet of paper from his jacket. On the paper he had written out the prayer he had intended to intone the next Sunday.

He glanced at it and read: "O God, who art the Author of peace and Lover of concord, pour down now upon the German people the blessing of Thy love and understanding, that their hearts may be touched by the grace of Thy Holy Spirit and their minds awakened to the recognition of the universal brotherhood of man. Grant that their eyes may be opened to the truth, and that they may rise from the plane on which men are separated from each other by their prejudices to that plane where they are united by good will and unselfish co-operation. Amen...."

He read the words a second time and shook his head with a deep sigh. Then he tore up the paper.

9. *At Sea*

IT WAS THE thirteenth day since he had set out from the base at Kiel. His instructions had been to cruise in Norwegian waters and watch for possible English raiders and for convoys on the way to and from the port of Murmansk. But only once in all those days since he had left the home station had he sighted an enemy craft. That had been on the third day out: a British destroyer racing at top speed through a choppy sea had betrayed itself by the thick clouds of smoke pouring from its funnels. For a few hours he had given chase in the hope of intercepting the English vessel. But towards evening, just after he had given the order to man the torpedo tubes, the Englishman had run into a fog bank; when it had lifted, there had been no trace of the enemy. Thereafter he had drifted lazily in the general direction of the Scandinavian coast. When the weather changed to clear sunshine, he had taken it easy on deck.

Lieutenant-Commander Gustav Mahrendorf was a Frisian. He had been an instructor at the Oberrealschule in Emden when the war broke out. Like all the men from his district, he had been appointed to one of the naval bases on the Baltic and had spent a year in training for submarine warfare in Kiel. He was now making his first trip as commander of the U206 and was secretly happy that so far there had been no occasion to give battle.

Not that he was afraid to fight. It was not that. He felt that there was something treacherous and shameful in the nature of submarine warfare. It did not comport with his ideas of chivalry and German frankness. He would much sooner have shipped on one of the battleships and sailed up to the enemy in full sight, decks cleared for action and the guns stripped for an honorable, aboveboard contest of skill and might. He loathed the idea of crawling over the bottom of the ocean and of sneaking up like a crouching tiger on some unsuspecting freighter and then of sending a torpedo crashing into his fragile hull. Of course, he realized that it had to be done. He knew, as did everyone else, that Germany was forced to make up for her naval weakness by craftiness and ruthlessness in order to break the stranglehold of the British blockade, but to say that he carried out his task with relish and pride would be wrong.

He hoped for a speedy end to the war. He wanted to go back to his study and his books and to complete the volume of poetry he had started just when the mobilization order had reached him. And then there was his wife Magda, of course, and their little girl Hilda, with the golden hair, who was just beginning to talk. He had been obliged to send them away from Kiel three months ago because of the constant air raids. They were staying with his parents now on the farm in Holstein. At least they were safe and had enough to eat, too. . . . How long would it be before he would see them again? He was wondering about that as he slowly paced the deck in his hip boots and looked on the endless expanse of gray-green water and on the waves splashing against the steel of the conning tower. He took a notebook from his pocket and wrote down a few words. He always did that when a thought or an idea for a poem crossed his mind. He would work it out later, he thought, tonight in his berth after they had come to a halt and most of the members of the crew had gone to sleep. . . .

If that Gestapo man would only go to sleep, too, or busy himself with something else besides sitting by his side and watching his every move. . . . Why had that man come with them on his journey, anyway? Was the government afraid that he would not carry out his duty or that his men would mutiny, as the Kaiser's sailors had done in the last war? Commander Mahrendorf resented the presence of that political commissar on board. The man himself was not a pleasant fellow in the first place, he was taciturn and morose. Surely not the ideal person to stimulate the morale of the crew or to keep them in good spirits with his short answers and freezing looks.

Kurt Seitz was the man's name. He hailed from Hamburg. At least, so he said. But that might well be a lie, too. For he could not understand a word of the Frisian or Holstein dialect. He spoke like a Prussian landlubber, like a Berliner. He said *"Yott"* instead of *"Gott,"* and *"yefunden"* instead of *"gefunden."* And then, those shifty evil eyes. The man behaved like a born spy. How many times had Commander Mahrendorf not looked up from his plate at the mess table to find the steely eyes of Seitz on him in a strange, quizzical, suspicious way. No, frankly he did not like the man. But then, what of it? The patrol would soon come to an end, and they would be in Kiel for two weeks' leave of absence, and he would run up to his parents' place in the country and see Magda and Hilda and forget about Seitz, and on the next trip there would probably be another political inspector along, a more amenable fellow. . . .

No, it would not be long now. He had just verified the contents of the oil tanks. They were half empty. He would have to run in at Trondheim or Bergen or preferably at Kiel, of course, in a few days, anyway. Perhaps he would find time on the next occasion he was ashore to finish that poem on the sea he had in mind. He ought not to delay long with that poem. He had it all in his head. He would tell the story of a half-ruined old castle on the sea-shore, one of those old fortresses of the Vikings he had spotted on the Norwegian coast last week. In one of the upper chambers of the castle he would place a man, a prisoner, a pale and somber man, who was loaded down with chains. That man would not hear anything but the howling of the wind and the roar of the sea, but in the night he would have him read songs of hope, songs that grew as fiery flowers out of the ashes after a prairie fire. . . .

He would have him read of the sea and of the gulls that swept by on lazy wings carried by the wind.

"The sea, the sea!" Commander Mahrendorf was speaking to himself. "The sea is a wheat field sprinkled with cornflowers, and the midday sun, as it now dances on the white plumes of the waves, is the scythe that mows down the white, blue harvest. . . . The sea is a wild ferocious animal that growls and rattles its chains, but also a little child that sings innocent lullabies and that weaves a garland of forget-me-nots. . . . The sea is a lascivious woman, an odalisque who tempts with the eyes of a gazelle, or an orchestra with copper cymbals and trumpets which blare of passion and tumult, or yet again a procession of pure virgins, who carry lilies and who wear long, still veils of transparent white. . . ."

He would have the prisoner in the castle see and feel the different moods of the sea and of the fleets that sailed by his window with swollen sails that glided off towards the horizon like white-winged swans. . . .

Lieutenant Mahrendorf broke off his murmurs suddenly and lifted his binoculars to his eyes. For a moment he stared and then hastily clambered down the conning tower, closing the steel lid above his head. As soon as he was below he gave the order to submerge and took up his position before the periscope.

"There's an Englishman about six miles off," he said to Seitz, who stood beside him. "It must be the ship about which headquarters radioed us this morning. We'll be in a position in less than an hour. It's strange, I had not noticed him before. . . ."

"You were probably occupied with other matters," returned the Gestapo official icily, and his eyes stopped significantly on Lieutenant Mahrendorf's big notebook, which protruded from the pocket of his jacket.

Mahrendorf flushed crimson but did not reply. His eyes were glued to the periscope. In the misty blurb on the sea-spattered glass above the surface he could see a black speck emerging. He turned the knobs on the instrument to get clearer visibility.

"Is it a freighter?" asked the man by his side.

"It's a passenger liner," returned Mahrendorf.

The Gestapo man grunted with satisfaction. "Must be a troopship bound for Russia," he said.

Mahrendorf shouted an order in the telephone. The ship lunged forwards and gathered speed.

"This will mean the Iron Cross for you," said Seitz to the Commander.

"That is, if I sink him," returned Mahrendorf. "And that is not so certain. He has seen us. He's beginning to zigzag. We'll have to be careful. He has a gun aft and may start to throw off depth bombs. I must get a mile closer anyway, before I can do anything. . . ."

The Commander grew suddenly silent. He wetted his lips and swallowed hard. He was almost crushing his forehead against the glass. He could see the deck of the steamer quite clearly now and the sailors stripping the tarpaulin from the gun on the afterdeck. He paid little attention to them. He turned the periscope so that the sight focused squarely on the bridge. There he could see a woman who was strapping a life belt on the shoulders of a little girl. The little girl's hair was blowing in the breeze. "She has the same hair as *meine kleine Hilda*," he thought. He turned away from the instrument and glanced at the Gestapo man. Their eyes met for a fraction of a second. . . . Then he looked into the glass again. . . . Once more he saw the little girl. A sailor was carrying her in his arms to one of the lifeboat stations.

Mahrendorf sighed and gritted his teeth. The Gestapo man by his side watched him like a cat. He could feel those steely eyes on the side of his face. He took another look into the periscope. He was beginning to feel seasick. "I do not see any flag," he said.

"Sufficient reason to send him down," replied the Gestapo man.

The Lieutenant's eyes flew along the ship's deck where the passengers now stood in line with their lifebelts on. He picked out the little girl easily. She was standing by her mother's side, and her hair was blowing in the sunny breeze. It seemed to him that she was looking straight into the periscope. He closed his eyes for an instant and then looked into the Gestapo man's face again. When he shouted the order to fire, his voice was a hoarse whisper.

The next instant he raced up the companion ladder and threw back the hood of the conning tower. Before looking at the sinking Englishman, he tossed his notebook into the water.

10. *Peradventure!*

In this, the tenth hour of the day, the sun was beginning to cross the Hudson River. The daily journey through a thousand centuries neared its end. Already the candles were being lit for the homecoming, and God was standing in the doorway looking for His messenger's return. Shadows were installing themselves on the New York side of the river as the roar of day softened to a zooming murmur. In the trees was heard the rustle of the wings of sparrows stirring in their first sleep. Objects were no longer isolated but were blending slowly in a gloom that was like a solemn anguish mounting in the measure that the light receded. Behind, in the sun's path lay the world as a dark, deep abyss. Quenched now were the red flames of noon. Where the zenith had been passed, torrents of rain washed the battlefields of the morning. Over the domed cathedrals and the teeming cities of Europe the moon had taken over the vigil, but the ocean lay wrapped in brooding darkness as in that timeless hour when the Spirit hovered over the waters. A bank of mist obscured the New Jersey shore. It was a cloud of midsummer vapor, soggy and heavy with moisture. Into this wall of white steam the sun moved like a dripping chariot and then disappeared as behind a vast curtain of luminous white. Even the strings of electric lights, which usually sparkled in the blue twilight like superimposed tiers of jewels, had become invisible, wrapped as they were in that liquid shroud of heat.

Thus, I recalled, I had one evening watched the Dead Sea vanish from sight on the road from Hebron, when I had set out to see the pillar of salt in the Valley of the

Plain. And there, too, I remembered, alone in the wilderness with a dooms-day color filling the sky, I had felt afraid as never before on any battlefield. From the flint-covered path that I was treading Abraham must have looked in the direction of Sodom, that morning when he rose early to see the smoke of the country go up like the smoke of a furnace. And I thought: if there had only been ten or even five righteous men in Sodom, this immense desolation before my eyes would not have come into existence, and here instead would be a plain filled with orchards and meadows and towering cities, with cool fountains and little children in the squares clapping their hands in joyous play.

Do not all the old legends say that it is for the sake of a handful of righteous men, not princes or mighty ones, but humble men in whose hearts there is no guile, that God until this day preserves the world from destruction? In the Talmud it is the *Lamed Vov,* the thirty-six unknown who live in each generation, to whose virtues and ideals we owe our continued existence. In the Bible their number is less. It was of that legend in Genesis that I thought on the road from Hebron. It came back to mind once more as I watched the sun become blotted out in a pall of white through which shimmered the lambent flush of distant flames.

And Abraham drew near, and said, Wilt thou also destroy the righteous with the wicked?

Peradventure there be fifty righteous men within the city: wilt thou also destroy and not spare the place for the fifty righteous that are therein?

That be far from thee to do after this manner, to slay the righteous with the wicked: and that the righteous should be as the wicked, that be far from thee: Shall not the Judge of all the earth do right?

And the Lord said, if I find in Sodom fifty righteous within the city, then I will spare all the place for their sakes.

And Abraham answered and said, Behold now, I have taken upon me to speak unto the Lord, which am but dust and ashes.

Peradventure there shall lack five of the fifty righteous: wilt thou destroy all the city for lack of five? And he said, If I find there forty and five, I will not destroy it.

And he spake unto him yet again, and said, Peradventure there shall be forty found there. And he said, I will not do it for forty's sake.

And he said unto him, Oh let not the Lord be angry, and I will speak: Peradventure there shall thirty be found there. And he said, I will not do it, if I find thirty there.

And he said, Behold now, I have taken upon me to speak unto the Lord: Peradventure there shall be twenty found there. And he said, I will not destroy it for twenty's sake.

And he said, Oh let not the Lord be angry, and I will speak yet but this once: Peradventure ten shall be found there. And he said, I will not destroy it for ten's sake.

When I had read the old story once more I fell to wondering: if Abraham should have taken his immense compassionate courage in his hands just once more and had asked the Eternal if for the sake of five or of four or three He would not have destroyed the city, what would have been the answer? And if we were to ask that question in our time, in this year of grace 1941, what would be the answer? And further again who are the few wholly righteous men for whose sake the Judge of all the world is willing to suspend judgment over a world that is wallowing in the blood of His children. And my mind's eye ran over the great and the mighty ones, the men in the first ranks, whom all the world sees and who are almost deified themselves in our time, the prelates in purple and the *duces* and *Fuehrers* and those that make the universe ring with the rattle of their sabers and with the clink of their spurs and with the thunder of their voices—the men who are like earthquakes and fires and who go through the world like a great storm wind. Is it for their sake?

God is not in the storm of passions raised by the different political movements, not in the earthquakes of those sudden national renewals that have not a single solid basis, not in the fire of demogogic words that inflame the crowds. God is in the murmur of the still small voice. He is not with the brilliant, loud-talking majorities, for there is nothing official about Him, and He does not conform to the fashion of the day. He loves to be allied with minorities. Is it not from extremely small minorities that the most worth-while things in life have come? It may well be that God again makes an alliance with a single individual, as with Abraham or Elijah, and, if so, it is to such a man that must be applied the word of John Knox which is inscribed on the Reformation monument in Geneva: *"Un homme avec Dieu est toujours dans la majorité!"* (A man with God is always in the majority!)

Leonhard Ragaz

The dead Beethoven was found in a half-sitting posture with his wide-open eyes frozen in a horrible stare. To the neighbors who opened the door of his room in the morning, it seemed that death had snatched him away while he was in the full fury of one of those leonine fits of rage which seized him more and more frequently during the latter part of his life. The body was seen to be leaning somewhat forward. His fist was clenched in an expressively menacing gesture towards heaven. This macabre spectacle of a dead man who seemed still to be speaking shocked Beethoven's good neighbors not a little. At once the thought of impious irreverence and blasphemy entered their minds. For no decent, God-fearing citizen of their acquaintance had ever fared forth to meet his Maker in so patently rebellious a disposition as the dead musician's defiant attitude but too clearly suggested. Fists should not be found clenched on deathbeds, but hands gently folded in pious resignation, as if imploring the divine mercy. Even a lifeless body should somehow indicate by a posture of decorum that in the last hour of consciousness there had been nothing like a battle or a stormy debate, but rather, filial submission to God's will and some evidence that he with the cruel reaper had been "greeted as feet of friend coming with welcome at our journey's end."

Yet, I have wondered more than once if, after all, there was anything impious in Beethoven's final gesture of angry protest—that is, if piety and godliness are not judged by the usual standards current in Christian circles, but when we measure them by the Bible, where men are to be found striving and battling with God and crying out: "I will not let Thee go, except Thou bless me"; where men do not long and languish, but where they hunger and thirst for righteousness; where insistently, night and day, the frenzied clamor goes up for justice, and where there is violent protest and direct opposition to God's decrees, even in the matter of death itself.

No, it is not impious, and surely not un-Biblical, when Franz Polgar, in reporting the circumstances of Beethoven's death, declares that the Last Judgment will consist not so much in man justifying himself before God as God justifying Himself to man—for instance, to Ludwig van Beethoven for having deprived him, him, of all human beings, of the power of hearing.

I know a man, the most modest, most self-effacing, and gentlest of human beings, who challenges God every day of the year, and who at times actually upbraids the Most High. That man is Leonhard Ragaz, the Swiss Apostle of the Social Gospel. At the same time, I must say that I do not think God is at all displeased with Ragaz' bursts of anger. For who, after all, implanted that immense passion for the Kingdom in the heart of the Swiss prophet —that overwhelming longing for a world of reason and justice in which the lie shall be broken, pride shall be turned to shame, and the last shall be the first? Who, but God Himself, the God of Moses and Isaiah, of Jesus and Akiba, of Cromwell and Francis of Assisi, men who bent the will of God, who were so insistent that they at times succeeded in changing the mind of the Master of the universe and who forced Him by prayer and persuasion, by imprecation and by threats, to set wrongs aright, to frustrate the plans of the evildoers, and to help in the advance of His own Kingdom.

"It is true, I do grow impatient at times," Ragaz said to me one day, just after the Nazi hordes had trodden into the mire the political structure in central Europe, which his friend and disciple, the late Thomas Masaryk, had set up and nurtured to life. "I grow impatient," he said, "when I do not immediately see the role God plays in this spectral agony of our dying world—that is, when I see injustice triumph and justice flung into the discard like a soiled rag. I cry out, 'Yes,' and I say to God: 'Why dost Thou not intervene? Art Thou asleep perchance or weary? Why dost Thou not rend the heavens and come down? Is this not Thy cause that is suffering and the advent of Thine own Kingdom that is being retarded, not to speak of the nameless sufferings of Thy children?'

"But today I see the light," Dr. Ragaz went on, after a pensive interruption. "The evil situation in the world will and must grow and become a great deal worse yet. Humanity will have to drain this cup to the bitter dregs. It cannot be otherwise. Let us be honest about it: the world will not accept Christ until the hour of its ultimate and supreme distress. Jesus acknowledged this Himself. Only when the terror of violence has become so great, so absolutely unbearable that men cry out: 'Mountains fall upon us and hills cover us,' only then, He said, will we see appear the sign of the Son of Man, the sign of the Cross.

"Did you ever hear that story," he asked suddenly, "the story of that priest in the Alcazar of Toledo who came to the commandant with a suggestion of surrender or, failing that, at least of sending the women and children away to safety? The commandant turned the priest away with the words, 'Man, don't bother me. Give us absolution, and we will all die together!' Well," resumed Ragaz, "if Christ is not able to inspire His followers with the same heroism as those Spaniards displayed, then His cause will not only be lost in our time—then it is lost now!"

Ragaz, for all those passionate outbursts, is not a ready conversationalist or even a constant talker like those politicians and literati one encountered in the salons of Paris before the debacle and whom one suspected either of indulging their vanity or seeking to hide their mortal ennui under a flow of brilliant conversation. Ragaz' interests, too, are universal, but he speaks somewhat haltingly and seems to experience difficulty in verbal communication—a circumstance that probably derives from his extreme shyness, the grave and sweet shyness of the Alpine peasant. There are moments when he appears hesitant or, one might say, *gêné*. In the midst of a serious argument he will suddenly leave a sentence unfinished and then blush like a boy, as if astonished by the boldness of his own assertions.

But there is an urbanity about his features, some kind of luminous gentleness, which is given life and meaning by the earnestness of his deep brown eyes when he speaks. Ragaz does not make a fiery nervous appearance in the pulpit, as did Savonarola, whose burning glance shining fiercely under his black cowl was said to have made men turn away in guilty consternation. Short of stature, Ragaz does not command physical attention, except, perhaps, as an ethnological type, for he is neither German nor French nor a mixture of the two, but of that race of almost swarthy mountaineers which the winds and the sun of the Swiss canton of Uri have produced.

Ragaz is more of a teacher than an exhorter: every form of artificiality or affectation is alien to him. Yet, without any of the professional orator's tricks, he fascinates his hearers by the sheer earnestness of his word. He repeats himself frequently, in fact he repeats *ad infinitum,* for he has only one theme and one theme only: the

Kingdom of God. Like Lenin, he restates and reshapes
and regroups his ideas, always in the simplest of language,
until his hearers not merely catch the drift of his argument, but become drenched and permeated with his
thoughts.

I never saw Dr. Ragaz in the pulpit of Basel's great
cathedral. When I came to know him he had long since
abandoned his chair in theology at the University of
Zurich in order to go to the proletariat, to the poorest
and the outcasts. My visits to him took place in the Gar-
tenhofstrasse, in the cloisteral study with the soundproof
doors and the dominating, life-size portrait of Blumhardt,
who was the first minister of the state church in Germany
to give up the pastorate in order to become a Socialist
deputy.

In his study Leonhard Ragaz was all serenity and peace.
Yet, he was visibly an extremely lonely man, as the
prophet must be lonely, because the people for whom
the prophet enters into battle can never rise to the dangerous life of the spirit. This, indeed, is the mark of
the true prophet in that, from his loneliness and bitterness, always and again he returns to the people with
renewed love, whereas the demagogic and egotistical agitator soon conceives contempt for the masses.

Ragaz is a prophet—that is, an activist: he demands
deeds, not words. To the prophet spiritual values exist
to be translated into reality; words must become flesh
and blood, ideals take tangible shape in human relationships. The prophet's activity is directed chiefly against
the existing, against the traditional, against the petrified
religion of which the priest is both the custodian and the
beneficiary. The prophet is the revolutionary who wants
to break up the old forms, to infuse new life into with-

ered bones. Ritual from which the spirit has departed is meaningless mummery to him. . . .

The prophet turns against the king and the state and the power of the state. He tolerates no betrayal of the basic values. Let your yes be yes and your no, no! What have politics and commerce to do with such absolute and unconditional principles? Aren't politics a game of give and take, of temporizing and compromise, and should not ideals be locked in the cupboard when not useful or when they are contrary to the material interests of the ruling castes?

Is it surprising that at all times the prophet has been denounced by politicians and statesmen and kings as a dangerous revolutionary?

Since he resigned his professoriate at the University of Zurich, Leonhard Ragaz has worked with imaginative sensibility in close harmony with the aspirations of the working class. He has sought to fructify the socialist search for justice by imbuing it with the message of the Kingdom of God and its justice in this world. He looks to see civilization and public and private life finding revivification in a sacredly revolutionary renewal of the cause of Jesus—*die Sache Christi*—as he puts it. What this has meant in public disdain, in suffering, in constant struggle, but also in outright persecution can scarcely be imagined by those who cling to the nation that the Swiss Republic carries on as an island of pure democracy in a sea of foul totalitarianism. Ragaz, for one, has known otherwise a long time. The general press long has tried to silence him by ignoring him. When this method of coercion failed, Swiss respectability had recourse first to ridicule and jeers, then to misrepresentation and violent denunciation. The cool and collected scholar was turned into a fever-brained zealot; the champion of nonviolence and spiritual defense was branded a destructive Bolshevik; the man with a European following and a world reputation was dismissed as a parochial little busybody who interfered vociferously in things of which he had no knowledge.

But at each new betrayal of the Swiss people's democratic faith, at each retreat from the ideal, Ragaz openly denounced the Bundesrat. And at each successive piece of brigandage pulled off by the international statesmen in Geneva, who were the honored guests of the Swiss Republic, the voice of Ragaz thundered through the city of Calvin like those storm winds in his native mountains on a fierce autumn night.

Then the man's mail began to be opened and his children ostracized from the society of *die Anständigen*. Of course, those Protestant ministers whose conception of the Kingdom of God, over there as over here, is personal tranquillity and respectability and unction and smugness, and comfortable parsonages and fat posts on educational boards, who deny Christ by the very fact that they have never known what it is to have oppression, let alone martyrdom, in this world, early took a hand in discrediting the upstart Prophet. They assailed Ragaz' interpretation of the texts, his unseemly familiarity with the deity, his orthodoxy, the unambiguity of his language, his repetitiousness. The little bookshop he ran for years was closed. His monthly magazine was censored. Alpine peasants turned into secret-service men noted down his sermons and searched for evidence of subversion in the Gospels. The Volkshochschule, where he lectured every night to crowds of workers, was taxed out of existence. His books were proscribed in a gesture of appeasement to the incendiaries of parliaments and libraries in the Reich. In the end the sons of William Tell, Zwingli, and Pestalozzi in the Federal Council forbade him to speak. Ragaz was reduced to starkest poverty.

His own personal well-being means nothing to the Prophet. He is not only doomed to loneliness, he is often an outcast from society. The public powers jeer at him as a Utopian dreamer and through their henchmen hound him from the market place where he would speak. Still he returns, in the teeth of opposition and popular disfavor. He takes his life in his hands. He whips his people because he loves them. He wants to see his people great and therefore belittles them. "He is a mere instrument, a trumpet through which the divine voice grows audible; a plow in the hands of the Eternal Plowman, perhaps only a combustible that must flare up on the pyre in order that God's fire may become visible."

But he is human, too, the prophet. He has his moments of anguish and doubt and lassitude. For the task is ungrateful, and he would fain be at peace with the world, not always striving and castigating and denouncing. Perhaps Thou wouldst send another, said Jeremiah. I have not the gift of language, demurred Moses. Perhaps the ideal could be stated less forcefully, less implicitly. Can we not compromise or condone just a little? Why should I incur the world's hatred and contempt?

The prophet has a dual battle to wage, against the world outside and against himself, to keep the faith, the certainty of salvation.

For years Ragaz has not only been predicting the catastrophe that has now befallen Western civilization, but he has warned his fellow citizens that neither the so-called neutrality policy pursued by the Federal Council simultaneously with its outright contradiction—the militarization of Swiss national life—would save the old democracy of William Tell from destruction by totalitarianism. In the end, he told the Bundesrat, which is composed of representatives of big business, you will not even resist the pressure from Berlin and Rome. You will capitulate voluntarily (as did actually happen on March 21, when the Swiss Federal Council voted unanimously to accept the New Order in Europe).

"And then it will be seen," he added, "that all the time you prided yourself on your ideals, you were, like the governments of Holland and Belgium and France, only paying lip service to democracy. Not force of arms or superarmaments were the safeguards of the small European countries, but an international order based on justice and respect for minorities. This order," he told the Federal Council, "you have always sabotaged. You ridiculed it, you called it unrealistic, you were embarrassed that the seat of the League of Nations happened to be on Swiss soil. You laughed about the dreamers of human brotherhood, all because you found it more profitable to have strife and war and bloodshed and misery in the world. You worshiped the totalitarian idol, which preserves your class interests, in your heart before you dared to set up in public your altars in its honor. . . ."

"Even so, is it not a pity," I would say to him, "that, in the disasters you see coming over mankind, the good must suffer with the bad, the innocent with the guilty?"

"But there are no innocents," Ragaz would reply. "The guilt of 'the good' resides in the fact that they have given power to the evildoers. It is through their cowardice and lukewarmness to the ideals of democracy that the forces of evil have gained the tremendous power they have at present. Fundamentally, it is a case of the good having made the evildoers what they are today. The peculiarity of present-day forms of evil is not the enormity of evil but the magnitude of its power. For who are these men, Hitler, Stalin, and Mussolini? Are they extraordinarily important or gifted men? In a moral sense, they are no more important than others. But they are filled with egoism, they have no sense of responsibility toward God, which means that they are not orientated toward their fellow human beings as brothers. In that way they are very much like ourselves. But they have been given power, power such as no human soul can bear, power without limit. This has led them to feel that they owe responsibility to no one, God or man. And this will yet lead to the notion that they are divine or semidivine.

"How did evil get on the throne? you ask me. Where were the good and the innocent of whom you speak, those who knew the difference between good and evil, between the lie and the truth. Did they speak, did they raise their voices . . . I mean the representatives of decency, of intelligence, of justice and religion? No, they were silent, silent in all languages. And I say that the root of present-day evil resides not only, as a Frenchman has said, in *la trahison des clercs,* but in the abdication of the decent. . . ."

But that is a long story. Ragaz does not believe that it started with Mussolini's march on Rome or with Hitler's accession to the chancellorship of the Reich, but much, very much earlier. It started at that point in history when Christianity, with its faith and love, withdrew from the world or, rather, created a private sphere for the exercise of Christian virtues. Quite consciously and emphatically did this occur in Lutheranism, though fundamentally this lies in the essence of ecclesiasticism and therefore has come to the fore everywhere. If the Roman Catholic Church, superficially seen, does make a claim to the moral leadership of society, this is fundamentally rather a hierarchal than a theocratic claim.

That, however, the same abdication should have followed in Protestantism is, according to Ragaz, the great catastrophe and the guilty tragedy of the Reformation and of Democracy. For it reduced the reformed church to a mere religious business, a private undertaking, whereas that church, as it started, was to have been an advance guard of God's Kingdom in this world.

It is more than a coincidence that what Ragaz calls the abdication of decency was preceded by decades wherein that abdication was preached and practiced in the most smug and self-satisfied manner in our Protestant churches. We have seen Protestant theologians declaring that the Reformation itself had been a mistake and that the church should confine itself to meditation, preaching of the word of God and letting it wax and grow as best it can (but not too high or too richly). Under this dispensation the prayer: "Thy Kingdom Come," has become as meaningless mumbo-jumbo as the jittery incantations of the Australian bushman.

"We have gone so far in our Protestant churches," he told me once, "as to damn and discredit profane humanitarianism, socialism, and education, forgetting that nothing else remained to the world-conquering di-

vine thought, which came into the world with Jesus,
but to take nonecclesiastical forms and to seek and manifest itself in other ways, since the church denied it the
light of day. Modernism and enlightenment and socialism had to do what the church neglected to do, for
humanity, for equality, for liberty. . . ."

Albert Schweitzer

The rich diversity of his talents is not the most important characteristic of Albert Schweitzer's personality.
Musician and historian, theologian, philosopher, and
medicus, European and African, a contemplative spirit
and yet an active man—all these qualities and attributes
may give the outsider an impression of confused interests
rather than of greatness. Schweitzer's life acquires its
great significance only because of the harmonious way
in which he combines these talents. In a pre-eminent
degree he has united the urge to self-realization with the
courage of self-restriction.

As a religious historian Schweitzer gained a more than
European renown before the First World War. His
works ushered in a new era of development in the department of historical criticism. Starting from the Messiah secret, he created that conception of the historical
Jesus which is based on the eschatological principle. He
elaborated this conception in a number of learned books
that gained him an immense respect. "The real understanding of Jesus is that of will to will," he said in his
Quest of the Historical Jesus. "We must try and come
to feel the heroic in Jesus."

When, after long years in Africa as a medical man,
Schweitzer published more religio-historical works,
among others his tremendous *Paul and His Interpreters,*

he had carried out that demand for the heroic by founding his mission station at Lambarene: he had brought
about a harmony of action and words.

World fame he first gained as a musician. In 1908
appeared Schweitzer's *J. S. Bach,* in which he explained
for the first time the colorful plastic style of a composer
whom men had seen previously only as the pure mathe-
matician of music. The book, rich in detail, led to a
new basis for the presentation of Bach's works. In Mühl-
hausen, under Münch, and in Paris, under Widor,
Schweitzer developed into one of the foremost organists
of our time. But not into an organist: Schweitzer, who
is a descendant of a long line of organ builders, wrote a
manual for the construction of these instruments. The
organ is a mysterious instrument that through long centuries of evolution grew from the shepherd's flute into
a mighty, seething sea of tones. Building one requires
a vast and comprehensive technical knowledge, though
factory construction has caused it to degenerate into a
banging rattlebox. In combating factory construction
and striving to return to the genuine old organ, with its
fine and beautiful sound, Schweitzer was struggling for
culture and tradition.

I recall how Dr. Schweitzer came once to Zutphen in
Holland to preach the Christmas sermon when I was a
guest at the manse. He arrived on a Monday, and Christmas fell on a Saturday. We did not see the great man
all week, until finally, passing by the cathedral and hearing the organ, we found Dr. Schweitzer, covered with
sweat and dirt, up in the loft busy cleaning the pipes.
On Christmas he not only preached the sermon, but also
played the organ to the astonishment of the churchgoers,
who, upon entering the cathedral, looked up in amaze-

ment when they heard the prelude and said: "Is that our old organ?" Archbishop Söderblom told me that Schweitzer did the same thing once in Upsala. But there he worked for two months before he had the organ back to what it should have been.

This man, who was professor of theology at the University of Strasbourg and to whom the whole theological world listened with respect, suddenly started to study medicine and after graduation went off to the darkest heart of Africa, to work there amongst one of the most backward tribes of blacks. His departure was called a breach with civilization, a flight from reality. But the contrary was true.

He did not formulate his plans. He did not say that he wanted to save souls or to bring joy and relief into the lives of the most underprivileged of human beings. He went away silently. But in his mind there was the feeling that he went to do his part in atoning for the Western world's treatment of the natives of the most ruthlessly exploited continent in the world.

Personally, I have too much faith in the moral future of mankind to look with much hope on the attempts to evangelize the non-Christian peoples (or the pagans, as they are still called) by endoctrinating them with that worn-out and antiquated mythology which is the chief stock in trade of the average missionary. The task of a Christianity conscious of its social calling is to bring religion down from heaven to earth—that is, from the realm of illusion to that of tangible reality. Exposition of doctrines and even radical criticism is not enough when it leaves untouched the moral abnorms and abnormalities of our Western Christian world. It is for that reason that I can muster no enthusiasm for the Christianizing of Moslem or Buddhist. Who needs the preaching of the Gospel more—the Chinese coolie who labors in the rice fields or the plantation owner with his passion for profits and that other passion for Oriental nanas. But whatever the answer may be, I believe with the Salvation Army that charity begins at home. The Apostles of Jesus also started their work in Jerusalem.

Can you think of the Twelve Apostles marching into Europe behind an army of triumphant plunderers, with the Gospel in one hand and the sword in the other? What kind of a civilization is this, which, while priding itself on its science, its culture, and its decency, seeks to make proselytes for the ideas of God's fatherhood and man's brotherhood in other parts of the earth, meanwhile hiding the poverty, the ignorance, and the race discrimination in its own bosom? It is a civilization with a popular standard of morality not quite on the level of the Ten Commandments—a morality allowing nations that invoke the friendly name of Jesus to arm themselves to the teeth and to play their gruesome game of blood and greed? It must be said with deep compassion and with a deep sense of shame also that our Western world, which seeks to convert the pagan East, itself swarms with pagans, both male and female.

Goethe wrote once: "Laws bring order and destruction, religion elevates and persecutes, morality ennobles and damns. In that way the letter, which in itself is indispensable, carries death into every domain of life. But the man of love, whether he be prince, statesman, soldier, laborer, or farmer, finds in life a thousandfold opportunity to be helpful where the state, religion, the law, and doctrine fall short. In stillness he becomes a friendly protector of the spiritual possessions which should be inviolable but which must always and again be disturbed. . . ."

In that sense Schweitzer's work should be evaluated: as that of a silent protective spirit who goes his way unobserved, whether he is misunderstood or not. Compassion and a profound feeling of responsibility for the harrowing condition of the peoples of Africa, which is for the most part the result of the influence of Western civilization, drove him to abandon his position in Europe and to take up the cause of "the brotherhood of those marked by suffering."

The right of the Western nations to dominate peoples that stand on a lower cultural level is accepted by Schweitzer, but only on condition that there is a serious intention to educate those peoples morally and materially. For Schweitzer missionary endeavor depends neither on dogma nor doctrine, but of the simple Gospel, that teaches the liberation of the world through the spirit of Jesus, as it went out to man in the Sermon on the Mount.

"The difference between white and colored falls away," Dr. Schweitzer wrote, "as it falls away between a cultured and an untutored man when one approaches the questions which deal with man's relationships with himself, his neighbor, and the eternal. Christianity is for him the light that shines in the darkness of his fear. In the measure that he becomes acquainted with the higher moral concepts of Jesus' teachings, something grows in him that was not there before, something becomes conscious and something is liberated. He experiences salvation in a double sense: his fear disappears, and he advances from a nonethical to an ethical idea of life and the world."

Schweitzer emerges from his isolation occasionally,

with a book on *Indian Thought and Development* or to lecture at Oxford as in 1940 or to undertake a series of organ concerts in Holland and Sweden, but only long enough to collect funds for his mission, where he is surgeon in chief in a hospital that he built with his own hands, preacher on Sundays, and also planter, smith, steamboat captain, pharmacist, treasurer, and judge. . . .

Yet, his life must not be considered in its separate parts, but in its unity and fullness and in its deep, comprehending humanity.

There is no sentimental piety in Albert Schweitzer, no fanaticism with rigorous demands. He goes his way calmly, is full of humor, has an extraordinary sense of adaptation, but also a mysterious shyness. He shrinks from publicity. In everything he undertakes he is animated by an incredible gentleness and an all-embracing sense of responsibility.

Respect for life! Respect for all that breathes! In this idea Schweitzer sees the real solution of the question of the relationship of man to the world. He is the missionary who has understood the true object of missionary endeavor: to bring light to those who sit in darkness and to redeem oneself by expiating the sins of Christendom.

Gunther Dehn

Then there is Gunther Dehn. I do not know if he is still alive. For he was one of the first men to be arrested by the Nazis when they came to power in 1933, and he has seldom been heard of since. Dr. Dehn was the pastor of the Lutheran church in Wedding, the working-class district in Berlin. He was the friend of "the proletarian youth" and had large numbers of Communists amongst his hearers and followers. Unlike Martin Niemöller, the minister of the church in the fashionable Dahlem suburb, who was removed from his charge by the Nazis because he objected to state control of ecclesiastical affairs, but who had no quarrel with and who never voiced a word of protest against the antidemocratic, antiparliamentarian, anti-Semitic and racialist theories and program of the Hitlerites. From the first hour Dr. Dehn was their opponent on social, political, and, above all, religious grounds.

He looked upon the totalitarian state, which confesses its own divinity and the nationalist deification of race and blood, as the resurrection of the pagan gods. Although ultraorthodox, a follower of Karl Barth in theology, Gunther Dehn saw in the efforts for peace, democracy, and socialism on the part of the workers' organizations an important phase—the most important in our time—of the struggle to translate into reality the reign of brotherhood and the Kingdom of God.

In Gunther Dehn's teaching the struggle against Fascism appeared in a totally new light. He showed the anti-Christian character of the growing Nazi power, not because of its interference in ecclesiastical affairs or its elimination of certain ministers, but because of Fascism's essential function, which is that of protecting the capitalist system against democratic control and the humanization of man's relationship to man.

What Jesus did, he told his working-class followers, was to found a new society. "Before Him the peoples belonged to their overlords as herds of cattle belong to their owners. . . . Princes and mighty ones oppressed the people with the full weight of their pride and their greed. Jesus made an end to this unsocial system. He lifted the bowed heads and made the slaves free. He taught men that if they were equal in God's sight, they were also to be free in their mutual relationships, that no man should have power over his brother, that freedom and equality were divine laws and as such that they were inviolate. He taught that might can never be right, but that in a well-ordered society power should be a service, to be taken up voluntarily for the sake of the common weal. That was the society Jesus founded.

"But what do we see in the world? What are the princes and those in authority amongst us, are they servants or overlords? For nineteen hundred years the one generation is passing the teachings of Christ to the next and all pretend to believe in it. Yet, what change did that faith bring about in the world? The oppressed and the suffering are still waiting for the promised liberation. And this is not because the word of Christ is untrue or impotent, but because the peoples have not understood that for the realization of those promises they must exert their entire energy and show their own unshakable will. Instead of being watchful, we have fallen asleep and have neglected to do the one thing which could have brought the victory of Christ's ideas—we were not ready to die for the truth. Now this has changed. The working class is on the march. To those who have ears to hear the voice of the future is audible as it says: 'The liberation is near.' "

Normally, a Christian should be loved and esteemed by everybody. He should be an ornament in society and looked upon with favor by his fellow men. Men should speak well of him and cite him as a model citizen. Gunther Dehn taught his hearers that such eulogies formally contradict the New Testament, which says: "You will be hated by all because of my name," and: "Woe to you if men speak well of you!"

He believed, as did Leonhard Ragaz in Zurich, that the days will return when anyone confessing the name of Christ will be hated of all. By the name of Christ he understood His cause. And he prophesied that the hatred would emanate from a so-called Christian society itself, from the state and from the official religions that have made common cause with the state. "The police stations are not the only places where those who are loyal to the cause of Christ will be subjected to dire punishment," Dr. Dehn warned. "The synods and the other ecclesiastical commissions will carry out the persecution. The concentration camp awaits the true Christian in our day. Not because he is baptized, or because he wears an ecclesiastical garb, or because he recites prayers and mumbles pious phrases, but because he declares himself for social justice, for peace, for democracy, for the brotherhood of man, against race hatred, for the rule [*Reich*] of God on earth and not the third Reich."

It is quite possible, Dr. Dehn believed, that those who are hated because of the name of Christ will be members of the society of the godless—Socialists, Communists, and unbelievers. The "good" believers, those who confess with their lips and conform in every way, would not be touched, he said, in the great wave persecution that was to come. On the contrary, great honors were awaiting them. Confessing the name of Christ would not cost them one hair on their heads. "They will preach profound sermons on the subject of the Cross, but they will not feel the Cross in their own lives, except, perhaps, the Iron Cross dangling on their chests. . . . The real adversary of Christ is the godlessness of pious formalism. . . ."

But who would accept with a calm conscience the hatred of everyone? Do we not all desire to be loved and esteemed? Who takes a delight in being calumniated and slandered and jeered at? Is it not easier and more pleasant to row with the stream than to be deprived of civic rights, to be dragged out in the middle of the night, and to be beaten up in a concentration camp? Why should a Christian, the man who believes in brotherhood and peace, be the subject of opprobrium and persecution? What gain is there in that? What profit?

Dr. Dehn's answers that only those who endure to the end will be saved. Whoever does not hold out is lost spiritually. Blessed are those who are persecuted for righteousness' sake, for theirs is the kingdom of heaven. Blessed are ye when men shall revile you and persecute you, and shall say all manner of evil against you falsely, for my sake. Rejoice, and be exceeding glad: for great is your reward. . . .

Dr. Dehn was arrested at the same time as the poet Erich Mühsam. Upon arrival in the concentration camp Mühsam's ears and nose were cut. Three days later he was trampled to death by a squad of Storm Troopers. Of Gunther Dehn his relatives heard only once. He sent word through a prisoner who was released that he was forced to scratch the dirt away between the cobblestones of the camp's parade ground with his fingernails. . . .

11. *The Soil's Blessing*

ALTHOUGH THE day was now far advanced, the long rays of the sinking sun were still coming over the rim of the darkened pine forest. They lightly touched the tips of the tallest trees and tainted them with a shimmering golden burnish. From a distance it looked as if the trees had been on fire and were now burning out with a last gleam of phosphorescence softly lighting up their needle-like extremities. High in the west, immobile in the dreamy twilight, stood some massive clouds limned in a thin frame of ocher and pink, like rocks rising abruptly from a pale blue sea. From the direction of the brook near the house could be heard the splash of a muskrat suddenly diving below the surface. In crazy curves a bat flapped in and out from under the eaves of the house. Beyond, on the edge of the forest, a cow was shaking the flies off her flanks, making the bell on her neck rattle in a succession of swift vigorous alarms.

At that same moment the door in the rear of the log house opened, and an old man could be seen dragging a heavy wooden chair over the rocky path that led from the house to the well. He was Herman de Vriendt, and this was the hour when he was in the habit of sitting outside for a spell if the weather permitted, to look at the sky, to smoke his pipe, and to dream a little.

And what did he dream about, this old man? Nothing in particular, you may be sure, nothing startling, nothing to excite interest. Herman de Vriendt had no strange visions or ambitious projects in his head. He just sat there thinking about tomorrow's work, about some trees he was going to cut down or about the new stable he would have to build the following spring. Those were the things that passed through his head, nothing of more consequence than that.

Herman de Vriendt always sat there by the side of the well in the evening, thinking and ruminating and turning things over in his mind. Sometimes, it is true, one of the men or women from the Irish settlement, eight miles up the road, his nearest neighbors, would pass by and, seeing him there, stop a moment to chat with him. But most evenings he was alone. It had always been that way, always, that is to say, since he had taken up the homestead thirty-eight years ago.

Now, was it thirty-eight years or was it thirty-nine? Let's see now: he was wondering himself. He had left Holland in the fall of 1902 and had come to this section of Timiskaming in northern Ontario the following spring, just when the snow was melting. The intervening winter he had spent in North Bay with his family. It had been a bad winter, cold and raw, a winter such as he had never seen in Holland, and they had been hungry more than once, he and his family. But in the spring he had gone to the land office, and the officials there had looked over the map with him and had pointed out a district where there were free homesteads for the taking. And then they had assigned an Indian guide to go with him, and this man had wandered through the forest with Herman de Vriendt and finally had shown him those places the men in the office had indicated on the map.

De Vriendt had been thirty years of age then, the father of three small children who had been born in a village near Zaandam in Holland, where he had been employed in a sawmill from the day he left school. It had taken all the money his wife had inherited from her parents to transfer the family to Canada, and they had known before they left Holland that on their arrival in North Bay, the town to which the Salvation Army's emigration bureau had directed them, they would be in a strange land, absolutely penniless, among people whose language they did not know. That forbidding knowledge had caused Herman to hesitate a long time. Should he venture it or should he rather wait till the children were a little older? Friends had told him that it would be like a leap in the dark and that Canada was an inhospitable country, dreary, with a climate as rigorous as that of Russia, inhabited by Eskimos and Indians.

But each time Herman had called at the Salvation Army's bureau in Amsterdam and had received renewed assurance that there was land available in Canada, that he could have a farm merely for the asking, the urge had come over him again, and he had returned home and told his wife: "We are going because we must go: we must go while I can still work." And yet, in spite of those determined words, it was Herman who had begun to tremble as the day for the departure grew nearer, and it was his wife in the end who had shown the greatest resolution by taking the envelope with the steamship tickets stealthily from his pocket so that he could not take them back to the office in Amsterdam and cancel the trip.

That was thirty-eight years ago, but Herman was thinking of it again as he sat by the well and let his eyes wander along the edge of the pine forest. It was he who had pushed that forest back with the strength of his two arms until it stood today half a mile distant from the road. The cleared-off space had been turned into as fine a farm as could be seen anywhere in northern Ontario. He felt grateful that evening, grateful, above all, to his wife Kee, who lay buried there not fifty paces from the well. If she had hesitated, if she had been as fearful back then in 1902 as he had been, he would not be sitting here now. He would still be in Koog, near Zaandam, a day laborer with his sons day laborers and his daughters married to other day laborers.

He lit his pipe, and his eye caught a couple of belated chickens coming in from the forest's edge. The birds disappeared into the door of the cellar that served as their coop. Herman thought of the time when he had dug that cellar. That had been in 1903. It was the first thing he had done after he had built the house and after he had made a small clearing in the forest.

Why had he dug that cellar and made it as wide as a barn and then roofed it over with a mound of earth? Why, you ask? He had simply dug it to have a place of refuge in case of a forest fire. Indeed, it had saved him and his family back in 1911 when the fire had swept through northern Ontario, consuming villages and settlements and mining camps and driving the people from their homes. How many had perished in the smoke and flame that year nobody would ever know: settlers in lonely cabins, prospectors caught staking out a claim somewhere in the depth of the forest. There must have been hundreds upon hundreds of victims. He did not like to think of that terrible summer when the sky had been purple for days and then gradually had turned black, and the flames had come bearing down on his house with the roar of a tornado. How had he saved the house? He had saved it by hanging wet blankets over the log walls and by standing on the roof with his boy Hendrik and spilling the water over the blankets from the barrel they had hoisted up. They had saved their lives and their house. It still stood there, and he still lived in it. You could see it there: a good, solid house, roomy, with neatly painted doors and windows.

Now there was no more danger from fire. The forest lay too far away. He had pushed the forest back. He liked to repeat those words: "I pushed that forest back." When he said those words to himself, his face grew hard, and he gritted his teeth and fell back into his old native language, into Dutch: *"Ja, ik heb dat bosch teruggeduwd. Ja, zoo is 't gegaan!"*

But he was not saying it this evening. He was silent and grateful. That day he had come in early from work. He had not felt quite himself. It had been the first time in thirty-eight years that he had felt tired and now that he sat by the well he thought of the feeling of weakness he had experienced in the afternoon, and he suddenly bethought himself that he was no longer a young man but well into his sixty-ninth year. He could expect nothing else but a slowing up of the machinery.

And then, too, this day had been the anniversary of Kee's death. That had made the day a heavy one, a day charged with thoughts and memories. Yes, here she had stood with him, here where the well was now, thirty-eight years ago when they had pitched their small tent, and he had trembled and been afraid and had asked her if she was not sorry to have left Holland. Kee had smiled back and had only said: "Tomorrow we start building our house."

It all came back to him now as he sat there by the well and smoked his pipe in quick, nervous little puffs. "Thirty-eight years," he muttered, "where is the time gone?" After they had built the house, they had made some furniture— bedsteads, a table and some benches—and had placed moss and pine needles in the bedsteads so that when winter and the snow came they had been warm and snug. Just when the credit at the grocery store in Charlton, sixteen miles distant, had run out, he had begun to cut the first big logs on his lot and had sold them to the storekeeper, who had them hauled away toward spring.

But that spring was also the time when they had lost their eldest boy. He did not like to think back to that tragedy, for there was always a lump in his throat when he thought of young Herman. That was the boy's name. Young Herman would have been forty-two years now, a man with a family of his own, living across the road maybe or up near the Irish settlement perhaps, not too far away. De Vriendt sighed. They had been digging the well together, young Herman and he, that spring. He had gone into the pit himself, shoring up the sides as the work progressed, and the boy had pulled up the pails of dirt that he sent up to the surface by means of a pulley. He had come up to get some nails from the house before hammering together another square of shoring when the boy must have stepped on the pail and slid down into the well. The shock of the pail striking the bottom had caused the lower walls to collapse, and young Herman had been crushed beneath the weight of mud and timber.

It had taken Kee and him two days to recover the body, and then they had buried the boy back of the cellar where there was a small garden now, which his daughter tended and where he had buried Kee also ten years later and the two children that had been born to them in Canada.

And then, the autumn following young Herman's death, there had been all that trouble with the police and the courts and the many days he had lost when he was summoned to appear before the investigating magistrate in Elkhart. It was all because he had buried the boy without first obtaining a death certificate from a physician.

The Mounted Police had stopped at the house one day, and one of the officers had walked over to Herman's grave and had asked the father: "And who is buried here?" He had told the man in his broken English, but the policeman must not have understood him clearly. He had asked for a shovel or a spade, and had begun to dig up the body. This, Herman de Vriendt had not permitted. He had ordered the policeman off his place, saying that this was his land and in the grave was his own boy—he was to sleep on without being disturbed. And all the things that followed: the journeys to Elkhart and finally the magistrate's suggestion that the body be dug up and transferred to the cemetery in the village.

Those people had not understood him at all when he had told them that he and Kee wanted to keep their boy near them and not far away in some strange cemetery, amid strange people. It had taken a long time to straighten out the affair. But in the end it had all blown over, and Herman was still there now in his grave next to his mother, and all was well.

But that had not been the only time when Herman de Vriendt had run up against the authorities. No, the police had paid him a second visit that might have been fraught with far more serious consequences. That had been several years later, in the course of the terrible year of 1921, when he could not sell any logs or timber, when the grocery store in Charlton had gone bankrupt, and when hundreds of settlers had left their holdings and had flocked to the cities, driven by hunger to join the crowds of unemployed in the mining centers and in North Bay, Toronto, and Montreal. That winter, when De Vriendt had learned that what remained of the grocery store's stock was to be shipped out from Charlton, he had walked to the village one night and broken into the freight shed by the side of the railway depot of the Timiskaming and Northern Ontario Railway, had taken a sack of flour, and had carried it home.

What else could he do? The children he had left at home were the small ones. Hendrik, his second boy, had served in the Canadian Expeditionary Force in France and had been so severely wounded that he was still in Christie Hospital in Toronto. Of course, Herman knew full well that he had committed a crime when he broke into the freight shed and stole the sack of flour. But again: what else could he do? His children were hungry, and Kee, sick with fever, lay in bed on the sack filled with pine needles. When the Mounted Policeman stopped at the house and asked him about the flour, he had not denied that he had taken it. "I took it," he said. "Where is the sack?" the man asked. Herman led him out to the cellar. He lit the lamp and showed the officer the sack standing against the wall. "What's in this vat?" the man had asked, pointing to a barrel. Herman had lifted the lid off the barrel. "That's all we had to eat this winter," said Herman, "pickled muskrats. . . ."

Then they had stood there silently, the policeman and Herman, for a moment looking squarely at each other. And then the policeman's eyes had suddenly become wet, and he had stalked out in big steps, saying: "God damn it, Mr. de Vriendt, this is a hell of a cold winter."

He was thinking of all these things now as he sat by the well. He chuckled a little when his mind reverted to the time when he hauled his own logs to the railway for the first time. He had hauled them on a sleigh drawn by a horse and an ox. He had not been able to buy a second horse, but, learning that a man in the Irish settlement had an ox for sale, he had bought the animal and hitched it to the sleigh alongside the horse. In that way he had gained two years, for it would have taken him that long to save up sufficient money to buy a second horse.

The other settlers had laughed at the combination of the ox and the horse and the extremely slow progress he was making in getting his logs out. But he had made an extra trip every second day and had made that trip late at night, when there were no other sleighs on the road, and in that way he had transferred more logs to the siding than anyone else that year. He chuckled when he thought of how he had beaten all the other settlers with his ox and his horse. It is true that Angus Macpherson, the Scottish settler, had tried to frighten him by saying that the Bible forbids the harnessing of an ox and a horse together and that, upon finding the passage in the Book, he had been sorely disturbed by it, but the Presbyterian dominie in Charlton whom he had consulted had reassured him that under the circumstances he had committed no offense.

Herman de Vriendt was a simple man. He let his eyes roam over the broad field of almost ripe wheat, splotched with daubs of gold that the sinking sun sprinkled by way of farewell to the world. How many stumps had he not pulled up from that field? Hundreds upon hundreds each year. People now came to look at his farm from great distances, and sometimes the Crown Agent would pass by and stop with him for a short while and shake his head in admiration and mutter that it was almost incredible. "And all this is the work of one man," the visitor would say, "those fields, those barns, those houses. And how do you get such fine wheat and that barley over there? There isn't any like it to be seen this side of Haileybury. . . ."

"Oh, I just plow a little deeper than the others," Herman would say. "I break it up. It's good land though, that's the main thing. You couldn't grow good wheat if the land was bad. I don't let it get hard and cake so that the melted snow and the rains run off. I let the water soak in. It's harder work, to be sure, but look . . . I have good wheat, too. That's my reward."

Good wheat! Why, Herman de Vriendt had not only good wheat. He had fine barns, for he had built some addition or other every winter. His farm looked like a small settlement now, where thirty-eight years ago there had been a dense virgin forest. There were five families living on his farm. Young farmers they were, who occupied De Vriendt's houses while they were clearing off their own places farther up the road. De Vriendt would not allow any settler to spend a winter in a tent. "That cost me my wife," he would say. "The winters are too severe in this part of the country for women and children to be exposed. You had better take this small house of mine for the winter. Next year you will have your own."

He was counting the buildings on the farm when he heard the door of the old log house open. His daughter came out to take him inside. "Come, Father," she said, "it's getting cool. You must come in. The sun is gone." But there was still some light over the dark pine forest in the distance. The large house across the road, which stood in the middle of another clearing, was the one occupied by his son Hendrik and his family. The lamps were being lit in that house. In the luminous haze that hung above the trees the smoke from several chimneys could be seen rising in straight candlelike pillars toward the darkened sky. Before walking back with his daughter, De Vriendt took a last glance at the scene: "Look, Cornelia," he said, "God helped me to push that forest back with my own hands." Then he smiled in the direction of the small garden: "Good night, Kee . . . good night, Herman," he said, and went inside.

12. *The Miracle of Arjuna*

THE WHITE men from the plantations would sometimes stop before the door of the old man's hut in the evening and call out: "Hali, Hali, *djangan takut!* Hali, do not be afraid! Do not be afraid at all!" But he would first send out his daughter Onahassan or his boy Urdu to see who they were and if they were not drunk. For Hali could not speak with men when they were drunk. He could not bear to look on their faces when they had lost their dignity, when their gestures had become those of monkeys and an ugly red glow tainted their cheeks. And then, the odor of their breaths made him quite fearful. It brought back sharp memories to him of the hospital in Magelang where he had once been taken to undergo a throat operation. When Hali spoke to a drunken man, the sickening smell in the room with the long white table and the glass cupboards with shining knives came back to him. He shuddered when he thought of it!

Often in the evening, when the white men came to bargain with him, that same pungent odor of the hospital in Magelang seemed to return. It floated in the air, and clung to the leaves and the branches of the great waringin tree in front of the hut for hours after they had left. Hali could not ask the white men to stay away from his place when they were drinking. They were the lords of Kedu and of Semarang and even of Surakarta (where there was a sultan) and of all Java. He needed their patronage. To whom else could he have sold the tiny figures of buffalos and monkeys and elephants that he carved from the black horn of the buffalo.

When one of the men of the plantation had completed

his term of five years and was about to leave for Holland, he would always come to Hali and lay in a stock of carved walking sticks and kris handles and fans and penholders and fine bamboo boxes to take away for his friends and relatives. But such a man would not come alone. When one of them was getting ready to leave, the white men were all in a joyful mood for weeks. They went around in groups, singing, talking loud, and always drinking that liquid whose smell Hali held in detestation. They would come riding to Hali's hut in an automobile, and he could hear them from afar, blowing their horn, shouting at the girls in the village square, and chasing the chickens in all directions through the village. When they were in that mood, Hali feared white men.

At other times he merely despised them and had as little to do with them as possible. He tried not to think of them when he was working. He had other things to think of. He was thinking of the profile of the all-wise and all-beautiful Arjuna, the god of his people, and of how to carve the face of the giver of life.

For years Hali had tried to give the god that vague, dream expression which, he knew in his heart, must be hovering on the face of Arjuna, who is to be found in the twilight where spirit merges with matter. That was Hali's sole thought, his obsession: to carve one perfect image of the god, an image wherein the gentleness of Arjuna would be visible on the face and his love for men would be seen to grow from the lips and the forehead itself.

Hali had tried many times, hundreds of times. Once or twice in forty years he had seemed on the point of succeeding. Then he had trembled in anticipation and had polished and rubbed and smoothed to give the right shadow to the nose and to implant that sad smile on the god's face. But always, at the last moment, something had gone wrong: the hair had not come out quite right or the chin had receded too far; in short, the god had escaped him. By a fraction of an inch only, it is true, but it had not been a perfect image. The god had not spoken to him. Never yet in all those years had Hali succeeded in producing an Arjuna to his own satisfaction. To others, the imperfections in the statues were invisible. His son Urdu would stand near him when an image was approaching completion, and the boy would say breathlessly: "That is Arjuna . . . there you have him . . . now he is here." But Hali would sigh: "Not yet. Do not be hasty. For if it is Arjuna, he will speak to me."

"Speak to you with the voice of man?" Urdu would ask.

"No, when Arjuna comes," said the father, "he will speak to my heart. I will know that my work is finished by the grace that descends in my heart."

"Then when will it be?" asked Urdu.

"Not until my knowledge is complete," answered Hali.

"And when is your knowledge complete, my father," Urdu would go on asking, as boys will ask questions and never end.

"Not until I understand suffering as Arjuna understands suffering," he would say mysteriously.

And so Hali went on carving. In the morning he cut from the buffalo horn the trinkets the white man bought from him, knobs for walking sticks, boxes for cigarets, supports for books, and other such things. But of afternoons he worked on a horn of ebony, black as the night. Then he went back in search of the smile of Arjuna, which is the answer to the mystery of life and death and of all the striving of man. He cut carefully, in small, deft strokes, tenderly holding up the figure to the light of the sun from

time to time. Sometimes, as he was carving, his breath
would come as that of a man who carries a heavy log to
the top of a hill and who is within reach of his goal. For
Hali knew that in the last hours of carving an image, the
slightest deviation of his knife, a mere slip or a scratch, as
thin as a hair, might equally well ruin the face as bring
forth the miracle of perfection. He knew that Arjuna
would come to him in a flash and that he would suddenly
hold the god in his hand as a materialized shadow.

He was a wrinkled little man, clad only in a loincloth.
His appearance filled the men of the plantations with
mirth. Some of them would stand by and look on while he
was carving. They would ask him why he did not send for
a model or for a picture of Arjuna so that he could imitate
the lines of the god's face with precision. But this question
only made Hali smile. He knew that they who asked were
only children. He could not explain to them that there was
no model for Arjuna in all the world, except the vision of
the god in his own heart. But in order to say this he did
not know enough words in the language of the strangers
and to hide his ignorance he would grin at his questioners,
and they would burst out laughing.

And then bad times came to the dessa of Pindoeng in the
province of Kedu, where Hali lived. First, the rice harvest
failed, and a sinister blight struck the leaves of the tea-
plant so that they shriveled up like old paper and crumpled
to dust. And then war broke out on the other end of the
world, and the white men stopped buying Hali's trinkets,
for they no longer made journeys to Holland. He could
not fathom the reason for the strange things that occurred,
and neither could Urdu or Onahassan his daughter,
though they spent the afternoons in the village square gossiping with the other women and girls.

The white lords came by frequently now, but not those of the plantations: other men, in khaki uniforms, who carried guns and sabers. And they looked in at Hali's workshop and took his son Urdu's printed papers away, those papers the boy had received from the village hairdresser. And they said to Hali: "Watch that boy of yours, now, Hali! See that he has nothing more to do with anyone who speaks of independence for Indonesia. For if he does it will go hard with him and with you all."

And Hali had pondered over these words until it occurred to him that independence might be a strange new god whom the *balandas* feared. But it was Onahassan who explained to him that independence was not a god, but the hope of the young men who gathered at nights in some clearing in the palm forest. Urdu was one of them.

Then Hali was sore afraid for his son's sake and he sat for days thinking of what his own father had told him of the times when the people of Kedu were happy and built great temples like that at Borobudur, where dances were held by thousands of maidens and princes came from all parts of Java. In those days every man had his own house and his own rice field. Now the strangers who had taken Kedu by force owned the rice fields and the roads and the water wells and even the air one breathed.

And times grew steadily worse. Not only were the white men no longer buying Hali's carvings, but they asked for their money back, the few cents and dimes and guldens that they had paid him for the trinkets. They said they needed the money to buy flying machines and steel wagons in order to protect Pindoeng and Kedu and Java. They were speaking by order of the great white prince who ruled in Batavia. And Hali knew that he, above all, must be obeyed.

"But how is it," asked Hali of the taxgatherer, "that you want to protect me and take the little money I have saved for my old age? You do not protect me, you take my protection away, you are evil."

Hali soon found out that those words had been taken as bad words by the taxgatherer. The dessa chief had come running to his hut to say that he, Hali, was now also classed as a strong head, as bad as his boy Urdu. . . .

Once he paid the taxes, twice he paid the taxes, three times he paid them, but then he had no more money. Hali went to the dessa chief and told him: "This is the end of my wealth I have no more. Will I not be protected any longer?"

But the dessa chief said: "O, we will see about that. You still have a buffalo, do you not?"

Upon hearing those words from the dessa chief, Hali had begun to shake as a leaf. For the buffalo, which grazed in the communal plot in the daytime and which stood by his bedside in the hut at nights, was the darling of the children. He could find no words to answer the dessa chief. It was as if lightning had struck him. He wanted to ask the dessa chief if he knew what the karbow meant to him and to his children, that it had come to them as a calf, that they had fed it and nourished it in their hut, that it understood their every word, that it was like a sister to them. But the dessa chief had already busied himself with other matters and did not seem to want to look in Hali's way.

How could he go home and tell his children. . . .? Could he take Shumi the buffalo and Urdu and Onahassan and hide in the palm woods, burn fires at nights to keep the tigers away, and go peddling his trinkets in other villages? No, for now he was too old for that. And then, every nook and corner of the land was being searched and scoured by the men of the government. They would find them in less than a week. The dessa chief would pass on the word that Hali and his children and their property had disappeared, and searching parties would be sent out after them. Shumi could not walk very fast, and they would all be brought back, and all the people would see them being led back by the police. And there would be the shame of it and the punishment that was bound to follow. No, that could not be. He could not leave the dessa. . . .

When Hali reached home, his children were sitting in the doorway. Shumi was standing near by, swishing her tail to keep the flies off. He went inside and brought his work bench into the open to profit by the few minutes of daylight that remained to work on his carving. But he could not work. He could only sigh, and each time that he looked at Shumi his eyes filled with tears. And then his children began to weep, for they understood that it was because of Shumi that he was sad.

And he said to his son Urdu: "Let us go into the fields, my son, and see the full moon." And when they walked out, Hali held his son's hand and told him that if the taxes were not paid by the morrow, the dessa chief would send his men to take Shumi away. They walked in silence for a long time, afraid to speak their thoughts. Then Hali looked at the moon and tried to pray, but his heart was as heavy as it had been in the dessa chief's office that afternoon. He could not find words to pray. He could only lift up his arms and sigh. But Urdu said: "If they dare to take Shumi, I will set the wheat fields on fire!" As he said these words, two men ran from behind the palm trees on the edge of the field and seized the boy and led him away. . . .

The trial came swiftly. It was held on the veranda of

the dessa house. All the people were present, and they heard the witnesses who declared that Urdu had been a leader in the independence movement, that he was an agitator and a strong head. And it did not take the judge long to render his verdict that Urdu was to be sent to the Djungel, to the concentration camp in the fever marshes of New Guinea for his opposition to the government and for his advocacy of violent measures. And they led the boy away. . . .

Finally the morning came when Urdu was to be taken to the railway station with some other men and boys, all chained together, and all destined to the prison camp. Hali saw his boy go by the hut, walking between rows of gendarmes with fixed bayonets, and he and Onahassan followed the procession from afar. In his hands Hali carried the image of Arjuna on which he had been working that morning. It was nearly completed. Another day, in another few hours it would have been finished. He was yet to bring out the shadow on the face. Hali held the statue against his breast as he walked to the railway station. He could see Urdu standing at the head of the procession of prisoners. . . .

From the distance came the whistle of a train, and Hali felt Onahassan's head against his shoulder. Her sobs shook him. Hali took the statue in one hand and placed his other arm around the girl's shoulder. With his gnarled and calloused thumb he rubbed the face of the god. The train passed. It had only been a string of oil cars. Soon another whistle was heard, and a passenger train came thundering into the station. Now the prisoners were marched to the last car, a small van with barred windows. He could see his boy Urdu mount the steps and disappear inside. Then the train moved off. Presently it passed the spot where Hali

and Onahassan were standing. Urdu pushed his face
against the bars of the window in the van and smiled at
them. Hali smiled back. As he did so, he crushed his nail
into the statue's face. When the train had passed, he looked
at Arjuna again. Then his breath stopped, and his heart
pounded in his throat. The miracle had occurred. The
god looked at him with the smile of one who has seen the
unseeable, of one who knows all the sorrows of man and
all the joys that shall be his when the new day comes.

V

Irrevocable Hours

Hitler did not drop ready-made from the sky, and the samurai of Japan are not swarming over the Asiatic continent in response to some mysterious urge to see the world. After a summer night's rain toadstools are plentiful in the forest, and tulips do not grow from crocodile eggs. There are no accidents either in the natural world or in human history, and the mystic doctrine of spontaneousness explains nothing. But if the raindrop, in falling from the clouds, could think and speak as you and I, it would probably say: "It is not an unconscious force directing me on my downward course; it is of my own free will that I have come to quench the thirst of the parched flowers."

Day follows night, and night follows day; the seasons succeed each other with unfailing regularity. Everything in nature, beginning with the majestic movement of the planets and ending with the grain of wheat fermenting in the furrow, is subject to established laws. It is the same with social phenomena. Wherever capitalism develops, a working class comes into existence and grows. Every phenomenon, whether it is a man on horseback, a famine, or a shortage in gasoline, has a cause. A particular phenomenon may be inexplicable and may remain inexplicable for a long time. We may not understand at first glance why Göring set the Reichstag on fire or why Rudolf Hess flew to Scotland. But if these phenomena are inexplicable, it is because the relationship between them and other phenomena escapes us for the moment. As long as the relationship is not established, a phenomenon, whether in nature or in human society, may remain inexplicable and a mystery. Once that relationship is discovered, we have what we call a scientific explanation of the phenomenon.

The will of man is not an exception. It, too, is subject to the general law of cause and effect. Man's sentiments and his will depend on the condition of his physical organism and the conditions in which he finds himself. Man's will and human nature are determined by definite causes, whether he scratches himself behind the ear because he has a pimple there, drinks a glass of water because he ate salt pork for dinner, or whether he runs a tank into a company of infantrymen because they are the enemies of his country. Sometimes it is difficult to discover the causes and motives that make men act. Because it is difficult to find an explanation, it does not follow that no explanation exists.

If man's every action is determined by a cause, it does not mean that he has no free will, that he exercises no choice in the matter, or that he is a helpless victim of blind forces. Society is made up of an infinite number of individuals, all with sentiments, a will, determination, and energy of their own. One man may have more energy than another. One man may wish to go one way, and another may wish to go off in another direction. There is a clash of will and of desire. Everyone consciously follows his own objective. But in an organized society men have also a common goal. They have a common method of settling certain difficulties or of solving certain problems. In common they make a decision that does not contradict the individual will of each. Five men decide to lift a stone. Not one of them can lift it alone, but the five of them lift it with ease. The common decision does not go contrary to individual desire. On the contrary, it helps fulfill the desire.

It is the combination but also the clash of wills and individual desires that makes history. Incidents occur in history that at the time of their taking place do not attract attention or do not appear significant. Some incidents pass unobserved and perhaps do not merit a second glance. It is only in their relation to and in the interplay with other incidents that they rise to significance, take on flesh and blood, and sometimes even assume a decisive character. History is an accumulation of related incidents, a molecular process in which some molecules assume momentarily the salient importance of the keystone in the arch.

In each century, Leon Trotsky said once, if not exactly in these words, there is one decade that decides the march of events. In each decade there is one year, in each year one week, in each week one day, in each day one hour, and in each hour one minute that has determining force and character. And he cited the case of the Cossack soldiers who, instead of riding into the crowds of revolutionaries on the Nevsky Prospekt in 1917, winked at them.

1. *The Rejected Masterpiece*

DURING THE LONG summer afternoons of 1919 a young man wearing a faded military greatcoat and battered felt hat could be seen wandering up and down the principal streets of Munich offering picture postcards for sale to the tourists and visitors who were plentiful in that city, in spite of the desperately bad times that had come over Germany. This young man was of ordinary height, but he walked with a slight stoop and coughed incessantly, the result, no doubt, of a whiff of poison gas that he had inhaled while on active service on the Western front. A heavy black mustache and long strands of unkempt hair made him look much older than he was in reality.

It was impossible to say whether the poison gas in his lungs or his naturally frail physique caused him to walk with a slow and slouching step. It was only certain that the years of service in the army had failed to leave its stamp upon his physical bearing.

Listlessly and almost surreptitiously, as if he were innerly ashamed of what he was doing, he drew the packet of postcards from the deep pocket of his overcoat whenever he saw a party of tourists approach. But although he praised his wares as original, hand-painted sketches and not merely colored photographs and reproductions, he had little luck in selling them.

Night after night he trudged back, forlorn and penniless, to his quarters in the Mustergasse, where he shared a room with five or six other young men who were, like himself, waifs of the great storm in Europe that had just been stilled. On the way home he would stop occasionally in front of a *Konditorei,* or bakery, and look over the delicacies and rolls spread out in the show window. Then with a sigh or with a nervous shrug of the shoulders, but always with a bitter smile that distorted his face, he continued on his way, muttering of the injustice that doomed a man who had served his fatherland faithfully and in perilous circumstances to wander through the streets of an opulent city as a hungry beggar.

He could not look forward with a feeling of relief or anticipation to the evening. For he could not even be sure that a meal or food of any kind awaited him at his lodgings. His fellow occupants of the room in the Mustergasse were, like himself, as poor as church mice. If one of them had luck in the course of the day in obtaining some work, running an errand or picking up some scraps in the market or at the kitchen door of one of the great hotels, they all had a feast in the evening. But this was a rare occurrence. Usually they shared a crust of dry bread that one of them had obtained at half price because it was stale or mildewed.

After sundown they sat in the dark on their cots, talking and smoking tobacco offal that they had picked up in the streets. Or they went to sleep. There was seldom the half shilling among the lot of them that the slot machine had to be fed before they could have a few hours of electric light in the evening.

According to their custom, one man had to remain in the room during the day to tidy up, to take messages, and to cook the evening meal—when and if the wherewithal was available. The young man with the bad cough was frequently selected for the job of housekeeper because he had periodically to stay in anyway to replenish his stock of picture postcards.

He painted those postcards himself: rural scenes of

Bavarian and Austrian farmhouses, snow-covered moun-
taintops, fields of ripe corn, and green hills with small
timbered chalets on their summit. These were his
themes. Yet, he never went out to sketch in the open.
His physical condition and a certain inborn listlessness
would not have permitted him to undertake excursions
to the countryside. Moreover, he complained frequently
that he had not the strength for long walks. He painted
from memory, and the finished products of his art looked
accordingly. They were crude, immature pictures that
might have been considered not without merit if they
had been done by schoolchildren.

Nevertheless, the young man entertained high illusions about his own capacities. He told his roommates
more than once that if he were given the opportunity
and the right kind of tools, he was sure that he could
make a name for himself in the world of art. He felt
sure though that he just had to keep on painting and
that in the end recognition would come his way. Besides,
he did not want to do anything else. He was an artist
and as an artist he would succeed in life or not at all.

Things went a little more prosperously with the six
companions the following winter. Two of them had
gained employment with the Black *Heimwehr,* a secret
terrorist organization of *Junker* and reactionaries that
aimed at the disruption of life under the Weimar Republic by waylaying and assassinating prominent labor
leaders and liberal intellectuals who had had a hand in
formulating the democratic policy of the new government.

It was a dangerous job, but it paid well, and all the
six companions in the Mustergasse profited by it, now
that two of their number had more or less regular em-

ployment. Now they could eat and buy a few clothes, instead of going around in their old army uniforms. They could also afford a little jollification from time to time and forget their troubles in drink or by bringing in a prostitute from the streets.

But in these celebrations the young painter never joined his companions. He remained morose and distant and frequently fell into long spells of silence. The more hilarious the party, the quieter he grew. More than anything else, he resented the presence of women in their communal room. He told his companions that he felt such a deep physical loathing for members of the opposite sex that their nearness nauseated him.

Nevertheless, he did not leave the quarters in the Mustergasse to seek an abode elsewhere. He had come to like the easy and Bohemian life. Now that money was coming in and his companions were generous enough to share their new wealth, he could lead a life of leisure and lie dreaming on his cot as long as he liked and paint a little too when the inspiration and the desire came over him.

The truth is, he could not have struck out for himself. He lacked the physical and spiritual stamina to stand on his own feet. For one thing, he could not have done a day's steady work. You could tell that by his thin arms and muscleless shoulders, a condition caused by attacks of rickets in his youth. He caught cold on the slightest exposure and had to watch himself carefully because of his weakened lungs.

He did not object to his two companions' criminal employment. It furnished him with bread and leisure. He had given up painting postcards and peddling them in the streets. He was at last enabled to work on a more ambitious composition. He worked in one of the corners of the room near the window. He painted in the afternoon when the others had gone out. In the morning he stayed in bed. At noon he ate some breakfast in a neighboring coffeehouse and in the afternoon he was at his easel for a few hours. But when his companions returned toward evening, he covered up the canvas and joined them in the discussions that ran to politics most of the time.

He agreed with his friends that something must be done to bring Germany back to a position of honor and greatness among the nations of Europe and that the Republic was not succeeding in that task. But he, no more than the others, knew how to go about it. There probably had to be a revolution, a thorough housecleaning. But he felt no inclination to take an active part in anything that called for physical energy and exertion.

Moreover, he had his own work to do now. He placed great hopes in the composition he had started. He did not conceal his expectation that the new painting he had started would set him on the road to fame. The painting represented a naked young man with blond hair tearing off a set of iron shackles that were fastened around his hands and feet. With his right hand the man in the painting had seized a hammer in apparent readiness to ward off an invisible foe. That blond young man was the symbol of the new Germany, and the red snake on which he was treading was the Weimar Republic. The painter hoped to submit this allegorical vision to the jury and to see it hung in a prominent place in the Munich Art Exhibition of the coming spring.

He worked at his composition all winter. Several times he changed the attitude of the blond young man, each time making him look stronger and more virile. He also enlarged the head of the snake and even introduced an angel in the background. The angel was seen to be urging the blond *Prometheus Bound* to greater deeds of valor.

The painting was finally finished, and a frame was bought for it from the money donated by one of the employed roommates.

On the evening of May 7 he carried the picture to the gallery. As he entered the building he was told by an attendant that the hanging committee was in session in one of the rooms on the first floor. He went up on the elevator and knocked at the door of the room the man had indicated. When he entered he stood before five gentlemen who sat ranged in a semicircle behind a large table. He said he had come with a picture that he hoped would get a place of honor in the exhibition of contemporary art. As he spoke he lifted the cloth from the painting and, holding it at arm's length, exposed it to the gaze of the judges.

One of the members of the jury put on his pince-nez and smiled. Another chuckled in a rather embarrassed way. But the president of the jury told the young man frankly that his picture could not be entered. "The composition is bad," he said, "the idea is crude, and the work is generally chaotic and disordered. . . ."

The young painter did not wait for the president to finish his criticism. For a moment he glowered at the members of the jury. Then without a word he picked up his canvas and ran out of the room. Downstairs he asked the attendant the names of the members of the jury. He was given a printed slip of paper containing the names. As he looked over the list he said to the attendant: "Three out of five are Jews, isn't that right?" The man nodded his head. The painter went home and wrote the chairman of the jury a short note. The note ran as follows: *"Dies werde ich diesen Juden niemals verzeihen*—This I will never forgive the Jews." Then he signed his name: Adolf Hitler.

2. *The Warden of the Inheritance*

WHEN WOODROW WILSON landed in Europe in December, 1918, Romain Rolland addressed the President in these moving words: "You alone, *monsieur le président,* among all those whose dreadful duty it now is to guide the policy of the nations, you alone enjoy world-wide moral authority. You inspire universal confidence. Answer the appeal of these passionate hopes! Take the hands which are stretched forth, help them to clasp one another. . . . Should this mediator fail to appear, the human masses, disarrayed and unbalanced, will almost inevitably break forth into excesses. The common people will welter in bloody chaos, while the parties of traditional order will fly to bloody reaction. . . . Heir of George Washington and Abraham Lincoln, take up the cause, not of a party, not of a single people, but of all! Summon the representatives of the peoples to the Congress of Mankind! Preside over it with the full authority you hold in virtue of your lofty moral consciousness and in virtue of the great future of America! Speak, speak to all! The world hungers for a voice which will overleap the frontiers of nations and classes. Be the arbiter of the free peoples! Thus may the future hail you by the name of the Reconciler! . . ."

I do not recall the newspaper in which I read this appeal at the time. It may have been only a pamphlet. But it was Laurie Scoville, the tallest sergeant in the 26th Canadian Infantry and former collaborator of Josef Urban, with whom I was engaged in painting a backdrop for a field theater, who brought it back with him from the village of Audenge, where he had gone to buy some

coloring material. Coming down the road, he waved the
document in his hand from afar and shouted at me:
"Pete, we will be senators yet! . . . President Wilson has
arrived to call the Parliament of Man! . . . This means,
in the first place, that you and I are going to celebrate
Christmas like real Pilgrim Fathers, for I have already
espied in yon farmyard the turkey you will be allowed
'to win' for us after dark, and I know the very pot in
which it is going to be cooked, namely: this old wash
boiler!" With these words Laurie pulled aside the flap
of the tent in front of which I had been taking it easy,
kicked both our rifles out into the mud, and with solemn
voice intoned *The Battle Hymn of the Republic:* "Mine
eyes have seen the glory of the coming of the Lord. . . ."

Along with Rolland's message the paper contained
some excerpts from Woodrow Wilson's speeches about
admitting the Latin American republics to partnership
in the Monroe Doctrine, about the New Freedom, about
the need to draw the free peoples of the world into some
covenant—some genuine and practical co-operation that
would in effect combine their forces to secure peace and
justice in the dealings of nations with one another. "The
brotherhood of man," he had said, "must no longer be
a fair but empty phrase—it must be given structure of
force and reality." The price of peace was stated to be
impartial justice in every item of settlement, no matter
whose interests were to be crossed. There was to be self-
determination for small peoples, a respect for the life
and culture of minorities. In the end the League of Nations, formed under covenants, was indicated as the only
instrumentality by which the agreements of the coming
peace would be honored and fulfilled.

Laurie Scoville was not the only one to be transported by joy over the news. Wherever we went in France and in the Rhineland to paint stage decorations for the theaters of different army units that had been scattered by the Armistice, we met people who spoke of Woodrow Wilson with words that betokened an almost religious veneration. They seemed to feel instinctively that Wilson, in thus stating the goal of American democracy, was giving voice to the ideals of humanity.

Here, it was felt, was a man who was more than a politician or a statesman. Here was a prophet. To Laurie and me he was the warden of the inheritance of the Puritans, of the Covenanters, of Jefferson and Tom Paine. His arrival made us feel for the first time that the war had not been in vain, that we had been like soldiers of the Lord in a great and holy cause. There was, it is true, somewhat of a dictatorial, an almost theocratic ring, to the President's words, but that we ascribed to the fact that he spoke with the authority of the chief of a nation that had brought the decision in the four-year conflict.

Laurie Scoville and I saw the presidential train pass through the railway station at Conches, in the *département* of the Eure, where thousands of Norman peasants, driven by I do not know what mysterious urge, had left their fields and workshops to stand for hours along the track and to kneel down when the coaches rolled by.

Why? Did those humble people understand one word of Wilson's tremendous phrases about open covenants openly arrived at, about victory in arms being disastrous to the ideal of an unselfish humanity, about making the world safe for democracy, or about a crusade to establish the reign of law in the world?

What interest had they in the theory of the freedom of the seas or in the doctrine of self-determination for Poles, Czechs, Yugoslavs, and Jews?

They had heard mere echoes of his words, yet it was in those words, they knew, that lay the power, more than the formidable military apparatus America had transferred across the ocean, that had brought about the collapse of the Teutonic alliance. They, the common people of France, no less than the common people of Germany, Italy, and eastern Europe, looked upon Woodrow Wilson as their spokesman, as their advocate and mediator. They felt that if he were allowed to carry his ideas into reality, that better day of which the generations of men have dreamed, and for the sake of which the martyrs and prophets of humanity have poured out their love and goodness, would dawn at last.

The superintendent of a mission station in India reported: "Somehow these people have heard extracts of what President Wilson has said, and it has gripped their hearts as nothing else has done since the war began." Writing in 1924, Dr. William T. Ellis said: * "The illiterate millions of the backward continents knew nothing of the men ordinarily called famous in civilized lands but because of the magic appeal to the sensibilities of all human life, which were given the wings of the morning by the unprecedented propaganda of the allies, the Wilson principles quickly spread to the uttermost parts of the earth. There the innate vitality of the ideals caused them to take root and to grow. As no other wholly

---

* Quoted by Denna Frank Fleming, Ph.D., in *The United States and the League of Nations*, G. P. Putnam's Sons, New York and London, 1932, p. 43.

human man has ever done, Woodrow Wilson voiced the basic instincts and desires of the race."

Of the human race! But not of the small minority of representatives of vested interests who, as always—*et pour cause!*—feared the triumph of the ideals of democracy in the world that was to emerge from the agony of four years of bloodshed.

The war was over, the Armistice had been signed. The murderous game had suddenly come to a stop, but the evil passions and the hatred at the moment of disappearing were fanned back into new flame. The voice of the prophet was lost in the void. The advocate of perfect justice was turned aside by a handful of Americans who spoke as chauvinistically as the worst European imperialists. Wilson became enmeshed in a web of intrigue that stretched from the American continent across the ocean to Europe. While he yet spoke, the Versailles Conference, behind his back, devoted itself to the installation of a new regime of force and to the humiliation of a defeated enemy.

Although the President's statements on America's war aims and the means he advocated to prevent a recurrence of the tragedy had evoked the almost unanimous concurrence of the American people, the Congressional elections of 1918 had brought a Republican majority to the Senate. This majority, which stood under the influence of his personal enemies, let it be known to the world that Woodrow Wilson, when he came to France in the winter of 1918, did not represent the sentiments of the American people. This was at best a half-truth: that infinitesimal section of the American people that he did not represent were the men who were fighting his every act and gesture by injecting false issues into the campaign. When Woodrow Wilson arrived in France, Clemenceau, who asked after the first session of the Peace Conference (at which he sat next to Wilson): "What am I to begin, wedged in as I am between Jesus Christ and Napoleon Bonaparte?" (Woodrow Wilson and David Lloyd George) was perfectly well aware of the Republican opposition to the President's plans. The old Tiger was on the alert the moment Woodrow Wilson set foot in France.

Fundamentally, he did not understand a single one of the President's motives. Clemenceau's conception of honor and loyalty was diametrically contrary to Wilson's. The men were of different texture, as far apart as heaven and earth. Old Clemenceau, who had already passed into legend, was in turn pathetic, stupefied, and ironic as he fought Woodrow Wilson in word and writing, in public and in secret, because Wilson, as he thought, quite sincerely no doubt, had come "to close a door behind which the best part of France's victory had been left outside."

His thesis, as it is set down in *Grandeurs et misères d'une victoire,* was: what do you Americans want here anyway at the Peace Conference? You did not make any contribution to speak of in the war. You hesitated too long, far too long before coming in. That delay cost France a million and a half dead. You lost a few men: fifty thousand or so. Now you want to shape the peace. What right have you to mix in our affairs? You have come with Fourteen Points and the plan for a League of Nations. We have agreed to negotiate on that basis not only to please you, but also to bring the German enemy to his knees. But do you now really expect us to conduct the negotiations on so narrow a basis, now that we have the upper hand? The Germans accepted your Fourteen

Points. That was a clever move on their part, at least so they think. We are of the opinion that they ran into a trap. In fact, we have them in the trap now. You do not think we are going to let them off as lightlv as you propose in your Fourteen Points, do you?

"*Ah, non, le Boche paiera!* The most criminal nation on earth will now have to pay for its misdeeds."

Under Wilson's pressure Clemenceau nevertheless withdrew his plans to make an independent republic out of the Rhineland and to carve Germany into its component parts. But only on the understanding that there would be a pact of guarantee—of French security—in return. This Wilson could not promise and would not promise, for he expected that America would become a member of the League of Nations and that a universal league would be the supreme guarantor of peace, not only of the peace of France but the peace of the world.

The treaty was signed: a bad treaty from Wilson's point of view because it was a complete negation of the ideals he had set forth in his Fourteen Points. As it stood there, the Treaty of Versailles was unquestionably the breeding ground of fresh hatreds and renewed acts of violence. Yet, the President felt that his League of Nations, as soon as it started to function, would be able to mitigate the evils of Versailles and to redeem its worst features by international collaboration, round-table conferences, and supplementary covenants and stipulations.

To make that League a reality he returned to America. He felt that all could be saved yet, that the Republican opposition could be overcome, and that the masses of the American people who had supported him could be persuaded that entrance into the League would assure the peace of the world.

It was to gain the people for his ideas that he started on that exhausting campaign in the West. He was a sick man at the time. But he felt that if the Treaty were defeated, "God alone knows what will happen to the world as a result of it. Even though, in my condition, it might mean the giving up of my life, I will gladly make the sacrifice to save the Treaty." He had grown old in the struggle, but the tom-toms were beating their trick music about the danger of entangling alliances, the adroitness and the pernicious intentions of Europe's politicians to drag America into new wars, and all the other appeals "in marked form" designed to delude the American people.

Nevertheless, Wilson was winning the day. Desperately ill, almost staggering on his feet, he continued to make speeches, saying on the last day in Pueblo: "I am thinking of my clients in this case. My clients are the children, my clients are the next generation. We said to the men who lie dead in France that they went over there not to prove the prowess of America or her readiness for another war but to see to it that there never was to be such a war again. The children do not know what promises and bonds I undertook when I ordered the armies of the United States to the soil of France, but I know, and I intend to redeem my pledges to the children: they shall not be sent upon a similar errand. . . ."

On September 26, 1919, he was struck with paralysis. His secretary, Joseph Tumulty, tells how he entered the presidential drawing room and found him fully dressed and seated in a chair. "His face was pale and wan. One side of it had fallen, and his condition was indeed pitiful to behold. . . . Looking at me, with great tears running down his face, he said: 'My dear boy, this has never happened to me before. I felt it coming on yesterday. I do not know what to do.' He then pleaded with us [Tumulty and Dr. Grayson] not to cut short the trip. Turning to both of us, he said: 'Don't you see that if you cancel this trip, Senator Lodge and his friends will say that I am a quitter and that the Western trip was a failure and the Treaty will be lost?' "

The Treaty was lost in that hour when Wilson fell sick.

Senator James Hamilton Lewis wrote later: "The former Presidents [William Howard Taft and Theodore Roosevelt] by their appeals in marked form, have deluded the people against themselves and caused the Republican voter to stab his own children with the sword of future wars!"

3. *Tiger in Slippers*

"I AM AN old man," said Georges Clemenceau. "In my day I have lived through a lot of noise. I cannot deny that my life has been an uninterrupted tumult. . . . But lately it seems to me that I am beginning to hear the muffled footsteps of the great silence. . . . You want to know how I spend my days? Very well, I sit here in my house and I wait. The summer I spend in the Vendée cultivating my roses and looking at the sea. That is all there is left to do: I look at the sea and I interrogate the heavens and I wait. From time to time I ask a few questions. I say to myself, now that the eventide draws to a close: what does it mean after all to have lived? What is life and what is death? Of what significance is it to have been born at all?

"You may think that these questions show that I am growing afraid, that fear has come over me as it comes over every man who grows aware that the end of his improvised existence is drawing near and that his personality is about to be annihilated. . . . It is not that I am afraid. No, I am stupefied. I am crushed by amazement. To have lived? It is no more than the sensation of an imaginary fixation in an endless revolution of that wheel of things of which India glimpsed the existence and then conceived the irresistible temptation to free itself. . . . To die? *Eh bien,* that is to continue, that is still continuation and so on forever in other forms that are eternally renewed. . . .

"In the course of his long sojourn on earth man has only learned recently—that is, within the last ten thousand years or so—to say the words 'beginning' and 'end,' the words 'creation' and 'annihilation.' But these conceptions are of no historical value, except as representations of primitive appearances. . . .

"What do we know? What is the sum total of our knowledge? We have not even the faintest idea of the meaning of life. We have guessed at it now and then, no more. . . . A few conjectures, that is all that can be offered to man in return for a bitter and harsh journey. It would be wonderfully pleasant to be able to say that there is a paradise of felicity without end in the offing. But that is merely an aspiration to satisfy ancestral puerilities, one of the illusions the medicinemen of the Church keep alive. . . . Man is a phenomenon, *voilà tout,* one of the phenomena of the universe, and he has to accommodate himself to the other phenomena, whether he likes it or not. His adventure is of no greater importance in the blind scheme of things than this or that organic or inorganic movement in the infinite world. . . .

"To suppose that this world exists in answer to or to fulfill human destiny is as infantile as to believe in oracles or in revelation. Go and ask your priests and pastors why he waited so long, their God I mean, why he waited until yesterday, after aeons and aeons of time, to make his revelation of salvation and of infinite happiness? What was he doing all that time, those hundreds of millions of years since this earth came into existence, and why did he finally decide to pay attention in the end to his insignificant cooled-off ball we call the earth and reveal his plan to the ridiculous creatures that walk around on this the smallest of worlds? Why? . . .

"*Tiens,* I have an idea: go and ask that question of the theologians, *ces messieurs de Saint-Sulpice,* yes, and publish their answer in the American press. That will be interesting. I am giving you an assignment. I have found something for you to do. Their answer, whatever it is, will create at least some diversion in this world which is dying of boredom. Their answer will be part of the procession with which humanity has amused itself since its infancy—the procession of hereditary emotions, presented with pomp and floating banners, with songs of glory and crashing cymbals and tom-tom frenzy and incense and tiaras and images and emblems, all those other fictions that have been invented to keep man's eyes away from the void, from the meaninglessness of existence. Do I see you shake your head? Ah, you do not wish to ask that question? You think he needs silence, *hein*, the God of the Christians, in order to gain the upper hand over us? Or do you also seek to retard the emergence of the thinking men after a hundred thousand years of man the dreamer? . . ."

He chuckled. I had not interrupted his monologue by so much as a word. I had come to the apartment in the Rue Franklin on the insistence of Harold S. Pollard, the editor of *The Evening World,* the newspaper I then represented in Europe. Mr. Pollard thought that it would be worth while to have an expression of opinion from Georges Clemenceau after his phenomenal defeat for the presidency of the French Republic, the position he had so ardently desired as the crown of the French people's approval on his life's work.

It was not the first time that I had been face to face with the Tiger of France. More than once I had heard him growl that in his day on the *Aurore* and *L'Homme Libre* journalists did not come to disturb old men for an interview but wrote their own opinions. I had come prepared to hear one sarcasm after another, especially at the expense of the American press, which Clemenceau knew well, having resided in the United States, and of which he nearly always spoke with withering contempt. But I had not expected that outpouring of pessimism. . . .

Perhaps it was the disillusion of the last few days that had made him doubly bitter. What had happened? Since the signing of the Treaty of Versailles, which was his handiwork, Georges Clemenceau had lived a retired life. He had begun to work on those monumental volumes: *Les Grandeurs et misères d'une victoire, Démosthène,* and *Au Soir de la pensée.* Politics still interested him. But he, as the author of the victory over Germany, had become a figure, probably intentionally so, *au-dessus de la mêlée,* above the everyday petty quarrels and wrangling of party politics. He had had his fill of parliamentary debates. The time for polemics was over. He had been in the thick of it since the days of the Commune of Paris in 1871, when he served as Mayor of Montmartre, the district where the barricades had held out longest and where the slaughter had been the most merciless. He had been in exile for his opinions and had returned to become *le tombeur des ministères:* Clemenceau had brought more ministries to fall than any other man.

Then in the end he had been the wheelman who had piloted France through the tempest of 1914-1918. He had been called to the bridge at the age of seventy-seven. When others faltered, he had kept the faith in final victory. When Pétain had suggested surrender, he had dismissed the ignoble maneuvering of the defeatists. Four long years he had been everywhere at once: day and night at the front, in the council of ministers, on the speakers' tribune in parliament, attending the sessions of the High

Command when important decisions had to be taken. He had brought the traitors to book and to all the schemes and tricks of the intrigants and politicians he had returned his eternal: *"Je fais la guerre!"* He had carried France under his heart for four years as a woman carries her unborn child.

Then peace had come at last, and France had been the first Power in Europe. But from the moment the document was signed in the Hall of Mirrors and even before that, during the negotiations, Clemenceau knew that France would have to exert all her energy to maintain herself in that dominant position, that there was a conspiracy on foot to rob France of the fruits of her victory. Lloyd George and the British government wanted to revert to the old British policy of the balance of power. He saw the first efforts to lighten Germany's burdens, the loosening of the shackles of Versailles: the surrender of the bridgeheads in the Rhineland by the British and Belgians, the whittling down of the sums of reparation the Reich was called on to pay, the initiation of the so-called policy of reconciliation with the enemy of yesterday by Aristide Briand. He was alarmed.

Had it all been for nothing, the immense suffering, the long years of bloodshed, the destruction of the fairest provinces? Could the new German leaders,—Stresemann, Müller, Brüning—be trusted? Were they different than those Prussian and Teutonic ancestors of theirs who had come smashing their way a hundred times from their arid soil toward the fat habitations of Celts and Gauls? Had the leopard changed its nature or only its spots? Did the world realize that France no longer had her allies of the war years by her side but that she stood alone, that the British persistently refused to guarantee French

security and that America, after making the world safe
for democracy, instead of keeping it safe had washed her
hands of Europe and was deploying her fantastic energy
in the pursuit of an ephemeral prosperity?

Although he had relinquished office, the Tiger was
watching carefully. Briand's attempts at *rapprochement*
with the Reich, the succession of concessions and allevia-
tions, filled him with concern. He was fully aware, of
course, that the policy of reconciliation pursued by Bri-
and and the permanent staff of the Quai d'Orsay was not
dictated by any sentiments of altruism, but was a *pis-aller*
to which France was forced to resort because of England's
new policy of restoring the balance of power, which under
the circumstances amounted to raising Germany from the
pit of impotence into which the defeat of 1918 had
plunged her. England wanted Germany to be a counter-
balance to French influence in Europe and to break
French military, economic, and political supremacy. For
dancing so slavishly to London's tune, Clemenceau
looked upon Aristide Briand as a weakling. France was
being robbed of the fruits of her victory by a Foreign
Minister who had not the gumption to tell the Foreign
Office that, if Britain would not support a realistic policy
in regard to the Reich, France would go it alone. It was
more than weakness to Clemenceau, it came close to
treason.

The Tiger had been near bringing Briand before the
High Court in the course of the war, along with Joseph
Caillaux and Jean Malvy, on a charge of treasonable
dealings with the enemy, and he had more than once expressed regret that he had not had the Foreign Minister
executed. And now that his back was turned and he had
retired, the game had started all over again, the game

of appeasement and surrender. They who were running the show must have thought that he, Clemenceau, was no more than a mummy, a tired old man who no longer paid attention, who was no longer on guard.

"They have never forgiven me the victory," he said. "They will yet take revenge by robbing France of the peace."

But he would show that he still had a few more tricks up his sleeve, that he had not been called a *tombeur de ministères* for nothing. He would be a candidate for the presidency, now that Poincaré's double term of office was running to a close, and he would resume his vigilance over France's foreign policy from the Élysée Palace. "If I can have one or two more years where I can supervise the business," he said, "the peace and security of France will be safe." Then they would see how long Aristide Briand would last and how much longer victorious France would trail as another Portugal or African colony at the coattails of Monsieur Lloyd George and the British Foreign Office. . . .

Père-la-Victoire was so certain that he would be elected to the presidency that he had put on his dress suit the afternoon the National Assembly met and had his limousine standing in readiness to speed out to Versailles the moment word came of his election to receive the acclaim of Senate and Chamber. It was Georges Mandel, his old collaborator, who mustered the courage to telephone the old Tiger from Versailles that Briand had outmaneuvered him and that Senator Paul Deschanel, an innocuous, meaningless, and shilly-shallying opportunist, who was to become insane within three months, had been raised to the dignity that Clemenceau had thought to be his as "an elementary recompense" for services rendered to the country. When the Tiger heard the news, he blurted out with characteristic terseness: "That's Briand's work!" and after a pause: *"Eh bien, la France est foutue! . . ."* *

My visit to the Rue Franklin took place a few days after these events. I was to pulse the mood of the disappointed old statesman and, if possible, have him say something about the future of France. This was not an easy task, for had he known the real object of my call, he would most certainly have refused point-blank to see me. A little stratagem was therefore employed. *M. le président* had been reported to be paying an occasional visit to the Folies-Bergères prior to retiring to the country for good. He was said to have ordered a coffin and to have given instructions that he was to be buried in a standing position, as his father had been. Those were the things I was to verify and to have him talk about, if he could be led to talk at all.

After the long monologue Clemenceau rose from his chair, signifying that the audience was at an end. He was going out for a drive, he said. He led me to the door of his study and I opened it. "You can say that I am in good health," he added. "Only, I will soon have to undergo an operation . . . on the prostate gland. That will make me a colleague at last of Raymond Poincaré. . . ."

"Monsieur Poincaré," I said, seizing the cue quickly, "is reported to have said to someone who came to see him on his estate at Sampigny in Lorraine that the Germans will most certainly come back again if they can. Does Your Excellency agree with that?"

"For once I agree with my future colleague," he answered with a smile. "Yes," he went on, "when I said to

---

* This may be translated as "Now France is sunk," though the connotation is far more Clemenceauistically rude.

you *tout à l'heure* that we do not know anything, I did not mean that we must not try to learn. . . . We can learn only by keeping our eyes open, by seeing, not by staring, for that will lead to blindness. Nor should we try to see as that philosopher who closed all the windows and then pushed his fists into his eyes in order to learn the secrets of the human soul and human destiny by interior observation. For we know this much today that the things which have to do with man's destiny can be discovered only in the light of his relationship with the universe. The first condition is to have the courage—and that is a rare thing in our time—to open the windows, all the windows, and to look out and then to say what we see.

"I am an old man," he went on, *"c'est évident,* I am like an old farmer who raises himself up at the end of a day, all stiffened by the effort at the plow. He looks at the fields and he wonders. He wonders what the harvest is going to be like. He wonders how much of the seed he has sown is going to be picked up by the birds and if those clouds massing on the horizon are not going to wash out his furrows. I, too, look to see what is coming. I want to know everything, the best that can happen and the worst. . . .

"Will the Germans come back? Well, history, I always say, is a succession of strong wills that have imposed themselves. That is the only way to look at the world. We have conquered the Germans, but they are a strong people. They have a will. Their will is to make a comeback, as you say in English. Why? . . . Modern psychology gives us the answer. Psychologists speak of individuals who have an inferiority complex—the term is very fashionable just now—a feeling of inferiority with, as compensation, an exaggerated need of recognition of superiority. Of course, every psychological comparison of the individual and the nation is a lame one. Nevertheless, there is no better image with which to explain German national sentiment at the present time. . . . They want to show us that they are not merely our equals, but our superiors. And they will not hesitate to beat this into the head of the whole world with hammer blows. If they cannot crush our ideas, our culture, they will strike at our skulls. That is the way the feeling of inferiority is going to express itself: by force. . . ."

I did not say what I thought at the moment—namely, that Monsieur Clemenceau's own Treaty of Versailles seemed to be the political instrument most apt to drive the German inferiority complex to the sickly height of a dangerous and mortal epilepsy. . . .

4. *The Price of Glory*

IN ROME there once lived a man by the name of Benito Mussolini. This Mussolini had the short bowlegs of a peasant, but his features startlingly resembled those of that crowned anarchist, Heliogabalus, who dressed up in harlot's finery and who sprinkled his posterior with powdered gold in order to make the populace and the Roman Senate believe it was the sun. In the dead of night, when poisonous vapors come up from the Tiber, this Mussolini sat alone in an enormous room in the Palazzo Chigi, reciting stanzas from Dante's *Commedia* to himself, brooding over a map of the world, and dreaming of an Italian imperium. From time to time he would step before a large mirror, glower at himself or strike the pose of Caesar's statue saluting the legions of Gaul. In the morning he put on a hat with a peacock feather, strutted past the ranks of the ten thousand dagger carriers, and smiled broadly when his followers shouted: *"Eia, eia, alala!"*

In Rome lived also Giacomo Matteotti. This Matteotti had the misfortune of knowing Mussolini's secret. He wrote sarcastically and with deliberate irony in the newspapers of the great imperium and of the warrior in the Chigi who was to conjure it into reality by a stroke of the magic sword. That was an error. The parades were not a burlesque, nor was the tarbush with the white plume a subject for ridicule. The fallacy may perhaps be overlooked, if it is taken into consideration that this Matteotti was an ordinary Socialist who quoted as gospel truth the resolutions of the international labor congresses, who invoked the legality of the democratic process, and who believed in the vote. A man of such dovelike simplicity could not be expected to understand that Mussolini was Mussolini and that castor oil may be utilized to other ends than that of export to America. Only the workers in the great factories of Fiat in Turin and Naples chuckled over Matteotti's biting monologues concerning Benito's toothaches, his preference for pig's liver, and his insane fears that the large doses of mercury he had taken in his youth had made his bones brittle.

Mussolini was chief of the government. This is a more exalted position than that of feuilletonist for struggling provincial journals that want proof for their readers, furnished in fifty-two weekly installments of equal length, that God does not exist. It is also more munificent. How the change came to be made was Mussolini's secret; his, the Lilliputian King's with the scrawny neck, and Matteotti's. To only one of the three was the secret a deadly possession, and he burned to reveal it to the world. Why should kings call in revolutionaries? And what had been the *quid pro quo* that had led Victor Emmanuel of Savoy to facilitate the blackshirts' march on Rome by furnishing a Pulmann de luxe to their leader?

When a man is charged with the conduct of the highest political office, he cannot be expected to occupy himself with petty, everyday details of statecraft—for instance, with so inconsequential a trifle as the size and the make of the instruments of torture to be used on political opponents in the cellars of the Regina Coeli. One has one's assistants when one is *capo del governo* and architect of a world imperium in the making. Mussolini's first helper was Filipelli, who published the *Corriere Italiano*. His task was to print at least once a day that the Duce was always right, that he was as good a musician as Beethoven, as holy a saint as Saint Francis, as profound a thinker as Nietzsche,

as courageous a soldier as Garibaldi, as immortal a hero
as Caesar, and as divine an empire builder as Alexander.
That was the ministry of culture: essentially a question
of a voluminous historical encyclopedia and a knowledge
of superlatives.

Then there was Signor Carlo Dumini. Dumini was
charged with a more virile mandate: he had been set to
watch and crush the Duce's enemies. The esthete of the
original Fascio—he never smoked a cigarette without first
putting on his gloves—Dumini could be relied upon to
proceed in all matters with refinement and discrimination.
He had practised vivisection on stray dogs at the Humane
Society before coming to the light. Mussolini made a
felicitous choice when he selected Dumini.

One day Matteotti wrote a new article. The workers of
the Fiat Motor Works pasted it up on the walls of their
factory. Its title was: "Mussolini Is a Humbug," and the
subtitle: "This Clown Will Steer Italy into the Bloodiest
Mess of All Times." Matteotti also interrupted the Duce's
speech in the Chamber of Deputies and thereafter
mounted the speaker's tribune himself. The Duce was
not so discourteous as to interrupt in turn. He observed
a perfect decorum. Arms folded, lips pursed, and chin in
air, he sat in stolid silence during Matteotti's harangue.
But his eyes traveled over the faces of the deputies until
they came to rest on Dumini. Then the Duce's chin came
down slowly, and he closed his eyes. Was this a gesture of
assent, of drowsy renunciation before the vibrant, incontrovertible accusations of Matteotti? It may have seemed
that way to a casual observer. To Dumini it was a signal.
And the signal read: the time has come.

Matteotti had not a few followers himself, many hundreds of thousands more, in fact, than Mussolini. It would

therefore be no easy task to put him out of the way. An attack on his person by *squadristi* as he was leaving the Chamber or the newspaper office was almost sure to be followed by popular demonstrations and . . . by retaliation —retaliation on the person of the *capo del governo* perhaps. Matteotti was known abroad. Vienna was even then awaiting his arrival. To make a move against Matteotti might conceivably lead to international complications. The regime was not strong enough yet to defy world opinion. Moreover, England had shown itself not quite unsympathetic, and a financial loan from London would by no means come amiss. A statesman must feel his way cautiously. Dumini's mind reverted to the past. In his grandfather's day a small white powder in the wine would have been sufficient. An agent could have been sent into the streets of the darkened old Borgo, a mask over his face and a poniard under his cape, to await and seize the propitious moment. Had that method not become antiquated? Would not the English see through it at once and laugh their cynical little laughs and—who knows?—kill the movement and the imperium with ridicule? Surely to make Matteotti disappear was not a matter to be undertaken singlehanded—at least, not without some advice from the Duce himself.

Mussolini had easily observed the worry on his helper's face. In the corridor of the Chamber of Deputies, just before stepping into his car, he remarked with a significant smile in Dumini's direction that an automobile is a most convenient accessory to politics. Was this the remark of a vulgar parvenu who had been a footloose vagabond all his life? Or another signal?

Dumini saw the point. Was not the Duce always right? Mussolini praised the laborer of the soil and rural poetry.

Nevertheless, he was not to be included among the enemies of the machine. He knew it, the Duce, that there can be no great imperium without big industry.

In Rome there is a Colosseum and an airdrome, antique shops with faked antiques and chemical laboratories in which a new brand of poison gas is being perfected. Everything has its rightful place in Rome. In the neighborhood of the Eternal City are some godforsaken districts, the fever-ridden Campagna, ghastly deserts, swamps stinking with miasma—for instance, Quartarella. But Signor Filipelli owns a magnificent motorcar, a red-lacquered Fiat, a twelve cylinder six-seater.

When Dumini praised the virtues of the automobile to his friend and colleague Filipelli in the Café Colonna, he was not talking heresy. He was an orthodox blackshirt. The automobile! Dumini blessed the new era. Only now did he understand the full beauty of Marinetti's futurist poetry.

It is a hot day in July. The crows sit yawning on Bernini's columns in the Piazza di San Pietro. The Pope's apartments bake in the merciless fire. Fortunate Romans roll away from the solar inferno to the Alban Mountains and the shores of Ostia. Those who remain in the city drink lemonade and sigh. The speculators' voices in the alleys have sunk to a whisper, for the sun burns, the lira melts, and the English loan is evaporating. Guides show visiting American women the ruins of Vesta's temple. The cats of the Forum have crawled into the deepest caverns. Those who are against the great imperium eat cheap water ice, and those who are for it do the same. The blackshirts are sticky with sweat. The sun of Italy rises, but nobody has the strength to yodel *Eia, eia, alala!*

Mussolini sits in the Palazzo Chigi. The building has cool chambers and white marble floors. The Duce holds water ice in contempt. Water ice has nothing in common with imperium and *mare nostrum* and forests of bayonets. The Duce thinks of Tunis and Nice, of Malta and Dalmatia. How can this clan of mandolinists be turned into a nation of steel and the picture-postcard peddler on the Corso be transformed into a legionnaire? The Duce thinks of the arch of Titus and of that other, more distant arch, on the Champs Élysées. He also thinks of Matteotti. What had that Socialist pig reproached him with that morning? That Fascism had no philosophy? Ah, that we will see. Mussolini begins to write. It is a letter to Giovanni Gentile. "What Fascism needs quickly and at once, Professor, is a philosophy. . . . Yours is the task to furnish the movement with a philosophy. . . . Fascism must have the historical tradition it lacks at present. . . . A philosophy to justify our existence!" . . .

To Mussolini this does not look like a tour de force. And to be sure, every realtor knows that if a suburban subdivision lacks a sewer, it can be dug. All you need is good will, co-operation, and a little money. When no historical tradition and philosophy exist, they can be created. If only the fundamental directive is kept in mind: to sidetrack the results of decades of proletarian history, to frustrate the solution of contradictions rooted in the country's social structure, and to prevent the triumph of the Socialist resurgence as against bourgeois decadence. When that is borne in mind, everything becomes permissible and possible: sophistry, misinterpretation of history, a false front, the Roman salute, the assassin's dagger, a Cossack beaver,

invincible legions, murder, and castor oil. Is that not a
dainty dish of philosophy to set before King, Pope, and
motor magnates?

Giovanni Gentile is one of the leading philosophers of
history of our time. But not even he can produce a theory
in justification of dictatorship and gangsterism—at least,
nothing better than what looks to the disinterested onlooker like a beggar's blanket consisting of patches of Con-
radini's Italian nationalism, Macchiavelli's principle of a
nonhereditary dictatorial leadership, and snatches of Gio-
berti, Mazzini, Sorel, Pareto, and Nietzsche. Fascism has
no theoretical past, and the only theoretical foundation it
can be given is that it has strengthened the omnipotence of
the state and that in its *carta del lavoro,* according to Wer-
ner Sombart's expression, it has given "the highest possible synthesis of the power and authority of the state still
compatible with the capitalist system."

Karl Marx, whom Mussolini called "our common teacher" in a letter to Lenin, analyzed, in *The Eighteenth of
Brumaire,* the natural inclination of the petty bourgeois
to hide behind the specters of the past when historical evolution pushes him into the political foreground. "Thus
Luther put on the mask of the Apostle Paul, the revolution
of 1789 till 1814 draped itself successively in the garb of
the Roman Republic and of the Roman Empire. . . . But
upon a closer inspection of this trick of political conjuring,
a startling difference is revealed. The heroes, Robespierre, Desmoulins, Danton, Saint-Just, Napoleon, as well as
the parties and the masses of the old French Revolution,
dressed as they were in the Roman costume and using a
Roman phraseology, nevertheless fulfilled the historic task
of their epoch: the reorganization of modern bourgeois
society. . . . No sooner was that task accomplished than the

antediluvian colossi and with them the resuscitated *Romanità*—the Brutuses, Gracchi, Publicolas, tribunes, senators, the Caesars even—disappeared."

Whereas the different layers of the middle class in the revolutions of the past quickly became aware of the significance of current events and utilized them in the name of a progressive ideal, Fascism, after fifteen or sixteen years of power, was not clear yet about its own ideological meaning, because its power remained uncertain and because it was unable to set up an ideal that reflected present-day reality. Fascism was a masquerade from beginning to end, a tragicomedy without precedent in history. It was forced to present itself, Ignazio Silone said once, as that character in one of Pirandello's plays who at a masquerade ball had dressed himself in the costume of Henry IV, the Holy Roman Emperor. In a fall from horseback, this person loses his mind and is thereafter convinced that he is in reality Henry IV. He has his house transformed into a medieval court. Pages speak to him in an archaic language, and messengers bring him letters from Matilda of Tuscany and from Pietro Damiani, who are both intriguing against him with the Pope. The folly does not last long, but in the meantime such curious events happen that the sick man cannot straighten things out again when he recovers his sanity. He remains the prisoner of his illusion and for the rest of his life is compelled to persist in the masquerade.

That is the way it has gone with Mussolini. He could no longer take off the makeup that he put on before the March on Rome. Having led his party to victory, he could no longer reveal what transpired in the wings and what was the object of the masquerade. He was doomed to play the Caesar of carnival till the end of his life, to twist his facial muscles in one grimace after another, now pushing the Roman chin forward, then assuming the Napoleonic stare. This obscene mixture of the past and the present made Italian national life resemble a film, unreal, impermanent. To millions it was a nightmare, and even to those in whose interest it existed it seemed like a phantasmagoria.

While Mussolini is ordering a philosophy by mail, Matteotti also writes. In his small apartment the atmosphere is suffocating. He must finish his article quickly. For tomorrow he is off for Vienna. Strange, is it not, that the passport should have arrived so promptly? He had expected a refusal. Mussolini must think that he is going to remain in Austria for good, that he is afraid to face the music. A fool, that Mussolini! But his days are numbered. In a week Matteotti's article will be in the press, and the world will know the Duce for the treacherous cowardly sycophant he is. He thinks of triumphators, does he? Well, the workers of Fiat and the Aventine Coalition will show him a triumph he has not bargained for.

Matteotti's thoughts also fly beyond the limits of the peninsular kingdom. He will show in his article that what the workers of Italy do will have an important bearing on the international situation. . . . In Germany the chances of revolution have been thrown away. But Russia is holding. All the interventionist armies could not crush Moscow. . . . The English dock workers have refused to load war material destined for the Soviet's foes. England is stirring. If England moves, Italy will be next. . . . And so far as the arch of Titus is concerned, had not the poverty-stricken, untutored sectarians of Judea proved themselves mightier than Rome's demigods?

Matteotti has written nineteen pages. He has shown in what direction Mussolini is leading the country. That will make the King look up and perhaps make him reconsider his choice for the premiership. Mussolini is heading for war. Sooner or later he will plunge the country into the abyss. War is the last thing that the House of Savoy wants. Little Victor Emmanuel still trembles when he thinks how near he came to losing his throne in the last. And now war again? After Caporetto and Gorizia? War! That specter would stir the workers. Did they remember: the frostbite in the Alps, the famine in the cities, the shells of the Austro-Germans, the hundred-mile-long strings of ambulances on the roads in the Venetian plain? . . . Yes, and after that he will show the world who this Mussolini really is, what a contemptible cur, what a Judas! . . .

Matteotti has smoked many cigarettes while writing the article. He has completed one page on which he had begun to reveal Mussolini's secret. Then he stretches out his hand for a fresh cigarette and frowns. The box is empty. He rises and says to his wife: "I will be back in a minute. Just going around the corner to buy some cigarettes. . . ." Quickly he walks along the blistering Lungo Michelangelo. Speed was the essence of the hour. By rapid maneuvering it is still possible to isolate the Fascists in the Chamber of Deputies and throughout the country. But in a week, perhaps two, Mussolini will surely dissolve the Chamber, put the press under the ban, and forbid the holding of meetings. One week, ten days, perhaps a month!

A red-lacquered Fiat limousine stops at the corner. Five men jump out and surround Matteotti. They do not wear blackshirts or uniforms, just ordinary civilian suits. They lift him bodily off the street and throw him into the car. The man at the wheel steps on the gas. The motor roars.

Nobody pays any particular attention to the red automobile. So many cars are racing for the mountains where it is cool or to the shore where the breeze comes in from the Tyrrhenian Sea. Moreover, the curtains of the car are drawn. Who knows if there is not a pair of lovers or newlyweds inside who do not wish to be seen. . . . Signor Filipelli's car swiftly serpentines its way through the narrow streets. Inside are Dumini, four of his assistants, and Matteotti. Filipelli is not of the party. He is waiting at the office of the *Corriere Italiano.*

Mussolini is waiting at the Palazzo Chigi, which takes its name from a Pope who always kept a coffin in his room and who drank from a cup shaped like a skull. Reports have come in that opposition to the brigands' regime is waxing in the country and that the movement is crystallizing itself around Matteotti. Matteotti is preparing for battle. Mussolini does not like battle. At the front he always managed to have himself transferred to the rear on some pretext or other when an offensive was impending. He attributes the glory to himself afterwards and will take responsibility for what is about to occur when it is quite safe, when Matteotti is dead, all the man's friends are assassinated, and the whole country is helpless in the strait jacket of Fascism.

Dumini works with precision. He has two extra pairs of gloves with him this July day. After throwing Matteotti to the floor of the car, three men sit on his chest, while a fourth forces a gag into his mouth. Dumini is on his knees at the chauffeur's side, facing backwards. He directs the struggle. Matteotti is fighting back. He has shaken off his assailants and succeeds in holding them off while he reaches for the doorknob. But Dumini is watching. Swiftly he reaches over and cuts the veins of the deputy's left hand. As Matteotti withdraws his hand in pain one of the helpers seizes him by the hair and holds his head down. Dumini reaches over again and drives his dagger into Matteotti's neck at the base of the brain. That is where the weapon sticks. When a man's ideas are too strong for you, strike at his skull, Stalin said once. Not the meek but the gorillas will inherit the earth.

Here is Quartarella. Here are neither tourists, nor passers-by, nor shepherds. Only clumps of thornbushes and sun. Silently the men drag the corpse from the limousine, over the asphalt into the shrubbery. Dumini has thought of everything. He produces two shovels from the baggage trunk. The men dig a grave. What they do is a noble task, one that will be well compensated by Mussolini and sung by all the poets of the *strapaese*—that is, the poets of rural, bucolic beauty. Is not digging related to agriculture? But it is easier to slaughter a human being than it is to dig a grave. The soil is arid, baked into brick-like hardness. The sun beats down on the gravediggers' heads. After an hour they have only a small, shallow hole. Dumini says it is sufficient. The body is forced in. It does not fit. Dumini jumps on it and breaks the backbone. Now it fits. A resourceful fellow, this Dumini. He will go far in life.

The red limousine roars back to Rome. It is growing dark. The car is one of many carrying people back to the city after having enjoyed the breezes of the country. The murderers are dismissed at the office of the *Corriere*. The reporters have long since left. Only Filipelli is still waiting.

Dumini holds up his blood-soaked gloves. "Everything went off well," he says, "except that there is some blood on the upholstery. Oh, yes, some women, too, were standing on the Lungo Michelangelo when we threw him in. They have seen, though they may not have recognized Matteotti."

"That is bad," says Filipelli. "Let me telephone a moment." He operates the switchboard himself. A moment later he is back smiling. "We are going to publish the news that Matteotti left for Austria without even informing his wife and will say that this is but another sample of Socialist heartlessness, cruelty, and materialism. Ha, ha!"

Dumini washes his hands, changes his shirt, and goes to the café. He drinks lemonade. The conversation turns to the Duce's plans to rebuild the Eternal City on the model of the Caesars.

Night descends on Rome. A fresh breeze blows through the streets. People breathe deeply. The ruins come to life: they are again the baths of Caracalla, the circus of Nero, the temple of Jupiter. The Arditi sit in the sidewalk cafés and watch the legs of passing women. Bats flap under the eaves of the Palazzo Chigi. The specter of the moon stands on the arch of Titus. The centuries play hide and seek and are mixed up in a jumble of shadows: Vestal virgins and blackshirts, Michelangelo and Marinetti, the Colosseum and the Café Aragno, marble and cement, centaurs and motorcycles, melancholy and dust.

In a high, cool chamber a man sits alone and reads. He has a bundle of papers on his table. The papers have just been brought in. There are nineteen pages of rapid script, difficult to decipher because obviously written in great haste. The nineteenth page interests him more than the others. There he reads: "It may well be that the fate of Italy was decided on that day when Mussolini accepted the seven-million-lira bribe from the Fiat Motor Works.

In that hour Fate began to write a new page of Italian history. . . ."

The night is calm. The moon is sailing through the ruins. Through the open window comes the sound of a motorcar halting in the Piazza Colonna. Filipelli and Dumini have come to bring their report. Mussolini looks on the column of Marcus Aurelius and thinks of the imperium and *mare nostrum*. He smiles. Danger is averted. Matteotti is no more.

5. *Failure and Success of a Putsch*

In 1888 General Boulanger was the hope of the French Monarchists. The *conferenciers* in the night clubs of Montmartre sang: *"Il est beau, il est bon, il est brave, not' petit général."* General Boulanger had indeed on one or two occasions called the Republic a pestilential disease. To call names is easier than winning battles and by itself is nothing extraordinary. In the witty *salons* of the Faubourg Saint-Honoré the *grandes dames* of the epoch often used expressions much more risqué when they referred to Marianne. It had been noticed, though, that when the General spoke he had placed his hand with a significantly bold gesture on the handle of his sword. That was more to the point. A good observer, say the Dutch, needs only half a wink.

Such an observer was a young man of swarthy features named Charles Maurras, who in years to come was to be recognized by both Mussolini and Franco as their personal teacher and mentor among antidemocrats. Maurras had his eye on General Boulanger from the moment the man began to rattle his saber. Maurras followed the General around, wrote to him, spoke of him, and in the end succeeded in creating a movement which came to be known as Boulangism. The General was this movement's solar plexus, its glory, and finally the cause of its eclipse.

Boulangism aimed at the restoration of the monarchy. Although there were not sufficient monarchists in France to go around and make this possible, Maurras claimed that all that was needed was a bold stroke by *une minorité agissante,* a small but militant minority, to set the ball rolling. The Bolsheviks have since proved Maurras' theory correct, though they have never given him credit for it. "Be resolute and the masses will follow you," the young agitator counseled the General. "You will get along without the masses afterwards. But of this they need not be told till the hour comes for telling them."

After months of prompting by Maurras, the General agreed to try his luck. He was to appear on horseback on the Rue Royale one evening, about the time when the theaters go out and the sidewalk cafés are crowded with patrons. Maurras would have his crowd of bravoes on hand and would raise the cry: *"A l'Élysée! A l'Élysée!"* The Élysée is the presidential palace. The crowd was to take up the cry and knock over the police, and some of the General's military friends were to keep the troops in barracks while the procession of insurgents made its way up the broad avenue. The General was then to take possession of the palace, chase out President Sadi-Carnot, and hold the place until one of the princes of the blood could come to Paris to claim the throne of Saint Louis.

All went according to program on the appointed day. The start was auspicious. Boulanger duly appeared in gala uniform. He trotted past the Madeleine and swung into the Rue Royale. Maurras raised the shout. Thousands joined, and the Republic began to totter.

It tottered for exactly half an hour. Then the oscillating needle steadied itself and remained that way for half a century. What had happened? The crowd had begun to sing: *"Il est beau, il est bon,"* etc. Everybody had shouted: "A l'Élysée," and the General had cantered boldly forward. Tens of thousands of sympathizers had come up through the side streets and now cluttered up the broad avenue. So great was the mob that it took General Boulanger half an hour to advance a quarter of a mile.

Just as he was turning the corner of the Place de la Concorde, a man fought himself through the crowd and handed him a telegram. He read the dispatch by the light of the street lamps. What he read there made him dismount at once, call for a fiacre, and return home. Two hours later he was in the night train for Brussels. Two years later he shot himself on his mistress' grave. It was the announcement of her illness that had turned him from his design to become a kingmaker.

The hope of the royalists died in Brussels in 1888. In the same city it was reborn in 1934. And again Charles Maurras was the impresario. For forty long years he had wandered in the desert in the cloak of a philosopher. Then in a flash he saw the promised land. In the solitude he had learned that neither kings nor revolutions are made on the whim of a moment; that, instead of a general with blond mustaches, one needs a pretorian guard and that the theory of a militant minority can best be translated into reality by a mob of gangsters.

The gangsters had been recruited and drilled. They were his own *camelots du roi,* or King's Henchmen; Pierre Taittinger's *Jeunesses patriotes,* or Patriotic Youth Society, and François de la Rocque's Legion of the Fiery Cross. The wait was only for a cause, an incident, the psychological moment. That, too, came in due time. It was the Stavisky scandal. Maurras felt so certain that the Republic could be brought to a fall over this affair that he notified the Manoir d'Anjou to be ready. The Manoir d'Anjou is an unpretentious château near Brussels in which lived the Duc de Guise and his son, the Comte de Paris. . . .

If Guise should have mounted the throne of France, he would have reigned under the name of Jean III and his son under the name of Henri V. At the height of the effervescence over the Stavisky affair, Maurras' newspaper announced in dramatic headlines that the skull measurements, the facial contour, the voice, the color of the eyes, and the size of the feet of the Comte de Paris were exactly like those of still-lamented King Henri IV. This was not precisely a recommendation from the point of view of pulchritude. Henri IV had not been an Adonis. But he had been popular: a generous lover, rough of language, but of good heart. He it was who said that he wanted to see a chicken in every pot on Sundays. . . .

The Duc de Guise, "heir to the forty kings who in a thousand years made France," was a collector of butterflies. This is an innocent hobby in itself and leaves a man ample time to administer some sugar plantations in Indo-China and two or three phosphate mines in Algiers and to clip a few coupons on Suez Canal bonds and Paris Gas and Electricity after supper if the mood strikes him. It is all in a day's work. Even pretenders must do something to keep themselves busy. How else keep up the pretense? Waiting to fill a throne is apt to be a tedious job these days when a paperhanger and a blacksmith's son have cornered the European market, so to speak.

It cannot be said that Guise received the long-awaited signal from Maurras with any show of exuberance. It may well be that the sickening pang of hope deferred had dulled the novelty. It may also be that as *chef de la maison de France,* he thought of his dignity. Whatever the case, Guise did think of one little matter which had entirely escaped the zealots of the royal cause in Paris.

Guise informed Maurras through the brother of Colonel de la Rocque, who at the time was working as the chief liaison officer between the Manoir d'Anjou and the King's Henchmen in Paris, that he would be willing to answer the call of his people. Before packing his grips, however, he wanted one thing cleared up. Then, as a good Bourbon, he showed that he had neither learned nor forgotten anything during the long years of exile.

Which flag, Guise wanted to know, would float over the Louvre and the royal palaces when he should make his joyous entry and hoist himself onto the throne of Saint Louis? The tricolor of the Republic, of Napoleon, and of the July Monarchy? If so, he, the Duc de Guise must be counted out. Never would he come to France so long as that infamous rag of international Freemasonry and the Sanhedrin remained the official standard. He would sooner stay with his butterflies and coupons.

Maurras was busy printing proclamations to the Parisians: "The King is here at last: *Vive Jean III!*" But the Pretender's message made him stop the presses. What? Start a debate in so solemn and sacred a moment, a quarrel over dressing before the goose was cooked, or plucked, or even caught? Monseigneur was really too particular. The main job was to get into the Louvre, flag or no flag. A minor detail like that about flags could easily be settled afterwards—for instance, after the hundred leading republicans, Herriot, Blum, and Daladier at their head (Maurras wrote), had been drowned like dogs in the Seine. Guise replied petulantly that the tricolor must come down before he would take one step on the road to Paris. With him it was the reverse of the case of General Boulanger. The General had dismounted too soon; the Duke would not stir from his high horse.

The matter would have ended right then and there, had it not been for the good sense of the Duke's son, Henri, Comte de Paris. The ancestor whom this young man was said to resemble had found Paris well worth a Mass. He,

Henri, thought it worth a flag and even a whole bushel of flags. He informed the disconcerted monarchists that he would come to Paris even if Beelzebub sat on the roof of the Louvre. In fact, the scepter and the diadem stood ready, next to his father's old butterfly boxes.

That was the language Maurras liked. Now he could start the ball rolling. The Parisians were informed through the medium of a series of articles in *l'Action Française* from the pen of Léon Daudet that the Pretender's son not only had the skull of *le vert galant*, but that he nourished some pretty progressive and advanced ideas. For example, the Comte de Paris had made a deep study of the Christian corporate state; he was an admirer of Mussolini; he furthermore believed in the family, in religion, in law, in order, in social justice, in peace with honor, in a big army, in a holy crusade against Moscow, in freedom of conscience for Jesuits, and in Paris Gas and Electricity. In other words, he was a unique young man, quite like the five hundred thousand members of the Fiery Cross. Maurras told me once that he detested Americans because he said they are always trying to sell something. While selling the Comte de Paris to the skeptical Parisians, Maurras launched the second grand coup of his life.

On February 6, 1934, his *camelots du roi* demonstrated on the Place de la Concorde in front of the Palais Bourbon, where the Chamber of Deputies was in session. Inside the building Daladier was defending some of his Radical friends against the Communists' accusations that they were implicated in the Stavisky scandal.

The demonstration took the government completely by surprise. Jean Chiappe, the police prefect, had gone on a vacation to Florence. It was not until he refused to return that it dawned on Daladier that there was a sinister connection between the man's absence and the riots that followed. The *camelots* demonstrated under the choral cries of: "France to the French! Down with the Jews! Hang the thieves on the lantern posts!" They came near breaking into the Palais Bourbon, whereupon Edouard Herriot, who presided, suspended the session and sent the deputies home for the day to their wives and mistresses.

On the following day, the Chamber went into session at two in the afternoon. By that time the quays leading to the Palais Bourbon were guarded by detachments of the Mobile Guard; units of the regular army were camped in the side avenues of the Champs Élysées, and patrols of dragoons were riding up and down the Place de la Concorde. Around six o'clock a group of young men, wearing the berets of the King's Henchmen and carrying walking sticks with razor blades fastened to the ends, made a descent on the Place de la Concorde from the direction of the Tuileries terraces and, rushing past the dragoons, attacked a couple of motor buses and set them on fire.

The dragoons promptly mounted and cleared the square with their swords. An hour later the Tuileries gardens were swarming with people. In one corner of the gardens I saw Maxime Réal del Sarte and Maurice Pujo, the commanders of the King's Henchmen, holding a conference with the organization's shock-troop leaders. In another section, near the Orangerie, were André Marty and Gabriel Péri, surrounded by so-called *"responsables"* of the Communist party. Slowly the crowd filtered into the square. When at seven o'clock the troopers received the order to clear the way, they were received with brickbats and burning hoops of straw, which the Henchmen deftly tossed around the horses' necks.

While this running fight was going on in the square,

a procession of ex-service men belonging to a Fascist veterans' organization, the Union Nationale des Combattants, came marching down the Champs Élysées and was halted by a cordon of police at the entrance of the square between the two statues of the Horses of Marly, which is the place where the guillotine stood in the days of Robespierre's Terror. Their leaders entered into an argument with the police inspectors. Claiming that Daladier had granted permission for their demonstration, they demanded passage.

While the debate was waxing hot, the Communists suddenly stormed into the square from the opposite side, sweeping the dragoons before them in one overwhelming mass movement. Only black-helmeted members of the Mobile Guard, Daladier's special police, stood their ground at the Pont de la Concorde. The Mobiles let the fleeing troopers pass through their ranks and fired a warning salvo into the air. That volley exasperated the crowd's temper. More thousands pressed into the square, with the result that the Mobiles were pressed so closely that they could not raise their carbines to fire but were forced to engage in hand-to-hand fighting with the mob.

In the meantime the mounted detachments, which had passed through the lines, had dismounted on the Quai d'Orsay. They were patting their horses and nursing their bruises when they were attacked by a section of the crowd that had come upon them by rushing across the Pont Royal, which connects the Right and the Left Bank of the Seine, from the Louvre's Pavillon de Flore to the Rue du Bac.

In a flash, dozens of horses were racing around with burning hoops of straw around their necks. The troopers had drawn their sabers, but they were being pushed into the river one by one. A good number of them were drowned. The government never published the number of casualties suffered by the police forces.

By that time fighting was general on the Place de la Concorde, on the *quais,* and the Champs Élysées. Some machine guns on the terrace walls of the Palais Bourbon had gone into action. They were still firing above the heads of the crowd. Had they not done so, they would have mowed down the Mobile Guards, who had their backs toward them holding off the mob.

But the firing did not disperse the mob. Something else did. A few minutes before ten o'clock, the Communists, who had taken the lead in the storming of the bridge in front of the Chamber of Deputies, suddenly withdrew from the battle. I saw the *"responsables"* going through the mob, ordering an immediate cessation of the attack. In less than an hour the Fascist organizations stood alone before the walls of armed men guarding the approaches to the Palais Bourbon.

What had happened to make the Leftists withdraw from the fight at a moment when it seemed that the next push, by sheer weight of numbers, would have carried the mob right into the corridors of the Palais Bourbon?

I asked Paul Vaillant-Couturier, the editor of *Humanité,* whom I encountered late that night "retreating" up the Avenue de l'Opéra. He said the whole fight had been a tactical error on the part of the Communists. They had not realized that they had become the unwitting instruments of Maurras and the Fascists in general.

"We thought at first that it was merely to be a demonstration against the government," he said. "In this we could join. But when we discovered that we were being pushed into something that was intended as a Fascist *coup d'état,* we stopped immediately."

"How did you find out that this was to have been a Fascist *Putsch?*" I asked.

"Through Weygand!" he said.

"How so Weygand?" I asked.

"Our men on the Place de la Concorde were told by the King's Henchmen and members of the Fiery Cross that if we could reach the Chamber gates, Weygand would send one or two regiments to help. . . ."

The fighting was not resumed the next day. Daladier resigned under the cry of "assassin of the people." Maurras raved and fumed in his newspaper, *l'Action Française.* He could hardly say that the failure of the *Putsch* was due to the defection of the Communists. His militant minority had simply failed to carry the masses along with it.

It was the second failure in forty years. But there was one phrase in Maurras' article which blew the gaff and which gave away the fundamental purpose of the bloody masquerade on the Place de la Concorde on February 7, 1934. It was this: "From this moment onward war with Germany becomes inevitable." That was true. Having failed to install a Fascist regime by their own strength, the French reactionaries could only hope that in a war with Hitler France would be defeated and that the Fuehrer would install the regime they desired.

On February 7, 1934, the basis was laid for what occurred in May and June, 1940.

6. *Politics and Souls*

THE BLOODY week of February, 1934, which saw the national army of Austria shoot down the Viennese Social Democrats has almost been forgotten in the presence of the mountains of human woe that the ensuing years have accumulated. And indeed, gruesome and shocking though it all was—the unprovoked attack on the working-class districts of the old Austrian capital, the bombardment by artillery of the apartment houses, and the subsequent hounding and hanging of the labor leaders—it appears as but a momentary and minor disturbance when viewed in the light of such appalling events as the systematic extermination of the conquered Slav nations—the Czechs, the Poles, and the Serbs—and the indescribable horrors inflicted on the Jews by the Nazi barbarians.

How trivial an impression does that distant week of fighting in Vienna make in the immense panorama of the world's tragedy today, when we see the shackles of slavery being forged around an entire continent?

Yet, the fatal hour wherein Dollfuss staged his sanguinary coup and destroyed what had been one of the most hopeful and successful experiments in social and economic planning of the postwar era, that hour is nevertheless one of the decisive moments in modern history in more than one respect.

For not only did the diminutive Chancellor, by his unprovoked assault on the workers of Vienna and on their democratic institutions, disarm and destroy the only force that would have enabled Austria to put up a desperate resistance against the Nazi invasion when it came four years later, but his action marked an important step forward in the Vatican's policy of reconquering what it had lost in Europe and in the world by the Reformation.

It is true that a great deal of what Rome lost by the Reformation had been recovered long before Dollfuss' exploit. Through the Counter Reformation and through the efforts of the nineteenth-century Popes, in all the countries that had remained Catholic and also in many territories that had become Protestant, the old authority had long since been re-established, albeit in new forms. For the Church had never abandoned its pretensions to domination. It had merely changed the methods and the tactics of regaining a dominant position in a changing world.*

The modern state grew up in the shadow of the Church. The noise of the struggle between Church and State fills the silent centuries of the later Middle Ages and the beginning of the modern era (silent, that is, in comparison with the tumult of our time). The Church definitely lost out in that struggle, but nevertheless this organization, whose motto is *semper eadem*, always the same, and which calmly attributes to itself divine approval, has never given up its ancient claims. These it has guarded till our day, along with the peculiarly ambiguous status of being both a world congregation of the faithful and a political institution chiefly concerned with gaining and regaining power.

If, after the Reformation, after the French and American Revolutions, the Era of Enlightenment, the Age of

---

* "Throughout the whole modern epoch and down to today the claim of the Papacy to authority has suffered not the smallest change, as may be studied conveniently in the well-known encyclical of Pius IX of December 8, 1864 . . . no historic document was ever more clear and precise." John Jay Chapman in *The Forum Magazine* of April 1925 on "America and Roman Catholicism."

A book proving again the papal yearning for temporal power is *The State and the Church* by Ryan and Millar. This book bears the imprimatur of the late Patrick Cardinal Hayes.

Reason, and the dawn of liberalism, the Church could no longer overcome her opponents by being against the state, it set out to try and overcome them with the help of the state. The goal had not changed, only the means to the goal. Of course, the Church denies this. Ostensibly, like any other religious body, it merely seeks the salvation of souls and the triumph of Christian principles in society. But the Roman Church also retains a political organization that all the other Christian bodies lack. It is this political organization which makes the Roman Church one of the most important factors in a period of historical transition such as ours, when humanity is faced with the decision of continuing its march on the road toward democracy or of reverting to a pattern of authoritarianism such as prevailed in those olden times when the sun of the Roman Church also stood highest.

Now, it is true that data supplied in the published works and in the public declarations of prelates and spokesmen to prove the ceaseless striving of the Roman Church for power cannot be so easily found as in the case of other political organizations, where one always finds some Professor Haushofer or Baron Tanaka letting the cat out of the bag. As the oldest international organization in existence, the Church has not only gained an incomparable authority and a respect, which in the case of American Protestants amounts to something like inviolability or untouchability, but it has also acquired a vast experience by virtue of which her prelates and princes with infallible instinct never say a word more than they wish the public to know. A bishop who told tales out of school in the same boyishly boastful manner as De Bono once spilled the beans about Mussolini's planned aggression against Ethiopia would be inconceivable.

Fortunately, however, not all Catholics are prelates, and therefore the world has come to know of the existence, in the bosom of the Church itself, of a critical attitude toward the Vatican's renewed and intensified interest and participation in world politics*. The actions of Dollfuss, to whom the pope's Secretary of State wired the papal blessing on the termination of the blood bath in Vienna†; the triumph of Fascism in Spain and the subsequent reception by the Supreme Pontiff of the leaders of the Falange; the praise periodically bestowed on the *Fascist* state of Portugal in the *Osservatore Romano;* the refusal of the French Benedictines to take up the task of "evangelizing" Russia‡, and the protests by the Patriarch of the Coptic Church against the Romanization of the Coptic communion in Ethiopia after the Italian conquest—these are but a few of the incidents that focused attention on the Vatican's profound interest and role in the major events of our time.

Although public pronouncements on this subject are not plentiful, actions, which speak louder than words, have incontrovertibly established the fact that the new world-political interventions of the Vatican date from the rise of Fascism. The predecessor of the present pontiff, Pius XI, initiated and intensified this new interest of the Vatican in world events. Before he commenced his reign in 1922, Pius XI, as Monsignor Achille Ratti, was nuncio to Poland. He was present in Warsaw in August, 1920, when the rapid advance of Simeon Budenny's Red cavalry brought the

---

* These critics are virtually all laymen: William Teeling, Georges Bernanos, José Bergamin, François Mauriac, Laurence Fernsworth, and others.

† Reported in the *Reichspost* of Vienna, *Neues Wiener Journal,* and *Neue freie Presse,* under date of February 14, 1934.

‡ Reported in the *Mercure de France,* issue of December, 1939, by Nicolas Brian-Chaninov.

Bolsheviks within sight of the Polish capital. While other diplomats fled, the nuncio remained behind. Polish history books assert that he, General Weygand, and Herbert Hoover are the men who organized the defense with Josef Pilsudski and that to their steadfastness and strategy must be attributed the "Miracle of the Vistula"—that is to say, the rolling back of the Red armies*.

Upon his appointment to the archbishopric of Milan, which was the center of the Fascist movement, Monsignor Ratti made the acquaintance of the leader of that movement, Signor Mussolini, and recognized in him the incorporation not only of anti-Bolshevik but of antidemocratic sentiments as well. Although he was an atheist, and even a militant one, Mussolini's offer to recognize the Church as an ally in the fight was not turned down. When, at the inauguration of the monument to the Unknown Soldier in Milan Cathedral, Mussolini asked the Archbishop if he could bring his blackshirts into the Duomo, Monsignor Ratti not only acceded to the request but saw to it that this band of notorious assassins occupied the seats of honor.

In June of 1921, Monsignor Ratti received the red hat from Pope Benedict XV and in January of the following year when the Pontiff died, the conclave elevated him to St. Peter's chair. In his reign, during the latter part of which Monsignor Pacelli, now, as they say in diplomatic language, *glorieusement règnant* under the title of Pius XII, functioned as secretary of state, the Vatican regained a mobility of political action that was reminiscent of its role in the Middle Ages.

Monsignor Ratti's mission as nuncio to Poland had been to win back that province of the Church, which had been

* Dr. Jan Romeyn, *Machten van onzen Tijd*, Wereldbibliotheek, Amsterdam, 1937.

lost in the eighteenth century. He fulfilled this task with success. The Polish Republic organized that campaign of terror and forceful conversion to Catholicism which *The Manchester Guardian,* the most fearless and honest newspaper in the world, fully reported (also, several books have been published on the subject). All the reports give one sad refrain of the persecution of the Ukrainian minority by the Poles. Here it was not a case of a few thousands but of a mass of ten million human beings who, in the years right after the First World War, and again in 1930-31, were subjected to a terroristic drive for conversion on the part of Church and State.

Those events, says Jan Romeyn, a Dutch professor who investigated the horrors and who has devoted a great deal of study* to the Vatican's activity in recent years, lead one to ask whether the great French historian of the nineteenth century was not right in saying that the misery of Poland began in the sixteenth century when the French candidate scorned the Polish throne, taking with him the crown jewels but leaving the Jesuits behind. The atrocities reported by *The Manchester Guardian,* Bochenfels†, and others are too harrowing to repeat; moreover, they are always the same. The result alone is important. The result was that the Ukrainian peasant who had escaped from the oppression of czarism fell back into the hands of Warsaw and Rome. It is hard to say which of them was worse.

His land trampled by the Polish soldiery, he himself impoverished, his Orthodox—Greek Catholic—clergy expelled, his schools and churches Romanized, it all meant a

* Dr. Jan Romeyn: *Gegist Bestek,* chapter: "De Paus in de Politiek" (The Pope in Politics). Uitgeversmaatschappy W. de Haan, Utrecht, 1939.

† Arthur von Bochenfels, *Das ist Poland!* Siemen Verlag, 1934, Berlin.

triumph for the Roman organization, which recouped the loss in souls it had suffered when the Ukrainian provinces had been attributed to Russia at the partition of Poland. The campaign of terror in the Ukraine, which was a ruthless attempt at Polonization of a racial and religious minority, was encouraged by Rome as an act *ad majorem Dei gloriam*. Did it not bring a few million schismatics back to the one true faith *?

Poland offers a sample of the way in which the Church works through the state and uses the state to gain her ends and also demonstrates the dual nature of the Roman *internationale*. Apologists of Catholic action never fail to admonish non-Catholics critical of the Vatican's history and its mode of procedure that it is time to forget the dark Middle Ages with their Inquisition and autos-da-fé, crusades against Albigenses, and campaigns of extermination in the Netherlands. Yet, in Poland it was shown that the Church is *semper eadem:* it never changes. It returns to the use of violence or at least condones it when it is a question of capturing souls or of extending its political power as soon as the opportunity presents itself.

Upon attaining the high dignity and authority of supreme leadership, Pius XI, encouraged by his success in eastern Europe, initiated a vast program of action† in the rest of the world. First came the integration of vast masses of laymen in the struggle for the Church, a move quite in conformity with the programs of other world-

---

* For propaganda purposes the Church has always had a great deal to say on the fate of the Christians in Russia, but that Rome has in reality no feeling of friendship or brotherhood for the Orthodox Church, but has persecuted its members when it gets its hands on them is passed over in silence.

† A study of the general policy of Pius XI may be found in Luigi Savatorelli, Pio XI e la sua eredita pontificale, Turin, Linandi, 1939.

political movements, such as Communism and Fascism, which had also come to the conclusion that nothing could be achieved without a mass basis. In the Church this movement has come to be known under the name of Catholic Action. The second point on the Pope's program was missions, with a hoped-for result of reconquering lost provinces of the Church. Finally, the third point was the restoration of the papal state.

The restoration of the papal state was accomplished in February, 1929, with the signing of the Lateran Treaty. Although the Pope's new kingdom was but of small area, the Roman Pontiff became once again a recognized sovereign. But with the signing of the Lateran Treaty, the Church also regained a second lost province—Italy.

The Vatican was given control of the Italian schools with exception of the universities; Catholicism was elevated to the position of a state religion, a device by which all criticism is squelched automatically; divorce was made impossible; the spirituals received a salary, and the monastic orders were recognized as legal entities and allowed to acquire property. The only one of the Pope's demands that was not acceded to by Mussolini was the incorporation of canon law in the civil code. So Italy became the second province Pius XI reconquered for the Church.

Although conflicts between the Vatican and the Italian state could scarcely be avoided while Mussolini was constantly intensifying the totalitarian character of the state, after 1931 little more was heard of friction between the two, a circumstance that would tend to show that there has since been a progressive Vaticanization of Italy as well as a Fascistization of the Vatican.

Austria was the third province reconquered by Rome. In that country the democratic evolution of social institutions was forcibly interrupted by Engelbert Dollfuss, who set out to build the corporate state on the basis of the ideals outlined by the Pope in his program, the encyclical *Quadragesimo Anno* of 1931. But in Austria the process of clericalization initiated by Dollfuss was interrupted when Austria was annexed by Hitler and the successor of Dollfuss, Kurt Schuschnigg, sent to a concentration camp.

Ethiopia was the fourth province the Pope reconquered in 1936. But with this advance came two disadvantages. In democratic countries papal policy began to be viewed with suspicion. Even in Catholic circles, the distinction between the Pope as spiritual head of the faithful and as a political figure was sharpened. The fear of some Catholic observers, expressed at the time of the signing of the Lateran Treaty, that the one Rome, in apparently regaining its independence, had in reality become the prisoner of the other Rome, seemed to be substantiated. The second disadvantage was that the ruthless conquest of a colored people by a white nation led to the gravest repercussions on the progress of missions amongst colored races elsewhere. The haste with which the Vatican strove to Catholicize the old Coptic Church of Ethiopia also produced considerable misgivings in Greek-Orthodox countries, as in Rumania, for instance, where the Vatican had initiated a movement looking to a healing of the Great Eastern Schism of the year 1054.

Spain was province number five regained from the clutches of democracy. Whether the Vatican was involved in the preparations for the rebellion of the generals in 1936 has not yet been established. But in Mussolini's shop across the street they were definitely involved and were scarcely trying to hide from the world what was planned in Spain. The higher Spanish clergy were also *au courant* with what the generals had in mind and took their side the moment Franco started his rebellion. No disavowal of their actions came from Rome. On the contrary. Although there lived in loyalist territory as many faithful Catholics as in the rest of Spain, although the loyal Catholic Basques chose, in close community of spirit with their clergy, the side of the government, although the inconceivably backward social conditions in Spain could not have been unknown to the Pope, the Vatican did not hesitate to take its stand on the side of the word- and oath-breaking generals. To Pius XI and his Secretary of State the Spanish government was "a Bolshevistic sympton," and apparently they agreed with Mussolini that no Bolshevism could be tolerated in the lands around the Mediterranean.

But the choice of the Pope in the Spanish civil war was determined by additional considerations: a Catholic Spain means a Catholic South America and in that lies the hope of a reactionary turnover in Mexico and the creation of a countercurrent to the opposing democratic currents that flow southwards from the great republic in North America.

In the matter of blocking democratic influences in Latin America, effective support for the Vatican's policy is also derived from Portugal, which is the mother country of the most powerful South American state, Brazil. Portugal, where the Church enjoys a virtual religious monopoly and where Protestant groups are persecuted, is the professed model and ideal of the Vatican and of American Catholics. It is a land where a rigorous press censorship holds sway, where education is degenerating, and where the standard of living could scarcely be lower*. The influence Portugal exercises on South America and especially on Brazil may best be illustrated by President Oliveira

---

* William C. Atkinson, Fortnightly Review, August 1937.

Salazar's summary of his policy in his book *Doctrine and Action*. He says: "We are antiparliamentarians, antidemocrats, antiliberals, and we are determined to establish the corporate state on the Italian model. . . . To believe that the liberty of the people is linked to democracy or parliamentarianism is to be blind to the evidence that the political and social life of every period of history affords."

At the Genoa Conference of March, 1922, the Vatican made its first efforts to establish contact with the Bolsheviks, its object being to review the question of a reunion of the two great halves of the Catholic body that had become separated in 1054. The Bolsheviks flatly refused to enter into negotiations. Result: the Pope's attitude toward Communism and toward the Soviet Union became more irreconcilable than ever and from time to time even assumed the form of preaching a crusade.

It was this anti-Soviet attitude that led the Vatican to see not only in Italian Fascism a natural ally but also a possible ally in German National Socialism. Pope Pius XII hastened, in spite of the hesitancy of his Secretary of State, who was conversant with conditions in the Reich, to enter into a concordat with the Reich, scarcely half a year after Hitler's accession to power. But this did not solve the difficulties. Quite the contrary. They were of a nature similar to those that had arisen in Italy in 1931, but of greater magnitude, for German fascism is more consistent, more thorough, than the Italian brand.

Although an authoritarian and a totalitarian state may look the same from a democratic point of view, there nevertheless exists a deep abyss between them. As ready as the Pope was to recognize in the authoritarian form of government his own ideal, he could not accept without important qualification the conception of the state as a totality. The education of the youth cannot be given up by the Church without giving itself up. Moreover, the Church as an international and in theory, supranational organization could never accept the Nazi doctrine of Nordic superiority. So while the Church's position in Germany remains uncertain, the drive continues in another direction.

Fascism is the synthesis of all the reactionary movements which were pitted against democracy in the last century and which were actively supported by Rome*. With the collapse of the French Republic and the introduction of the corporate state by Pétain, another province was brought back to the bosom of the church. In the first week after his elevation to the dignity of *chef d'état,* Pétain restored the crucifixes to the schoolrooms and the courts and brought back the monastic orders. He received the blessing of Pope Pius XII ten days after he came to power: the Vatican knew well what the old man was up to. The public-school system of France, which was the most carefully nurtured institution under the Republic and which Rome never ceased to attack and undermine, is being clericalized, while the Vatican, with its eyes to the east, trains teachers and priests† for the moment when Germany shall have conquered the western part of the Soviet Union.

---

* Charles Guignebert, professor at the Sorbonne, *Le Christianisme mediéval et môderne,* Flammarion, Paris, 1927, p. 267; Ignazio Silone, *Der Fascismus,* Europa-Verlag, Zurich, 1934, p. 233 *et seq.*

† During the pontificate of Pius XI several pedagogic and religious institutions were set up in Rome for the formation of a clergy and a body of missionaries that would be ready to take the field in Russia the moment the opportunity should present itself. This work is carried on under the direction of the pontifical commission *"Pro Russia"* in the Collegium Russicum, the Congregation of the Eastern Church, and the Abbey of Grotta Ferrata. Three periodicals are published dealing with the Russian phase of the Church's activity: *Orientalia Christiana, Irenikon,* and *Russie et Chrétienté.*

7. *A Pious Fraud That Is a Real Threat*

IN THE twenty-second and twenty-third chapters of the Second Book of Kings, the story is told how, in the eighteenth year of the life of King Josiah, i.e., in the year 622 B.C., Shaphan, the King's secretary, was sent to the Temple to collect from the public offertories the money deposited by worshipers for the repair and maintenance of the sanctuary. When Shaphan arrived at the Temple, the High Priest Hilkiah met him and said: "I have found the book of the law in the house of the Lord." With these words he handed him the document. After having given an account of his financial mission, Shaphan read the newly found law to the King. Upon hearing the word of God, Josiah was thrown into consternation. He tore his garments in token of distress and said to Shaphan: "Great is the wrath of the Lord that is kindled against us, because our fathers have not hearkened unto the words of this book, to do according unto all that which is written concerning us."

After that Josiah proceeded to acquaint the people with contents of the scroll, for he seems to have made up his mind at once to make it the fundamental code of his kingdom. It is written that he concluded an alliance with his people before Yahveh, which means that he exacted a solemn promise from his subjects to observe all the prescriptions of the new code.

The adoption of the newly found law as the supreme code of the land was followed by a number of radical reforms: the quarters of the temple prostitutes were de-

stroyed; the altars to the astral gods were leveled with
the ground; the chariots and the horses consecrated to
the sun, which Solomon had introduced into the sanctuary, were removed; the practice of necromancy, sooth-
saying, and magic was forbidden; the groves in the valley
of Hinnom, where children had been immolated, were
disturbed, and finally, the priests and levites serving
throughout the land on the hills and in the gardens dedi-
cated to strange deities were ordered to come into Jerusalem, where they were placed in the service of Yahveh
alone.

What King Josiah, or, rather, the priest Hilkiah, had
discovered was part of the codex known as the Law of
Moses, and can be found in Deuteronomy, the fifth book
of the Pentateuch. Not that Moses was the author of
that book, or that he had received it in some supernatural
revelation on top of a smoking mountain in the heart of
the desert of Sinai. The law that Hilkiah and his colleagues had secretly drawn up in the colleges of the
temple was simply attributed to Moses in order to give
it the prestige of ancient authority and divine inspiration.

As preliminary to their monotheistic reforms, Josiah
and Hilkiah suddenly produced the Law of God as revealed unto Moses and declared to the astonished people
that it had just been recovered from some dust-covered
corner of the Temple library. A reading of that law
showed that it was dead set against the polytheistic abomi-
nations to which the Hebraic tribes abandoned themselves in imitation of the Canaanites amongst whom they
had come to dwell and whom they had partly conquered
and absorbed. The law, curiously enough, set forth precisely those reforms which the prophetic school had been
urging in vain on Josiah's royal predecessors.

The discovery of that law was a pious fraud. Former attempts to banish the worship of foreign deities had failed. But the program of national religious reform, as advocated by the zealots of the prophetic school and accepted by Josiah (which involved, also, profound changes in the Judean social order), could no longer be stayed or opposed. The program had divine sanction.

Hilkiah knew what he was about when he suddenly stumbled on the scroll in a forgotten nook of the Temple. He produced the program that was to guide the people of Judea in the organization of the future theocratic state. What Hilkiah had "found" was a national religious and political program.

That pious fraud of antiquity, which must be considered one of the major blessings bestowed on humanity in that it constituted the primary impulse in the spiritual evolution that led to and blossomed in Christianity, may well have served as model and inspiration to Baron Tanaka, when he submitted a memorial to the Mikado in 1927. This document of the Nipponese Foreign Minister outlined in detail a program of Japanese imperialist expansion, beginning with establishment of Japanese control over Manchuria and leading eventually to domination over all China, Indonesia, Siam and Indo-China, the South Sea Islands, India, Australia, the Far Eastern Region of the USSR, the whole Pacific basin, and, finally, Japanese control of Europe and America.

This program was presented as the testament of the Emperor Meiji, who was supposed to have conceived its terms through direct inspiration from his deified ancestors. In other words, it was "the way of the gods" revealed in a supernatural manner: a schema and program to be followed and carried out by the Japanese warrior caste and the people in fulfillment of Japan's divinely appointed destiny.

As such, it is as much of a myth as Hilkiah's discovery in the Temple of Jerusalem. We may be quite sure that the gods of Japan, whoever they are, had nothing to do with the Tanaka Memorial. In reality, Baron Tanaka's document is a generalization of the plans and aspirations of the not-so-prophetic school of Japanese big business-men and of the army and navy leaders. The purpose of the mythical *mise en scène* was to affix the imperial ap-proval and, through the peculiar half-divine aura that surrounds the Emperor, to establish divine sanction for the long-range plans of economic domination by the Mit-sui and Mitsubishi banking, steamship, and mining trusts.

Just as the prophetic monotheists in Jerusalem invoked the authority of Moses and of Yahveh for the reforms contemplated and carried out by Josiah, so the Japanese imperialists palmed off their vast expansionist program as a command from the deities. Even as the torah of the Lord was to set the Jews on the way to building a theo-cratic state, so the Tanaka Memorial maps out the na-tional vocation of the Japanese people: taking possession of the better part of the habitable globe and of the seas.

In America the Tanaka Memorial has never been taken as a serious document. To the sober-minded Occi-dental this chart of imperialist policy, wrapped in a mythological package and passed off as the last will and testament of an Emperor whose mind had been wander-ing for years, seemed too much like the stuff that dreams are made of and to belong rather to the realm of fancy than to a world of factual reality. It is also true that the Japanese themselves have time and again branded the Tanaka Memorial as a Chinese forgery, a spurious document concocted by Chinese propagandists to arouse the suspicions of the United States as to Japan's intentions with regard to the Anglo-American spheres of interest in the Pacific.

The document came to light in 1927. Although its authenticity was immediately denied by Japan, the Japanese army nevertheless invaded Manchuria in 1931. That was the first phase of the plan as laid down in the Tanaka Memorial, which says that Japan's first step toward the conquest of China must be the occupation of Manchuria. That done, Japan has scrupulously adhered to the program of expansion as laid down in the Memorial, following its directions step by step.

But in the case of Japan, as in the case of the ambitions of the Pan-Germans, who through their incredible Fuehrer openly spoke for years of their intention to set up *das Weltreich der Deutschen*—the world empire of the Germans—and who, within view of the whole world, have come a long way in carrying that plan into execution, the peoples and the governments of western Europe and of the Americas have always behaved as if there was not a cloud on their horizon.

Publication of the Tanaka Memorial, in spite of the substantiation of its authenticity, if by no other evidence than the advances of the Japanese army into Manchuria, China, and Indo-China, was for a long time discouraged in America and in Britain and Russia as well.

The hush around the Memorial was imposed, I imagine, in order not to give offense to the Japanese war lords. As late as April, 1940, Rear Admiral Taussig, an authority on Pacific affairs, referred to the Tanaka Memorial in his report to the Senate Committee on Naval

Affairs. Taussig was promptly disavowed by his own department.

On the other hand, the Soviet government, which possesses a photostated copy of the Memorial in the archives of the Commissariat of Foreign Affairs, could scarcely reveal its existence as long as Stalin's appeasement policy, which culminated in the nonaggression pact of 1941, held sway.

But whereas the silence maintained on the incriminating document has not done either the Anglo-Saxon powers or the Soviet Union any good, it has been of considerable service to Japan, for the failure to take it seriously allowed every move of the Japanese army to come to the democratic peoples as a surprise. Future moves, though clearly set forth in the Memorial, are still the subject of speculation on the part of political analysts and molders of public opinion because of their ignorance of or disbelief in this document.

In one of his last articles* Leon Trotsky wrote that he could vouch for the fact that the Tanaka Memorial was first photographed in the Ministry of Naval affairs in Tokyo and brought to Moscow as an undeveloped film. He was the first person to see the document in English and Russian translations of the Japanese text.

Trotsky wrote that it would have required a genius to execute so complete a forgery with such penetration into the objective situation and the political psychology of Japan's ruling circles, and he added that geniuses as a rule do not occupy themselves with forgeries but devote their energies to other pursuits. "To be sure," he goes

---

* *The Fourth International,* June 1941.

on to say, "there was no scarcity of forgeries during the last war and the ensuing postwar years. Suffice it to recall the notorious Sisson documents on the Soviet Republic. As a general rule—and I know of no exceptions—documents of this type are extremely crude. They tend to reveal the psychology of the forgers themselves or of the circles for whom they are intended rather than the psychology of those individuals or groups in whose name the forgeries are committed*. If such documents meet with credibility, it is only because of lack of familiarity with the milieu from which they reportedly emanate. The Soviet Government," Trotsky goes on to say, "consisted of individuals completely unknown to world public opinion. Small wonder that it was possible to ascribe to them any goal or aim whatsoever, and depict these things in any kind of language.

"It is otherwise with the Imperial Government of Japan. It constitutes an ancient and traditional milieu. Whoever has carefully followed the evolution of Japanese politics cannot fail to recognize that the document, with its cynical realism and icy fanaticism of the ruling caste, originates in this milieu. The document is credible. The text is valid. The contents gain credence because they speak for themselves."

Then he tells the story of how the Tanaka Memorial fell into the hands of the Soviet Foreign Office. It appears that Felix Dzerzhinsky, who was head of the GPU and the Russian Intelligence Service back in 1925, enjoyed the services of a very trusted functionary who had direct access to the secret archives of the Japanese Ministry of Foreign Affairs. This man had over a certain length of

---

* A case in point is the forgery known as "The Protocols of the Elders of Zion."

time furnished the Soviet government with some very valuable information. His work as a foreign spy, says Trotsky, was marked by great precision and conscientiousness in fulfilling his obligations. He had informed Dzerzhinsky, through other agents, of course, that there existed in the Tokyo archives a document of the greatest importance. Dzerzhinsky, in describing to his colleagues in the Politbureau what he had learned of the contents of the secret document, thought that in and of itself it could provoke international upheavals, events of vast importance, even war between Japan and the United States. Trotsky remained skeptical.

"Wars are not produced by documents," Trotsky objected to Dzerzhinsky. But the chief of the GPU insisted: "You have no conception of the importance of this document: it is the program of the ruling circles, approved by the Mikado himself; it embraces the seizure of China, the destruction of the United States, world domination."

"Mightn't your agent be duped?" Trotsky asked. "No one writes such documents as a rule. Why should such plans be put down on paper?"

The Japanese functionary had offered to copy the document, but the GPU representative in Japan, on instructions from Moscow, demanded photographic copies. This was much more difficult. To photograph the Memorial it was necessary either to introduce a GPU technician into the premises of the Ministry of Foreign Affairs or to teach the Japanese functionary the art of photography. These technical difficulties caused a delay in obtaining the document. In the end, however, several photographic copies of each page were taken, and the film was then forwarded by two or three different routes. All the copies arrived safely in Moscow.

When the document was translated, it staggered the readers among whom were, first of all, Trotsky and Dzerzhinsky, but also Chicherin, Voroshilov, Stalin, and other members of the Politbureau. Bukharin believed so little in its authenticity on first sight that he expressed the thought that it was perhaps a poem. Trotsky, too, was astonished by the contents of the Memorial, but he did not in the least doubt its authenticity, acquainted as he was with the history of the document, the way it came into Soviet hands, and its internal validity.

"If we grant," Trotsky wrote after the Japanese had branded the Memorial a Chinese forgery, "if we grant that the Chinese did manage to find an ideal forger who fabricated this document, then the question still remains just how this Chinese forgery turned up in the Japanese Ministry of Foreign Affairs as a special, secret document? Did the Ministry of Foreign Affairs itself arrange to transmit the falsified Chinese document and pass it off as a genuine Japanese document? This supposition is utterly fantastic. The Japanese could not have been in the least interested in circulating such a document and arousing belief in it. They demonstrated this most graphically by branding it a forgery the moment it was published."

Now came the question of publishing the document and acquainting the world with the secret bellicose plans of Japan. It was impossible to publish the Memorial in Russia. Relations between the Soviets and Japan were strained to the utmost in those years. Moscow was making concession after concession to Japan. It had its ablest diplomat in Tokyo to smooth the ruffled Japanese temper. To have published the document in Moscow would have been tantamount to provoking Japan to open conflict. It was necessary, therefore, to publish the document abroad and, in publishing it, to avoid giving the Japanese the slightest inkling of the existence of a link between Moscow and the document.

"We were under the impression," says Trotsky, "that the document would literally be torn from our hands. . . . But things did not turn out that way at all. It was not easy to provide a credible version of how the document was obtained from Tokyo. Any reference to the real source, i.e., the GPU, would arouse additional distrust. In America the suspicion would naturally arise that the GPU itself had simply manufactured the document in order to poison relations between Japan and the United States."

The translated document was nevertheless shipped to New York, but not directly from Moscow. It came to America from Tokyo. The American press, in publishing it, made no reference to Moscow whatever.

However that may be, this also may be said: if it was the Bolsheviks' intention to relieve Japanese pressure on the Soviet state by creating bad blood between the U.S.A. and Japan, their gun missed fire entirely. In America the Tanaka Memorial was then—and still is—treated with considerable suspicion. This is not surprising, for, as Trotsky points out himself, it is a fact that fraudulent documents are sometimes acknowledged to be genuine while authentic documents are not infrequently labeled as forgeries. To this must be added that ever since the outbreak of the Second World War in Europe, America, in order to prevent the spreading of the war against Britain in the Far East, for a long time did her utmost to spare Japanese sensibilities. This is one reason why Admiral Taussig was disavowed by the Navy Department, which preferred to ignore—at least publicly—the existence of the Tanaka Memorial.

When the Japanese authorities denounced the Tanaka Memorial as a Chinese and not as a Soviet forgery, they showed that they were unaware of Moscow's role in the publication of the document. The appearance of the Memorial first of all in the American press naturally led the Japanese to suspect that the document had fallen into Chinese hands and that it had been forwarded from China to New York via Tokyo.

Although there was ample reason for the Soviets not to publish the document back in 1925-27, afterwards, when Japan moved into Manchuria and from there advanced into Jehol and into China proper, the silence of Moscow becomes inexplicable. Trotsky ascribed that silence to "the excessive caution which often drives Stalin to ignore major considerations for the sake of secondary and petty ones."

All these considerations receded into the background, however, as Japan moved slowly forward in the execution of a plan of conquest which was drawn up by Baron Tanaka in a decisive hour of modern history, back in 1925. There may be lulls in the battle for Asia and the Pacific, temporary setbacks and cautious delays, but one glance at the map in this month of August, 1941, shows that Japan, like a tiger, has slowly crawled to within easy striking distance of Singapore, the Pacific's passkey. If that great naval base can be destroyed or made untenable for the British and American fleets by land bombers based on southern Indo-China, Japan will have gone a long way in driving the Anglo-Saxons from the Asiatic continent, which is Nippon's by divine sanction, as set forth in the Tanaka Memorial.

8. *Why Alexander Was Killed*

ANTON PAVELIC is the model Fascist: ruthless and utterly unscrupulous, boundlessly ambitious and cruel. He had violated every law and he has never needed a pretext when he sought to betray. His cruelties spring not from the heat of his blood, but from cool, calculating meditation. Tall, well-built, good-looking, and possessing an ingratiating manner, Pavelic lived on the fringe of an international society which had its centers in Berlin, Paris, Deauville, and Monte Carlo in the postwar years. An adventurer of sharp practices and equally dubious antecedents, he lived tortuously on his wits, sold himself brazenly to the highest bidder, and had a very foul reputation.

I knew the man when he was in the employ of Juan March, the owner of Spanish steamship lines, who became the financier of Franco's rebel revolt. At the time, it was around 1924-26, Señor March was gathering in his first millions. He was engaged in the white-slave traffic, and Anton Pavelic was his chief purveyor of women in France. Marseilles was the headquarters of the business with South America. The late Albert Londres exposed the traffic, and Primo de Rivera put Señor March in jail. But not Pavelic, because Pavelic got away.

Before he came west in Europe, Anton Pavelic had been a member of the Skupshohtina, the Yugoslav parliament, where he led a small party of extremist Croat nationalist revolutionaries. The aims of this group were frankly separatist. He was obliged, owing to his seditious program, to leave Yugoslavia and to take the road of exile. The business connection with Juan March having come to an end with the arrest of the Spanish banker, Pavelic entered the service of the Hungarian government. In 1930 he was installed in Budapest as *poglavnik,* or supreme leader, of the Ustacia terrorist movement. *Poglavnik* is the same word as *Fuehrer,* or *Duce,* or *Caudillo.* It is the title under which he came to rule in Croatia after the destruction of the Yugoslav state by Hitler.

This secret society of the Ustacia sought to undermine the foundations of the kingdom of Yugoslavia. The Hungarian government paid the expenses, but acted in the matter as an agent for Italy. Assisted by Kvaternik and Gustav Percec, Pavelic began actively to foment armed rebellion in Croatia. Provided with ample funds, his agents carried on an extensive propaganda all over the country, especially among men of a suspicious character or in needy circumstances, whose support could be purchased. All political refugees, moreover, who crossed the Yugoslav frontier, whether into Hungary or Italy, or into Rumania, were taken to Anton Pavelic, who, after pointing out that their arrest and extradition were imminent, promised them immunity if only they joined his movement. Very soon Pavelic had at his disposal a fairly large body of men, dispersed over the principal capitals of Europe, who could be depended upon to carry out his instructions because their immunity from arrest lasted only as long as they faithfully served their chief.

Pavelic himself was on good terms with the police of Hungary, Rumania, Italy, and Germany (after Hitler's accession to power) and with certain high-placed pro-Italian personages in France, among them Jean Chiappe, head of the Paris police, and Pierre Laval. Switzerland barred him, but in Holland he sought to establish a branch of his organization under the guise of a news agency. The agency was indeed established—that is to say, a building was rented in The Hague. But it was a news agency without newspapermen.

One day, on a visit to Holland, I happened to read an ad in the Dutch newspaper *Het Vaderland,* a most respectable and conservative journal, calling for candidates to fill the position of chief correspondent in a newly established newsgathering organization. I called at the indicated address and was received by an individual who could speak neither Dutch nor English. I asked this man what sort of news he expected to get in Holland, and he replied that the job of chief correspondent merely entailed co-ordinating dispatches that would come from Eastern Europe. The summary was to be cabled to America. If I wanted the job, he said, I was to come back to be interviewed by the chief, who would be in The Hague in a week's time. The man was about to hand me his card when a piece of paper fluttered to the floor from his wallet. I picked it up and handed it back to him. On that piece of cardboard was the emblem of the VMRO, the Vontresna Makedonska Revolutionna Organizatsia— the Interior Macedonian Revolutionary Organization: a dagger lying on a Bible.

I did not want the job, but I was curious to discover what news agency recruited its correspondents by advertising. A week later when I called, the office had been newly furnished and decorated. An information clerk had been installed behind a gleaming mahogany desk. Above the young man's head hung a life-sized portrait of . . . the late Czar Nicholas II. I asked the man whom I had seen on the previous occasion what the significance could be of the picture of the dead Russian Czar in a newspaper bureau, and he said to me, with a smile, that it was a mere symbol.

"A symbol of what?" I asked.

"Of glory!" said the man.

"Past glory?"

"No, glory to come," said the man.

As he led me towards the room where I was to see the chief, the man confided that several high-placed Hollanders were financially interested in the new venture. He cited several names. In the editor's sanctum, I found myself face to face with Anton Pavelic.

"In what way," said I, in the course of the conversation, "will this news agency further your plans of achieving Croat independence, for that is your chief ambition in life, is it not?"

"It is," he replied, "but our chief aim here is to gather news from Russia."

"Aren't we a long way from Russia here in The Hague?"

"We will have our correspondents in Riga in due course of time."

"But why Russia, of all places?"

"Preparations," Pavelic said mysteriously. "Preparations for the future, for the redivision of the oil wells. That is why the Dutch capitalists are interested and backing us."

"But how can the Russian oil wells be redivided so long as the Bolsheviks hold them?"

"Oh, they won't be there much longer," Pavelic assured me. "There is going to be a war before long that will end the Red Terror. We have at last a champion of decency in Europe. . . ."

"Who is that?"

"Adolf Hitler!"

I left him on that note. Two months later when I passed the place again, I noticed that it was closed. That was in July, 1934.

From Holland Pavelic seems to have returned to eastern Europe. At any rate, he was soon thereafter reported engaged in rounding up his revolutionaries and refugees and bringing them together in large camps. In those camps, located in Hungary and Italy, Pavelic set about teaching the novices the elements of the profession of banditry. The best known of these training camps was Janka Puszta, a farm lying in close proximity to the Yugoslav border. Pavelic commuted between Hungary and Italy. When in Rome he moved in the select circles of the blackshirt hierarchy. He was a frequent visitor to the Palazzo di Venezia and once had an audience with Pope Pius XI, who, it should be said, was not aware of the man's evil reputation.

To break the Yugoslav state, Pavelic held that assassination as well as armed sedition was indispensable. In many of his pamphlets and newssheets, such as *Ustacia* and *Gric,* which his agents distributed secretly in the Hungarian-Yugoslav frontier zone, frequent appeals were made to the Croat population to kill King Alexander and the members of his government as the only means of securing their independence.

To kill Alexander became, in fact, the chief object of the entire bandit organization. It was Anton Pavelic who personally took the matter in hand. To prove to the world that if the King were assassinated this would be simply the expression of popular anger roused to desperation by oppression, he first sent small groups of terrorists into Croatia. These, according to plan, proceeded to attack military and police posts and to blow up bridges and tunnels. Upon learning of Alexander's forthcoming visit to Paris, Pavelic, with the aid of Budapest and Rome (which provided the false passports and visas), dispatched two groups of assassins especially selected for the murder. One group proceeded to Paris where they were to take action if a previous attempt at Marseilles failed.

The three assassins detailed for Marseilles crossed Switzerland and, traveling as tourists, arrived by car at a French village, where rooms at the local hotel had been booked in advance for them. From the village they went singly to Marseilles. In the Hotel Victoria, near the Cannebière, the southern city's main thoroughfare, they met a mysterious blonde woman, whose identity as Pavelic's mistress was later established. To each of the conspirators she presented a revolver. The leader of the three, Kvaternik, who was raised to the dignity of Governor of Croatia after the conquest of Yugoslavia by Hitler, prospected the route of the royal procession and selected the spot from which the attempt was to be made.

When Alexander came driving up from the Vieux-Port, where he had landed, he was accompanied by Louis Barthou, the French Foreign Minister. The King was killed outright, and Barthou expired in an ambulance on the way to the prefecture. General Georges, chief of the French General Staff, was seriously wounded.

After the crime Pavelic fled to Italy, where he was accidentally arrested by the police in Turin. He was immediately set free when Count Galeazzo Ciano learned the prisoner's identity. A telegram invited him to proceed to Rome at once. In that city Pavelic lived in a villa luxuriously furnished by the Italian Foreign Minister until the German armies marched into Croatia. But before that France made an attempt to have him extradited.

The widowed Queen of Yugoslavia caused a charge of murder to be laid against Pavelic and Kvaternik and entrusted the case to her attorney, Joseph Paul-Boncour, the former Prime Minister and Foreign Minister of France. Paul-Boncour filed a demand for extradition with the Ministry of Justice in Rome. Rome would have had to give up the murderers if it had not been for Pierre Laval. This gentleman, upon becoming Prime Minister of France, persuaded or ordered Paul-Boncour to drop the case for *raisons d'état*. Laval's policy was aimed at placing Franco-Italian relations on a "realistic footing."

In 1941 Pavelic, gangster and ruffian, was made *poglavnik* of Croatia, the land he had dishonored by his sordid and criminal existence. No more suitable person could be found by Duce and Fuehrer than this individual who had rendered them so great a service.

For what had Anton Pavelic accomplished in that decisive hour when the shots rang out on the Cannebière in Marseilles?

He had killed Alexander of Yugoslavia, France's most dependable ally in eastern Europe, the man who was, so to speak, the keystone in the arch of France's eastern system of alliances. Alexander alone could have held the kingdom of the Serbs, Croats, and Slovenes together.

After his death Yugoslavia sank through discord and strife from the position of the major military state in the Balkans into impotence. Alexander's death removed the danger to Italy of being caught some day in the Franco-Yugoslav pincers.

Pavelic also removed Barthou, the statesman who

aimed at linking France and the Soviet Union in a defensive alliance. Had that alliance become a reality, it would have assured peace in Europe for a long time. For, with France and Russia united, Herr Hitler would have been hemmed in by a circle of steel.

9. *"Thou Art The Man!"*

IN SPITE of his eminent services in the war of 1914-18 as Marshal Foch's chief collaborator and his own expressed desire to remain in active service, the government of the Popular Front, mindful of the warning of Georges Clemenceau that Weygand was "the most dangerous of the clerical-military clique," placed him on the retired list the moment he attained the age of sixty-five.

Monarchist, anti-Semite, contemptuously anti-British, with important connections in the world of finance and industry, Maxime Weygand was, on the word of Foch himself, unquestionably the ablest military strategist that the last war produced. For that reason alone, perhaps, he was the more to be feared.

Ever since the Boulanger affair in the eighties the government and the republican association had with more than a suspicious eye followed the political activities and public conduct of prominent military men. When, after the First World War, the question arose of recompensing the victorious military chiefs by granting them the title of Marshal of France, Clemenceau first objected on the ground that the new dignity would render these men more popular than was desirable from a political point of view. In the end he compromised by agreeing to confer the baton on Joffre, Foch, Fayolle Lyautey, Franchet d'Esperey, and Pétain.

When it was suggested that Weygand deserved the honor more than anyone else (which was undoubtedly true, for he had been the brains of the Allied campaign, as much as Ludendorff had been the supreme tactician on the German side), Clemenceau burst into a fit of violent anger. It was on that occasion that the Tiger urged the retirement of Weygand as soon as possible. "Weygand has gone far enough," said Clemenceau. "To allow that man to grow in popularity may prove more dangerous to the life of the Republic than poor old Boulanger. . . . Weygand is brilliant. He is resolute. He knows what he wants, and he is up to his neck in the Jesuits. And of the Jesuits we know what they think of republics and of the French Republic in particular." What Weygand wanted and thought was clear from his published works on Turenne, Vauban, Condé, and the other great captains of the epoch of Louis XVI, in which there is an idealization of the Grand Monarque and the period when France as a kingdom dominated the European scene.

I once had an opportunity of observing General Weygand at close range. That was in 1937, when, after considerable effort, I succeeded in obtaining an interview with him on the subject of the state of the defenses of different European countries. I saw a little man, extraordinarily lithe and supple for his age, with a wizened face, shrewd, intelligent, clearly xenophobe, who spoke with just the merest soupçon of the accent of the north country. Weygand was born in Belgium and was brought up on the estate of the late Empress of Mexico, the demented Carlotta.

He explained the strength of the various European armies to me in quick, snappy sentences. I recall how he said that the French Intelligence Service had precise knowledge of what was going on in Germany in the line of military preparations and that Goering had set aside 1500 planes "to launch a surprise attack on France."

"But," Weygand assured me, "France is fully prepared and constantly on the alert so that there is little danger of the Germans overwhelming us in a sudden attack. We know what they have; fortunately, we could see them coming if they should make a move in our direction." He would say nothing of the surrender of Czechoslovakia and the loss of its forty-five divisions and splendid mechanical equipment to the democracies in the event of a war with Germany.

He reminded me that Frederick the Great had once written to his envoy in Paris that even if the royal budget did not permit him a large enough allowance to ride in as fine a carriage as the diplomatic representatives of other countries, the ambassador was to bear in mind that behind the Prussian ambassador, even if he went on foot, there stood the thirty thousand bayonets of the Prussian monarch.

"Today," said Weygand, "it is not bayonets, but tanks and airplanes that give France a voice in the concert of the nations. They are of such numbers and of such quality that France can afford to speak calmly and look toward the future without anxiety."

I noticed that Weygand referred to Mussolini several times as "the eminent chief of the Italian nation, who follows a realistic policy." But the point that seemed to give the General the greatest concern, it appeared, had nothing at all to do with military affairs and with the relative strength of eventual future combatants. He was worried over the French system of education. He clenched his fists and dug his fingernails into his hands as he spoke fiercely of teachers who had come under the influence of alien cults and who no longer honored the traditions of the French family and of the French fatherland.

It was obvious that he had the neutral school in mind, *l'école laïque,* whose teachers at that time had just joined the trade union movement and whose congress had sent a call for fraternal co-operation between the educators of all lands to the end that "peace might be preserved and the nations advance together on the road to the human ideal."

"Teachers," said Weygand, "should instill the old patriotic virtues. What kind of soldiers is France to have in the future," he asked, "if its children are inculcated with such doctrines, as are now rampant, about international fraternization." I said to *monsieur le Général* that I had attended the teachers' congress and that I heard Monsieur Delmas, the chairman, put the motion of greeting to the pedagogues of the world. . . .

"*Ah, oui?*" he arched his eyebrows. "*Disgusting!* What did you think?"

"I thought," I said, "that it was rather a pleasant idea to see the teachers of the world fraternize rather than the cannon makers." That was the end of the interview.

After his retirement, Weygand was elected a member of the French Academy. That made him one of the forty living Immortals. His election was not, however, intended by the academic body as a tribute to his great proficiency in the art of war. It was a tacit rebuke to the government for having removed him from active participation in the administration of the nation's military affairs.

Released from the army and from the restrictions placed on army men in the political arena, Weygand became an assiduous attendant at the mass meetings held by the organization of the *Croix de Feu*, the Fiery Cross, of which his friend and fellow director of Paris Gas and Electricity, Colonel François de la Rocque, was the leader. Although he did not make speeches, he sat on the platform and contented himself, on the sole occasion I attended one of the meetings of the *Croix de feu* in the Salle Wagram with paying a few words of tribute to De la Rocque, to whom he referred as "a chief, a patriot, and a realist." It was evident that Weygand liked realists of the colored-shirt variety.

Toward the end both he and Marshal Pétain found their way into the high conclave of the *Cagoulards*, the anti-Semitic, Fascist, terroristic organization that affected the paraphernalia—the hood and cloak—worn by the now-dissolved Legion of Death. So many high-ranking military men were on the supreme council of the hooded order that the government had to proceed with the greatest caution in investigating the bomb outrages committed in Paris by members of that organization in 1938. When the police stumbled on a list of the directors of the *Cagoulards*, Weygand was suddenly recalled to active service and sent to Syria to reorganize the armies of the Levant.

From Syria Weygand returned helter-skelter by airplane on May 17, 1940, when Paul Reynaud had taken over the reins of government from Edouard Daladier and after the German armies had broken through the Dutch and Belgian defenses. Weygand immediately set out for a tour of inspection of the front lines. Reynaud had announced that the military situation was grave but by no means desperate. Moreover, he announced, General Weygand had now taken command: Weygand, the man of mystery, who had helped Foch win his phenomenal successes, the man who, when the Bolsheviks were in the suburbs of Warsaw, had shown by a mere stroke of the pen on the maps of the Polish general staff the way in which the Red army could be rolled back. . . .

Weygand flew to Ypres where Viscount Gort, commander in chief of the British Expeditionary Force, the Bel-

gian General Michiels, and General Billotte awaited them.
Leopold III, King of the Belgians, explained the military
situation. According to one of those present, the King expressed himself with moderation and great restraint, but
he pointed out to Weygand that whereas the Belgians and
the British were fighting heroically and were making enormous sacrifices, the French were falling back without giving battle at a single spot. The King remarked: "The
French have fallen back two hundred and fifty kilometers
[about 155 miles] in seven days. . . . My army has suffered
enormous losses in covering the French retreat, but these
operations will be absolutely futile if the French do not
make a stand. We cannot go on holding the entire German
army alone. Why do not the French stop retreating when
the enemy has not even made contact with them?" Viscount
Gort, the English commander, supported the King but
used more vigorous language.

Leopold then offered to take over the line held by the
16th French Army Corps, which stood on the left wing
of the Belgians in the Dutch province of Zeeland, "but
Monsieur Weygand politely refused that generous offer."
Within an hour of the conference the 16th French Army
Corps received orders to fall back, without having fired
a shot and leaving the British and Belgians to withstand
the German onslaught alone.

It is commonly supposed that General Weygand, who
had been instructed to reorganize the French Army of the
Levant and to work out, conjointly with General Sir Archibald Wavell, British commander in chief in the Near East,
a plan for the defense of the Suez Canal and its approaches,
remained at his post during the first nine months of the
war assiduously occupied with his important task. Nothing is farther from the truth. Weygand did make a tour of

inspection of the disposition of French and British forces in the Near Eastern theater, and he actually had one conference with General Wavell in January, 1940. But that conference was a dismal failure. For it was on that occasion that Wavell proposed, at the behest of the British War Office, to pool Franco-British resources in the Near and Middle East and to present a common front in whatever direction danger might be lurking. Wavell suggested, as a practical step toward a complete co-ordination of effort, that some of France's best combat troops, notably the mechanized equipment, be forthwith transferred from Syria to the western desert of Egypt to confront the Italian barbed-wire line in Libya.

The British officer expressed the opinion that the first move Mussolini was most likely to make, upon coming into the war on Germany's side, would be to create a diversion from the front in western Europe if fighting should break out there and become particularly heavy. It was true, General Wavell argued, that Mussolini had kept thirty-five thousand men on the island of Rhodes ever since the beginning of the Ethiopian campaign and that it was quite clearly intended that these troops were to be used to threaten Cyprus, Crete, and the Lebanese coast and were eventually to try to land at those points. On the other hand, he had been assured by the British Admiralty, naval units could quite easily prevent the Italian army on Rhodes from leaving that island. The reality to be reckoned with was that the greatest Italian troop concentration had occurred in Libya. In other words, Syria was not in such immediate danger as Egypt. The former country could, moreover, be patroled by machines based on the Damascus and Palestinian airdromes, whereas Egypt, it had been known since the Ethiopian campaign, figured at the top of Mussolini's list of revendications in the Mediterranean area.

To the amazement of the British staff officers, Weygand hotly disputed General Wavell's allegations that the Duce had anything but the best intentions toward France. There was no reason to suppose, he said, that Mussolini intended to throw in his lot with Berlin. The British officers, who knew no better than that the mobs in the Italian cities were clamoring for Tunisia, Nice, Savoy, Djibouti, and Corsica, all of them French, not British possessions, were stupefied to hear the French commander dismiss these chauvinistic outbreaks in Italy as insignificant demonstrations by irresponsible elements. He further claimed to have positive information from his friends Pierre Laval and François-Poncet, the French ambassador to Rome, that the Duce harbored no evil intentions against France. The upshot was that further discussions of close Franco-British collaboration in the Near East were dropped.

Thereafter, when Weygand had occasion to refer to military operations in the Near East, he spoke in downright scurrilous terms of General Wavell and his staff. But he made these contemptuous declarations in Paris, for he remained in the Near East but for brief periods of two and three weeks. Most of General Weygand's time as commander in chief of France's Near Eastern forces was spent in France, where he carried on a frenzied campaign for a declaration of war against . . . the Soviet Union. He urged that an expedition be sent to Norway to strike at the Soviet Union in the neighborhood of Murmansk and simultaneously that an attack be launched in the Caucasus and the Crimea. The French navy was to sail up the Aegean, through the Dardanelles and the Hellespont, bombard

Odessa, and land an expeditionary force on Russia's Black Sea shores.

One can hardly see how an expedition of that sort would have affected (except adversely) the military situation of France, menaced, as that country was, by the bulk of the German army mobilized on her borders. Could it be that after the partition of Poland Weygand considered Russia such a valuable supporter of Germany that, by attacking the Soviet Union, he thought to weaken the Reich? Or did he think that a French expeditionary force steaming up the Aegean or landing on the coast of Norway would in a flash be followed by Stalin hoisting the white flag on the Kremlin? Nothing of the sort. Weygand was too good a strategist not to know that the Red army of Russia could not be beaten by the kind of expeditionary force France, under the most favorable circumstances, could have mustered against it.

In an article published in the *Revue des Deux Mondes* under a three-star pseudonym, Maxime Weygand himself had remarked upon the effectiveness and the precision of Russia's artillery on Finland's Mannerheim Line. He also knew full well what had happened in 1919, when an attempt was made to land a French army at Odessa, at a time when the Red army consisted of mere irregular crowds of partisans. In fine, General Weygand was perfectly well aware that an expedition against the Soviet Union would be no walkover, even if he succeeded in the most improbable feat of landing an army on Russian soil.

Then, what was his aim in abandoning his important post in the Near East, where France was menaced as much as Britain (for the Suez Canal is the gateway to the French Far Eastern possessions as much as it is England's and Holland's road to their Asiatic empire), and come to Paris to engage in political intrigue and create even more dissension in French councils?

Every politician and general in France was harping on one subject and one subject only: the urgent necessity of having the nation present a united front to the German enemy, who had crushed France's only ally in eastern Europe and who was now gathering his resources on the borders of Holland, Belgium, and Luxemburg for a drive toward the Channel ports and Paris. Everyone in France knew and saw that the danger was near at home and that it was immense, and yet here was a general, the greatest strategist of the previous war, moving heaven and earth to deplete France's resources in manpower and armored equipment for what seemed a foolhardy and risky military undertaking two thousand miles away against Russia, which was not mobilized on France's borders, which was not at war with France, and which had given not the slightest indication that it might become a belligerent in any war that Germany unleashed against the French.

The world has heard ad infinitum that the defeat of France must be attributed to inner disruption, to the fact that the people were split into opposing political groups, to the growth of pacifism and the spirit of internationalism, or even—most cynical lie of all—to a growth of luxury and indolence among the French masses. Discord there unquestionably was, but that discord did not manifest itself in the French masses.

There was not a single antiwar demonstration in Paris or in any of the metropolitan centers of the provinces, not even in the municipalities that constituted the so-called "Red belt" around the capital. Not a single political party voted against war credits. It is not true, either, as it is so often alleged, that the Communists sabotaged France's war effort. One has only to consult Winston Churchill's *Step by Step* to learn what attitude the French Communists took and how the British Prime Minister lauded their patriotism and included them amongst the best soldiers of France. No, the crux lay elsewhere.

It was Weygand and Laval, Pétain and Flandin, Badouin and Bonnet, who sabotaged the French war effort. It was the French General Staff and the officers' corps, the Roman Catholic hierarchy, and the trust magnates and utility directors who were afraid to fight Hitler. Not that they were afraid of being defeated. They were afraid that the phenomenal Gallic fury, the revolutionary fervor of the French people, would, once the country was seriously menaced, gain the upper hand and not only hurl back the Nazi hordes, but run over into the Reich and liberate the German people from the spiritual and physical tyranny of Fascism. They were afraid of victory. They did not want to see Herr Hitler, the man who had vowed to eradicate democracy, eliminated. They hated democracy as much as he. They considered democracy, and rightly so, a greater threat than Hitler to their own class hegemony in French society. Thierry Maulnier, who wrote, in justification of the surrender of France, that a victory of French arms would have meant a victory for democratic principles, which would in turn have led straight to the ruin of France and of Europe, effectively blew the gaff with those words and unconsciously showed up the falsity of the explanations and analyses of the "explainers" who came to America after the fall of France to befuddle the judgment of the American people.

Maxime Weygand, in advocating an expedition against the Soviet Union, merely sought to get into Herr Hitler's good graces. He wanted to make an attempt to change and transform the war into a holy alliance against Russia. In a late hour, when the armies of German Fascism were poised for a mortal blow against the French, Dutch, Belgian, and Scandinavian democracies, he sought to divert the Teutonic fury by offering collaboration with Germany. He thought that, in taking the lead against Russia, he could turn the full might of the mobilized armies of Europe against that country. In other words, he attempted to incorporate France into the Fascist bloc by a detour. He tried to convey the message to Hitler that France—at least, the French ruling clique—had no desire to fight him and that he and his friends did not look on Fascism as an evil, but as the supreme good—the only remedy, in fact, to save the privileged position of the *bourgeoisie* against the progressive democratization of life.

Incidentally, Weygand's foolish suggestion—or was it so foolish?—to occupy Norway naturally reached the ears of the German High Command and gave Adolf Hitler sufficient justification to claim that, in invading the Scandinavian kingdom, the Germans had merely stolen a march on the Franco-British allies.

This General Weygand, who, to the knowledge of every informed man in France, looked upon defense against Germany as a waste of effort because Russia, not Hitler, was the real enemy in his eyes; who held the French Republic and republican institutions in execration; who was a member of the Academie Française, which was a center of pro-German and pro-Italian elements that held victory over the Germans undesirable and dictatorship the perfect form of social order as opposed to "democratic decadence"; who, moreover, was one of the animating spirits in a Fascist organization openly calling for collaboration with Germany and Italy in the establishment of a new order in Europe, and which, through its newspapers, had more than once suggested that it might become advisable to call in Adolf Hitler to establish order in France (that is, to crush the democracy that the native French Fascists had not been able to crush): this General Weygand was entrusted with the sole responsibility of defending France against the German onslaught in May, 1940.

Upon his arrival at the front, Weygand began by quarreling with the British over the technique of the withdrawal from Belgium and then ordered French divisions to fall back without first informing either the Belgians or the British of his decisions. The front was therewith thrown into hopeless confusion. But Weygand was playing his own game. At last he had the reins in his hand and was steering the French Republic toward the harbor into which he had wanted to steer her for a long time—perdition. In the cabinet he had an able second in *le faux frère*, Marshal Henri Philippe Pétain, the mythical hero of Verdun, who had counseled surrender in the previous war, back in 1917 and 1918.

The French government, headed by Paul Reynaud, a vain litle parvenu who had gained some notoriety as the advocate of monetary inflation and who was consumed by ambitions of power and wealth, had been transferred to Tours on the night of June 10. Before leaving the capital, the majority of the members of the government, besides the presidents of the Chamber of Deputies and of the Senate, Messrs. Herriot and Jeanneney, had elaborated a plan to fight the Germans in a delaying action, first on the Aisne, then on the Seine, then on the Loire, and finally on the Garonne-Gironde line in order to enable as much of the army as possible to embark at the southern and southwestern ports for the purpose of continuing the war from Africa.

When this plan was brought to the attention of Weygand at Tours on June 13 in a cabinet meeting, both he and Pétain immediately vetoed it. One who was present at that session has declared that the attitude of General Weygand not only surprised the cabinet members, but "filled every man present with stupefaction." Their stupefaction turned to silent horror when Weygand in icy tones mentioned capitulation.

The General was asked if in his opinion the military situation had degenerated to such a point that no other course of action was left. It was then that he gave the answer that unmasked him and his intentions. "It is not the military situation that is so bad," he replied, "but if you gentlemen do not ask for an armistice there will be Communism in France. Maurice Thorez [the secretary of the Communist party] has already established himself at the Élysée [the presidential residence in Paris]. Riots have broken out in the capital. We must hurry if we are to save France. Only capitulation can save us! . . ."

Georges Mandel, Minister of the Interior and therefore chief of the Paris *service de sécurité,* immediately challenged Weygand's tale of a Communist uprising in Paris. He said that but an hour before he had been in telephonic communication with Monsieur Langeron, the Prefect of Police in Paris, who had been ordered to stay behind to assure order in the capital until the Germans arrived. Langeron had assured Mandel, his chief, that all was quiet in Paris and that the city was virtually deserted.

"That was only an hour ago," said Georges Mandel.

General Weygand could scarcely control himself upon hearing those words. He grew red in the face and began to say something that sounded like: "You, Monsieur Mandel, you are . . ." But he checked himself. The time had not come yet to say openly to a minister of the government what the members of the *Croix de Feu* had so often shouted at Leon Blum in public meetings: *"Vous n'êtes pas un Français des Français, Monsieur Blum,"* in other words: "You are a Jew!" Weygand, after beginning to say it, bethought himself, stuttered, coughed, and finally flung out: "Do you doubt the word of an officer?"

"Not at all," Mandel replied coolly. "Shall I telephone the Prefect again?" he asked. *"Monsieur le général* could then speak to Monsieur Langeron himself. I would like to have the President of the Republic [who was present] and all you gentlemen [members of the cabinet and of the Supreme War Council] hear what the Prefect has to say." And, joining action to words, Mandel called Paris, spoke to Langeron, and once again heard the Prefect of Police say that all was quiet.

"But there are rumors that the boulevards are swarming with Communists!" Mandel insisted.

"There is not a soul in the streets, from the Porte Dauphine to the Porte de Charenton," came back Langeron. "The city is as dead as a cemetery!"

"Where are you now, Monsieur Langeron?"

"At the prefecture."

"On the Boulevard du Palais, are there any crowds about in the Latin quarter?"

"Not a soul, *monsieur le ministre!"*

"Monsieur Langeron, it is rumored here in Tours that Maurice Thorez, the secretary of the Communist party, has installed himself at the Élysée; also, that important buildings have been occupied, that there are riots. . . ."

"Absolutely nothing to that, *monsieur le ministre:* everything is quiet here. We are awaiting the entry of the Germans tomorrow morning. There is no panic, no disturbance, no sign of Communists. Everything is normal."

That spiked Weygand's maneuver to force the government to ask for an armistice. Nevertheless, both he and Pétain resumed their pressure on Paul Reynaud to bring the war to a quick conclusion. After hours of deliberation, it was decided to move the seat of government to Bordeaux the moment the Germans should reach Chartres. Before moving to Bordeaux the cabinet had another session at the Château de Saint-Avestin, President Lebrun's country place. When Weygand was not present, Lebrun seemed to agree that the best course would be to move over to Africa, save the fleet and the colonies, and continue the fight on England's side. But the moment Weygand made his reappearance and began insisting again that France capitulate before exasperating Hitler by her resistance and making the Fuehrer's armistice conditions more severe, Lebrun weakened. Still, he insisted that he wanted the consent of the British government to an armistice.

In the meantime the Germans had entered Paris, and the French armies were in headlong retreat. Division after division passed through the cities of the rear without a single officer. Stephan Lauzanne, former editor of *Le Matin* and one of the most careful observers, reported that wherever he stopped to watch the retreating army go by, he was struck by the total absence of officers. In several places he questioned the soldiers as to the whereabouts of their superiors. In each case he received the same reply: "We haven't seen our officers for weeks." Other reporters, who watched at other points, have remarked on that same circumstance. Yet, there was no panic among the troops. Panic was confined to the civilians. The soldiers had no orders except the last order given them by their fugitive officers: to fall back and to keep on falling back. I have in my possession fifteen letters from personal acquaintances who served in the French army. In different terms they confirmed what Lauzanne had written: the officers abandoned their men to their fate.

When the government of France reached Bordeaux on June 14, it was found that a rump parliament was in session in the *mairie*. That rump parliament was headed by Pierre Laval and was made up of all the appeasers, the anti-British elements in high politics, and the other friends of Hitler and Mussolini. They gathered in the office of Adrien Marquet, Mayor of Bordeaux, a Fascist stalwart of long standing. For a few hours, which seemed interminable, the debate raged between these groups and the members of the regular government as to what course to pursue. Paul Reynaud was still in favor then of heading for Africa, and several of his ministers had already set out for the transmarine colonies to get things in readiness. Amongst them was Georges Mandel and Edouard Daladier. These men were later arrested and, among other things, charged with desertion by the supreme deserters, Henri Philippe Pétain and Maxime Weygand.

Weygand and Pétain had almost won their battle for surrender when Great Britain entered upon the scene on June 14. Its envoys were Lord Lloyd, personal friend of Winston Churchill, General Spears, and Mr. Alexander Union. They arrived by plane and were immediately brought into the presence of the President of the Republic, the cabinet ministers, the presidents of the chamber and the Senate, General Weygand, and Marshal Pétain.

Lord Lloyd explained the British proposition with fine tact and sensitiveness. He brought word that Great Britain proposed an immediate union of the French and British Empires. Hitler might have overrun a good part of France: that was a disaster of which he would not deny the magnitude or mitigate the gravity. Yet, nothing was lost. The French army, as well as the British, was virtually intact. The French army could yet be extricated and at a word from him, George Ambrose Lloyd, the signal would be flashed from London for the entire British navy—the Home Fleet, the Mediterranean squadrons, and the Atlantic patrols, probably a thousand ships in all—to rush to France's western and southern ports to begin the evacuation of the French armed forces. Two or three French army corps were to be halted in their retreat to face the oncoming foe and try to hold him until the bulk of the army and most of the material and stocks were embarked for Africa. Once established there, the forces were to be reorganized, and the French navy was to join with the British in driving the Italians, who had entered the war a few days before, from the Mediterranean.

Paul Reynaud took the offer under advisement, and the debate resumed once more: the government sitting in the Bordeaux prefecture, Laval and his satellites in the city hall, with Weygand serving as go-between and military adviser to both groups.

Laval and his friends were for breaking off the British alliance at once, for setting up an antidemocratic govern-

ment in unoccupied France, and for entering into negotiations with the Germans with a view to bringing France
eventually into the Axis combination. Reynaud favored
transferring the government to London, as Poland and
Holland had done, to accept the British offer of union,
and to evacuate the army to Africa. The three British
representatives remained in constant touch with the government and on June 15 were asked to submit their
propositions once more, this time in writing. When they
delivered their document to the cabinet, Weygand received it from the hands of General Spears. As he took
the papers, Weygand remarked: "This is the offer to
France to give up her independence and become a
British dominion."

The British took the insult calmly and withdrew to
allow the cabinet to deliberate. For a few hours the
majority seems to have been in favor of accepting the
British plan. Then Weygand, who had gone to fetch
Laval, reappeared and began to expostulate on the impossibility of withdrawing the French army. Reynaud,
hearing this, again began to waver. Someone said to
Pierre Laval: "But if you accept the German conditions
you connive at the total collapse of France for at least
fifty years." To which Laval returned: "That is true,
but we shall at last be able to take the working class in
hand."

"With Germany?" asked the diplomat, who had spoken
first. "With Germany against the French people?"

"With Germany to eradicate the pestilence," Laval
came back.

After hearing this conversation, Paul Reynaud resigned, and Marshal Pétain agreed to head the ministry.
Pétain named Weygand his first assistant and the advo-

cates of complete capitulation and collaboration with Fascist Germany were at last in the saddle.

For more than a year thereafter the world looked with hope and expectation to Weygand. Would he save France's honor by making a stand across the Mediterranean in Morocco, which Germany had not been able to touch; or would he, in spite of the humiliation of France and of Hitler's subsequent betrayal of the hopes of the French Fascists, carry out his new master's wishes. He was a free man. He did not have a large army at his disposal in Morocco, it is true. But it was an army large enough to keep Hitler in Europe and, in collaboration with Wavell, to throw Mussolini out of Tripoli. He chose the road of dishonor. He facilitated the Duce's attack on Egypt by allowing Italian and, later, German armored equipment to be landed in Tunis.

He next permitted German troops to filter into Morocco, into Algiers, and into Senegal for the occupation of strategic positions in the Reich's eventual drive against the Western Hemisphere—the goal of all Germany's stirring.

It is Weygand who, without being compelled to do so, handed Hitler the pistol directed at the heart of America.

10. *Hess Flies to Scotland*

NOBODY WHO knows anything about Rudolf Hess, about his character and about his position in the Nazi hierarchy will seriously entertain the thought that his flight to Scotland was desertion or that he intended to transfer himself, with all his influence and all his secrets, to the enemy's camp. Not that the man is incapable of treason. Rudolf Hess is capable of every foul deed under the sun. He is a killer—a killer of his closest collaborators and of men who had long considered themselves his most intimate friends.

When it is a question of serving the Fuehrer's interests, Hess will do anything and take any risk, even if it involves placing himself in the enemy's power. He it was who carried out the purge in Munich and in southern Germany in June, 1934, while Göring attended to the bloody business up north. It was Rudolf Hess who walked into Ernst Röhm's room at Hitler's behest and silently placed the loaded revolver on the table and who, upon hearing Röhm say: *"Nein, aber diese Dienst werde ich dem Adolf nicht erweisen*—this service I will not render Adolf," deliberately took aim and kept firing until the chief of the S.A. lay riddled on the floor. It was Hess who thereupon calmly reloaded his revolver and drove to the inn where the Nazi chiefs had often foregathered. There he killed the innkeeper in the presence of the man's wife and children, not because he was a member of the opposition, but because of the possibility that the innkeeper had overheard some snatches of conversation between the Nazi leaders as he waited on them personally in their rooms.

Hess had none of the glamor of a Göring or the influence of a Göbbels on public opinion. He always avoided the full glare of Nazi publicity. He did not possess any of the castles and estates and art treasures with which Robert Ley, Joachim von Ribbentrop, and Göring have enriched themselves. To the public he remained somewhat colorless. He was never included in the pantheon of living Nazi idols.

Nevertheless, he was the Fuehrer's confidant, Adolf Hitler's alter ego, and that he remains, even in his captivity in Britain.

The local Nazi bosses would call him *der Aegypter,* the Egyptian, a name suggested by his birthplace, Alexandria, and by his inscrutable demeanor. Men higher up, who envied this young man his unique position as Deputy Fuehrer of the whole party, used to call him patronizingly Fräulein Rudi, suggesting with true Nazi tact that he owed his influence to his personal charm and captivating smile.

For a time Hess was assistant to Professor Karl Haushofer, the director of the Geopolitical Institute in Munich. Haushofer, who made his debut in life as attaché to the Germany embassy in Tokyo, preached the doctrine (since taught to the world by its grim Nazi interpreters) of *Lebensraum*—living space. Many of Haushofer's plans and schemes found their way into *Mein Kampf,* as it was Hess who took dictation from Hitler for this book when they were both locked up under the Weimar Republic for participation in the Kapp *Putsch.* There is no doubt that Hess is the author of whole passages in the work. He wrote the first publisher's prospectus to the volume, which was then called *Four Years and a Half of Struggle against Lies, Stupidity, and Cowardice.*

Hess is the creator of the *Verbindungsstab*, the liaison office between party and state. Ostensibly designed to supervise the ordinary state departments, it is in reality a spying system that has superseded Himmler's Gestapo. The *Verbindungsstab* has its checking bureau in the *Aussenpolitisches Amt*, where Alfred Rosenberg is the head, but it also maintains a *Dienststelle* in the Foreign Office to keep tab on Herr von Ribbentrop. Through Gauleiter Karl Böhle, Hess exercised an influence on the *Auslandorganisation*, which, besides regulating the activities of German nationals in foreign countries, develops sabotage and espionage abroad and keeps a careful watch over enemies or potential enemies of a Nazi world order in every land under the sun.

Through his position in the party and its elaborate spy system, which stretched its antennae and tentacles into every nook and corner of the various state departments, Rudolf Hess knew, therefore, more about the real state of feeling in Germany than anybody else, including Hitler himself. He also knew, more than any other man, the innermost thoughts of his master. There was no major military plan and secret of the Third Reich of which he was unaware.

Did he cross the North Sea in order to reveal these things to the British? Did this man, who owes everything to Hitler and who has been uninterruptedly at his Fuehrer's side from the beginning of the Nazi adventure, through prison and humiliation, through the long years of *Vehmgerichte*, conspiracy, assassination and plotting, through the blood purge, the murder of Dollfuss, the Czech tragedy, the campaigns in Poland and France and Rumania, suddenly fly off to tell the British Intelligence Service something that could just as well have been confided to its agents in neutral Sweden, Switzerland, Spain, or Portugal? Was Hess planted in Britain or was he a rat that tried to get away from the sinking ship?

Winston Churchill promised to reveal the purpose and object of the flight to Scotland as soon as Rudolf Hess should have been questioned by an official of the Foreign Office. But after it was learned from the Deputy Fuehrer's own mouth why he had made the hazardous trip, Winston Churchill became strangely silent.

British and American observers, after weeks of guessing and being left in the dark, advanced the suggestion that the Hess affair was a sign that the Nazi machine would not survive a major German military defeat. This did not sound very convincing in the light of subsequent events: the German armies smashed Yugoslavia and Greece in a couple of weeks, took the isle of Crete to close the Aegean against the British navy, wrenched Turkey out of the British system of alliances, and, on top of that, deliberately took on the colossus of the Red Army. The explanatory tune was therefore changed: Hess had come because he had quarreled with Hitler or because he had grown afraid that Hitler would heed the reckless advice of extremists like Ribbentrop and Göring, who would throw the might of the *Wehrmacht* against Russia and thus ask of the armies and of the German people that extra spurt that Hess, with his finger on the pulse of the German people, feared to ask. In other words, the world was invited to see the trip to Scotland as evidence of fear in high German circles or, at least, of uncertainty and disquietude over the outcome of a new offensive that was being envisaged.

What is incontrovertible about the flight to Scotland

is the fact that the cruel bombing of London and of various British port cities, which had, in the few weeks preceding Hess' journey, threatened to disrupt all of England's industrial and commercial apparatus, ceased abruptly. With Hess' arrival in Scotland came a breathing spell for the people of England that was to last for several months. Hitler turned the Luftwaffe's striking power in another direction. First, he sent it to central Poland to engage in battle practice for six weeks and then, to carry out the newly learned lessons, against the Soviet Union.

Rudolf Hess did not fly to Britain on his own initiative. That would have been an act wholly at variance with what is known of the man's character. All the years he spent in the Nazi party, from the days of the Kapp *Putsch* till the moment he left Germany by plane, Hess was not merely one of the Fuehrer's most faithful followers: he was his watchdog and bodyguard, devoted to his master in an unquestioning, almost slavish way. In the inner councils of the Nazi party, Hess did not formulate policies or project plans. He carried out orders, and he did this ruthlessly, to the letter, regardless of personal predilections or sympathies. Hess had but one loyalty: to the Fuehrer; but one aim in life: to execute Hitler's commands.

There had been no break between the Fuehrer and Hess before the latter left for Scotland, and there was no evidence of indignation or surprise in official Nazi circles after it had become generally known that Hess had voluntarily landed on enemy territory. Not a single German newspaper as much as whispered a word of condemnation or disapproval. On the contrary. The commentaries in the Nazi journals on the flight to Scot-

land were studiously sympathetic: Hess was an idealist,
it was said, a great humanitarian who had lately been
somewhat overwrought and nervous. That was the worst
that was said of him and his amazing flight. There was
not the faintest trace of that crepitating kind of invective
of which Dr. Göbbels and his associates in the Ministry
of Enlightenment are unquestionably the masters in
Europe. While Göbbels and his crew of propagandists
never miss an opportunity to indulge their particular
genius, in the case of Hess they scrupulously refrained
from using that one word "traitor" which is always on
the tip of their pens. In fact, the editorials and commentaries on the Hess affair astonished the world with
their obvious insouciance. Yet, for Hess to have for-
saken Hitler's cause was just as if one of the most obviously *papabile* cardinals had left Rome to embrace the
Moslem faith.

Hess flew to Scotland on Hitler's orders. The notion
that he suddenly packed up and departed because there
had been a falling-out between gangsters is not borne out
by subsequent events. Over what should they have fallen
out? The German army was marching from strength to
strength. London, England's ports, and English industries were being reduced to heaps of rubble by Luftwaffe
raids that were far from having reached their fullest
possible intensity. The submarine campaign against
British shipping was reaching proportions that would
have proved fatal to Britain had the tempo been kept up.

Were the commanders of the *Reichswehr* again in disagreement with the Fuehrer on the next move in the
campaign of world conquest, as overseas reporters, for
lack of a more plausible story, were reporting whenever
there happened to be a lull in the actual fighting? Some

day the Nazi gangsters may have a falling out. But this had not occurred when Hess took off for Scotland. Generals, especially generals of the Prussian tradition, and an officers' corps which is not of the Chocolate-Soldier or opera-bouffe variety do not revolt when engaged in campaigns replete with victory, loot, and promotion.

"Do our enemies entertain the hope of a revolution in the Reich?" asked Gustav Frensen, the gentle author of *Hillegenlei* grown virulent chauvinist, just about the time when Hess flew off. "Do they expect a wedge to be driven between the Fuehrer and the people? From which section of the people would such action proceed? From the Sudeten Germans, whose thousand-year-old passionate desire to return into the bosom of the Reich Hitler fulfilled? From the army, which he had created and restored to honor and might? From the workers, whose comrade and hero he is? From the farmers, whom he has set on their feet and given their rightful position in society? From the women and children, who love him as a brother? A revolution? Let the world know that one does not make revolution against oneself, against one's own heart!"

Rudolf Hess was sent to Britain because he is the Fuehrer's most intimate confidant, the one man who could be relied upon to carry out instructions to the letter. The message Herr Hitler wanted to convey to the British government, especially to the ladies and gentlemen of the former Cliveden set and of the former Anglo-German fellowship, could not be conveyed through neutral diplomatic channels. The slightest hint that Hitler desired to enter into *pourparlers* or negotiations or merely to re-establish contact with the British authorities or with certain representatives of an influential group in the British nation would at once have been greeted as a sign of weakness on Germany's part, as an indication that the Reich was at the end of its resources or out of breath and that the Fuehrer wanted to bring the hostilities to an end while he still had the upper hand. Moreover, rumors and hints that Hitler was desirous of establishing contact would have been promptly squelched by resolutions and by motions in the British Parliament to go on fighting to the bitter end, especially in view of the hypothesis, which would naturally have been advanced, that the Reich was tired.

The faithful Hess was chosen because Herr Hitler did not want to receive a rebuff before he had at least made it clear to his friendly enemies of the appeasement mentality in England what was on his mind, what turn his campaigns must inevitably take, and what Britain must expect if she persisted in challenging the Fuehrer's mastery of Europe, now that this was a *fait accompli*.

Hess did not come to Britain with a threat. He came, in his own words, to save humanity. He came with the proposal that the Reich be given a free hand in eastern Europe to destroy the Soviet Power and that she share the mastery of the world with Britain. Hitler figured that a battered and tottering British Empire would be only too willing to listen to the allurements of a German policy that had been for years the fundamental directive of tory Continental diplomacy: turn Germany in easterly direction and allow her to carve for herself a *Lebensraum* from the Ukraine to the Urals and the Caucasus.

The message Rudolf Hess brought from the Fuehrer was substantially this: Germany does not want to destroy the British Empire. During the negotiations over Dantzig the Fuehrer made it abundantly clear that he would guarantee the territorial integrity of the Empire; in fact, he offered to become the Empire's protector. In return for this, the Fuehrer asked that Britain abdicate her role as the supreme arbiter of the fate and destiny of Europe. Germany could no longer tolerate British interference on the Continent.

This proposition was turned down by the British government, and it went to war with Germany. Since that day in September, 1939, Hess was to say, British hegemony over Europe has been destroyed by German arms. France no longer exists, militarily speaking. The Fuehrer deprived Britain of the possible assistance of the Soviet Union by revealing to Stalin what the tories' secret objectives were with respect to Russia. We Germans, on the other hand, offered Stalin peace and a nonaggression pact because we wanted our rear covered while we dealt with France and her satellites in the west and east and established our military domination of the Continent.

Stalin accepted our proposal and was of invaluable aid to us in protecting our left flank while our armies brought Hungary into our new order and while they overran Rumania, Bulgaria, Yugoslavia, and Greece. We occupied Crete and thereby isolated Turkey, Britain's last potential ally in Europe and the Near East.

Wavell's recent retreat from Cyrenaica proves, moreover, that the German army has crossed the Mediterranean and that we can advance to the Suez Canal when we decide the time has come. Spain we can occupy in twenty-four hours. Franco is wholly in the Fuehrer's power. Germans run the air service in Spain, the railroads, the telegraph, the mines, the ports, the customs. We are fast filtering into Morocco. Weygand has been collaborating with the Reich from the moment he was brought from Syria to take over from Gamelin. All this means that we can close the Mediterranean at will. Such a move would cut your Empire in twain. Somewhere, either through Iraq or Syria or the Caucasus, we can advance on India. Your navy is powerless to prevent that. . . .

As to armies, you have not sufficient man power and equipment to defend Palestine if we should take it into our minds to occupy that country. We are building a railway, in collaboration with Weygand, from Algiers to Dakar. Here again your fleet will be powerless to prevent us from establishing an aerial base and a submarine base on your long route to India and the Far East. In the Pacific the Japanese are with us. They are waiting for our troops to appear at the gates of India before marching down through Indo-China and over the Malay Peninsula to Singapore. Your navy will be of no avail there either, not even if America should come in to help you. We will have our land-based bombers on hand in Siam and Indo-China to keep your naval units far out at sea, as we did in the case of Crete. All this we can do before American aid becomes of any real value to you. Whether you agree or not, that is the situation in brief. . . .

But why not come to a compromise now? You have lost Europe. You have shown yourselves valiant opponents, the only enemies worthy of the German sword. Germany recognizes your heroism, your endurance, and your determination. But you have been outplayed and outmaneuvered. Your allies failed you. France was rotten. The East European ententes collapsed like a house of cards under our diplomatic pressure. . . . Have you now the man power to stage an invasion of the Continent

and drive us out of France and Scandinavia and recon-
quer the European Continent? You know you cannot
do it, surely not alone. Do you expect American troops
to come to your aid? Please do not fool yourselves on
the subject of America. American aid is a long way off.
The Americans will have their hands full at home. For
we have the power to plunge America into civil war.
We know whereof we speak: all this talk of America
coming to your aid is *Zukunftsmusik*. . . .

On the other hand, we offer you an alternative: we
are going to attack Russia. We prefer our *Lebensraum*
right next door. We want the iron ore of the Urals, the
oil of the Caucasus, the wheat of the Ukraine. You have
India, nearly all of Africa, Australia, Canada. Let us
have Russia for a colony. As evidence of our good faith
we shall forthwith cease our bombing of the British Isles.
What do you say? The war is over if you give the word.
We cannot expect you to veer around in one week or
in a month. We will advance against Russia in the meantime. We will show you that we are in earnest. England
has nothing more to fear of us. You will have time to
make up your minds. . . .

This was the sum and substance of the message from
the Fuehrer that Rudolf Hess was to deliver to Winston
Churchill.

It goes without saying that the Deputy Leader of the
German National Socialist party would have preferred
to state the object of his visit first of all, as he had intended to do, in some select gathering of British friends
of the new Germany—for instance, in the hunting lodge
of the Duke of Hamilton, on whose vast estate he had
landed for that very purpose. But that little scheme of
coming to Britain incognito and flying off again after

a day or two had been frustrated by the unfortunate circumstance that Hess had been seen alighting from his plane by a stupid Scottish tenant of the Duke's and that this foolish man had taken the regulations about descending enemy flyers quite seriously and had notified the police.

"Take me to the Duke of Hamilton," the Scotsman was told by Hess, who was wearing all his medals and who must have thought that this Highlander, like any other Prussian peasant under the circumstances, would have clicked his heels with the words: *"Zu Befehl, Herr Obergeneral des Dritten Reich! Be pleased to follow me!"* Instead, that obstinate Calvinist came on with his pitchfork and made the Deputy Fuehrer put up his hands and stand in that humiliating attitude until his wife came back with the rural constable. Those simple-minded Scots apparently took the war seriously. Instead of seeing the Duke of Hamilton, Hess landed in the local jail. That was a miscalculation. He had expected more considerate treatment.

With the Duke of Hamilton, a British Fascist, Rudolf Hess had carried on an assiduous correspondence ever since the beginning of the war. Before September, 1939, they visited each other, hunted together, planned together, and held discussions and conferences with mutual British friends. Discussions on what? On the prevalence of the boll weevil in Georgia's cotton fields or on the measuring the pants of the man in the moon perhaps? God forbid! Nothing as treasonable as that! Those two gentlemen had merely bewailed the fact that their respective countries should have drifted into a war, which was from the point of view of both—the appeasement group in Britain and the men around the Fuehrer—a wasteful and futile struggle, something almost unnatural. This touching harmony of view on the nature of the war had led them most naturally to explore possibilities of terminating the conflict or diverting it in another direction.

One thing had led to another. Hess had kept the Fuehrer fully informed of his British friend's anxiety and his sincere desire for peace. The Fuehrer had learned what Lord Redesdale, the Duke of Hamilton's neighbor and the father of Unity Freeman-Mitford, thought about the war, and what Lady Astor said in private, and what Sir Nevile Henderson (who, when he was still ambassador to Berlin, had been frankly in favor of letting Germany take the whole of Europe) and that other good friend of the Fuehrer's, Lord Runciman (who had been so helpful in the matter of Czechoslovakia), what these gentlemen and Lords Londonderry, Stamp, and Brocket were telling the Foreign Office now. In that way Hitler had gained the impression that there was quite a little appeasement sentiment left among the people who count in England, and he conceived the notion that, with the aid of some tactful suggestions about turning the war into an anti-Bolshevik crusade, the good old spirit of Munich might be revived and that even stubborn Winston Churchill might yet come to see the light.

The confidential information reaching Rudolf Hess became so encouraging that the Fuehrer and the men of his entourage—Göring, Ribbentrop, Göbbels, and Himmler—began to hunt for a stratagem that would turn British public opinion still more in Germany's favor. Of the select British circles that had formerly furnished the membership for the Anglo-German Fellowship and the smaller Cliveden set, the Fuehrer need not worry. They had considered the war a foolish undertaking from the beginning. Now, with its devastating progress—France knocked out and the whole Continent passed under German domination—the Cliveden set must have grown more convinced than ever of the truth of the Fuehrer's remarks to Monsieur Coulondre, a French diplomat, when he stopped off in Berlin on his way to Paris in August, 1939. Monsieur had said to Hitler: "Do you know, *monsieur le chancelier,* who will be the sole beneficiary if Germany and England go to war?"

"Of course I know," the Fuehrer had replied: "the sole beneficiary will be Trotsky!"

Those gentlemen like to give a personal touch to their figures of speech, but their fears are genuine. Wars are the beginning of revolution. What could the British upper classes expect from the war if it ended at once? Why, the best thing possible for them—a return to the *status quo ante.* On the other hand, what was in store for Britain if the struggle continued? Loss of territory, blasted cities, a ruined commerce, perhaps India in turmoil, the rise of revolutionary sentiment, and the triumph of socialism? In order to keep the morale of the British people at a high pitch, Winston would sooner or later have to state his war aims; he would not be able to avoid promises of a better life, of more democracy, of a wider distribution of wealth. . . .

If the Fuehrer, who believed so fanatically in the power of his own word, could only talk to England, he felt certain that he could convince even the most skeptical. Had he not prevailed over the old man with the umbrella and over Simon and Halifax, Henderson, Daladier, and so many others? Yet, personally he could not go to England. He could not suddenly call a halt to the

war and say: "That is all." Those Englishmen would
take that for a sign of exhaustion. And Germany was
by no means exhausted. The German war machine was
intact, in perfect order. In perfect order, except the
brakes. They were missing. The Fuehrer knew that he
must go on from victory to victory, or the machine might
disintegrate, or the tension in which the German people
have lived since 1933 might snap.

He needed oil now, oil and ore and wheat. Those
things could not be obtained by a successful invasion of
England. For that he must go to Russia. But if he
attacked Russia before he had subdued England, he
might himself call up the specter of a double front—the
danger against which Bismarck had warned and which
had broken Wilhelm.

No, England must be lulled to sleep first. England and
America must be made to believe that they need have
no further fear of German aggression.

If England could be pacified now, Roosevelt would be
left with a useless armaments program on his hands and
would be utterly discredited while America would be
plunged into an economic crisis from which there would
be no exit. That would give him, the Fuehrer, time to
conquer Russia, transform that country into a vast arsenal
in a few years' time in collaboration with all the conquered countries, weld the European states together in
one common task, and then . . . why, after that the
United States could build all the fleets it wanted and
turn out all the bombers possible, it would not be able
to outbuild a united Asia and Europe. Both America
and England would be at Germany's mercy. . . . But
England must first be got out of the way.

Hitler said to Hess: "Rudolf, go to your friends! Say that I am ready to come to an understanding and say that I am in earnest about it! . . ."

"Before we enter into negotiations," Winston Churchill said to Hess, "we want to have some evidence of the Fuehrer's good faith. For years he has promised to attack Russia and build his colonial empire in the Ukraine. Former British governments did all in their power to facilitate the Fuehrer's march eastward. In the end your Fuehrer betrayed Britain. This time we want to see Herr Hitler act and not merely hold out promises."

Churchill made no promises. But in that hour, when he spoke to Hess, he made five decisive gains: he acquired an ally in Russia, he turned the Nazi war machine in an easterly direction, he postponed the invasion of England, he gave America an opportunity to perfect her war machine, and he started Hitler on the long road that leads to perdition.

VI

The River Flows Home

In the daytime there are tugs on the river towing long strings of flat-bottomed barges and swift, black-painted naval sloops that send up whorling tufts of white spray. When those boiling woolsacks fall asunder, the floating strings of foam give the surface the appearance of green-veined marble. The gulls fly low, but they venture farther upstream than they did a month ago. They now come as far as the George Washington Bridge. Before winter is over they will be seen in Yonkers and beyond. Returning from their inland errand, they sit on lumps of driftwood that rock and sway unsteadily on the swift current. Sounds are growing sharper, and the signal blasts of the river boats startle with their harsh and strident wails. When it is still, you can hear the sea from afar. But it is no longer the sustained drowsy murmur that rose from the heart of summer. The song has moved up to a higher note, fresher, more penetrating.

The trees along the drive are turning russet and yellow. Any night now may come the storm that will strip them of their leaves. There are moments when the trees begin to tremble as in a sudden panic, only to return quickly to their former splendid serenity. Do they feel the approach of death, and would they once more stand forth in their most festive array before bidding adieu? They greet the cool dawn with a deep sigh, as if relieved that another night has passed without torment.

The light of autumn lends a clearer outline to the

buildings on the New Jersey shore. They are the color of steel with thin pink edges. Now that the soggy haze of summer is dissipated, that land over there looks too hard and rocky. The small church without a steeple, straight across from my window, makes me think of a ship that has been thrown up on the shore—a ship that is awaiting the arrival of the crew to set it afloat again. Now I can see why those Hollanders and Zeelanders who sailed with Hendrick Hudson in the *Half Moon* hugged the eastern shore of the river. It was the fat and pleasant land that drew them, not those forbidding, towering cliffs across.

There are freighters gliding by, empty, high out of the water, with strange flags painted on their hulls, the flags of nonseafaring nations: Switzerland, Bolivia. They move to the basin above the bridge to wait for a call to take in cargo. Tomorrow or the next day the bustling little tugs will scream and yell at them and push them in between the piers on the opposite bank, where endless trains of heavily loaded flatcars are edging up to the shore.

The river is gray and melancholy. The golden luster of high summer that glittered on its surface has sunk to the depths. There is now a mercury-silver sheen over the water. But it is still warm in the daytime. It is still growing weather. . . .

It is always growing weather. Only the ignorant and the blind believe that the soil ever comes to rest. Never is it in such intense travail as in autumn. The heart of the earth never stops beating. Scarcely is the harvest home than the promise of future wheat fields is visible in the dark clods of earth. Everything ferments and germinates, always. The autumn distills the sap that will

feed the young life in the coming spring. That is the life of
the earth. That life also pulsates in us, an intensely profound and irresistible force. We belong to the earth as
she belongs to us. We are permeated with the earth.
It is through her that mounts in us the spirit of our fore-
bears.

Half of our misery and weakness derives from the fact
that we have broken with the soil and that we have
allowed the roots that bound us to the earth to rot. We
have become detached from the earth, we have abandoned her. And a man who abandons nature has begun
to abandon himself. It is in the moment when we realize
the dire consequences of our having lost contact with
nature that we must begin to think of returning to her.
And not merely in a haphazard or sentimental manner,
but wholeheartedly and entirely.

I know full well that one may dwell in a cement cave
in a great city and still be close to nature. One can find
solitude in the midst of crowds and tumult. There are
always heroes and saints or, at any rate, strong souls. But
mankind does not live on heroism and saintliness. Man
is weak. Man must be brought back to the start. He
must be put in a state of grace. . . .

Slowly the night descends. Like the sunlight at dawn,
it comes over the northern peoples softly and on slippered feet. The white domes of the oil reservoirs on the
other shore are imperceptibly turned into hooded
mosques. The chimney stacks become slender minarets.
In the gathering darkness the hoisting cranes and steel
trestles across the river are weird creatures signaling to
each other with sharply pointed fingers. The whistle of
the trains sounds far off.

The current runs swiftly, and the waves of the river go by like the serried ranks of a vast host. The sun is gone. The shadows deepen. Night will soon be here.

Let us not speak evil of the night! The night is rich in mysteries and in revelation. The night reflects the secret thought of the day. The night is the day's sub-consciousness. When life began, the night was there. The night was his horizon for every man who ever lived. The far-off ancestor feared the night because he dreaded to meet the spirits of the dead. And we? Are we not afraid of the night? We think and we guess, we believe and we deny, but do we really know anything more than that distant father? We know that the night is a great sea, a never-ending stream that bears all that lives away. No more than the waves that pass by in never-ending procession know that they will be thrown into the sea and be dissolved and vanish from their own ken do we know where we are going. We know that death is a gateway that opens for everybody, but we do not know whither the gate leads: to annihilation of consciousness or to a transformation of consciousness.

We do not know. We guess and we believe, we surmise and we suppose, we float and sway to and fro like driftwood, but we know not. We know that worlds are born and perish, that suns and solar systems grow, flourish, and wither, just as all things blossom and die in the great garden of the universe. We know that nothing remains unchanged, that all things constantly undergo transformations, that soil and sunlight become flowers and grass, and these the bodies of men and animals, and that they change back again to grass and flowers and insects and birds and color and perfume and voice. We know that steaming vapors and red-hot clumps of metal change into planets. But of ourselves we know nothing. We do not know whether the flame we feel in us will be extinguished or burn with a new brilliance. We surmise, we hope, we believe, but know we do not. . . .

The chaos and anarchy of the era through which we are passing, the apparently directionless drifting of human society, are indications of the growth of a new culture. We are witnessing the bloody and catastrophic birth pangs of a new world order. We see before our eyes that the peculiarities of different national cultures, as those of Britain, France, Germany, and Italy, are rapidly dissolving and disappearing. Through a number of factors, not the least of which is the fantastic tempo of the evolution of the technique of transportation, the different parts of humanity are growing into one body and organism.

"The unification of the world," wrote Guglielmo Ferrero many years ago, "through scientific expeditions, colonization, emigration, world religions, wars, commerce, diplomacy, railways, telegraph [and he may well have added, "through aerotechnical progress"] must inevitably lead to a culture of universal character. . . . But the world which becomes a single body," he added, "cannot possibly live with a number of mutually hostile and contradictory forms of consciousness. The body of the world must have a soul." This new soul of the world, the Italian historian and philosopher thought, would consist of the best of all the old cultures harmoniously blended together.

Of course, this is but wishful dreaming. There can be no question of a harmonious blending of different old and new, European and Oriental, technical and spiritual cultural elements so long as the capitalistic culture of the West is utilized by a caste minority to enrich itself at the expense of the majority and so long as the dominant white race utilizes that culture to oppress and exploit other races.

In western Europe, moreover, capitalistic culture has virtually destroyed the remnants of the precapitalistic popular cultures, while outside Europe it has entered into conflict with age-old, profoundly rooted agrarian cultures, with a different basis, a different evaluation of moral values, and an entirely different goal.

Those ancient cultures have been thrown out of their course by the rapid transformation of their production economy into a money economy: the making of profit has become the one and only goal. Nearly everywhere in the world the spontaneous, organic growth of society has been disturbed by capitalism foisting on the peoples a need for money. Through the impoverishment of the masses by constantly more refined means of exploitation, as well as by the importation of machine-made commodities, the old native craft culture is being killed. This tragedy is being enacted in British India, in the Dutch East Indies, and all over Africa. The East is being Westernized, which means that it is being imperialized and militarized. This phenomenon, on the other hand, is coupled with a violent reaction against the spiritual content of European civilization and with a striving for a renewal of the old native cultures. This is the case in India, in Indonesia, and, to a lesser degree, in Africa. In Asia Japanese imperialism has seized upon these native movements to further its own ambitions of expansion and domination with the slogan: "Asia for the Asiatics."

Even so, everywhere we look we see that Western

pseudo culture is exerting a disintegrating influence on the old social relationships and on what, in the old native cultures, gave form, sense, and value to life. A disintegrating influence brings overestimation of riches, of comfort, of luxury, and of sensual pleasure and the underestimation of peace of mind, concentration, inner harmony, and the satisfaction over good work well executed. It brings mechanization of labor, of industrial organization, and speeds up the tempo of life by the anarchistic production methods and by economic rivalry.

The result is that all those native peoples are being robbed of what once made them valuable as human beings, no matter how impressive and materially great they now may be made to appear.

To speak, therefore, of a melting pot, of a synthesis of East and West, is absurd. The very opposite is taking place: it is confusion, dissatisfaction, opposition, and hatred that are growing.

Age-old concepts and social relationships that we held sacred and immutable are falling away. Ultimate certainties and transcendental values which for centuries have been laid down in terms such as God, fate, destiny, freedom, sin, have become petrified and are no longer considered vital concepts. In an autarchy different groups and nations stubbornly seek to maintain and to safeguard what they consider the highest good, whether it be race, honor, dogma, system, capital, or power. This is taking place in a world which through technical progress is becoming more and more a unity, a single body whose separate organs are getting more and more indispensable to one another.

Is it to be wondered at that this harsh self-satisfaction,

this self-righteous, intolerant mentality in the religious, spiritual, economic, and cultural spheres, has plunged the world in chaos and misery?

Yet, still we talk of fighting to preserve the *status quo*, this system which is stuck in a mire of its own making and which can move neither backward nor forward without producing new disasters, new depressions, new wars, and more mass misery.

The dominating economic motif of our time is mass production of each article of merchandise where it can be produced under the most favorable conditions and with the least possible effort and then its distribution over the length and breadth of the earth. But this economic motif cannot be fully developed because the world is split up into a number of independent and sovereign states, every one of which nourishes the absurd pretension of being self-sufficient and of being able to produce inside its own frontiers and by its own means everything it needs, besides a surplus for export. Every state barricades itself behind its own frontiers against foreign products and against human beings.

Whereas at the beginning of the century man could still travel from one end of the earth to the other without a passport, whereas at that time anyone could work anywhere and do business, except in some backward countries which were regarded as backward precisely for that reason, man can now no longer circulate at will. He has become more and more restricted in his movements until today he has come to a complete standstill.

Merchandise moves with even greater difficulty than man. While in the last century merchandise could enter foreign countries without charge or on payment of very modest imposts in so-called protectionist states, today scarcely a product enters a foreign country without its quantity being severely rationed by quotas and contingents and without paying almost prohibitive import duties, which cause it to be sold at twice, thrice, and even ten times its intrinsic value.

Thus, while technical progress tends more and more to impose a single world economy—in truth, a universal economy—politics impose a constantly widening estrangement between the hundred and one different national compartments into which the world was divided at a time when there were neither steam nor electricity, neither automobiles nor flying machines.

Capitalist economists have themselves pointed out the folly, the wastefulness, and the inconsistency of this immense and flagrant contradiction. In the years following the First World War various remedies were indeed suggested to put an end to it. But the ruling classes of the different countries showed themselves unwilling to sacrifice the least particle of their interests. It is true that some international cartels were formed, but, besides being extremely precarious in character, besides ignoring that immense section of industry which remains in the hands of small-time enterprise, those cartels did not eliminate the barriers that the various states had built against other nations. In fact, the barriers were fortified since every one of the copartners in the international cartels sought to use those barriers (which preserved and protected them within their own borders) as means of putting pressure on its foreign partners to obtain more advantages in the division of other markets.

The last and most important step taken by big business in the direction of creating an international economic organism was the establishment in 1929 of the Bank of International Settlement in Basel. But this institution had scarcely started to function when the crisis came.

The crisis! That was a signal for everyone to lock his doors more tightly than ever. From that moment dates the system of contingents and quotas. Since the crisis the control of exchange has become the rule in most countries, while hunting the foreigner has become almost everywhere a sort of national sport.

For different reasons, principally because they possessed no colonies, the central European countries suffered most from this splitting up of the markets, for it prevented them from selling outside and caused them to starve while sitting on top of mountains of their own manufactured products.

Germany armed to put an end to this process of splitting up. In Europe the German industrialists envisaged a division of labor, so to speak. Rumania and France were to restrict themselves to agriculture, for instance. Norway was to supply fish and lumber, oils and fat, Holland vegetables and shipping facilities, in exchange for Germany's manufactured articles. Germany aimed at an economic order that would be more in conformity with the conditions and progress of modern technique.

Today Hitlerian and Mussolinian Caesarism are on the way to realizing by methods of constraint those United States of Europe which had failed to materialize by peaceful means.

If the lifting of national trade barriers was more urgent in central Europe than anywhere else, it is equally necessary everywhere. The contradiction between the international tendency toward perfecting technique and the particularist reactions that the different national states put in its way is a general phenomenon, a universal problem that must be solved everywhere.

It must be solved in a very short time outside Europe. But that it will be solved, one way or the other, of that we may be quite certain. For that solution is a social and a historic necessity. The curtain which shrouds the future is not entirely impenetrable. When it became necessary for man to scratch the soil in order to produce his food, he invented a plow. When it became necessary for him to fly, he invented the airplane. When he no longer can dispense with international collaboration, he will find a way for the simple reason that a way exists. . . .

Darkness lies on the deep like an impenetrable shroud. The river is a black mirror over which moves the cool breath of the autumn night. The only sound is the lapping and gurgling of the waves against the granite and basalt rocks under my feet. Is there a ship passing by in the gloom of midstream, or has the wind risen that there should be this ghostly stir in the water? The yonder shore is blotted out in Stygian shadows. The almost palpable clouds of night close in with menacing intent. . . .

Then the moon comes rolling in from the ocean, and his friendly face bends over the world to whisper words of love. The river comes to life. The silver confetti sprinkled on the surface are a million tiny lanterns lighting up the running tide. Under my gaze the river turns into a highway, a broad, dark street whose name is life. The white-plumed waves that rise and fall softly in even cadence are the generations of man pushing each other on, overtaking each other on the way to their eternal home. Here passes everything that dreaming thought conceived and what the heart sought to know: the glory of the world and the sorrow of man, the ecstasies of those who saw the Eternal in the burning bush and in the intoxication of the tripod.

The soft wind brings the music of flutes and the distant thunder of flaming forests. For that still water which now stifles its sobs can also boil. When the storm awakens, you can hear the cry of the blood of the millions who could not be because their fathers were slain. . . .

Now the river is placid. The waves move on in orderly rhythm. On their tops float the ruins of all that has been: the hieroglyphs of Egypt, the emperors of China, the yogis of India who spent their lives sitting on ashes in the wilderness; all the myths of the wondrous gods, sphinxes, and chimeras, creatures with the trunks of elephants and the bodies of humans, gods who changed into mice and stones, gods who were both man and woman, gods who mutilated themselves or who gleamed as scarabs in the sand.

Forward rolls the stream. I see the movement of creation, the never-resting, eternal urge of genesis.

Is that man, is that the king of creation, the father of Plato and Solomon, that creature moving by there? His forehead recedes, and his teeth protrude in a simian grin. Hear his groans and grunts as he tries to walk by throwing himself upward at every painful step with a quick touch of his long arm on the earth. Is that dull noise which rattles in the back of his throat the voice that will intone a Te Deum tomorrow? Throw him a deerskin for his naked loins and some raw fruit that he may devour it. For what are his eyes in their deep sockets searching in yon clumps of bushes? Let him have his female, let him run after her into the woods, and over-whelm her and hold her captive with his hairy knees in wild pairing heat! Do not prevent him, for of that hasty mating will be born Michelangelo and Beethoven and Einstein. . . .

I hear voices. I catch the sound of articulate words. There is a new man. His eye is clearer. His shoulders are covered with a sheepskin. He carries a bronze ax and a sharply filed stone. He sits down to weave a basket. He puts twig and loam together. I see his brothers. They wear a band around their waist and an apron. There is custom among them and law and orderliness. They rub two sticks together, and a flame dances in the dry moss. Now the smell of burning fat drifts over towards me.

There is a group of shepherds coming next. They drive a herd of cattle before them. They are white of skin, and their bodies are well formed. They pull a shawl over their heads as they face the sharp, dry prairie wind. They crouch around a fire in front of a tent. Tomorrow they will move on to fatter land, to the edge of rivers. They glance at the stars before going to sleep and lift their arms in mute appeal for solace and warmth and safety. . . .

A funeral procession moves by. Women weep. Priests mumble incantations. On that stretcher is a mummy. Oxen draw the solid heavy cart. These know of immor-tality. They have invented the wheel. "Friend, thy man-sion awaits thee, comfortable is thy dwelling. Judge gently, Osiris," the priests mumble. "We commend him to thy loving-kindness. Do not eject him from thy palace of light and return him to the sorrowful cycle of this life. . . ."

Who is that man alone in the desert? Why is he untying his sandals and crossing his hands on his breast with eyes closed? Has anyone called him? Why does he bow his head? Has he heard a voice in his own heart? . . .

They pass by: fierce warriors with black, square-trimmed beards, the bowmen of Assyria, the charioteers of Mizraim, the Hittites building cities with walls. Who is that one with the royal diadem on his forehead who crawls in the grass like an animal? Is it you, Nebuchad-nezzar? And you there, with your eyes bulging with fright because of the hand on the wall? Have courage, Belshazzar! The night will cover you!

Did you hear that laughter? Say, did you hear it? Hellas! Hellas! The garlands are placed around the heads, the crown of laurel leaf and oak. Golden bracelets are fastened around the arms. Now dance! Now has happiness come! Sing the chorus and the antichorus! Go into your temples . . . there is the myrtle leaf and the mixed wine. Sprinkle it on the altars! High the apple and the phallus! The god is born again. . . . New life, better life begins. . . .

But who are those somber figures? Those men in camel-hair cloaks? What is it he of Tekoa says? "I hate, I despise your feast days. . . . I will not hear the melody of thy viols. . . . Take away from me the noise of thy songs. . . . I will not accept your offerings. But let judgment run down as waters and righteousness as a mighty stream!" And he there, who goes naked through the streets of Jerusalem: "Behold, I create new heavens and a new earth and the former shall not be remembered. . . . Ye shall turn your swords into plowshares. . . . They shall not build, and another inhabit."

The moon is passing behind a cloud. The air is damp with the drizzle that rises from the stream. The wind has come up and sighs plaintively through the tree branches behind me. It will soon be time to turn in. There is a storm coming up. I can hear its distant roar gathering strength as a wail that travels over wide fields. The waves roll on, uniform, equal in height and shape. With the waves pass the armies of slaves. There is struggle but no hope of victory. Chained together, they march to the ends of the earth. . . .

Now I feel the air growing colder. A Cross comes into sight. I hear the groans of the Man on the Cross. I see the blood on His face. He turns His head from side to side in nameless pain. His lips move. Hear! He speaks: *"Eli, Eli, lama sabachtani!"* A dark mist descends. The song of the birds is silenced, and the forests cease their rustling. The moon's rays are frozen, and the earth stands still. There is nothing but the wood and the Man who suffers on the Cross in eternal torment. The river moves on, but the Cross remains, now as a vague vision that recedes in the night, then moving forward in stark reality.

When the strong torture the weak, when the poor cry for bread, when the innocent languish in dungeons, when mothers go insane because they see their children die, when the outcasts roam in the wilderness, when the soldiers go to battle, when those who sit in darkness pray for light, the Cross returns, and the head of the Man on the Cross sinks deeper on the tired breast. . . .

The river flows on. The sound of trumpets is heard. I hear the scratching of pens as men bend over manuscripts. I see a monk haranguing a crowd in the market place, and a moment later great hosts of men, and even children, come marching by. Knights in armor lead the procession, which is preceded by all the banners of Christendom, and the cry goes up: "God wills it! God wills it!"

The world becomes a tumult. Peasants are fighting. Jacques Bonhomme has risen in revolt. I see the flames of a burning pile of wood and a man in the midst of the fire tied to a stake, and I can hear him say: *"Sancta simplicitas!"* before the smoke blots out the sight. The flames leap over to a hundred, a thousand other places. All Europe is covered with burning piles. . . .

Now there is more light on the river. The moon has come through the clouds for a brief moment. There go Lorenzo, Newton, and Columbus. Life becomes freedom, thought. . . . Fleets swarm out to all parts of the world. Cities leap from the ground. Treasures pour in. Men from the most remote corners of the earth begin to trade and meet and talk together.

Then the moon goes in hiding again, and darkness returns. The river flows swifter. The wind drives it on. I hear a voice which says: "We must overcome the disease of poverty. Man is born to be happy. . . ." and I recognize the speaker by his thin sarcastic lips and his leering smile: Voltaire. The tumult breaks out once more. A mob storms the Bastille, and a king's head rolls into the dust.

Man will be happy yet. He will never rest until he has found the way of happiness. You too, workers of the world, in your slums and lightless factories, you will know the light. Science will find the long-sought peace and glory. That is the word of the new prophets who float by silently: Saint-Simon, Fourier, Faraday, Darwin, Kropotkine, Tolstoy, Huxley. . . .

Yet, the sky grows darker, the moon is now hidden entirely. A storm has come up. I can no longer see the waves. The wind howls with fierce, frightening lament. Bolts of purple lightning fly through the obscurity. Their lurid flash lights up the houses across the river with the color of blood and sulphur. . . .

> *Neen, het is nog geen nacht.*
> *twee of drie staan er nog op wacht.*
> *maar het is verdomd donker aan 't worden—*
> *en misschien*
> *worden zij afgeslacht*
> *vóór dat zij den morgen zien.*

> No, it is not yet night.
> Two or three are still standing guard.
> But it is growing damned dark
> and perhaps
> they, the watchmen, too, will be slaughtered
> before they see the morning.

These lines, which I copied from an inscription on the wall of the People's Hall in the town of Breskens during the last hour I spent on Dutch soil, give a pointed and complete expression of the sentiments one feels if but one glance is taken at the future, or even at the present status of European culture—that is to say, of the state of Christendom. A few years ago the cry of the young French intellectuals was still: *"Faire l'Europe!* Build a Europe!" They bewailed the fact that Europe was innerly torn apart and solemnly warned us that a demoniacal apparatus of violence was being set up that would threaten seriously all the norms of justice and morality. They asked the world if it realized what was at stake, what treasures of truth, justice, morality, philosophy, and religion were in danger. They asked if it was realized that such words and concepts as culture,

spirit, idea, God, Christ—all these things which are permeated with the spirit of eternity—would become meaningless. Did we realize that their disappearance would
signify the definite end of the Christian era, that human-
ism and idealism would be things of the past, and that
the future would belong to blood and race? Those young
men still saw the menace in the future and grew almost
frantic at the prospect of seeing the lights of the spirit
being menaced with extinction.

But today all that is an accomplished fact. The lights
are out. The night has come. The last watchmen are
being slaughtered. And not only on the battlefields of
Europe and Asia, but wherever an emasculated tolerance and cowardly liberalism permit the undermining
of the democratic ideal by leaving it unstated.

For merely to say that the struggle raging in the
universe is one to save democracy, or to preserve the
American way of life, or to beat Hitler, is beside the
point, because it would mean that the chief aim and
object of the battle waged by the democratic states is to
bring back the *status quo ante bellum,* which is precisely the state of affairs which produced the calamities
that have overwhelmed humanity.

It would mean what is impossible of achievement:
turning back to what once has been. We cannot return
to what has been, because that is what this war has
already destroyed. What has been destroyed is, in the
first place, the imperialist concept of Europe. Never
again will Europe be a beggar's blanket of small sovereign independent states. Technical progress has made
a return of that constellation impossible. Hitler, who
was the tool of destiny in this matter, and only to that

extent a personification of "the wave of the future," may be defeated, or he may be victorious. The unification of Europe will remain.

Through the mist of blood and tears the peoples of Europe have caught a glimpse of the future. The barriers of the frontiers, which hemmed them in and which divided the Continent into an infinitesimal number of nationally independent cubicles, have fallen away. Unified customs regulations have been introduced. Europe has visibly become one single, unified economic organism.

Nazi Germany has unwittingly and unintentionally supplied proof that there will be no need and no occasion for the peoples to fly periodically at each other's throats once the element of economic rivalry between their respective ruling classes is permanently removed. But by that revelation Germany has also sealed the doom of her own new ruling class.

The Reich's temporary leadership in Europe, wholly immoral and objectionable though it is, has nevertheless shown the direction in which the peoples will move, because it is the direction in which they must move. A new concept of national independence and security through a unified economy and a sharing of the common task looms in the offing. For the chief question a generation should ask of the future is not what will happen but what should happen. And then it is no longer a matter for debate whether Europe or the world has a special predilection or not for a planned international economy, for that has become an ineluctable historical demand. It is merely a question of whether that new economy shall function by the free will and moral consent of all the peoples or whether it shall continue to be imposed on them by the military machine and the police regime of Nazi Germany and operate as a slave economy for the sole benefit of the new German ruling class. . . .

There is a historic precedent for the transformation of human and international relations as we see it taking place in our time. In the Middle Ages, too, a totally new spirit slowly conquered man and society. But then it did not come about "by itself," either; here and there the early capitalist economy had to force commercial and industrial enterprise to behave capitalistically. In our time it is the Hitler flood of violence, brutality, and terror that is changing the motive complex that has been uppermost for the last hundred years or so. It is teaching the peoples solidarity through blood and tears. Through rivers of blood and oceans of tears, it is true. Nevertheless, it is implanting the sentiment in their hearts that their merits and achievements, their faults and sins, their aspirations and their hopes, not only do not mutually exclude each other, but complement each other.

Through its berserker rage, which was born of the desperation of a great people hemmed in on all sides by walls of steel, and which, like an angry flood, has spilled over and effaced the frontiers, Hitlerism has given the decisive impetus to a functional reorganization of society on an international scale.

Wars are the thresholds of revolutions. With the war it unleased in 1939 Nazi Germany has cleared the way for the advent of a new dispensation. Hitlerism itself is not that new dispensation. In fact, Hitlerism, after releasing the floodgates, has itself become the greatest single obstacle barring the road to the wave of the future by its monopolization of the role of innovator.

That is why Hitlerism must be swept aside and eradicated root and branch and in all its ramifications both abroad and in our own midst. That is the first and principal task of the democracies-in-arms and of the democratic spirit. To that end democracy must not only fight Hitlerism with force of arms and with all its might, but it must also attack and purge itself of the enemy in its own bosom. It must remove and overcome the conditions from which the great catastrophe originated. For "these conditions," as Dr. Paul Tillich has pointed out, "are not bad accidents, but structured trends, rooted in the very essence of bourgeois democracy. In the case of the Second World War," he said, "those who are attacked had the attacker in themselves, consciously or unconsciously. They have created Communism by the social injustice they defended with all their power, and they have nourished Fascism to use it as a tool against Communism. . . ."

What the peoples have found in the hour of their greatest sorrow and anguish, they must and, I think, will never lose again. They must remain united economically and to the sense of commonal interest and common destiny must be added a desire to do justice—to feel a social international responsibility. Instead of satisfying by force the needs, the whims, and the lusts of a nation which in an unholy hour of history allowed itself to be called *"das Herrenvolk,"* the nations ought to aid and contribute to each other's development.

It is true perhaps that the demands of the world of tomorrow do not harmonize with our subjective desires. Perhaps we would like to see the world turn in a wholly different direction. But that question is not asked of us, any more than a child is asked whether it wants to become an adult or an adult whether he wants to die some day. All that is asked of us is to place ourselves and our actions under the norm of the dispensation of God.

Under a new international social policy the duty will rest on the more mature, more powerful, and richer nations to support and lead the others. To this end, and in order that a real world economy may become a working possibility, an immense amount of preparation, education, and study of such problems as functional organization and transformation will be required. The first structural requirements, no doubt, would be a permanent international economic council and, above that, a universal society of nations built on the regional principle—two organisms to direct, guide, co-ordinate and educate. One of them, however, should also be equipped with the power to compel.

For in the planned economy of the future, which is coming in one form or another—that is to say, either as a free association of all the peoples of the earth or as the enslavement of the nations by one dominant race—the merging, co-ordination, and integration of different cultures, varying economic capacities, and so-called hereditary enmities cannot be expected to come about entirely without friction. An association of free nations, which are fundamentally, i.e., economically bound together, must overcome the egocentrism of the haves, the greed of the have-nots, the amorality of the imperialist states, the striving for autarchy, and the return to armaments. In the transition period leading to a world community, therefore, instruments such as international courts of arbitration and even an international armed force to impose the decisions of the majority on any eventual recalcitrant member will be indispensable.

"Whoever understands the signs of the times," said Queen Wilhelmina of the Netherlands once, "knows that of this generation will be asked an act of confidence, of self-sacrifice and moral courage, and of faith." We know that a new world order is in gestation. We should also have learned from the past and from the present that the durability of the success of international social measures stands in reversed ratio to the degree of violence employed. This is not sentimental romanticism, but realistic, technical common sense, which says that the essence of renovation is not destruction but reorganization and that its strength depends on the creative force of the idea realized.

We know that we cannot entrust leadership to Nazi Germany in the new world order that stands before the door. We cannot submissively accept being turned into slave nations. To whom, then, must the world turn?

I think that the supreme direction of the new international organisms must be placed in the hands of the two great English-speaking commonwealths, the British and the American. Britain and America—with their balanced, cumulative Anglo-Saxon culture; with their relatively healthy religious and moral conditions; with their gentleman ideal, which is extremely useful as a rule for international conduct; with their clear insight into political and economic world relationships; with England's experience as the leader of a great Empire and America's experience of abstention from the worst features of imperialism; with America's prominent position in international cartels and England's aristodemocratic mentality and the immense moral prestige of both, which will be greater even when victory is won over the Axis—Britain and the U.S.A., more than any other single country or combination of countries, possess the qualities and the position and the power to direct the evolution of the world's reorganization.

Not as domineering imperialisms, however, but as leaders! They must secure the collaboration of the elite of European and Asiatic countries. Their statesmen must learn to think in terms of the universal commonweal and not in terms of particularist nationalist interests. German thought and superb organizational qualities, French spirit, Italian sense of form, Japanese industry, Dutch humanitarianism, Russian patience, mysticism, and vision—all should be combined in a system of interrelated and interpenetrated continental economic units and mandated territories. That is the vision of the future.

The nations must be given "a vision beyond and above the present status of the world," if they are to fight their way through the dark night of the dying world order. Germany and Russia in one way, France and Britain in another, have shown the world that unless man believes and works for something higher and greater than Germany, Russia, France, or England, his strength fails him: he will not fight, suffer, much less die. . . .

It is not given to man to predict the future. But while keeping our mind on the reality, we must nevertheless place our ideal as high as possible. Knowing that not a single ethicosocial ideal can ever be fully realized, we must yet await the outcome of our striving in its direction by accepting the result in anticipation. We should not need hope in order to make an effort, or succeed in order to persevere.

In the combat that lies before us we must make the Gospel our ideal, "as [did] the early Christian church which waged a war against the pagan world, guided by the vision of the Kingdom of God." The Gospel alone has a tender and profound sympathy for everything that bears the name of man, for everything that is human, and for everything that concerns the community of man. The Gospel alone takes man seriously as an individual while holding the totality of men in sacred respect. It is through the Gospel that we are held accountable the one for the other and the entire human race in principle is conceived as one single household under the sovereignty of God.

Through the Gospel we feel the lack of justice and brotherliness of man for his brother and also shame and anger over the fact that men are cold and hungry, that they suffer and go to war against each other.

The Gospel invokes a terrible malediction on all situations, all persons and all powers which enslave men instead of setting them free or which separate men instead of uniting them. Through the Gospel we know that humanity in its entirety is created for one solidary union, because it considers the triumph over everything that is inhuman or antihuman or humanly antisolidary a duty of conscience and faith. Seek first the Kingdom of God and its righteousness—that is, try to regulate the common life on the basis of the demands of the most elementary humanity. With that precept the Gospel has not only set up *a* social ideal, but *the* social ideal of all times and of all races and peoples. Nor is that ideal to be understood as an unrealizable dream, but as the real goal of humanity to which it comes ever nearer in the measure that its members unite in a serious sentiment of reciprocal responsibility, mutual aid, and a common will. . . .

In the terrific tension and upheaval of our time, every man should stay with his own task. For whoever performs well the daily work, as the sculptor Rodin once said, may expect to see the mold break to pieces one day and the statue appear. No energy is lost in the universe: the tears of a child in China may light the flame in the heart of America, the prayer of a Hindu saint may bless the prisoners of Europe. Tears will become rocks, and prayers will be turned into weapons of war.

Slowly the hopes and aspirations of mankind turn into concrete achievements. There is something utterly pathetic in all of man's individual endeavor. But not in the collective march of humanity to its ideal.

A day will surely come when man, having grown tired of walking alone, will turn to his brother. On the day when we shall have learned to feel the sorrows and the joys, the suffering and the hope of others, as our very own, that world order of love and justice for which the universe yearns and of which the planets in the stillest night are the splendid but imperfect symbol, shall have come nearer.

On *that day alone* the brotherhood of man will have become a reality!

New York, September 4, 1941